A Short History of English Literature

A Short History of English Literature

Harry Blamires

820.
9
BLA

Methuen & Co Ltd

First published in 1974 by Methuen & Co Ltd
11 New Fetter Lane London EC4P 4EE
© 1974 Harry Blamires
Printed in Great Britain by
Richard Clay (The Chaucer Press), Ltd., Bungay, Suffolk

ISBN 0 416 24110 7 hardbound
ISBN 0 416 24120 4 paperback

Distributed in the USA by
HARPER & ROW PUBLISHERS INC.
BARNES & NOBLE IMPORT DIVISION

Contents

Preface

This work of introduction is designed to escort the reader through some six centuries of English literature. It begins in the fourteenth century at the point at which the language written in our country is recognizably our own, and ends in the 1950s. It is a compact survey, summing up the substance and quality of the individual achievements that make up our literature. The aim is to leave the reader informed about each writer's main output, sensitive to the special character of his gifts, and aware of his place in the story of our literature as a whole. No artificial schematization is imposed, but a pattern emerges naturally from considering writers in the groupings into which they fall by virtue of their historical context and their special interests.

Chapter headings do not define strict watertight divisions. Each one denotes the central interest of a chapter without being exclusive. The bibliography at the end provides chapter-by-chapter reading lists which guide the reader to a sample of texts, mostly inexpensive, and to a few relevant works of critical, historical, or biographical interest. Very many of the listed books are paperbacks.

I gratefully acknowledge the valuable critical help I have received from Professor Harold F. Brooks, and from my son, Alcuin Blamires. Professor Brooks in particular has been most generous in drawing attention to matters in my manuscript that called for re-consideration; but of course I am myself responsible for anything in the book that is amiss.

1
The fourteenth century

The fourteenth century was an age of healthy literary productivity dominated by four major poets – Chaucer, Langland, Gower and the anonymous 'Gawayne-poet'. There were also significant religious writers and the unknown makers of Miracle plays.

Geoffrey Chaucer (c.1340–1400) had an important career in public service. He was fighting in France by 1359–60, was taken prisoner and ransomed. No doubt his career benefited from his marriage, for his wife, Philippa, was lady-in-waiting to Queen Philippa. He was early attached to the royal household and went abroad on diplomatic work. His sister-in-law, Catherine, became John of Gaunt's mistress, then his third wife. These influential connections, together with his important civil and diplomatic appointments (including missions to Italy), gave Chaucer a wide knowledge of the world, strangely unrestricted, it would seem, by the limitations of outlook which in later ages social class might well have imposed.

The Book of the Duchess, Chaucer's earliest work, is an elegy in memory of John of Gaunt's first wife, Blanche, who died in 1369. Its purpose is to praise the deceased and console the bereaved. Chaucer uses the convention of the dream-allegory. The poet falls asleep while reading the very relevant story of 'Ceyx and Alcione', in which Alcione sees her husband in a dream and learns from his own lips of his death at sea. The poet's dream takes him to the countryside on a May morning. There is a hunt in progress; but the poet meets a disconsolate young knight sitting apart, clad all in black and abstracted with grief. The succeeding dialogue between poet and mourner, though its structure owes much to the rhetorical rule-book, is marked by striking touches as the tentativeness, simplicity, and even obtuseness of the inquiring poet are offset by the deep grief of the widower. For at first the knight distances the presentation of his sorrow in artifice: he is the victim of false Fortune who has bereft him of his queen and checkmated him at chess. But the narrator's probing questions then elicit a full and touching account of his lady's beauty, of her wooing and her winning. The reliving of past happiness seems to enable the knight for the first time to confront the stark fact:

> 'She ys ded!' 'Nay!' 'Yis, be my trouthe!'
> 'Is that youre los? Be God, hyt ys routhe!'

A light counterpoint balances the black grief of the 'man in blak' with the white of the lost one, White in name and white in complexion, white-necked and white-handed, and with the white walls of the hill-castle to which the hunters return at the fading of the dream.

This poem illustrates the way Chaucer blends the conventional literary forms with a lively realism and a psychological subtlety that speak to us across the centuries, making the modern reader feel very close to him. We have to forget our prejudices: we must not think of the stylized medieval framework as fettering the poet's spontaneity. For though Chaucer's work throughout shows him to be a craftsman well versed in all the devices prescribed in the study of rhetoric,[1] it does not give us any sense of an inner impulse striving to break out of a literary straitjacket. Rather the antithetic balance between formality and vigorous realism is something that Chaucer seems to have relished, and it gives his poetry a peculiar charm and piquancy.

Some poets overpower us with their presence or their passion, but Chaucer worms his way into the hearts of his readers, and one key to his insinuating charm is the delightful self-projection that is effected with amusing self-deprecation, even self-mockery. In *The House of Fame* a comically ironic self-portrait emerges in contrast to the solemn machinery of a love dream enriched with the paraphernalia of classical epic. The poet's dream takes him to the Temple of Venus, where he studies a pictorial representation of the story of Dido and Aeneas from the *Aeneid*. An Eagle, sent from heaven, takes him up to the House of Fame, and then to the House of Twigs, where the fortuitousness of earthly fame and fortune is allegorized in the concourse he encounters. The attractiveness of this unfinished poem is enhanced by the comic correspondence between the English poet's guide (the Eagle) and Dante's guide (Virgil) on his parallel ascent in the *Divine Comedy*. There is no depreciative mockery, except of Geoffrey himself. The humour lies

[1] In the Middle Ages all modes of literary expression were codified in the study of *rhetoric*. The codification included what we now call 'figures of speech' as well as techniques like allegory, devices like digression and illustration, and regulations for presenting material in a clear, comprehensive and interestingly varied way.

in the contrast between the devices of high literature and the fumbling poet at the receiving end of the talkative Eagle's disquisitions.

Chaucer used the form of the love vision again, though with different purpose, in *The Parliament of Fowls*. The narrator is taken to a dream-garden, sees the voluptuous goddess in the Temple of Venus, where paintings display victims of tragic love, and then by contrast comes to the fresh outdoor Court of Nature. Here birds of all kinds are engaged in a St Valentine's Day council to choose their respective mates. Three eagles stake their rival claims to the female eagle. After debate the decision is referred to the female eagle herself, and she calls for a year's deferment for reflection. Topical readings of the poem have been hazarded with reference to contemporary royal love-suits; but the tendency now is to emphasize the thematic interest in the way various views of love are voiced and represented. There is a dream-allegory again as prologue to the stories of nine heroines in *The Legend of Good Women*. The poet is taken to task by the god of love for heresy against the law of love in his translation of the *Romaunt of the Rose* and for representation of feminine misdeeds in *Troilus and Criseyde*. He is charged to write of good women, and the stories follow duly, beginning with that of Cleopatra.

Troilus and Criseyde, Chaucer's great completed poem, is a much expanded version of Boccaccio's *Il Filostrato*, about two thirds of the work being Chaucer's own additional material. Troilus is the son of Priam, king of Troy. Criseyde is the daughter of Calchas, a Trojan priest who has gone over to the Greeks, leaving her behind in Troy. Troilus falls in love with her and Pandarus brings the two of them together for a night in his home, where their love is consummated. Pandarus, the archetypal go-between, is a great humorous study in knowing contrivance and zestful avuncularity, and he manages the lovers with breathless dexterity. But an exchange of prisoners is arranged by Calchas: his daughter is to be brought over from Troy in return for an important Trojan prisoner, Antenor. Troilus is heart-broken at the news:

> And as in wynter leves ben bireft
> Ech after other, til the tree be bare,
> So that ther nys but bark and braunche ilaft,
> Lith Troilus, byraft of ech welfare,
> Ibounden in the blake bark of care ...

Criseyde promises to return soon and passionate vows of fidelity are exchanged; then she departs from Troy under the care of Diomede, and it is Diomede who seduces her. As Troilus gradually realizes what has happened, the slow agony is recounted with unforgettable acuteness:

> The lettres ek that she of olde tyme
> Hadde hym ysent, he wolde allone rede
> An hondred sithe atwixen noon and prime ...

The pathos is deepened by Chaucer's unerring presentation of Criseyde as a study in weakness rather than falsehood. The frailty of her defences and her resolution is portrayed without rancour. But Troilus's despair is eased only by rushing into battle and eventually meeting death at the hands of Achilles. Chaucer concludes his poem by shifting the viewpoint and urging young people to forsake earthly loves and set their hearts on the love of Christ. The rich personal experience recorded, and the high codes served by it, belong to a world that fades like a flower. The poem ends in prayer.

The first reading of *Troilus and Criseyde* is one of life's great narrative experiences. The subtlety and power of the characterization, the fine penetration revealed in the developing sequence of mood and emotion, and perhaps above all the rapturous tenderness sustained in recording the lovers' joy in each other – these qualities give a rare intensity to the work. It has been called a 'psychological novel', and the words give an accurate suggestion of the reader's close encounter with its personalities. The sustaining of a deeply intimate tone through 1,177 stanzas of fluent yet dignified rhyme royal[2] is a remarkable achievement.

The *Canterbury Tales* is Chaucer's most celebrated work. The *Prologue* establishes the framework by presenting a party of pilgrims who have gathered at the Tabard Inn in Southwark to make their way to the shrine of St Thomas à Becket at Canterbury. It is a motley assembly of men and women, portrayed in the *Prologue* with relish and vitality, though deadly satire is directed at corrupt ecclesiastics. Harry Bailly, the pilgrims' host at the inn, suggests that, to pass the time agreeably, they should each tell stories on the outward journey and on the return journey. He himself will go with them, and he promises a supper to the one who tells the best stories. This vast scheme was not completed. The twenty-nine pilgrims are represented by only twenty-three tales, not all of them finished. Links between the tales do something to give order to the collection by sketching in a continuing interchange of banter and crosstalk between the pilgrims, but the series of links is too incomplete to do more than whet the appetite for an accomplishment unrealized. The incompleteness of the interconnecting material leaves room for doubt in some cases about the order in which the stories should occur and about how they fit into the various stages of the pilgrims' journey.

Nevertheless, the *Canterbury Tales* leaves the impression of a work unified in spirit as well as diverse in riches. A cluster of varied and vivid personalities and a sequence of delightfully contrasting stories are together put before us, and the mixture is so winningly contrived that the reader forgets the missing machinery and the imperfect fabric. The design seems to be such that groups of tales are concerned with specific human problems and contrasting attitudes are juxtaposed. The Knight, model of chivalry and gentility, as 'meeke as is a mayde' in his bearing, who 'nevere yet no

[2] *rhyme royal:* a seven-line stanza of decasyllabics, rhyming *ababbcc.*

vileynye ne sayde / In al his lyf unto no maner wight', tells a tale of chivalrous rivalry in love, of tournament, tragedy and noble marriage. Its philosophic reflections, like those of *Troilus and Criseyde*, remind us that Chaucer was also the translator of Boethius's *De Consolatione Philosophiae*. In immediate contrast, the brawny thickset Miller, with a wart and a tuft of hairs on the tip of his nose, and a head that could batter any door off its hinges when he took it at a run, tells a tale at a level of earthiness parodic of the Knight's high seriousness. A young Oxford scholar, Nicholas, sets his heart on the wife of a carpenter with whom he is lodging, and induces the carpenter to take precautions against a coming second Flood by suspending tubs in the attic, so that the three of them can safely float. While the carpenter sleeps in his tub, Nicholas and Alison get out of theirs and go to bed together. But Nicholas pays for his deception. Absalon, the parish clerk, comes to beg a kiss from Alison and she rebuffs him by sticking her bare buttocks out of the window. In revenge Absalon returns with a red-hot iron and asks again for a kiss. This time Nicholas sticks out his buttocks, and he is branded. His shrieks waken the carpenter, who hears the desperate cry, 'Help! water! water!', assumes that the promised Flood is at hand, cuts his tub from the roof so that it can safely float, and comes crashing down.

One of the pilgrims, the Reeve, is himself a carpenter and not unnaturally the story affronts him. He responds with a story at the expense of a miller, exchanging Oxford for Cambridge. Two students deceive a miller by getting into bed with his wife and his daughters in the darkness. This tit-for-tat rejoinder indicates the potential of the whole work. Like the Miller and the Reeve, the Friar and the Summoner, two ecclesiastical rogues who are rivals for money and past masters at turning piety to personal advantage, tell crude yarns at each other's expense.

No person in the company comes more vigorously to life than the Wife of Bath, a bold, showy woman with scarlet complexion and scarlet stockings, a hat as big as a shield and hips of comparable proportions. A hearty chatterbox and a scathing foe of celibacy, she treats her companions to a detailed account of her life with five successive husbands, pointing the forceful moral that woman must wear the trousers in married life. This formidable exponent of medieval Women's Lib tells a tale that drives the lesson home. One of King Arthur's knights is reprieved from the death penalty for rape and given a year to find out what women love most. A hideous hag gives him the answer ('Sovereignty') in return for a pledge of obedience, and then, exacting what is due, requires him to marry her. In bed she offers him two alternatives – shall she remain hideous and faithful, or shall she become beautiful and perhaps unfaithful? Exercising all his faculties at this crucial juncture, the knight asks her to make the choice herself. He is duly rewarded for his acumen: she both becomes beautiful and promises fidelity.

In strong contrast the Clerk of Oxford, an earnest, unworldly and bookish man who does not waste words but is worth listening to when he does speak, tells the story of patient Griselda, whose wifely submissiveness is the antithesis of what the Wife of Bath advocates. Her virtue and love are tested by harrowing trials, including the supposed loss of her children. A happy ending is miraculously contrived, and the touching beauty of the tale moves even the rugged Host. 'By Goddes bones, / Me were levere than a barel ale / My wyf at hoom had herd this legende ones!' The recurring theme of marriage and fidelity is taken up again by the Merchant. He tells the story of January and May, wintery old husband and fresh young wife who, by a complex contrivance, is helped up into a tree by her husband, there to enjoy her youthful lover. The Franklin ends the marriage controversy on a happy note with a tale that exemplifies married loyalty sustained by generosity of spirit. Dorigen, the loving wife of Arveragus, fobs off the persistent appeals of the devoted squire, Aurelius, with the playful oath that she will succumb to his love only when all the rocks on the coast of Brittany are removed. The strange fulfilment of this condition by magical means produces, at the climax, a delightful interchange of magnanimities. Arveragus will not let his wife break her word: whereupon Aurelius remorsefully releases her from the commitment and in turn is released from his bond to pay the magician who served him.

Chaucer's versatility may be further exemplified by the *Nun's Priest's Tale* of Chauntecleer and Pertelote, cock and hen, whose farmyard dialogue brings the domestic situation into new focus within a delicious mock-heroic framework. Chauntecleer has had a bad dream of a fox: Pertelote puts it down to indigestion. Chauntecleer delivers a solemn lecture on dreams, well-documented by reference to the learned authorities. For there *is* a menacing fox; and soon he tricks Chauntecleer and captures him. A lively chase ensues, with shrill shouts reminiscent of 'Jakke Straw and his meynee'. It culminates in a cunning escape on Chauntecleer's part. From the irony and farce of this rollicking earthy fable, one might turn to the opposite extreme of earnestness and pathos, and hear the Prioress, a lady of tender-hearted delicacy who 'wolde wepe, if that she saugh a mous / Kaught in a trappe', tell a tale closely resembling that of St Hugh of Lincoln. A young Christian boy is murdered by Jews for singing a hymn to the Virgin Mary. His body is thrown into a pit, where it miraculously sings still, so that the murder is discovered and the perpetrators are executed.

Chaucer's multifarious diversity puts him among the first three or four English poets. It used to be argued that he had every literary talent except that of encompassing the tragic and that he was deficient in philosophical profundity. It is doubtful whether these two charges could stand up against a sensitive reading of *Troilus and Criseyde* and a comprehensive grasp of the *Canterbury Tales*.

There can be no question about the profundity and universality of *Piers Plowman*, a deeply religious poem by

William Langland (*c.*1332–*c.*1400). Langland came from Malvern to London, took minor orders, acquired a wife and daughter, and seems to have lived by praying for patrons. A man of fervent Christian conviction, Langland was no stained-glass-window figure. He tells us how in old age the 'limb' that his wife loved him for and liked to feel in bed at night could no longer be made to serve her wishes (*Passus* XX). This frank personality sets the opening scene of his great poem in the homely Malvern Hills. There he has a vision of the threefold universe, earth pitched between Heaven and Hell. There is a Field full of Folk, a packed and bustling concourse of worldly rogues, lay and clerical. In their portrayal harsh judgement upon the corrupt is intensified by compassion for the poor. Over against the bitter survey of scoundrels and hypocrites the poet presents those worthy souls who live prayerful lives in love of God; for the moral and social satire is subordinate to a vast allegorical search for Truth. A beautiful lady, Holy Church, comes to help the seeker, proclaiming that God is Love; but first she shows him the world dominated by Falsehood and Flattery. He sees the perverters of justice, servants all of Lady Meed, rich in jewelled robes of scarlet and gold. We watch her, the symbol of worldly gain and corruption, taken before the king and rebuked by Conscience. Then we return to the Field full of Folk to see Reason preaching repentance. Responsive penitents are directed to seek for Saint Truth; and the only guide they can find is the simple plowman, Piers. He can direct the pilgrims to Truth if they will lend a hand with the ploughing. The symbolical significance of ploughing takes in the whole sphere of good works meekly and faithfully performed. Some pilgrims work eagerly and Truth delivers a pardon into Piers's hands for all who help. When the document is opened, it promises eternal life to those who do good and damnation to those who do evil. This rigorous legalism is no true pardon and Piers tears the document to pieces, quoting, 'Yea though I walk through the valley of the shadow of death, I will fear no evil, for thou art with me ...' His dissatisfaction is apparently over the terms of the Old Law on which salvation is offered. The gospels teach the love of God and recommend the example of the birds of the air who neither sow nor reap.

The problem thus posed provides the substance of the second part of the poem, which pursues the quest of doing good and so attaining salvation. The quest becomes a three-fold one, the stages of spiritual progress being to Do Well, Do Bet(ter) and Do Best. There is argument on sin and salvation, on faith and works, on the spiritual importance of learning and the function of grace; then Faith (Abraham), Hope (Moses) and Love (the Good Samaritan) are introduced and in culmination the dreamer has visions of the Cruci-fixion, the Harrowing of Hell, the Resurrection, the Ascen-sion and the coming of the Holy Spirit. The suffering and redeeming Christ is seen wearing the humanity of Piers him-self, to whom the power of absolution is granted and on whom the onus is laid for construction on earth of the house of Unity. Correspondences thus build into the figure of Piers (Peter, the rock) the symbolism of Incarnation and the Church of Christ, for the house of 'Unité, holicherche on [in] Englisshe' is a barn where harvested Christian souls are to be garnered. But the attack of Antichrist and the Seven Sins wreaks devastation among 'the crop of treuthe', and at the end of the poem Conscience turns pilgrim, to walk the world in search again of the saving Piers Plowman. Langland thus completed, in a style of extraordinary imagin-ative vigour and clarity, the one great comprehensive poem of the age containing a profound consideration of the good life and of man's religious vocation.

To John Gower (c.1330–1408) also goes the credit for hav-ing realized a massive conception in verse. His great Eng-lish poem is *Confessio Amantis* (The Lover's Confession) in which he presents a comprehensive vision of life within the framework of a dramatic sequence in the Courtly Love tradition. Gower's connecting theme is the confession of an ageing lover afflicted with a passion, humble and devout, for a beautiful but unresponsive young lady, sympathetic enough to be tantalizing to him, but restrained enough to throw him into despair. His confessor, Genius, is at once a minister of Love able to direct him in the way of her service, and a moral priest who can broaden the particular lesson for a lover into a principle for all mankind. The scheme takes us through the Seven Deadly Sins: the confessor probes the lover's conscience, examines each sin under five different heads, and proceeds to a twofold analysis of each sin within the moral code and within the love code respectively. In each case separate stories are told to illustrate moral and amatory instruction. By this means Gower fulfils his design, stated at the beginning of the prologue, to write a book which mixes pleasure with instruction ('Somewhat of lust, somewhat of lore').

Gower succeeds in presenting a lover moved by real emotion and responding to it in little acts that are unforgettable. He is delighted to be able to help his beloved on to her horse or accompany her to church. He reads the Tale of Troilus to her and recalls gazing on her slender white fingers as she busied herself with her embroidery. He delays his partings from her, returns on makeshift excuses, and always finds himself unable to utter in her presence the fine things he intended to say to her. The persisting dialogue with the lover is not without its touches of wry humour when he bemoans his ineffectiveness; but the work as a whole is too formalized to catch fire. Thirty thousand lines in octosyllabic couplets strain the reader's sensitivity for all their fluency. Nevertheless, through the stories themselves, the poet's high seriousness does acquire imaginative and emotional vigour in its expression. Not that Gower has technical subtlety in presentation; for his strength as a story-teller is not that of narrating events with notable dramatic effect. Rather he pinpoints emotions and dilemmas of the characters so as to moralize their experience humanely and wisely. The direct style is unexcitingly serviceable, but

Gower's eye for detail can delight, as when he records Jason's toilet after gaining the Golden Fleece:

> And Jason was unarmed sone
> And dide as it befell to done;
> Into his bathe he went anone
> And wisshe him clene as any bone,
> He toke a soppe and out he cam
> And on his best array he nam
> And kempt his hede when he was clad ...

The story of Medea is told under the general heading of Avarice to illustrate False Witness and Perjury. The stories of Ulysses's return and of the Wise and Foolish Virgins are told under the general heading of Sloth to illustrate the dangers of Delay. It was the lengthy story of Apollonius of Tyre (Book XVIII) from which Shakespeare drew the plot of *Pericles, Prince of Tyre*.

Outstanding among the substantial fourteenth-century poems of unknown authorship is *Sir Gawayne and the Green Knight*. A chivalrous romance written in vigorous alliterative verse, it is a carefully structured narrative, vividly conceived and sharply visualized. King Arthur and his knights are feasting at Camelot in the Christmas season: there is meat and mirth, exchanging of gifts and of salutations, blaring of trumpets and leaping of hearts. Queen Guinevere sits on a richly canopied dais, Agravayne and Gawayne on either side of her. A massive, fearsome intruder rides in, clad in green: everything about him is green, even the horse's mane and his own shoulder-length hair. Chatter and minstrelsy are hushed. The brawny warrior arrogantly challenges one of the company to take his own mighty axe and give him a blow on the neck, then to meet him a year hence and receive a return blow. This is the Beheading Test, a test of knightly courage. Sir Gawayne rises to it, decapitates the knight and buries the axe in the floor of the hall. The body gropes and picks up the severed head by the hair: its lips repeat the pledge of an appointment at the Green Chapel in a year's time: then body and head ride away. The seasons pass and the time comes for Gawayne to ride out to his appointment. He goes towards North Wales and, as Christmas approaches, he is warmly received at a castle where a lady even lovelier than Guinevere is his hostess. Here the second phase in the knight's quest for honour begins – the Chastity Test. The lord of the castle tells Gawayne that the Green Chapel is near at hand, and requests him to stay. Tomorrow the lord is to go hunting and he pledges whatever quarry falls to him as a gift to Gawayne. In return Gawayne promises to his host anything he himself wins. There follow on successive days three attempts on Gawayne's chastity by his hostess, and Gawayne is placed in a testing dilemma where the demands of courtesy and chastity seem to conflict. On the first return the host puts a deer at Gawayne's feet, on the second presents him with a boar, and on the third day brings back only a fox. On each occasion Gawayne keeps his pledge by giving kisses to the lord which he has accepted from the lady; but a green girdle, given to him on the third day to make him invulnerable, he does not hand over. The poem does not flag for a moment, in spirit or technique, throughout these events. The vitality of the outdoor hunting scenes is matched by the tensely sensuous blend of verbal and physical seductiveness to which Gawayne is submitted indoors. The interlacing of these two motifs represents literary craftsmanship unsurpassed in the age. Moreover the blended interdependence of the beheading game and the chastity test makes a comprehensive trial of Gawayne's virtues. And the climax of the poem fulfils all expectations. Gawayne sets out to keep his tryst at the Green Chapel and rides through the desolate countryside on a wintry morning:

> Mist muged on the mor, malt on the mountes,
> Uch hille hade a hatte, a myst-hakel huge.
> Brokes byled and breke bi bonkkes aboute,

Schyre schaterande on schores, ther they doun
     schowved.

The Green Knight arrives true to his word. He wounds
Gawayne and then reveals himself as his host. Host and
hostess have conspired to submit Gawayne to the tests.
Through failing to hand over the girdle Gawayne has suffered a wound: otherwise he has come honourably through
the trial. But Gawayne's pride is wounded too. In shame he
flings down the girdle which has reduced him to the act
of breaking his knightly compact. But the Green Knight
restores it to him, for confession has put all to rights. In
Gawayne's eyes his weakness has linked him with Adam,
David, Samson and Solomon as men tricked by feminine
guile: but his reacceptance of the girdle seems to crown the
tests of courage and chastity with the due humbling of that
pride which aspiration to knightly perfection builds into the
chivalric code. The sign of the humbling becomes the badge
of his glory on his return to Camelot, for when he has
recounted his story, the knights all bind green baldricks on
their own breasts.

If, as is considered likely, the author of *Sir Gawayne and
the Green Knight* is also the author of the three other
poems contained in the same manuscript (*Pearl*, *Patience*
and *Purity*), then indeed he is a poet of outstanding imaginative power and technical skill. *Pearl* is an intricately
constructed poem and plainly the work of a writer highly
sensitive to the potentialities of words. Stanzas are linked in
groups, and groups themselves related, by the forceful reiteration of keywords with subtly modulated connotative
emphases. The virtuosity with which both rhyme and alliteration are exploited in twelve-line octosyllabic stanzas is
closely congruous with the organized complexity of the
thought and feeling conveyed. The lost pearl the poet
laments is symbol of a lost daughter and perhaps of lost
spiritual grace. As he mourns the young girl, he falls asleep
on her grave and is granted a vision. He sees a river border-

ing Paradise and on the other side Pearl herself. She is adorned with bright raiment ornamented with pearls. She comforts him, for she is now in blessedness as the bride of the Lamb. He is given a lavish glimpse of the New Jerusalem, and the city is suddenly filled with maidens all dressed and crowned like his own beloved, decked with pearls and each with a pearl at her breast. The sight of these, and of the Elders, the angels and the Lamb Himself, makes him desperate to join them:

> Delyt me drof in yye and ere;
> My manes mynde to maddyng malte;
> Quen I sey my frely, I wolde be there,
> Byyonde the water thagh ho were walte.

But he is recalled to the realization that it is not the Prince's will that he should cross, and he awakes consoled.

In *Pearl* we are near to the spirit of those contemporary contemplative writers who produced mystical treatises. It is refreshing to turn from the satire of ecclesiastical rogues in Chaucer and Langland to this evidence of a strong and persistent current of sincere spirituality within the Church. The anonymous *Cloud of Unknowing* is a specialized call to the life of the spirit. It accepts that to penetrate the cloud that separates man from God something more than intellectual understanding is required. The disciplines of the contemplative are demandingly defined; but there is a clarity and concreteness in the thinking that confirms the impression of a writer with his feet on the ground. Richard Rolle of Hampole (1295–1349, so-called because he spent the last years of his life at Hampole Priory in Yorkshire) forsook home to live as a hermit and excited eager discipleship. It is understandable that he should have done so, for the emotional and rhetorical quality of his English work (he wrote in Latin too), such as the *Meditation of the Passion*, probes the feelings disturbingly. Correspondingly his lyrical vein when describing experiences of spiritual exaltation is rich in imagery. The soul in ecstasy is 'like a burning fire or like a nightingale that delights in love, song, and melody, and faints from excess of love'[3] (*The Form of Loving*). Walter Hilton (d.1396) is a lively and clear-headed teacher whose study, *The Scale of Perfection*, traces the spiritual pilgrimage through detachment from earthly interests to the true knowledge of God, a knowledge that cannot be separated from true knowledge of the self which He made. Hilton is sober and orderly in instruction, and has a gift for apt imagery. 'Sweep your soul clean with a broom of the fear of God', he writes, 'and wash it with your tears, and so you shall find your coin, Jesus.'

Perhaps the most fascinating personality in this group of mystical writers is Julian of Norwich (b. 1342). She eventually lived as an anchoress in a cell at Norwich but the mystical experiences recorded in *Revelations of Divine Love* took place at an earlier date (1373) and the book is a mature reflection on these visions. There is a remarkable blend in her work of simplicity with sharpness of intellect, of imaginative sensitivity with hard-headed logicality. She records fifteen revelations, or 'Shewings', and meditates reflectively on what they mean. In this way she provides guidance not only to those seeking to practise the art of prayer and to grow in faith, but also to those grappling with the problem of evil. She is forceful when dwelling on the physical sufferings of Christ on the cross ('The skin of the flesh ... was small-wrinkled with a tanned colour, like a dry board when it is skinned') yet inspiringly jubilant when she discerns evil as a perversion that is wholly offset by God's goodness and love:

> One time our good Lord said: 'All thing shall be well;' and another time he said: 'Thou shalt see thyself that all *manner* thing shall be well:' and in these two sayings the soul took sundry understandings. (Chapter 36)

[3] Quotations from Richard Rolle and Walter Hilton have been modernized.

The drama is our next consideration – a consideration which cannot be contained strictly within the compass set by our chapter heading, for the Miracle plays belong as much to the fifteenth as to the fourteenth century. They were performed by various guilds, like Glovers, Tanners, Dyers, Grocers, Shearers and Tailors, Shipwrights and Tile-thatchers, who (at least at York and Chester) presented them on wagons at strategic points of their town. Summer festivals, especially that of Corpus Christi, saw connected sequences of such performances on Old and New Testament themes. In subject the plays were essentially instructive and theological, but by treatment they were also down-to-earth, contemporary and amusing. They were the outcome of combined ecclesiastical and social developments. Dramatization of Christian teaching in the sequences of the Church's year, and in the symbolic summary of human redemption played out in the Mass, encouraged the habit of concretely realizing the pattern of historic and individual salvation and of participating in its reactivation. The practice of emphasizing the message of Christmas, Easter and other feasts by dramatizing such events as the meeting of the women and the angel at the empty tomb created an appetite among performers and spectators that could be fully satisfied only outside the walls of the church and the limitations of the liturgy.

The genesis of the Miracle plays, then, ensured that the little dramas illustrative of biblical events should be grasped as connected together within an all-embracing drama of man's history and destiny from Creation to Doomsday. Hence the notion of a cycle of plays was a logical expression of the theology from which they ultimately derived. But social, no less than specifically religious, causes influenced the development of the cycles. Play-production involves organization and discipline, and outside the Church no doubt guilds were the only bodies which could cope with such demands. The specialization of human activities represented by the guilds fitted neatly into the requirement for diversified contributions to a single corporate endeavour.

There is sometimes a touching literalness about the link between the guild and its particular contribution to the cycle. It is the 'Waterleaders and Drawers in Dye of Chester' to whom is assigned the third pageant of Noah's Flood, *The Deluge*. And indeed the peculiar blend of religious and secular, of cosmic conflict and homely comedy, is deeply engrained in the cycles.

> I, God, that all the world have wrought,
> Heaven and earth, and all of nought,
> I see my people, in deede and thought,
> Are sett fowle in sinne.[4]

It is on this solemn note of universal judgement that Deus in *The Deluge* begins his proclamation that is to bring destruction to 'all the world' except Noah and his family; but it does not prevent the 'Good Gossips' of Noah's wife from comforting themselves, as 'the Flood comes in, full fleetinge fast', with a good swig at the madeira:

> Here is a pottell of malmsey good and stronge,
> It will rejoice both hart and tong.

If the Chester Waterleaders were the right men to tackle the Flood, the Tile-thatchers of York were appropriately put in charge of *The Birth of Jesus*, whose scene is set 'in a cattle-shed', while, at Chester again, the Cooks and Inn-keepers, accustomed to internal heating, were aptly entrusted with responsibility for *The Harrowing of Hell*: its scene is 'The Interior of Hell', where 'a great light begins to shine'.

In the Miracle plays, for all their lack of sophistication and polish, there is often a simple sublimity in the presentation of God and his angels; and in plays such as *The Betraying of Christ* (from the N. town cycle) the sufferings of Jesus and St Peter, St Mary Magdalen and the Virgin Mary, are represented with sensitivity. On the other hand Satan and evil characters like Herod generally obtrude as roister-

[4] Miracle plays are quoted from J. Q. Adams, *Chief Pre-Shakespearean Dramas* (Harrap, London), 1924.

ous exponents of slapstick. Crude fisticuffs and hearty back-chat are notably indulged in the famous *Second Shepherds' Play*[5] in the Wakefield cycle, where a comic plot of contemporary life is interwoven with the presentation of the Nativity, so that farce and ritual meet and mix. For the farce is not irrelevant. It involves theft of a sheep by one, Mak, whose wife, Gill, hides it in a cradle as though it were a baby. This use of the symbolic Lamb in homely, inoffensive parody of the Nativity is noteworthy. Squabbling and horseplay dominate domestic scenes between Noah and his wife in the Wakefield *Play of Noah*. The Wakefield cycle, sometimes called the 'Towneley cycle' because the manuscript was for long preserved at Towneley Hall, Lancashire, contains individual plays strikingly developed as dramas in themselves. It is later than the Chester and York cycles and dates from the fifteenth century. Accretions to the specifically religious basis have by this time achieved a vitality of their own.

Among non-cycle plays surviving from this period is one, *The Play of the Sacrament,* in which Jews mock and misuse the host and wine of the sacrament and are rewarded by a series of crude miraculous signs. The host and the wine bleed; the sacrament sticks to Jonathas's hand, and when they nail it to a post and drag Jonathas's arm away, his hand is left behind. It will be evident that the religious material has become little more than an excuse for grotesque horseplay.

A more significant development is the emergence of the Morality play, in which the Bible is forsaken and a new inventiveness is applied to allegorical treatment of the human situation. The earliest Morality surviving in a complete text is *The Castle of Perseverance*, dating from about 1425. It is ambitious in conception and lavish in declamation. A diagram, giving instructions for production, sets the castle in the middle with Mankind's bed sheltering beneath it, while

[5] The manuscript has two plays about the shepherds coming to the manger.

'scaffolds' to east, north-east, north, west and south are respectively assigned to God, Covetousness, Belial, World (Mundus) and Flesh (Caro). World, Flesh and Devil each have their followers. World's attendants are Lust and Folly, his treasurer is Covetousness and his messenger is Backbiter. Mankind has his advisers, Good Angel and Bad Angel. There are also the Seven Virtues, keepers of the castle, and the Four Daughters of God – Mercy, Peace, Truth and Righteousness. The conflict for possession of Mankind is conducted in formal versification that is more like alternate speechifying than living dialogue; but by the very nature of the 'characterization' in types (Gluttony, Lust, Sloth, and the like), it is possible to stage the work impressively; and the excitement that may have been engendered at contemporary performances can perhaps best be gauged by noting the stage direction for Belial when the evil powers assault the castle:

> He that shall play Belial, look that he have gunpowder burning in pipes in his hands and in his ears and in his arse, when he goeth to battle.

It seems something of an anticlimax after this that the 'Virtues beat them back with roses, emblematic of Christ's passion'.

A frequently revived Morality play is *Everyman*, and it belongs to the very end of the fifteenth century. It is a play that can stand on its own literary merit and does not require of the modern reader that connivance at crudities in deference to antiquity which some early drama elicits. At the beginning God sends Death to summon Everyman to come and render account of his life in the world. Everyman turns to Fellowship, then to Kindred and Cousin, to accompany him on his journey, but all make excuses. By this time the urgency of Everyman's need is conveyed with an intensity that compels involvement, and the suspense, heightened by further appeals to Goods, has bred a mood of desperation when Everyman stumbles on Good-Deeds lying on the ground, anxious to help, but 'sore bound' by Everyman's sins, so that he cannot stir. But Knowledge, the sister of Good-Deeds, leads Everyman to Confession and, after his penance, Good-Deeds is enabled to join him. Other companions accrue – Discretion, Strength, Beauty and Five Wits – but these forsake him at the grave. Knowledge however is still with him when he finally entrusts himself into God's hands, and Good-Deeds remains to speak for him as the Angel receives him.

2
Fifteenth-century poetry and prose

Our survey of drama has taken us up to the end of the fifteenth century, and we may now consider what else was happening in the literary field in a century which saw the most important literary event of our civilization, namely the invention of printing. It is a period of which we have a peculiarly thorough record of domestic life in the *Paston Letters*, a collection covering three generations of family life in Norfolk. The public life of the same age is perhaps coloured in our imaginations by the recollections of Shakespeare's historical plays, covering the reigns of Henry IV, Henry V, Henry VI and Richard III. But it is not a great century for English literature. In Sir Thomas Malory we have one writer of the first rank, and there is a small group of gifted poets in Scotland.

John Lydgate (?1370–1452) deserves mention too. He is one of those writers who achieve in their own day an immense reputation that posterity fails to confirm. His output was enormous. His biggest poem, *The Fall of Princes*, contains some 36,000 lines. It is three times as long as *Paradise Lost*. The work known as the *Troy-book* has over 30,000 lines. Some of his 'lesser' poems are big by normal standards, and he wrote plenty of short poems too. The *Troy-book* tells the story of the Trojan War. It contains a version of the story of Troilus and Cressida, and comparison of Lydgate's treatment with Chaucer's brings out Chaucer's insight into emotion and psychology as against Lydgate's method of submerging individual characterization under a codified sequence of moral generalities. Of course twentieth-century prejudice is weighted against appreciation of Lydgate. His idea of poetry is not our idea, but an idea rooted in the medieval philosophy of universal order. He moralizes and philosophizes the human scene into a grand organized literary fabric whose sections and sub-sections exploit the techniques of the rhetorical rule-book as formally as they exploit the cosmic medieval view of ordered life within an ordered universe. Some who have studied Lydgate attentively, however, claim that his systematized work, in spite of its artificialities, deserves something better than to be fashionably dismissed.

A name usually associated with Lydgate's is that of John Hoccleve (?1370–?1450), like Lydgate a disciple of Chaucer. His didactic work, *The Regement of Princes* (a translation from the Latin of Aegidius Romanus) was written for Henry, Prince of Wales, the future Henry V. Hoccleve has interest as a portrayer of his times, but distinctive literary quality was beyond his reach. He does however frequently tap a vein of self-revelation, and the self revealed, though neither modest nor subtle, confronts the reader vividly, notably in *La Male Regle*.

We may well introduce the Scottish poets of the fifteenth century by looking back and incorporating at their side a poet of the previous century, John Barbour (?1316–95), for his poem, *The Bruce*, written about 1375, achieved something of the status of a national epic. It covers events during the period 1304 to 1333, mostly in the reign of Robert the Bruce, taking in the Battle of Bannockburn. Fact and legend are combined in a romantically heroic account of the deeds of King Robert and James Douglas. The work has been criticized for its shapelessness and for the unevenness of its poetic quality, but its stories have fed the popular historical mind.

Poethood embraces royalty in the person of King James I of Scotland (1394–1437). Young James fell into English hands while making his way to France at the age of about twelve. He was kept in England for nineteen years and in 1424 married Lady Jane Beaufort. His poem, *The Kingis Quair* (The King's Book), celebrates his love of Lady Jane. It tells how, as a prisoner, he sees a beautiful lady in a garden from his tower (the incident is reminiscent of Chaucer's *Knight's Tale*) and is transported to celestial realms where Venus and Minerva advise him. There is a strong didactic vein, emphasizing the fickleness of Fortune. The combination of pagan divinities with Christian sentiments (Minerva quotes Ecclesiastes and urges the lover to act as a 'Christin') is incongruous perhaps only to the very literal. There is a touching authenticity in places, notably in the final fresh account of the lover's happiness, but elsewhere perhaps James is too conscious an imitator of Chaucer and Gower, to whom he pays tribute as:

> Superlative as poets laureate
> In moralitee and eloquence ornate.

Robert Henryson (*c*.1430–1506) is a man about whose life little is known, but it appears that he was a schoolmaster in Dunfermline. His distinction is to have excelled in two literary forms, his *Moral Fables* and his *Testament of Cresseid*.

The *Fables* (the tale of the Cock and the Hen, the tale of the Town Mouse and the Country Mouse, the tale of the Fox and the Wolf, and so on) give to the animals the kind of human characteristics that Chaucer gave to Chauntecleer and Pertelote. Hear how the town mouse declines the food offered by the country mouse:

> 'My fair sister' (quod scho) 'have me excusit,
> 'This rude dyat and I can not accord,
> 'To tender meit my stomok is ay usit,
> 'For quhylis I fair alsweill as ony lord
> 'Thir wydderit peis, and nuttis, or thay be bord
> 'Wil brek my teith, and mak my wame ful sklender,
> 'Quhilk wes before usit to meitis tender.'

By deft touches of description and felicitously phrased dialogue Henryson enlivens the situations and relationships of the animals, and he presses home his moral in a concluding section at the end of the tale, labelled *Moralitas*. Humour and quiet irony pervade his stories, but the social and moral conscience evident in his implicit and explicit commentary is a deeply concerned one. Henryson knows intimately the world he is writing about; the animals, the people, the country, the weather: he has got the feel of them and can convey it:

> The wynter come, the wickit wind gan blaw,
> The woddis grene were wallowit with the weit,
> Baith frith and fell with froistys were maid faw,
> Slonkis and slaik maid slidderie with the sleit.

Such descriptions, like the wintry landscapes in *Sir Gawayne and the Green Knight*, are refreshingly different from the standard May scenes of medieval poetry.

The *Testament of Cresseid* is a sequel to Chaucer's *Troilus and Criseyde* written in the same stanza form. It tells how Diomede wearies of Cresseid and leaves her. She returns to Calchas, and to his temple, and there, on her knees, vents her anger in reproaches against Venus and Cupid. Then, in a vision, Cupid summons the seven Planets to hear of Cresseid's blasphemy, and she is condemned to suffering and incurable disease. She wakes in grief to find herself a leper. She goes to a hospital, but moans there so lamentably that she is driven out and becomes a beggar. By this point the poem is already heavy with sadness, its heroine weighed down under the burden of suffering and remorse alike; for Henryson's oppressively moralistic tone matches the intensity of his feeling: but now the agony becomes something rarely fine and dramatic, for Troilus passes by the hideous beggar: something faintly reminds him of his darling Cresseid and he gives a generous sum. When Cresseid asks who it is that was so kind, another leper identifies Troilus. Cresseid is overcome by grief and remorse: she writes a will bequeathing a ring to Troilus, and dies. The ring is taken to Troilus, who has an inscription put on her tomb. It commemorates Cresseid of Troy town, once the flower of womanhood, who died a leper. Here, as elsewhere, one admires that discipline of mind in Henryson that cherished concentration and economy.

King James, Henryson and Dunbar have been called the 'Scottish Chaucerians', and indeed each of them paid tribute to Chaucer. At the beginning of the *Testament of Cresseid* the poet is reading the poem 'writtin be worthie Chaucer glorius', and in *The Goldyn Targe* Dunbar exclaims:

> O reverend Chaucere, rose of rethoris all,
> As in oure tong ane flour imperiall.

The words remind us that fifteenth-century poets looked to Chaucer as the great master of *rhetoric*, sadly undervaluing perhaps the qualities that have appealed to later ages. William Dunbar (*c.*1460–*c.*1530) seems to have been employed in the service of King James IV as Chaucer was employed by the English court, and like Chaucer he became the recipient of a royal pension. His high connections can be measured by the fact that *The Thrissil and the Rois*, a dream-allegory in which 'fresche May' wakens the poet and calls him to a gathering of articulate birds and beasts and flowers, is concerned with the marriage of James IV to Henry VII's daughter, Margaret. *The Goldyn Targe* is a bigger essay in the same artificial form, handling classical gods and goddesses alongside 'Nature', 'dame Beautee', 'Fair Having', 'Benigne Luke' and many other comparable personifications. At the opposite extreme *The Tua Mariit Wemen and the Wedo* is an exercise in ripe realism. It is a private conversation and the poet is an eavesdropper. Its subject is married life, chiefly bed-life, and the women exchange their confidences with a frankness and crudity that contrasts harshly with their external beauty, dignity and sweetness as they appear before the world. In this sharp ironical antithesis the power of the poem resides. The two married women are revealed as comparative novices in the art of getting the maximum sexual pleasure and personal advantage from men. The widow's lurid record illustrates the paradoxical moral that, with a husband out of the way, one can give delight all round.

Dunbar's excellence is a gift for descriptive writing that intermittently throws a flash of colour before the reader such that his eyes dazzle:

> The roses yong, new spreding of thair knopis
> War powderit brycht with hevinly beriall droppis,
> Throu bemes rede birnying as ruby sperkis.
> (The Goldyn Targe)

He has neatness in handling well-balanced stanza forms and, at his best, a dexterous control of rhythm and a ready adaptability of technique to a variety of moods and purposes. There is not much in fifteenth-century poetry more memorable than his tribute to fellow poets now dead, *Lament for the Makaris*, with its opening epigraph 'When He Wes Sek':

> The stait of man dois change and vary
> Now sound, now seik, now blith, now sary,
> Now dansand mery, now like to dee;
> *Timor mortis conturbat me.*

With Dunbar we have moved into the sixteenth century and it is fitting to link Gavin Douglas (1475–1522) with his fellow Scottish makers. He was of high birth (son of the Earl of Angus), was educated at St Andrews, and held Church appointments while also involving himself in the political struggles of the day. His poem, *Palice of Honour*, is a dream-allegory in which various routes to honour are explored – the way of study, of statecraft, of virginity – and the way of poetry chosen. But Douglas's great achievement is his translation of Virgil's *Aeneid* which he completed in 1513. The work is not a bare translation, for it includes passages of commentary and prologues to individual books: these sometimes have a personal flavour and discuss the task of interpretation or describe the passing season. The vigour and versatility of Douglas's version are indisputable, though it is medieval in rendering and in presuppositional outlook.

We return to England and to the mid fifteenth century to look at the work of Sir Thomas Malory (c.1408–71). Malory lived through the Wars of the Roses and spent some time in prison, where *Le Morte Darthur* was composed. He has been conjecturally identified with a Sir Thomas Malory whose recorded career of violence, theft and even rape seems incongruous for the exponent of chivalrous idealism, and the identification has been disputed. *Le Morte Darthur* uses stories from the vast cycles of Arthurian chronicles and works them into a single fabric, made coherent by its central concern with the conflicts which bring about the dissolution of the Round Table. Superimposed on this material is the quest for the Holy Grail, and the tragic figure of Launcelot links the two elements together, for it is his adulterous relationship with Queen Guenever that unfits him for the sacred quest; and his unsullied son Galahad finally achieves it.

Heroic tales of Arthur appear in the twelfth-century *History of the Kings of Britain* by Geoffrey of Monmouth, who ended his life as Bishop of St Asaph. One of the 'books' of the history is concerned with the 'Prophecies of Merlin', another with the reign of Arthur's father, Uther Pendragon, and two others provide a substantial record of the exploits of Arthur, already a highly romantic figure. In the same century Wace of Jersey used the Arthurian legends in his *Roman de Brut*, and soon afterwards (about the turn of the century) appeared Layamon's *Brut*, a verse history of England connecting the British kingdom with the ancient world by linking the first legendary British king Brut with Aeneas. The poem takes in the reigns of King Lear and Cymbeline. Arthur is the great national figure, and the crucial story of his passing is included. There was some indebtedness by Malory to a fourteenth-century poem in alliterative verse, *Morte Arthure*, whose material resembles what was to be found in Geoffrey of Monmouth and Layamon; but Malory also followed French sources closely.

It can be argued that *Le Morte Darthur* is rather a collection of tales than a single integrated work. The early books, dealing with Arthur's first battles, his marriage, his establishment of the Round Table, and the extension of his conquests into Italy, are interwoven with fully developed tales like that of Balin and Balan (brothers who fight to the death and learn one another's identity only when the fatal wounds have been dealt) and that of Sir Gareth. The saga of Tristram and Isoud then intrudes at length upon the developing story of Sir Launcelot and Guenever. It is only perhaps in the last books that the sense of an integrated artistic whole is conveyed. The culminating events of Malory's chronicle put an end to a great venture in fellowship sustained by many individuals of unquestioning loyalty, unselfish courage and high idealism. The tragic irony of the conclusion inevitably carries a fatalistic flavour. The larger moral issue, involving the gradual growth of mistrust and jealous disloyalty, and the persisting infidelity of Guenever, asserts itself notably in those passages where the central story of Arthur and Launcelot is worked out, and it overshadows the ending. The unity sensed retrospectively by the reader at the end is less apparent as one moves through the maze of adventures in which the various knights pursue their heroic quests, dealing death to dragons and giants, encountering deception, magic and sorcery, their days punctuated by wayside fights to the death, their years by feasts and tournaments.

Malory's fusion of the Holy Grail story with the Arthurian material creates difficulties, for it introduces the Christian ethic in such a way as to disturb the moral consistency of the whole. Chivalric idealism had its Christian basis in the knight's pledge to defend the weak, suppress the wicked, and honour God in noble acts. Courtly Love, in so far as it exalted fidelity and unselfish service, was in tune with Christian idealism, but the cult of adultery was not. Malory spells out the Christian ethic of the Grail episode, exalting virginity. As a result there is an uncomfortable clash with the Courtly Love code implicit in other parts of the book. The devotion of Launcelot and Tristram to their loves is the source and inspiration of their heroic deeds: it is disquieting to see this devotion dragged through the mire by the high hand of chastity. Our eyes are forcibly opened to the discrepancy between Camelot and Carbonek over this issue.

Perhaps such discrepancies were unavoidable unless the tales were to be told on a level of shallow narrative interest alone. Malory's instinct and artistry gave to his treatment of the cycle the kind of depth that raises awkward moral questions: but the depth, and the unity it seeks to establish, make the book memorable. By making Arthur the centre of things and his court the locus for annual review of achievements, Malory gave a thread of connection to all the adventures. The early deeds of valour, however disconnected outwardly, tend to the glorification of Arthur's ideals and the rise of his kingdom. Thus a narrative rhythm emerges. The rot sets in; the knights begin to be jealous and critical of each other, and after triumphs of worldly pageantry and of spiritual exaltation before the Holy Grail, there is a collapse.

Intrigue and counter-intrigue tear the fabric of chivalrous achievement to tatters. Old loyalties are forgotten. Ultimately it is not so much Launcelot's love that causes the disintegration as the evil-minded spite of those who reveal it to the king and use it as a cloak for their designs:

> Ah, Agravaine, Agravaine, said the king, Jesu forgive it thy soul, for thine evil will that thou and thy brother Sir Mordred hadst unto Sir Launcelot hath caused all this sorrow.

During the decades when the 'Scottish Chaucerians' were at work there was only one poet in the south to break through the mediocrity of what was a dull period for English poetry, and that was John Skelton (c.1460–1529). Skelton won a 'laureateship' at both Oxford and Cambridge, and became tutor to Prince Henry, later Henry VIII. He took holy orders and was rector of Diss, Norfolk, for about ten years, and then returned to court where he acquired the title of *Orator Regius* in about 1512. (The *Bouge of Court* is a dream-allegory satirizing the life of the court.) As parish priest of Diss, Skelton earned some notoriety. He kept a mistress by whom he had a child, and complaints were made to the bishop. It is said that he responded by showing the naked baby to his congregation from the pulpit and protesting: 'If I had ... broughte forthe thys chylde without arms or legges, or that it was deformed ... I wolde never have blamed you to have complayned to the bishop of me; but to complayne without a cause, I say ... you be, and have be, & wyll and shall be knaves ...'[1]

Here speaks the extraordinary character who invented 'Skeltonics', if *invented* is the right term to apply to the devising of a formless form in which rhythmically anarchic short lines are spilt down the page so indiscriminately that rhyme seems to provide the sole discipline. *Philip Sparow* probably displays this style at its best. It is a mock-heroic

[1] The story is told in *Merye Tales of Skelton* (1567).

elegy, in part a burlesque requiem, for the deceased pet bird of a young lady, Jane Scrope. Skelton's persistent hammering and jingle are perhaps not out of place in this playful if tediously protracted burst of gentle mockery. And perhaps the battering of crude, tumbling jingles is not unsuited to its purpose in *The Tunning of Elinor Rumming*. It describes the keeper of an alehouse, a dirty woman with a dirty female clientele who pay for their drinks either by notching up credit or by depositing goods.

> Some brought their clipping shears,
> Some brought this and that,
> Some brought I wot n'ere what;
> Some brought their husband's hat ...

It is a rollicking, disorderly scene, full of quarrelling and drunkenness, spattered with bad language, bad smells, and obscenities:

> Maude Ruggy thither skipped:
> She was ugly hipped,
> And ugly thick lipped,
> Like an onion sided,
> Like tan leather hided ...

There is a more serious purpose in the two satires, *Colyn Clout* and *Why Come Ye not to Court?* The defiant battery of invective hurled at corruption in high places shows Skelton to be a master of vituperation. It is not difficult to understand how he earned Wolsey's hostility and was at some risk as a result. Indeed the elaborate play, *Magnificence*, is a Morality converted into a means of satirizing the powers that be. But neither this nor the stiltedly formalized *Garden of Laurel* is readily palatable except to the antiquarian. *Speke Parot* is unintelligible. It has been compared to *The Waste Land* because of the tangle of contemporary references its cryptic form conceals.

Many English ballads have come down to us in a form that dates from the fifteenth century. Oral transmission has left questions of authorship wrapped in mystery. It also accounts for the simple memorability of the stanzaic patterns and for the existence of the same 'poem' in different versions. Ballads have to be accepted on their own terms. By its very simplicity the form easily lapses into doggerel. Yet the impersonal presentation of a story, uncluttered by reflection and bare of psychological elaboration, can make a telling emotional impact. The better ballads contain beauty and pathos peculiar to the genre. In *Lord Thomas and Fair Annie* this is Annie's response when her lover asks her to receive the wife he is determined to take:

> 'But how can I gang maiden-like
> When maiden I am nane?
> Have I not born seven sons to thee,
> And am with child again?'

Sometimes highly dramatic use of the simplest devices of repetition and alliteration may create a pulsing sense of dash and urgency at a moment of crisis. Just so, in *Lady Maisry*, Lord William learns that Lady Maisry, his mistress, is being tortured for her love:

> 'O saddle me the black, the black,
> O saddle me the brown;
> O saddle me the swiftest steed
> That ever rade frae a town.'

Often a momentous scene of crucial action may be condensed into a few short lines that do their work obliquely and make a curiously concentrated impact. In *A Gest of Robyn Hode* the knight returns home to his wife after having been helped at the last moment to pay his debt to the Abbot of St Mary's, York. His lands are thereby saved from confiscation:

> 'Welcome, my lorde' sayd his lady:
> 'Syr, lost is all your good?'
> 'Be mery, dame' sayd the knyght
> 'And pray for Robin Hode.'

The oblique revelation can serve a tragic purpose too. The dying bride in *The Cruel Brother* brings the murder to light only as she is pressed with questions about her will:

> 'What will you leave to your brother John?'
> 'The gallows-tree to hang him on.'

The technique is a by-product of eschewing step-by-step narration. The ballads tend to focus attention lingeringly on moments of crisis without explicitly filling out connecting events. There is no accumulation of detail, but a deft selectivity and a weighted use of things basic to life's turning-points, happy and tragic; cradles, bride-beds, shrouds, graves and gallows-trees. The intimate emotional intensity of short ballads of personal distress, like *Fair Margaret and Sweet William*, complements the obvious thrust and excitement of longer narrative ballads that celebrate deeds of courage. Battles on the Scottish border, like the doings in Sherwood Forest, provided a lively impetus to balladry, which did not quickly die. Percy, the Earl of Northumberland, goes hunting in the borderland with 'fifteen hundred bowmen bold' in *Chevy Chase* and is confronted by Earl Douglas with a muster of 'twenty hundred Scottish speres'. The ensuing slaughter involves the deaths of both Percy and Douglas, and many bold and bloody deeds are vigorously enacted;

> For Withrington needs must I wayle
> As one in dolefull dumpes,
> For when his leggs were smitten of
> He fought upon his stumpes.[2]

Alongside the anonymous ballad there flourished the largely anonymous lyric. Of the lyrics that have survived many date from the fourteenth century, but most from the fifteenth and sixteenth centuries. The subjects are as various

[2] Ballads are quoted from F. J. Childs (ed.), *English and Scottish Popular Ballads* (Harrap, London, 1904).

as no doubt their authorship was. Many of the religious lyrics are songs to the Virgin Mary or to Christ, to the Cross or to the Sacrament. One of the loveliest, 'I sing of a maiden / That is makeles' presents the Incarnation in imagery as rich and as simple as the movements of nature's own life:

> He cam also stille
> Ther his moder was,
> As dew in Aprille
> That falleth on the grass.[3]

That the lyrical tradition did not lack exploration of verbal ambiguity as well as of imaginative natural correspondence is plain from a surviving thirteenth-century verse to Mary:

> Now goth sonne under wod:
> Me reweth, Marye, thy faire rode.
> Now goth sonne under Tre:
> Me reweth, Marye, thy sone and thee.

There are secular lyrics in praise of the natural world, of ale, of flowers and of women ('A woman is a worthy wight: / She serveth a man both daye and night'). There are sober reflections on death, and saddened outbursts against the female sex. But perhaps the most touching of all are those in which the religious and the secular meet and mix, sometimes joyfully, and sometimes wryly, as in the girl's outcry about Jankin who sings and serves so impressively at Mass:

> Jankin at the Agnus
> Bereth the pax-brede:
> He twinkled but said nowt,
> And on my fot he trede,
> Kyrieleyson.

[3] Lyrics are quoted from R. T. Davies (ed.), *Mediaeval English Lyrics* (Faber and Faber, London, 1963).

Benedicamus Domino
Christ from shame me shilde:
Deo gracias therto –
Alas! I go with childe,
Kyrieleyson.

3
The early sixteenth century

No literary personality of the early sixteenth century stands
out more impressively than Sir Thomas More (1478–1535).
He wrote his best-known book, *Utopia*, in Latin, but it was
translated into English in 1551. Interpretation of the book has
led to controversy. It cannot be treated as a straightforward
representation of an imaginary perfect state. C. S. Lewis
has observed that 'if it were intended as a serious treatise it
would be very confused indeed.'[1] Lewis regards it as the
playful product of intellectual high spirits, closer to satires
like *Gulliver's Travels* than to serious philosophical works

[1] C. S. Lewis, *English Literature in the Sixteenth Century* (Clarendon Press, Oxford, 1954).

like Plato's *Republic*. For More's imaginary state is sustained by slave labour, there is no private property, there is tedious uniformity of dress, attachment to home and to family is decried, euthanasia is recommended, divorce is by mutual consent, gold and silver are used to make chamber pots. These practices do not represent the values that More stood for. William Roper (1496–1578), his son-in-law and devoted disciple, left a delightful picture of More in his *Life of Sir Thomas More*. More emerges in it as a man eminently able to enjoy life yet profoundly aware of its transitoriness, a man whose joy was in simple things like love of his family and the pleasures of reading, yet who long sensed the inevitability of an ultimate clash between service to Henry and his religious faith. The picture reinforces Erasmus's exclamation: 'What did nature ever create milder, sweeter or happier than the character of Thomas More?'[2]

More's *Life of Richard III* is a knowledgeable historical study which has real dramatic power, both grave and comic, and it provided the source for Shakespeare's tragedy; but otherwise More's direct claim to be a contributor to English literature must depend on the controversial religious works he wrote in refutation of the opponents of orthodoxy, and for the most part they appeal only to the historian. But the *Dialogue of Comfort against Tribulation*, which he wrote in prison while awaiting execution for refusal to take the oath of supremacy to the king, is a moving and sensitive work. More unblinkingly faces what is before him while keeping a clear head and making every effort to be cheerful. Though he points patiently to the blessings of earthly tribulation, the Devil's power against the suffering Christian is fully reckoned with. The persistent humour and merriment are awesomely real, and the inevitable urgency is undergirded by a deep assurance and inner peace.

One of More's opponents in religious controversy was the

[2] Letter to Robert Fisher, 5 December 1499, quoted in J. Huizinga, *Erasmus of Rotterdam* (Phaidon Press, London, 1952).

Reformer, William Tyndale (?1494–1536). Like More's, his polemical works are of theological and historical rather than of literary significance, but his insistence on scriptural authority made him anxious to have a translation of the Bible. When the Bishop of London opposed his plan, he went to Germany and in 1526 his translation of the New Testament was issued at Worms, to be followed by the Pentateuch in 1530 and Jonah in 1531. Later revisions followed. Tyndale was indebted to Erasmus's Latin version of the New Testament and to Luther's German version, but he worked directly from the Greek and the Hebrew. There is a vigour and homeliness about his style which helped to determine the character of the Authorized Version. Some unforgettable words and phrases are his own inventions, such as 'passover', 'long-suffering', 'scapegoat', 'the Lord's anointed', 'flowing with milk and honey' and 'filthy lucre'.

Tyndale's work was taken up by Miles Coverdale (1488–1568), who published the first complete English Bible in 1535. Coverdale was not a linguistic scholar comparable to Tyndale: his version incorporated Tyndale's work and was otherwise indebted to the Vulgate, to Luther and to other sources. The revision of this version which he made at Thomas Cromwell's request was known as 'The Great Bible' (1539). Coverdale's importance is that he had a sensitive ear for English prose rhythm and a gift for felicitous phrasing, not always reliably grounded in scholarship, but contributing to the rich quality of the English Bible nevertheless. The expressions 'tender mercies' and 'loving kindness' are his. So too are the haunting phrases, 'His leaf also shall not wither' and 'my beauty is gone for very trouble'. It was the Great Bible which was revised under the direction of Archbishop Parker in 1568 and called the 'Bishops' Bible', and on this text the Authorized Version (1611) was to be based.

The one book of comparable significance in English literary history to that of the Bible is the Book of Common Prayer. Thomas Cranmer (1489–1556) was in charge of the preparation of the Prayer Book of 1549 (in the reign of

Edward VI) on which the Prayer Book of 1662 was based. What cannot be ascertained with confidence is the extent of Cranmer's personal contribution to the production of the text. His own original literary work in the field of theological controversy is not inspiring. Yet the achievement of the Book of Common Prayer in matching the Latin liturgy with an English rendering that has solemnity, beauty and sublimity, and yet is fresh and sinewy in its Englishness, is a remarkable one. The clarity of the English liturgy, its rhythmic vitality, its sonority and its rich compactness, have left their mark on our literature.

There are two prose writers of the period whose work was done in the educational field, Elyot and Ascham. Sir Thomas Elyot (c.1490–1546) published *The Boke Named the Governour* in 1531, and in the 'Proheme' dedicated it to Henry VIII as a work that 'treateth of the education of them that hereafter may be demed worthy to be governours of the publike weale'. The influence of the classics is evident; the philosophical and social emphasis on order is important: it was a book that Shakespeare evidently knew well, and the symbolization of order in the passage on 'The Good Order of Dancing' has left its imprint on the work of T. S. Eliot (*Four Quartets*). Roger Ascham, another humanist scholar, held a readership in Greek at Cambridge, and became tutor to Princess Elizabeth, the future queen, in her teens. Ascham managed to be a Protestant and Latin Secretary to Queen Mary at the same time, an indication perhaps of the charm of manner of which his contemporaries speak, though Camden observes that he was 'too much given to dicing and cockfighting'.[3] His book. *Toxophilus* (1545), is in praise of archery and in particular a defence of the English long-bow. It is written in the form of a dialogue and deals delightfully with the activities that might compete with Ascham's devotion to the bow – music, gaming and the up-and-coming

[3] Quoted by C. S. Lewis, *English Literature in the Sixteenth Century* (Clarendon Press, Oxford, 1954).

gun. But Ascham's best-known work, *The Schoolmaster*, on the education of boys, was not published until after his death, in 1570. In its attitude to the young it is a practical and sensitive book; but Ascham's humanist bias plays havoc with his literary judgement in some instances. He objects that the whole pleasure of Malory's *Morte Darthur* 'standeth in two special points, in open manslaughter and bold bawdery'. 'Those be counted the noblest knights', he complains, 'that do kill most men without any quarrel, and commit foulest adulteries by subtlest shifts.'

We turn to the poetry of the age, and that means chiefly to the work of Wyatt and Surrey, poets who had been dead ten years or more when their poems were first published in *Tottels Miscellany* in 1557. This collection is regarded as the prologue to the great burst of lyrical productivity that came in the reign of Elizabeth. Sir Thomas Wyatt (?1503–42) rose through a number of court appointments and took part in a diplomatic mission to Paris in 1526. In the same year an unhappy early marriage broke down. Later he was High Marshal of Calais, but came back to England in 1532. He was imprisoned for a short time on three occasions, but each time he was quickly restored to favour. He died of pneumonia in 1542. An urgent ride through bad weather to Falmouth, on diplomatic business, was the cause. Wyatt's relationship with Ann Boleyn, its possible connection with his second imprisonment (it came as she was arrested), and its more likely connection with some of his lyrics, has been the subject of much conjecture. If we compare his poems with the anonymous lyrics of the previous century we recognize a new sophistication of form and substance. The cultivated yet none the less authentic contrivances are presented sometimes with a swinging metrical regularity which reminds us that Wyatt often wrote his verses to be sung:

> My lute awake, perform the last
> Labour that thou and I shall waste;
> And end that I have now begonne:

And when this song is sung and past:
My lute be styll for I have done.

Wyatt has been compared to Donne for his capacity to
pack a lyric with dramatic power. The initial impact of *To
his unkind love* has Donne's thrust:

What rage is this? what furor? of what kinde?
What power, what plage doth wery thus my minde ...

And there is similar emotional force in the complaint of the
forsaken lover:

They flee from me, that sometime did me seek
With naked foot stalking within my chamber.

At his best Wyatt has an intensity of feeling, an unaffectedness of phrase, and a directness of tone which, contained
within a pressurized rhythmic pattern, sweep the reader
into intimate involvement with him. One is carried on the
tide. But it must be admitted that he is often not at his best.
Moreover he is always complaining, as a disappointed, ill-
treated lover. The melancholy is all-pervasive. Successive
titles read like a record of misery: *The lover forsaketh his
unkind love ... describeth his restless state ... laments the
death of his love ... blameth his love ... curseth the time
when he first fell in love ...* When Wyatt does turn aside
from his own miseries to be objective, the result is scarcely
more cheerful: *Of the mother that eat her child at the siege
of Jerusalem.*

Of course the suffering lover is a conventionalized figure in
the poetry of the period, and perhaps it is wrong to criticize
Wyatt for realizing the role with such intimate authenticity
that we seem to be in touch with an unhappy man. Such
convincing intensity is lacking in the work of Henry Howard,
Earl of Surrey (1517-47) who is to some extent Wyatt's
disciple, though more decisively under the influence of the
classics. He translated Books II and IV of Virgil's *Aeneid* in
unrhymed iambic pentameters, to earn for himself the

reputation of having invented blank verse. In his best lyrics he has a smoothness and polish that compare favourably with Wyatt's:

> O happy dames, that may embrace
> The fruit of your delight,
> Help to bewail the woeful case
> And eke the heavy plight
> Of me, that wonted to rejoice
> The fortune of my pleasant choice:
> Good ladies help to fill my mourning voice.

And there is a well-known sonnet on spring ('The soote season, that bud and bloom forth brings') that is vigorously fresh and observant, a model of compactness and control. Along with Surrey, other named poets represented in *Tottel's Miscellany* are Thomas Churchyard (*c.*1520–1604), Lord Vaux (1510–56) and Nicholas Grimald (1519–62).

The drama of this period is important, not for its intrinsic quality, but for its significance in linking the age of the Miracles and the Moralities with the magnificent outburst of dramatic literature in the Elizabethan Age. We take up the story of its development with an account of the Interludes, dramatic entertainments for a small cast, that were performed indoors at court and in colleges. They represent a movement away from the stylized allegory of the Moralities, for though some had a strong didactic element, others were lively farces, briefly working out a single situation or anecdotal argument in down-to-earth dialogue. John Heywood (?1497–?1580), husband of Sir Thomas More's niece and a skilled singer and virginalist, became a favoured courtier under both Henry VIII and Queen Mary. His play, *The Four P's*, dating from about 1522, is a lively specimen of the Interlude form. A Palmer, a Pardoner, and a 'Pothecary meet and excitedly dispute in defence of their respective callings. A Pedlar joins them and arranges a competition for the maximum achievement in lying. The discussion is earthy and frank. The ability of the contestants to lie, and the rabelaisian flavour of the inventiveness, may be illustrated by the 'Pothecary's story of how he cured a woman by plugging her up behind with a tampion, which was fired so explosively that it was propelled ten miles across country and demolished a castle. But it is the Palmer who wins the prize for the biggest whopper of all: he has never in all his life seen a woman 'out of patience'.

The brief Interlude, *A Mery Play between Johan Johan, the Husband, Tyb his Wife, and Sir Johan the Priest* (in print by 1533), is generally attributed to Heywood. There are only three characters; terrified, hen-pecked husband, shrewish wife and parish priest. The slapstick in this domestic triangle is hearty, the irony knocked home with a sledge-hammer. The husband is a bully, full of talk about wife-beating, until his wife actually appears: then he is the poor cuckold who is kept busy at the chores while Tyb and the priest feast on a pie. The use of asides enlivens the situation:

JOHAN (*aside*):
    If that parish priest, Sir John
    Did not see her now and then
    And give her absolution upon a bed
    For woe and pain she would soon be dead.

The priest is a smooth, amusing rogue. The sore-tried husband rebels at the end, takes up a shovel of coal and drives wife and priest out of the house.

The more respectable vein in Heywood's work can be seen in *The Play of the Weather* (also published in 1533), which opens with Jupiter speaking from his throne (as earlier plays began with a speech from God). Jupiter proclaims his intention to conduct an opinion poll about reforming the weather. Mery-report is the pollster who interviews various people with their conflicting requirements – a Merchant, a Ranger, a Water-Miller, a Wind-Miller, a Launder and so on. Jupiter finally earns the gratitude of all by proclaiming a balanced mixture of weather calculated to serve the needs of each in turn.

Ralph Roister Doister is know as the first English comedy. It was written by Nicholas Udall (1505–56) headmaster of Eton for seven years, but dismissed as a flogger. The work is indebted to Plautus and Terence. It is a five-act comedy in rather crude rhymed verse with a good deal of horseplay. Dame Christian Custance is a wealthy widow affianced to Gawin Goodlucke, a London merchant who is away from home. Roister Doister is a braggart and a dunderhead, but Mathew Merygreek, 'the fun-maker', encourages him to woo her. The Dame is in the plot and Ralph's attempt to take her by storm 'in martial array' is forcefully repulsed. Another comedy acted in the 1550s was *Gammer Gurton's Needle*, sometimes attributed to William Stevenson, a fellow of Christ's College, Cambridge. Gammer Gurton has been mending Hodge's breeches and has lost her needle. First the household, then the village, is thrown into confusion by the search, the false accusations, the mischievous elaborations, assaults and counter-assaults, until finally a hand is laid forcefully on Hodge's buttocks and the needle is painfully discovered. Diccon, the vagabond Bedlamite, in the role of mischief-maker, adds salt to this farce of coarse village life played out between Gammer Gurton's house and Dame Chat's ale-house. It is a display of cumulative horseplay on a studiedly structured classical base. The rhyming couplets are crude and the idiom coarse. Listen to Hodge:

> My guts they yawl-crawl, and all my belly rumbleth,
> The puddings cannot lie still, each one over other
> tumbleth.

A parallel development in tragedy was marked by the acting of *Gorboduc* at the Inner Temple in 1561. Regarded as 'the first English tragedy', it was the fruit of a collaboration between Thomas Norton (1532–84), who wrote the first three acts, and Thomas Sackville, Earl of Dorset (1536–1608), who wrote the last two acts. The play is modelled on Seneca and thus matches Udall's imitation of Plautus and Terence: indeed the action takes place offstage and is then presented to the audience in narration. But there are important native influences too. The story of Gorboduc appears in Geoffrey of Monmouth. The authors of the play sum up the argument themselves:

> Gorboduc, king of Britain, divided his realm in his lifetime to his sons, Ferrex and Porrex; the sons fell to division; the younger killed the elder; the mother, that more dearly loved the elder, for revenge killed the younger; the people, moved with the cruelty of the fact, rose in rebellion and slew both father and mother ...

Civil war and devastation follow.

The moral pattern determines the play's structure. Each development in the plot is given its appropriate moral, a moral emphasized in the dumb shows that introduce each act and in the speeches of the Chorus that round each act off. Finally the moral of the whole is summed up in six points at the end with a precision befitting the pulpit. And the general message had special contemporary political implications in drawing attention to the dangers of disputed sucession at a time when Queen Elizabeth was being urged to marry. The influence of the Morality play is evident. Ferrex stands listening to the alternating advice of good and evil counsellors, Dordan and Hermon, the one urging restraint, the other inciting to strife by flattery and slander. Porrex too stands between a wise counsellor, Philander, and a parasite, Tynder. The fusion of classical form with native legendary history and features of medieval dramatic presentation is interesting, and the play's blank verse, if it lacks all variety, does not lack force or dignity.

George Gascoigne (c.1530–77) adapted Ariosto's *Suppositi* as a prose comedy under the title, *Supposes*. In writing *Jocasta*, a version of the *Phoenissae* by Euripides, Gascoigne gave the English theatre its first tragedy from the Greek.

(The play was translated from an Italian version.) But more significant in itself is *Cambises* (*c*.1560) by Thomas Preston (1537–98). Half Morality play and half tragedy, it is an unpolished and ill-planned work often extravagantly written and crudely conceived. When Marian-be-good deals roughly with Ambidexter, the direction reads: *'Here let her swinge him in her brome: she gets him down, and he her down, – thus one on top of another make pastime.'* Allegorical personifications like Shame, Diligence and Execution play their part, and there are ruffians called Huf, Ruf and Snuf. The action is heavily moralistic. King Cambises, tempted by Vice, gives way to cruelty and murder. Sisamnes, the judge, also tempted by Vice, gives way to injustice. The two meet their doom. Both *Gorboduc* and *Cambises* deal with a divided kingdom, a theme which is to be important in Elizabethan tragedy. However, it is impossible to take the bombast of *Cambises* seriously. 'With velvet paps I gave thee suck', laments the mother of a brutally murdered child, and 'Oh, oh! my hart, my hart! O, my bum will break', cries Ambidexter at the end. We can understand Falstaff's mockery in *1 Henry IV*, 2, iv: 'I must speak in passion, and I will do it in King Cambyses' vein.'

4
Elizabethan drama
(Shakespeare and his predecessors)

The English literature of the Elizabethan and Jacobean Ages is one of the great phenomena of European culture. The period was one of immense and concentrated literary activity. Nor did the activity end with the death of James I, convenient as that may be as a dividing line, for the work of the Cavalier poets as well as *Paradise Lost* was to follow. If we consider what was written in English between the birth of Spenser in 1552 and the death of Milton in 1674 we find ourselves confronted by a great concourse of major and minor writers of astonishing variety. It is necessary to pick one's way through the mass of material with guide lines that are rough and ready. Even the convenient distinction between drama and poetry is imprecise. A very large proportion of the drama was in verse. The great dramatists were poets.

There was a group of young writers at the beginning of this period who have come to be known as the 'University Wits' because, after studying at Oxford or Cambridge, they moved to London to take up writing professionally. Greene, Lyly, Nashe, Lodge and Peele, as well as Marlowe, are classed among them. They represent an interesting cultural development in their attempt to put the fruits of their education before the public and to professionalize their enthusiasm for literature and ideas. They worked as prose-writers and poets as well as for the theatre, and so in some cases their names will recur later in our study. The blend of university culture and gentlemanly sophistication which some of them brought to bear on the popular theatre is significant, while Greene and Nashe may be credited with the achievement of marrying university culture and popular tradition.

John Lyly (c. 1554–1606) wrote prose fiction (*Euphues*)[1] as well as plays. His prose comedy, *Campaspe*, was performed publicly in Blackfriars Hall in 1583, then before the queen at court on New Year's Day, 1584. The choirboys of St Paul's were the performers. The story comes from Pliny. Alexander the Great has a Theban beauty, Campaspe, among his prisoners: he frees her and orders Apelles to paint her portrait. Painter and sitter fall in love, and Apelles delays completion of the portrait by spoiling it intentionally, so as to go on seeing her. Alexander sees through the ruse, but nobly surrenders Campaspe to the artist. The play is far from being an exercise in 'euphuism'. There *is* mannered prose, of course. 'I cannot tell, Alexander,' says Hephestion, 'whether the report be more shameful to be heard or the cause sorrowful to be believed.' But there is also brisk exchange of concise dialogue, notably between Alexander and the philosopher, Diogenes, who sits on stage in his tub:

ALEXANDER; What dost thou want?

[1] For *Euphues* and 'euphuism' see chapter 8.

DIOGENES: Nothing that you have.
ALEXANDER: I have the world at command.
DIOGENES: And I in contempt.
ALEXANDER: How should I learn to be content?
DIOGENES: Unlearn to covet.

This is a far cry from the crudity of *The Four P's* or the pomposity of *Cambises*.

Lyly's later plays, *Midas* (1592) and *Endimion* (1591), are based on classical legend, the former on the story of the king who was granted his wish that everything he touched should turn to gold – and had to beg release from the boon when he found that even the food he tried to eat became gold – the latter on the story of Endimion's passion for the moon, Cynthia, a story which was later to be told by Keats. In both plays Lyly allegorizes the material shrewdly so as to point to contemporary affairs. Midas is a satirical study of Philip of Spain and his covetous imperialism. The king is touched with bitter remorse for his lust for gold, and there are echoes of the destruction of the Armada in his outburst:

> I have written my laws in blood, and made my gods of gold. Have I not made the sea to groan under the number of my ships, and have they not perished that there was not two left to make a number?

Likewise *Endimion* has allegorical parallels pointing at the relationship between Elizabeth and Leicester.

George Peele (1556–?97) was a less original writer than Lyly, but he was prolific both as poet and playwright. The link with Lyly is evident in *The Arraignment of Paris*, which was performed before Queen Elizabeth about the same time as Lyly's *Campaspe*. It tells of Paris's call to judge the beauty contest between Juno, Pallas and Venus. When his choice falls on Venus the defeated competitors call him to judgement before Zeus and the gods. The decision is eventually put in the hands of Diana, who graciously and tactfully gives the prize apple to Queen Elizabeth. The tone and atmosphere are those of the romantic pastoral, and the play is enlivened with song, dance and spectacle. *The Battle of Alcazar* (1594), a verse tragedy in Marlovian vein, dealing with recent history and centred on Sebastian, king of Portugal, is too extravagant in its rhetoric to be convincing (it is one of the plays quoted in parodic bombast by Pistol in *Henry IV Part 2*), but the contrast between it and *The Arraignment of Paris* is remarkable, as is the contrast between it and *The Old Wives' Tale*. Peele's versatility in assaying forms so diverse is commendable, even if it is the versatility of the competent imitator. *The Old Wive's Tale*, in which two brothers (like those in *Comus*) are seeking a lady held captive by a magician, is a complex synthesis of fairytale material, astonishing in its variety.

The most successful plays by Lyly and Peele were comedies and, before we look at Greene, another of the 'University Wits', we may usefully turn to note the developments made by Shakespeare's predecessors in tragedy, Kyd and Marlowe. To Thomas Kyd (1558–93) goes the credit for having launched the Elizabethan revenge tragedy on its course. *The Spanish Tragedy* is a masterly play in which event is piled on event in a cumulative tangle of injury, conspiracy and vengeance, and in which rivalries and jealousies, frustration and ambition, intensify the emotional escalation to multiple murder. Bel-imperia, a lady of royal blood, has lost her lover, Don Andrea, killed in battle by Balthazar (of Portugal). Horatio, Hieronimo's son, and Lorenzo, Bel-imperia's brother, have taken Balthazar prisoner. Balthazar falls in love with Bel-imperia, who hates him. Lorenzo, a villain, abets him. The two men murder Bel-imperia's chosen lover, Horatio; and Horatio's father, Hieronimo, finds the hanging corpse. Here begins a long campaign by Hieronimo to discover the identity of the murderers and to exact vengeance, a campaign carried on, like Hamlet's, with subterfuge and plotting, and culminating in a play within the play. This inner play suddenly moves from fantasy to reality when stage murder becomes real murder: Lorenzo and Balthazar, who have agreed to take part, are stabbed to death. Kyd had little to match the poetic gifts of Shakespeare and Marlowe, but his theatrical sense, his powerful use of dramatic irony and his skilful management of plot make his play a notable breakthrough when measured against its predecessors.

In strong contrast to the cultivated literary tone and foreign aristocratic setting of *The Spanish Tragedy*, the anonymous play, *Arden of Feversham* (1592) is a domestic tragedy of contemporary English life based on an actual murder committed in 1551. Mistress Arden and her lover, Mosbie, make repeated attempts to have her husband murdered. A series of failures on the part of the men they employ, Black Will and Shakebag, adds to the tension and suspense. After much protraction, the combined efforts of four conspirators, including Alice Arden herself, do Arden to death in his own home. There is psychological reality in the central theme, and the characters as a whole belong to the world immediately outside the Elizabethan theatre. Arden himself is a gentleman landowner: a landlord, a painter, a goldsmith and a sailor appear among the cast. The straightforwardness of the issues, the naturalness of the social background and the directness of the passion aroused, give conviction to the play. The blank verse is fluent in rhythm, fresh and uncontrived in idiom.

With the work of Christopher Marlowe (1564–93), however, we reach a far higher level of theatrical skill and accomplishment. The new grandeur is grandly heralded in the prologue to *Tamburlaine the Great*, which was performed in about 1587:

> From jigging veins of rhyming mother-wits,
> And such conceits as clownage keeps in pay,
> We'll lead you to the stately tent of war ...

The play was such a success that a sequel was written, *Tamburlaine Part 2*. The two do not form a cunningly structured drama, but present a succession of adventures.

Tamburlaine makes his grandiose progress through a sequence of battles, achieving more and bigger victories, greater and greater power. There is no human retribution at the end: Tamburlaine does not lose a battle; he dies in the midst of another victory. Each battle is introduced by a poetic survey of the forces involved – long geographical catalogues in which Marlowe's rhetoric surges, wave upon wave. Between the battles Tamburlaine rages about his future conquests, and his arrogant lust for destruction leads to a hideous orgy of excess. The climax of indignities inflicted in *Part 1* is when Tamburlaine has the conquered Turkish emperor, Bajazet, dragged about in a cage. 'Bring out my footstool', Tamburlaine cries, and Bajazet is let out so that Tamburlaine can tread on him in mounting his throne. Eventually Bajazet ends his humiliation by beating his own brains out against the side of the cage. Thereupon his wife, Zabina, runs against the cage and brains herself too. In *Part 2* conquered kings are harnessed, bitted, reined and whipped: they draw Tamburlaine's chariot. But for all the excesses of action and rhetoric, Marlowe's 'mighty line' and his instinct for what tells on the stage made a powerful impact on the Elizabethans. Moreover a meaningful moral pattern emerges in the spectacle of the would-be world-conqueror's impotence to save either the beloved Zenocrate or himself from man's last enemy. Tamburlaine is undefeated by man, but the 'ugly monster Death', whom he has regarded as his slave, puts an end to his immoderate claim to exercise the 'power of Heaven's eternal majesty' as the 'scourge of God and terror of the world'.

The Jew of Malta was first performed in about 1592. Ferneze, governor of Malta, extracts money from the Jews in order to pay tribute due to Turkey. Barabas is deprived of all his wealth, and embarks on a complex career of revenge in which ultimately he kills even his own daughter, Abigail. Eventually he himself becomes governor of Malta and plots to kill the Turkish commander. He is foolish enough to involve Ferneze and is out-plotted. The drama is a series of episodes strung together and, as each one ends, there is a sense of completion. The play seems to be continually starting again. As for the moral drift of the work, we seem to enter a society of rogues seen through the eyes of a cynic. A significant prologue is spoken by Machiavel himself, summing up the philosophy of unprincipled opportunism (religion is a 'childish toy' and there is 'no sin but ignorance') which he came to represent for the Elizabethans. He has been the inspiration of the Duke of Guise (in Marlowe's *The Massacre at Paris*), he claims, and now the Jew is his disciple.

The tone of *Edward II* (1593) is graver and its commentary on life more profound. Reflection towards the end, especially by Edward, on the emptiness of earthly joys, the paradox of earthly power, and the transience of earthly good fortune, add to the play's tragic dimensions. The construction is episodic, in that there is a series of conflicts between the king and his nobles (Young Mortimer is another 'machiavellian'), with victory alternating between the two sides. Nevertheless the personality of Edward gives unity to the play. He is conceived as a weak yet not insensitive man goaded to desperation by his scheming opponents. Though he asserts that the 'griefs of private men are soon allayed / But not of kings', it is very much a personal tragedy, the tragedy of one who has worshipped a favourite as Tamburlaine worshipped physical power and Faustus spiritual power; and the pathos is acute at the end, when the king is imprisoned and murdered. Having stood ten days 'in mire and puddle', kept awake by a ceaseless drum-beat, he contemplates his dripping, tattered clothes and says:

> Tell Isabel the queen, I looked not thus,
> When for her sake I ran at tilt in France
> And there unhorsed the Duke of Cleremont.

The sad picture of the deposed monarch effects a shift in the audience's feelings towards a victim whose weakness and stupidity as king alienated sympathy. In this respect, as in the abdication scene, the play anticipates Shakespeare's *Richard II*.

Dr Faustus contains Marlowe's finest work. The hero sells his soul to the Devil in exchange for twenty-four years of life in which the demon Mephistophilis will be at his disposal. Aristotle laid down that a play should have a beginning, a middle and an end. The proposition might seem superfluous until one has read *Dr Faustus*, whose middle is mostly so poor by comparison with the beginning and the end that the whole seems like a mutilated masterpiece, and Marlowe's collaborator is assumed to have been largely responsible for the central scenes. All that leads up to the making of the diabolical contract, together with the representation of Faustus's last agonies, represents dramatic poetry that matches the intensity of Shakespeare. But between these magnificent extremes the inner episodes, displaying Faustus's years of pleasure, are disfigured by crude slapstick and farcical conjuring tricks. A papal banquet is interrupted by invisible food-snatching, and Faustus enjoys the dubious privilege of giving the pontiff a box on the ears. But at the play's extremes, in mature Marlovian verse, now as flexible as it is powerful, the sense of cosmic conflict involving the powers of darkness is potent and pervasive. 'This is hell', says Mephistophilis, giving expression to the conception of unlocalized damnation:

> Thinkst thou that I, who saw the face of God,
> And tasted the eternal joys of heaven,
> Am not tormented with ten thousand hells
> In being depriv'd of everlasting bliss.

When Marlowe's hand is recognizably at work we are in a world with heights above and depths beneath. In the closing soliloquy Faustus's final agony is voiced with tormenting acuteness in imagery of tumultuous power. Such poetry, coming from the pen of a man who was dead before he was thirty, compels one to speculate on what literature lost when Marlowe was stabbed to death in a tavern in Deptford.

Robert Greene (*c.*1560–92) is much quoted for his disparagement of Shakespeare in his autobiographical work, *Greene's Groatsworth of Wit, bought with a Million of Repentance.* Shakespeare is 'an upstart crow, beautified with our feathers that with his *Tygers hart wrapt in a Players hyde*' imagines he can 'bombast out a blank verse as the best of you', and thinks he is 'the only Shakescene in the country'. In the comedy, *Friar Bacon and Friar Bungay*, Greene makes use of the kind of legendary stories of necromancy that gathered around the two medieval scholars, Roger Bacon and Thomas Bungay. Friar Bacon manufactures a brass head that will speak by diabolical power and:

> tell out strange and uncouth aphorisms
> And girt fair England with a wall of brass.

Bacon and Bungay keep watch for sixty nights and days respectively, awaiting the message: then Bacon goes to sleep, ordering his man, Miles, to awaken him when the head utters. Miles thinks it futile to call Bacon for the first two brief utterances ('Time is' and 'Time was') and at the third utterance ('Time is past') lightning destroys the head so that all Bacon's work is brought to nothing. The accompanying love story of Lacy, Earl of Lincoln, for Margaret of Fressingfield, a keeper's daughter and a delightful romantic heroine, is managed with freshness and charm. The touch is a light one, and Greene is at his best. We are in the reign of Henry III and Friar Bacon's closing prophecy foresees the golden age of England's peace and prosperity under the queen whose 'brightness shall deface proud Phoebus' flower', Elizabeth.

Greene's satire, *A Looking Glass for London*, has its setting in Nineveh. Pictures of corruption are interspersed with moral exhortations from Oseas, who acts as chorus and pricks the conscience of Londoners. Finally the prophet Jonas arrives and persuades court and city to a general repentance. The play's lesson is pressed home in a series of extravagant spectacles requiring elaborate stage machinery.

One character is struck dead by lightning, another swallowed into the earth by fire; a prophet descends from the sky; and a hand issues from a cloud, gripping a flaming sword. There is neater workmanship in *James IV*. The Scottish king is married to Dorothea, daughter of Henry VII, but his wayward passion for Ida, daughter of the Countess of Arran, is fanned by the villainous Ateukin (another disciple of Machiavel). The queen remains faithful and devoted even after an attempt on her life. Ida is chaste against royal pressure and marries Eustace for love. The two firm and attractive women are finely portrayed. The blank verse is more disciplined and, at suitable points, veers into tidy couplets.

William Shakespeare (1564–1616) was the son of a Stratford-on-Avon tradesman important enough to hold the highest municipal office. He was probably educated at Stratford Grammar School, and at the age of eighteen married Anne Hathaway, a young woman of twenty-six. They had three children of whom one (Hamnet) died in childhood. Shakespeare had made his name in London by 1592 when Greene attacked him, parodying a line from the first act of *Henry VI Part 3* ('O tiger's heart, wrapp'd in a woman's hide'). Nashe, in the same year, plainly seems to allude to the popularity of *Henry VI Part 1* when he speaks (in *Pierce Pennilesse*) of 'ten thousand spectators at least (at several times)' beholding the scenes of Talbot's death. Shakespeare joined the theatrical company known as the Lord Chamberlain's Men, and in 1599 he and others from this company built the Globe Theatre and made it the outstanding theatre of the day. The company became the King's Men in 1603 and continued to dominate theatrical life. Meanwhile his share in this company and its theatre had made Shakespeare affluent, and he bought a fine house in Stratford. The King's Men took over a further theatre, Blackfriars, in 1608, but Shakespeare retired to Stratford in 1611, where he died five years later.

Shakespeare's attachment to a particular company in

which he had a financial interest supplied him with the kind of opportunity and motive which stimulate a writer. The Shakesperian phenomenon is not solely a matter of individual genius. Commercial and technical conditions were congenial. Moreover the form (the drama) had got through its teething stages and was ripe for high fulfilments, and the medium (the English language) was at a point of rich potential in terms of its historical development. We shall consider, in order, Shakespeare's early and mature comedies, his histories, his tragedies and problem plays, and his last romances.

The four early comedies, belonging to the years 1592 to 1595, only fitfully foreshadow the achievement of the mature comedies that followed in the subsequent five years. *The Comedy of Errors* is an adaptation of Plautus's *Menaechmi* and his *Amphitruo*. The search for lost and separated twin sons, with their respective lost and separated twin servants, while the pairs are in the same city of Ephesus, has farcical possibilities that are fully exploited in the comic entanglements, though the whole is contained within the grave framework of a threat hanging over the seeker. In *Love's Labour's Lost* the King of Navarre and three nobles pledge themselves to live without women for three years, turning the court into 'a little Academe / Still and contemplative in living art'. A royal feminine embassy arrives from France, and the young men quickly learn that young blood 'doth not obey an old decree'. They must needs lose their oaths to find themselves, or lose themselves to keep their oaths. Nor is their education complete when they have understood that withdrawal and book-learning are not the route to all knowledge. The visiting Princess hears of her father's death: there is a change of tone and the young lovers are submitted to a twelve-month probationary test of their love. The need for education by experience is the unifying theme. There is plenty of wit and much charming rhymed verse, and there is no dearth of topicality. Contemporary affectations of speech come in for some hearty parody. There is less verbal brilliance in *The Two Gentlemen of Verona*: it is more like a character play. Proteus, who is faithless to his mistress Julia, faithless in wooing his dear friend Valentine's beloved, Silvia, and faithless in betraying Valentine to Silvia's father, is, happily, faithless to his own villainy at the end in timely repentance and re-conversion to love of constant Julia. (Julia does her stint as a disguised pageboy in Proteus's service.) The balanced exploration of love and friendship is expeditiously contrived, and not on one social level alone. Masculine fidelity is touchingly evident in the devotion of Proteus's 'clownish servant' Launce to his pet dog Crab, a sour, dumb partner in much drollery. ('I have sat in the stocks for puddings he hath eaten: otherwise he had been executed.')

Petruchio is the energetic and resourceful gentleman who brings the termagant Katherina to heel in *The Taming of the Shrew*, an anti-feminist tract to delight the male heart. Katherina has some psychological basis for her tantrums in the masculine competition for the hand of her attractive younger sister, Bianca ('She is your treasure, she must have a husband'). The crudity of the methods employed to humiliate the woman who is 'renowned in Padua for her scolding tongue' is somewhat offset by Petruchio's masterful irony – first in pretending to find her a gentle creature, later in irresistibly denying her food and clothes on the grounds that they are not good enough for her, and making a noble virtue out of it:

> Well, come, my Kate; we will unto your father's,
> Even in these honest mean habiliments:
> Our purses shall be proud, our garments poor,
> For 'tis the mind that makes the body rich.

Thus handled, 'Katherina the curst' is fully subjugated. And she is also established in the family hierarchy as daughter number one.

A Midsummer Night's Dream marks the change to maturity. The workmanship is deft, the poetry almost unfailing. Three strands of action are skilfully woven together, the first a crossed pattern of love between two pairs of lovers who are brought together in a wood at night. Here their story is interwoven with that of the fairy king Oberon and his queen Titania, who are quarrelling. A misapplied fairy love-juice complicates the entanglement of the human lovers further. The third strand in the plot is supplied by Bottom and his fellow tradesmen who are rehearsing a play for the wedding of the Duke of Athens. Shakespeare gives the love plot an appropriate semi-stylized flavour by his use of rhymed couplets. The neat coincidences and contrived conflicts of affection are worked out with the formal musical structure of a ballet. Thus handled, they tone in well with the fantasy world of fairies, charms and potions. A greater contrast is provided by Bottom and his fellow mechanicals, whose performance of the play 'Pyramus and Thisbe' is hilarious. The simple-minded, managerial Bottom reflects a close, compassionate, yet wryly humorous study of the working man.

The very different fantastic element in *The Merchant of Venice* requires us to accept a world where a suitor may win or lose a wealthy bride by opening the right casket, or one of two wrong ones – the three made of lead, silver and gold respectively. We are also asked to accept that a Jewish moneylender is a fit object for Christian contempt, and that if his daughter runs away with a Christian lover and takes her father's moneybags with her, she is to be congratulated on both counts. We know from Marlowe's *The Jew of Malta* that the Jew was a fit target for the groundlings' hostility; and the implication of the Portuguese Jew, Roderigo Lopez, in a plot to poison Queen Elizabeth, gave a fillip to anti-Jewish themes for a time. But the play performs convincingly: the stereotyped 'wicked Jew' of literature is perhaps no more offensive to Semites than the stereotyped 'wicked stepmother' of fairy stories is damaging to second wives; and Shakespeare of course made Shylock more complex than that. He is not only the repellently vengeful moneylender who can relish the prospect of having a pound of his debtor's flesh in lieu of payment; he is also the victim of anti-Semite contempt who can cry out in protest that the Jew has eyes and hands, senses and passions, like other men, is 'fed with the same food, hurt with the same weapons ... warmed and cooled by the same winter and summer as a Christian is'.

The three comedies, *Much Ado about Nothing, As You Like It* and *Twelfth Night,* give astonishing proof of Shakespeare's now established virtuosity. In the first the device by which Beatrice and Benedick, arch-enemies of each other and of marriage, are tricked into believing in each other's devotion, and then led to acceptance of each other, is managed with courtly adroitness and high spirits. The other plot, whereby an arch-villain deceives Claudio into believing his beloved Hero unfaithful even on the eve of her wedding (he displays a night tryst in which she is impersonated by her maid), leads to a painful rejection before the altar of a finely presented woman, and a tragic note is sounded. Beatrice and Benedick are at once united in the conviction that Hero has been wronged, and that alliance helps to make the transformation of their relationship plausible. The parallelism between the plot to deceive a light-hearted couple (Beatrice and Benedick) into love and happiness, and the plot to deceive an earnest couple out of happiness, is balanced by the parallelism between the ready assumption of each other's enmity that so long divides Beatrice from Benedick, and the ready credence given to Hero's infidelity that so long divides Hero from Claudio. Dogberry and Verges, a blundering constable and his colleague, are a delightful answer to the technical question of how to bring the deception of the hero to light. Dogberry's heavy-footed, heavy-worded helpfulness and obtuseness leave us wondering why we do not call a malapropism a dogberryism.

As You Like It and *Twelfth Night* represent the peak of Shakespeare's achievement in pure comedy. Most of the action of the former takes place in the Forest of Arden, another idealized woodland, inhabited by a banished Duke who holds court there 'like the old Robin Hood of England'. Hither come those who have good reason to flee the world's injustices: Orlando, brutally done out of his due inheritance by his elder brother; Rosalind (the Duke's daughter), invidiously cast out by the usurper, her uncle; and Celia, her cousin, determined to share her fate. Orlando and Rosalind are in love, and Rosalind escapes to the forest in the disguise of a young man, Ganymede. As such, she encourages Orlando to find solace in treating her as his lost lady, Rosalind. The situation thus contrived is the extreme instance of Shakesperian multiple irony in exploiting female impersonation by boy actors. A boy actor impersonates a girl (Rosalind) who impersonates a boy (Ganymede) who impersonates a girl ('You must call me Rosalind'). The complications and dénouements are managed by wilful and playful human contrivances with some help from 'an old religious man' who, in the nick of time, converts the wicked uncle 'from his enterprise (i.e. vengeance) and from the world'. Shakespeare took his material from Lodge's *Rosalynde*, but the two characters who spice the play with melancholy disillusionment and caustic humour, Jaques and Touchstone, are Shakespeare's inventions.

What makes *As You Like It* and *Twelfth Night* outstanding is the prevailing imaginative control of word and idea by which everything is contained within a single living whole. We spoke of Shakespeare's success in weaving diverse themes together in earlier comedies. 'Interweaving' would be an inadequate word to use of the artistry that makes a harmony of the variety of these two plays: rather there is fusion. In *Twelfth Night* the theme of identities confused in separated twins (Sebastian and Viola) recalls *The Comedy of Errors* just as the theme of a girl in male disguise (Viola as Cesario) harks back to *The Two Gentlemen of Verona*. *Twelfth Night* touches such themes with a new freshness. Duke Orsino uses faithful 'Cesario' (Viola, who loves him deeply) to press his suit with the unresponsive Olivia, and Olivia falls in love with the go-between. The discovery of the genuinely masculine twin, Sebastian, enables both Orsino and Olivia to be happily partnered at the end. We see Shakespeare's comic characterization at full maturity in the persons of Sir Toby Belch, Sir Andrew Aguecheek and Malvolio; and this is the play where Feste, the clown, sings 'O mistress mine' and 'Come away, death'. It is packed with riches.

To read Shakespeare's histories in chronological sequence enables the reader to get a bird's eye view of political history (as seen through Elizabethan eyes) from the time of the composition of *The Canterbury Tales* to the reign of Henry VIII. But Shakespeare composed the 'later' cycle (*Henry VI* and *Richard III*) before the 'earlier' and much superior cycle (*Richard II*, *Henry IV* and *Henry V*). Moreover there is some dispute about the authorship of *Henry VI* and the extent to which other hands than Shakespeare's were involved in its composition. Two plays stand apart from these two tetralogies, *King John* and *Henry VIII*. *King John* has nothing to do with Magna Carta, but a good deal to do with John's right to the throne, over against the claim of Arthur, his nephew. The French are an additional external threat. Two forceful mothers, Queen Elinor and Constance, are powerful contenders for their respective sons, the king and the king's nephew. Unforgettable elements in the play are the tender feeling for gentle Prince Arthur's suffering and the bold wit of Philip Faulconbridge, bastard son of Cœur de Lion. *Henry VIII*, in which Shakespeare collaborated with Fletcher, is memorable for the dignity in distress of Queen Katharine and for Wolsey's bearing at his fall. He has ventured like a swimming boy 'many summers in a sea of glory' far beyond his depth. But the man that hangs on princes' favours – 'when he falls, he falls like Lucifer, / Never to hope again'. An odd interest of the play is that at a performance at the Globe Theatre in 1613 the firing of a cannon at the end of Act I brought the house down in flames.

'During the time of the civil wars of York and Lancaster, England was a perfect bear-garden, and Shakespeare has given us a very lively picture of the scene.' Such was Haz-litt's summing up of the three parts of *Henry VI*. In *Part 1* white and red roses are plucked by Richard Plantagenet and the Earl of Somerset, the seeds of disintegration are sown at home, and the rot sets in, while abroad French cities change hands with dizzying rapidity. A potted history lesson in Act II sorts out the genealogies that supply the country with rivals for the crown. *Part 2* traces the growing intrigue of the Duke of York and his allies, and the defeat and death of Humphrey, Duke of Gloucester, the king's uncle and Pro-tector. In *Part 3*, after the king's surrender of the future succession, the swaying fortunes of the two factions in suc-cessive battles, in strategic moves and counter-moves, cul-minate in the murder of Henry VI. Edward IV's power is established, but the traitor Richard (the future Richard III) is in the nest. In spite of the 'bitty' character of the dramatic treatment, there is an overall rhythm and a unity of tone in the work as a whole. Henry VI, for all his imperfections as a monarch ('I'll leave my son my virtuous deeds behind, / And would my father had left me no more!'), is depicted as a standard of personal Christian goodness. He and his coun-try are gradually stripped of those bright luminaries of heroic and loyal action on which the health of the body politic depends. Thus Talbot, the warrior symbol of courage, is killed in *Part 1* and Humphrey, the honest Protector, is killed in *Part 2*. On the ensuing darkness a gleam of new light breaks towards the end of *Part 3* in the young person of Henry, Earl of Richmond, the future Henry VII, 'Eng-land's hope'. An interesting feature throughout is the sig-nificant part played by strong-minded, ambitious women in England's descent into national disarray. Joan of Arc's witch-ery in *Part 1* is succeeded by Eleanor Duchess of Glouces-ter's witchery in *Part 2*, and the king's wife, Queen Margaret, is as evil a genius as is the Protector's wife (Eleanor).

As deeds of individual and party vengeance accumulate, the comments of participants remind us how evil leads to remorse and suffering, and a massive pattern of retribution is worked out whose climax is before us in *Richard III*, where evil is clarified and concentrated into the person of Richard, part machiavellian villain, part Morality Devil. Each part of *Henry VI* leaves us waiting for the next instalment, but *Richard III* is a tragedy complete in itself. There is single-minded representation of human evil in Richard, and a mythic record of its cost in the memories of Queen Margaret. At Bosworth Field the gathered ghosts of Richard's past victims come crowding back before he is slain; but Richmond, the new Henry VII, brings this time immediate prospect of 'smooth-fac'd peace, / With smiling plenty and fair prosperous days'.

Shakespeare's second tetralogy represents his finest work in the historical drama. The plays are based on Holinshed's *Chronicles* and they frankly put the emphasis on public action rather than on inner conflict. The dominant characters are key men in whom the kingdom's continuing destiny is worked out. This does not mean that the characterization necessarily lacks subtlety, for the study of the king in *Richard II* is a complex blend of traits that attract and repel sympathy; but such psychological interest is subordinate to the issue of hereditary duty in relation to the demands of sovereignty and of national well-being. The imaginative glorification of England in passages like John of Gaunt's speech, 'This royal throne of kings …' and of kingship in Richard's own fine declamations:

> Not all the water in the rough, rude sea
> Can wash the balm from an anointed king,

sets the tone for an epic cycle whose grandeur is not that of individual heroism alone (though there is no lack of it) but of a kingdom, triumphing and suffering. *Richard II* traces the replacement of King Richard by Henry Bolingbroke as an easily explicable sequence in view of Richard's waywardness and ineffectiveness, the need for firm rule, and the flexible strength of character that gains Bolingbroke his popularity. In itself the play is a moving study in the fall and death of an engaging man unequipped to rule. But it is the first play of the tetralogy too: we hear of Bolingbroke's young son Hal as a tavern-haunter among the dissolute, we glimpse young Harry Hotspur in devoted service to Bolingbroke, and we listen to ominous prophecies of the price that will have to be paid in English blood for the uncrowning of an anointed king and for the raising up of house against house. Thus in the two parts of *Henry IV* the king is the wearer of a burdensome crown. The rebellion of the offended Percys in *Part 1* can justify itself by the putting down of Richard, 'that sweet lovely rose', and the planting of the thorn and canker, Bolingbroke. Yet Shakespeare's poetic emphasis is on the nobility of spirit common to young warriors on both sides, Hal and Harry Hotspur, over against vacillation, cowardice and trickery, rather than on obligation to a specific crowned head. The sincere supporter of Henry IV now takes his stand on 'anointed majesty'. *Part 2* continues the tale of frustrated rebellion with a slightly stronger hint that Henry's kingship is rooted in cheap popularity and that the 'commonwealth is sick of their own choice'. But the king's dignity and integrity are maintained partly by his own consciousness of burden ('Uneasy lies the head that wears a crown') and even more so by his long memory for fateful prophecies that clouded his accession in *Richard II*. Moreover, he is the worried father of a young prince who has a misspent youth in the company of Falstaff and his associates to redeem. For Shakespeare gives an additional dimension to his survey of the nation's life by counter-balancing the scenes of political struggle and military conflict with the boisterous and even criminal activities of Falstaff and his companions. Here is a level of attitudinizing on which the great national issues are measuresd by different yardsticks. Their effects are subject to the earthier evaluations of the citizen who likes his drink and his joke, his dinner and his woman. Appeals to high-sounding criteria like 'honour' ring hollowly in the ears of such. The contrast between the high poetry of the nobles and the racy backchat in the Boar's Head tavern, or the cowardly mugging on Gadshill, is something more than an entertaining study in extremes, precisely because the Prince of Wales is involved in the hilarious escapades of Falstaff, Poins, Bardolph and Pistol before the graver demands of royalty claim him. We are witnessing not only the testing of a kingdom but the comprehensive personal and political education of its future ruler. A man must make his choice and a nation must make its choice. At the end of *Henry IV Part 2*, when the king dies, the young Henry V finally rejects his former boon companion in levity and dissipation. Falstaff and his friends belong essentially to those plays whose subject is internal unrest and where the health of the body politic is at issue. It is true that we meet a somewhat degenerate Falstaff, duped, mocked and brought low, in *The Merry Wives of Windsor*, a (largely prose) comedy reputedly written to satisfy Queen Elizabeth's wish to see the fat knight in love, but the real Falstaff dies early in *Henry V*, a play which clears the air of that sense of a diseased kingdom and a guilty nobility that infects *Henry IV Part 2*. A new inspiration is let loose by the rule of a firm king whose enemy is a foreigner and whose awareness of dependence upon God is persistent. *Henry V* contains a surging tide of rhetoric, grave and high-spirited. The enemy is without, once an initial attempt at conspiracy has been summarily nipped in the bud. The army that finally confronts the enemy at Agincourt may be physically exhausted, but it is the arm of a spiritually healthy nation where the morale of nobility and commonalty matches that of the king – a king who prays:

> Not today, O Lord,
> O, not today, think not upon the fault
> My father made in compassing the crown.

The years 1600 to 1605 were the years of Shakespeare's great tragedies and problem plays. Shakespeare had earlier written *Romeo and Juliet* (probably in 1595), a limpidly unproblematical play in which the young lovers are hounded out of life by the reasonless feuding of their respective families, Montague and Capulet. Rich as it is in lyrical beauty, in passion and pathos, the tragedy does not show man divided against himself. There is distress and disaster, but not torment of the soul. The three great tragedies, *Othello*, *Macbeth* and *King Lear*, explore the spread of disorder within the individual, the family, the state and indeed the universe. The correspondences which Shakespeare, in common with many who held fast in this respect to medieval traditions, read into the stresses of the world, the body politic, the body domestic and the microcosmic human soul, are explicated in summary in the famous 'Order' speech by Ulysses in *Troilus and Cressida*. What the rule of the sun is among the planets, the rule of the monarch is among his nobles. And the 'unity and *married* calm of states' is paralleled in the order of marriage and legitimacy in private life. The 'primogeniture and due of birth', along with the 'prerogative of age, crowns, sceptres, laurels', duly observed by the preservation of hierarchical degree, are guarantees of civilization and rationality, without which there would only be the law of the jungle, of superior brute force. 'Strength should be lord of imbecility / And the rude son should strike his father dead.' *Othello* is the intensest study in disorder in that sexual and domestic life are the field of operation, but the threat of treachery within it can, for Othello, reduce all creation to 'Chaos'. In *Macbeth* the canvas is bigger: the career of a single man and the history of a kingdom are set poetically within a framework that reaches to heaven and to hell. In *King Lear* the abdication of kingship in the body politic is prelude to, and symbol of, the abdication of fatherhood in the body domestic, and the abdication of reason in the microcosmic human soul. The surrender of kingship into the hands of unworthy subordinates is a moral as well as a political disaster by virtue of the corresponding usurpation of reason's throne in the soul of man by the forces of unrestrained animality. The tragedy of

King Lear is the tragedy of regress from the stability of true civilization to the chaotic disorder of unredeemed nature.

The three tragedies form a remarkably balanced triptych. The key event of *Othello*, on which the entire action hinges, is the murder of Desdemona, and this takes place at the end of the play. The key event of *King Lear*, on which the entire action hinges, is the abdication of Lear and the division of his kingdom, and this takes place at the beginning of the play. The moral pattern of *Othello* is that of temptation: Iago is the tempter and deceiver determined to destroy the hero's faith in the 'divine Desdemona'. Conversely the moral pattern of *King Lear* is that of retribution and purgation. There is no place for a tempter here. Edmund does not exist to lead Lear to commit a grave sin: he exists to indicate the kind of power into whose keeping the king has committed his kingless kingdom ('Thou, Nature, art my goddess'). Lear's subsequent pilgrimage is a painful progress towards self-knowledge. *Macbeth* stands between these extremes. The key event is the murder of Duncan, which takes place towards the middle of the play. Up to that point there is a pattern of temptation: after that point there is a pattern of retribution. The temptation luring Macbeth to murder his king, his kinsman, his guest, his benefactor, is notably comprehensive. He is assailed by the World, the Flesh and the Devil; the lure of kingship ('the golden round'), the seductive pull of Lady Macbeth, and the preternatural evil rampant on the heath in the three Weird Sisters. Nothing more clearly illustrates the Shakespearian blend of act and symbol than the rich web of imagery of which the poetry of *Macbeth* is fashioned; the fine counterpoint played out on the themes of blood and wine, food and sleep, interrupted banquets and broken slumber.

Hamlet has its roots in the pagan ethic of revenge, so that the dualistic moral patterning which gives a fundamentally Christian flavour to the poetic worlds of *Macbeth*, *Othello* and *King Lear* is less evident, and less congruous when it is evident. The doom is laid on the hero in Senecan fashion by a visitant from another world. What complicates the treatment is that the moral burden of revenge is matched by an intellectual burden; the realization that one 'may smile and smile, and be a villain', the evidence of total dissociation between the outer appearance and the inner reality. This revelation of untruth obsesses Hamlet so that every relationship he has with others is affected by the will to tear away the pretence that veils truth. The king's guilt must be unkennelled, the queen must be shown her true picture, and the 'deceits', harmless or damaging, real or imputed, of Polonius, Rosencrantz, Guildenstern, Ophelia and Osric must be ruthlessly probed and exposed. But neither a moral obligation nor an intellectual obsession will create tragedy's oscillating path to catastrophe. A conflict has to be found: and Shakespeare, following the tradition of revenge tragedy, imposes some kind of dualism on the pattern by the variously motivated system of delays. Where to kill or not to kill cannot appropriately be the question, to kill now or to kill later can be the issue.

The basic theme of *Troilus and Cressida* (the play most helpful to the understanding of *Hamlet*) is the antithesis between truth and falsehood. Troilus is true: Cressida is false. Truth is the harmony of the outer and the inner, the word and the deed, the action and the emotion, the expression and the thought. Cressida in the love story, Achilles in the war story, represent the dissociation between outer and inner, fame and fact, which is falsehood. Nor are these the only dissociations explored. There is a gap between aspiration and achievement, whether you are an impatiently wooing lover or a soldier battering many years at the gates of Troy; between end and means, whether you are Troilus having to use Pandarus, or Ulysses having to use trickery to bring Achilles down a peg; and of course between the physical and the rational, the crude manpower of an army and its leadership in strategy. There are two forces militating against the achievement of that harmony and unity which is truth. One of them is time, which devours good deeds and delays realization of hopes. The other is human weakness; the frailty of Cressida and the pride of Achilles. At the climax of disillusionment Troilus sees Cressida's falsehood as a denial of the harmony between beauty and spirit, as a rejection of the fundamental principle that the word should be at one with the deed.

Troilus and Cressida is a play of problems in the sense that the characters are disturbed by the problems of life. *Measure for Measure* is a problem play in that it sets a special problem of moral duty before the main character. While deputizing for the absent Duke of Vienna, Angelo enforces laws against unchastity which had fallen into desuetude. Claudio is sentenced to death for anticipating the marriage rite, and his sister Isabella, a novice, prays Angelo to pardon him. Angelo is affected by her beauty and offers to grant her wish if she will sacrifice her virginity to him. Isabella refuses, though Claudio for a time weakly begs her to pity him. An elaborate contrivance, involving a willing substitute for Angelo's bed, produces a happy ending. The contrivance is aided by the Duke who has returned to Vienna in disguise to observe events. The undoubted allegorical flavour of the play in plot and characterization, and the suggestiveness of the poetry, have led to somewhat rash religious readings of its significance which make much of the Duke as a symbol of divinity, and of his anonymous saving presence in the city. Chapter mottoes from the play in Scott's *The Heart of Midlothian* show Scott's awareness of the parallel between Isabella's dilemma and that of Jeanie Deans in having to choose between a moral obligation and the apparent claims of another's well-being.[2]

All's Well that Ends Well, a problem play that cannot be dated with certainty, makes use of the 'bed-trick' again. Rightful but rejected wife (wedded, but not bedded) is sub-

---

[2] For that matter, the influence of the play is evident again in the motto to chapter 1 of Lewis's *The Monk* ('Lord Angelo is precise . . .'). Angelo too has his successor, in Ambrosio.

stituted for unwilling maiden in the bed of Bertram, Count of Rossillion. Thus Helena eventually wins over the heart of the husband whose hand she won by curing the ailing king of France. The play is uneven in quality. Bertram's character is unattractively marred by petulance, unreliability and dishonesty. But Helena, a great initiator in healing and loving, has a nice Shakespearian blend of charm with capability; and the Countess, Bertram's mother, is a woman of commanding dignity and genuine warm-heartedness.

Of the three Roman plays two belong to the next quinquennium (*Antony and Cleopatra*, 1606–7, and *Coriolanus*, 1608) but *Julius Caesar* was written in 1599. In each case the events are taken from Plutarch's *Lives*. The plays represent a fusion between the characteristics of the histories and those of the great tragedies. They have clearly outlined events chronicled with a sense of urgency and contained within the sweep of a historic process whose inevitabilities one never quite forgets; yet Shakespeare gives to the central characters a depth and cogency of reasoning and feeling that makes them as freshly and convincingly realized as those of *Hamlet* or *King Lear*. Again the imagery reaches out to parallel the upheavals of persons and states with those of the world of nature. There is thunder, lions in the streets, and the opening of graves in *Julius Caesar* to match the conspiracy of Brutus and Cassius, just as storm and darkness and horses that turn on their masters match the assassination of guest and king in *Macbeth*.

Coriolanus is perhaps the most powerful of the three plays, though the hero's domination of the action and the intense concentration upon his dilemma and his destiny give the tragedy a monochromatic flavour at the opposite end of the spectrum from the colourful variety of *Antony and Cleopatra*. Coriolanus's great military services to Rome have won him its gratitude and applause: but he cannot bring himself to play the politician and flatter the rabble he despises in order to be chosen as Consul, and his arrogance leads to his banishment. In revenge he joins Rome's enemies, the Volscians and leads their attack on the city. His mother, his wife and his son come out to plead with him and he spares the city, only to be afterwards accused of treachery by the Volscians, and killed. There is a virility about this Roman play that shows up interestingly against the tone of *Antony and Cleopatra* where the charm lies in the fact that the Roman world is offset by the East. Shakespeare fastened on the opposition between the two to turn the text of his tragedy into unsurpassed poetry. The story of the break-up of the triumvirate established by Octavius, Antony and Lepidus after the defeat of Brutus and Cassius at Philippi, and of the subsequent rivalry between Antony and Octavius for mastery of the Roman world, is shot through with a strand of magic. Antony is enthralled by the seductive queen of Egypt, Cleopatra, and every movement in the struggle for power is coloured by her irresistible claim upon him, pressed with every ingenuity of feminine allure. Imagery and symbolism build up the collision between Rome and Egypt, the realm of the masculine and the realm of the feminine, the firm-set earth on which Roman power has footing and the unsteady waters of the Nile on which the shifty queen of the East receives her lover, into a verbal pattern of extraordinary complexity, unmatched for richness of texture. The inextricable entanglement of good with evil is a major concern. Antony's career as warrior and ruler is sacrificed to a love which, for all Cleopatra's defects, is at the last so lavishly enriched and universalized by the poetry that the world seems well lost.

Shakespeare's last plays, the romantic tragicomedies, belong to the years 1608 to 1611, when the Blackfriars Theatre had been taken over by the King's Men and indoor performances were possible. That there was a change in taste at this time is evidenced by the popularity of Beaumont and Fletcher. Like them, Shakespeare experimented with a kind of play in which a developing tragic situation is marvellously turned to a happy conclusion. *Pericles, Prince of Tyre*, however antedates the other plays in this group and was written perhaps as early as 1606. Its story is told in Gower's *Confessio Amantis* and Shakespeare brings Gower in as chorus to introduce the play. Pericles loses his wife, Thaisa, for she appears to die in childbirth on a voyage and is committed to the sea in a chest. It floats to shore at Ephesus, and a physician restores Thaisa, who assumes that she is a widow and becomes a priestess. Pericles also loses his daughter Marina. He entrusts her to the care of the governor of Tarsus and his wife, Dionyza, who is envious of her gifts (for they outshine her own daughter's), and orders her death. But pirates carry her off and sell her to a brothel in Mytilene. Her purity earns the astonishment of customers, preserves her chastity, and wins her release. Pericles is led by a dream to Ephesus where he recovers his wife too. The extraordinary diversity of the material does not detract from the charm of the play, though the text we have is a bad one. The wry ironies that affect brothel-keepers who find themselves with a beginner on their hands preaching sermons to their clients and giving them a distaste for their wickedness lead on without offence to a lovely scene of discovery and reunion between father and daughter:

> My dearest wife was like this maid, and such a one
> My daughter might have been.

The Winter's Tale, a play based on Greene's prose romance, *Pandosto*, most forcefully illustrates the combination of tragedy and comedy. The first three acts seem like a miniature *Othello*. Leontes, king of Sicily, is overcome with baseless suspicion of his wife Hermione's infidelity and tries to poison his innocent and suspected friend and guest, Polixenes, king of Bohemia. Against all reason he obstinately orders his wife's new-born baby daughter to be cast on a desert shore. Only after his son has died and his wife (as he is led to believe) as well, does remorse hit him. The years pass. We enter a different world. The abandoned child, a daughter called Perdita, is brought up by a poor shepherd in Bohemia. Polixenes's son Florizel falls in love with her.

Polixenes discovers the prince's attachment. Florizel and Perdita flee to Sicily and are received by Leontes. Perdita's identity is revealed and finally a 'statue' of the 'dead' queen Hermione turns out to be the living queen herself, kept in hiding while the next generation has grown to nubility. This wiping out of the evils and suffering of one generation in the happy reconciliation achieved by the next, as it sums up the character of Shakespeare's latest work, so it seems to stand as a commentary on the development of his own experience and outlook. In *The Winter's Tale* we are suddenly transported from the world of *Othello*, of suffocating, hot-house passion, to the world of *As You Like It*, of fresh pastoral comedy full of the perfume of flowers, dancing shepherds and shepherdesses, and a rogue pedlar hawking his ribbons and gloves.

In *Cymbeline* the villainous Iachimo hides in a trunk in Imogen's bedroom in order to get factual personal details about her that enable him to claim her unfaithful to her husband, Posthumus Leonatus. Threading her way through perhaps the most complex of Shakespearian plots, Imogen, daughter to Britain's king, Cymbeline, is an impressive study in fine firm womanhood who gives charm and authenticity to the scene whenever she appears. In this case the tragicomic sequence is worked through without recourse to a second generation, but in *The Tempest*, perhaps Shakespeare's last play, the pattern is comparable to that of *The Winter's Tale*. This time, however, the action opens on the eve of reconciliation and the wickedness that was perpetrated twelve years before is revealed through reminiscence. So we find Prospero, the rightful Duke of Milan, living on an island with his daughter Miranda, while his brother Antonio holds his dukedom in usurpation. Prospero's knowledge of magic has put spirits like Ariel and even the monster Caliban at his disposal. Prospero contrives that his usurping brother and his ally, Alonso the king of Naples, are wrecked on the island. There the old wickedness is renewed before us, Antonio plotting against Alonso with Sebastian (Alonso's brother) as once he plotted against Prospero with Alonso. The story unfolds the love of the king's son, Ferdinand, for Miranda, the frustration of the plotters, the repentance of Alonso, the restoration of the dukedom, and Prospero's final renunciation of magic. There is perhaps greater unity of tone than in the other late plays. Prospero is the dominant figure throughout. He has achieved the dream of Faustus without any recourse to the Devil. Now he commands even the elements. This unique personality once firmly established before us, the plausibility of the miraculous events he contrives is ensured. Acceptability is sustained by the fine delicacy of the poetry and the moral gravity of the contriver.

5
Jacobean drama (Shakespeare's contemporaries and successors)

Chapman apart, the dramatists we now turn to were born later than Shakespeare and their mature work belongs to the Jacobean and Caroline periods. Throughout the seventeenth century Ben Jonson (1572–1637) was considered by some to be England's leading dramatist and by many to share an equality with Shakespeare. It is sometimes said that he has now been unjustly overshadowed by Shakespeare; but his plays lack certain qualities which have made Shakespeare's appeal a lasting one. In particular Shakespeare's poetry makes a profound exploration of the connotative, associative and symbolic power of words and consequently operates at a level of human interest that transcends historicity and topicality. No one would claim this gift for Jonson to anything like the same degree.

Jonson was educated at Westminster School and worked briefly in his stepfather's trade of bricklaying, then served as a soldier in the Netherlands, but was soon back in England, acting and writing plays. He seems to have been a man of great self-assurance, confident in his own learning and in his own ability to instruct his fellows and lash the follies of the age. He spent some time in prison after killing a man in a duel. The picture we have of him – immensely competent and intellectually fertile, effervescent and prickly but generous and fundamentally large-minded – is a commanding one.

Jonson's best works are his comedies. He wrote many of them according to a prescription that has earned them the label 'comedy of humours'. The 'humours' of which a man's body was supposedly compounded, according to their relative predominance, determined his disposition – choleric, melancholic, phlegmatic or sanguine. Jonson applied the term metaphorically to what we should now call a man's obsession or his 'complex', and he explained his theory in the prologue to *Every Man Out of His Humour*:

> As when some one peculiar quality
> Doth so possess a man, that it doth draw
> All his effects, his spirits, and his powers,
> In their confluctions, all to run one way,
> This may be truly said to be a humour.

Thus, in *The Silent Woman*, the central character, Morose, cannot endure noise. He plots to marry a silent woman and thereby disappoint his nephew of his expected inheritance. But his agents are counter-agents, and the selected silent woman, once the knot is tied, turns out to have a very noisy tongue. Her female friends come along *en masse* to add to an ever-increasing hubbub. Morose is desperate for divorce or annulment and humiliates himself in staking his claim to nullity on the grounds of impotence. But finally the 'bride' turns out to be a boy after all. There is maximal exploitation of deception and counter-deception and a cunning network of manipulative devices by which the farcical moments of ironical discovery are produced.

Ben Jonson's theatrical virtuosity is unquestionable. There is a dazzling quality about his accomplishment. If we cannot warm to his characters as we warm to Shakespeare's, there is a response of hearty admiration to replace the response of involvement and sympathy. It is not surprising that Shakespeare is said to have encouraged him. We know that Shakespeare acted in the first production of *Every Man in His Humour* in 1598, and tradition has it that he took the part of Knowall, an old gentleman much given to solicitous concern for his son's behaviour. Young Knowall and his friends gather at the house of Kitely, a merchant perpetually suspicious of designs on his wife. A web of intrigue is woven on this promising basis, reaching a climax of misunderstanding that is finally resolved in the exposure of the foolish and the hypocritical. Jonson's polished plots depend for their speed and ease of development on the presence in them of a character whose function it is to plot and scheme and entangle others in an imbroglio. Such a person is Knowall's man, Brainworm.

Such too is Mosca, the servant in *Volpone*, a play whose satirical vein is bitterer. Volpone is rich and childless. Aided by Mosca, he pretends to be dying, then sits back to receive expensive gifts from greedy would-be heirs who visit him, and before whom he dangles the prospect of becoming his legatee. In the play's harshest and yet most moving episode, one of the friends, Corvino, is induced to offer his wife, Celia; and indeed Volpone is forcing her against all entreaty when a virtuous youth, Bonario, intervenes. Savage as the satire is, it is essentially moral, directed at avarice and hypocrisy. We can understand Jonson's claim, in his dedication of the play to 'The Two Famous Universities', that he has laboured for the 'instruction and amendment of his audience'.

The Alchemist is a comparable study in swindling, though its tone is less severe. An outbreak of the plague causes Lovewit to leave his London house in the care of Face, his servant. Face, together with Subtle, the alchemist, and Dol Common, embarks on a scheme for trading phoney alchemical expertise and so cheating gullible people who want to advance their affairs or satisfy their desires. Clients include the clerk, Dapper, who is promised infallible success at gaming, and the tobacco man, Drugger, seeking prosperity in business and marriage with a rich widow. Sir Epicure Mammon is lured by the prospect of infinite riches obtained through possession of the philosopher's stone. Two Puritan clerics from Amsterdam, Tribulation Wholesome and Ananias, seek the powers of the stone ostensibly to advance the cause. Greed and hypocrisy are pilloried, as ludicrous prescriptive demands are imposed and victims are bubbled out of their cash. Pertinax Surly alone is not duped. He turns the tables; but Face's brilliant extemporization in trickery quickly, though precariously, restores the *status quo*. Lovewit's return puts an end to a better-humoured frolic than Mosca's, and one in which Jonson contrives as hilarious a series of comic stage situations as is to be found in our literature. It was Coleridge's view that the *Oedipus Tyrannus*, the *Alchemist* and *Tom Jones* were 'the three most perfect plots ever planned'.

Along with power of construction Jonson has an unfailing fertility of verbal output which exploits the language of the day at all social levels and in every sphere of life. The slang of the underworld, the jargon of the professions, the colloquialisms appropriate to every mood or eccentricity seem to be illimitably at his disposal. Nowhere does his ear for living idiom serve him better than in *Bartholomew Fair*, a panoramic theatrical picture gallery of a London fair, its boisterous scenes packed with the riffraff of the underworld.

Jonson's tragedies, *Sejanus: his Fall* and *Catiline: his Conspiracy*, are scholarly reproductions of history but not effective theatre. The first traces the career of Sejanus as he gradually improves his position and his influence over his master, the Emperor Tiberius, till the tables are turned and he is put to death. The play suffers from stiltedness in the rhetoric: there is too much static speechifying and too little action. There is also no adequate focus for the audience's sympathy. The two opposed protagonists are matched in wickedness. The same complaint cannot be made against *Catiline*, for Catiline represents destruction, anarchy and selfish ambition, while Cicero stands for order and freedom in the republic. But Jonson's recipe for a dramatic text was not a happy one. He follows Sallust's account of the Catiline conspiracy closely and takes over large passages from Cicero's speeches verbatim.

Many less celebrated dramatists fed the hungry theatres throughout the Elizabethan and Jacobean period. Though plays were sometimes the fruit of collaborative effort, the writers are too individual for us to dismiss them in groups. Contemporary rivalries and surviving gossip direct our attention at clamorous personalities who cannot be merged in communal anonymity. Thomas Dekker (?1570–1632) was among the writers ridiculed by Jonson in his comedy, *The Poetaster*, one of the exchanges in the long verbal ding-dong between Jonson and Marston. Dekker seems to have been easygoing by nature and less than rigorously disciplined as a writer, and this puts him in a different class from the redoubtable Ben. He replied to *The Poetaster* with *Satiromastix or the Untrussing of the Humorous Poet*. Jonson had represented himself in *The Poetaster* as Horace at the court of Augustus, with Crispinus and Demetrius (Marston and Dekker) conspiring against him. Dekker in turn drew a picture of a conceited, eccentric, bitter Horace vainly seeking a rhyme while engaged in the laborious composition of an epithalamium.

Dekker's most celebrated achievement is his comedy, *The Shoemaker's Holiday*. It is a rollicking, genial play exuding the confidence and vitality of the new trading classes and craftsmen; for a hero with love trouble is hidden in London disguised as a cobbler. Simon Eyre, the master shoemaker, himself becomes Lord Mayor amid a refreshing outburst of egalitarianism. The rest of Dekker's plays leave us with a sneaking sympathy for Jonson's impatience with him. For when Dekker writes on his own elsewhere, as in *Old Fortunatus*, the product is marred by inconsistencies and haphazard workmanship. It is notable that *The Honest Whore Part 1* reveals competence in craftsmanship, whereas *The Honest Whore Part 2* is structurally and morally incoherent, and we learn from Henslowe's diary that Dekker collaborated with Middleton in writing the first part. The whore is Bellafront, who falls in love with Hippolito and attempts to win him. He responds by preaching a long sermon on the evils of harlotry, and she reforms, eventually to find a bridegroom in her first lover. The sequel, *The Honest Whore Part 2*, vulgarizes this material retrospectively where it touches it, and the whole is a confusion of ill-worked-out plot material. On the other hand *The Witch of Edmonton*, in which Dekker collaborated with Ford and Rowley, is a homely play that gives a taste of Jacobean domesticity. It involves a sympathetic study of a young man whose generosity first, then his weakness, leads him into the situation in which he commits murder.

Dekker's fellow victim of Jonson's ridicule in *The Poetaster* was John Marston (1576–1634). We have Jonson's own word, recorded in Drummond of Hawthornden's *Ben Jonson's Conversations with William Drummond of Hawthornden*, for this phase in the War of the Theatres. 'He had many quarrels with Marston, beat him, and took his pistol from him; the beginning of them were that Marston represented him in the stage.' In *The Poetaster* Horace (Jonson) gives Crispinus (Marston) a pill, forcing him to vomit up his turgid vocabulary. However, the two enemies were friends again by 1605 when they both collaborated with Chapman in writing the comedy, *Eastward Ho!*

Marston's *Antonio and Mellida* exemplifies the verbal idosyncrasies that Jonson mocked in *The Poetaster*. It is not a good play, but its sequel, the revenge tragedy *Antonio's Revenge*, is interesting as illustrating some of the features common to *Hamlet* and other plays of the same genre. Antonio, the revenge hero, in conversation with his mother, might be Hamlet in conversation with Gertrude:

MARIA: What my good boy, stark mad?

ANTONIO: I am not.

MARIA: Alas, is that strange news?

ANTONIO: Strange news? why, mother, is't not wondrous strange
 I am not mad – I run not frantic, ha?
 Knowing my fathers trunk scarce cold, your love
 Is sought by him that doth pursue my life.

Instances of such parallels could be multiplied.

The Malcontent is a better play, but defective even so. It shows us the rightful Duke of Genoa, Altofronto, present in the court of the Duke, Pietro Jacomo, and disguised as Malevole. Thus, at first, Pietro is the machiavellian villain and Malevole the revenge hero biding his time, feigning 'oddness', and sometimes torturing the guilty ruler as the opportunity arises. In his pose, half fool and half cynic, he is a useful mouthpiece for Marston's satire, social and moral. But the central theme is overlaid with a mass of material, some of it so ill-fused that the roles and relationship of Pietro and Malevole are incongruously transformed. For a time Malevole is virtually working in league with his foe.

The Insatiate Countess is a female rake's progress pervaded by moral insistence that increasing lust brings unhappiness and death. The countess ensnares one man after another, winning each by the shameless arts of the courtesan. It is the problem of getting rid of the second (Massino) by persuading the fourth (Don Sago) to slay him that leads to her execution. Isabella (the Countess) concisely sums up her character and attitude:

 Fair women play: she's chaste whom none will have.

The final moral judgement is as brief:

> She died deservedly. and may like fate
> Attend all women so insatiate.

Perhaps *Wonder of Women or Sophonisba* is artistically the most coherent of Marston's plays. It is more homogeneous in tone and more shapely in construction than any of the others. The story of Sophonisba, daughter of Hasdrubal of Carthage, forcefully married to Syphax and torn from his rival Masinissia, whom she loved, is treated dramatically again by Nathaniel Lee and by James Thomson. In Marston's play, a very free rendering of the story, Sophonisba's genuineness and nobility are effectively conveyed and Masinissia is an idealized study in courage and honour. The tone is lofty: and there is throughout an interesting undercurrent of comment asserting that the simple life is more genuine than court life; that love is there free from intrigue and policy, and mere reputation does not matter.

George Chapman (*c.*1560–?1634) was another writer with whom Jonson quarrelled, but only after years of friendship. He comes in for special praise in the *Conversations* with Drummond. Although Chapman wrote original poems and several comedies, it is his translations of Homer and his tragedies for which he is chiefly remembered. In the tragedies, *Bussy D'Ambois* and *The Revenge of Bussy D'Ambois*, we meet a new version of the Marlovian superman. Bussy D'Ambois is a fiery-spirited individualist at the court of Henri III of France, and he kills three rivals with the claim:

> When I am wrong'd, and that law fails to right me,
> Let me be king myself (as man was made)
> And do a justice that exceeds the law ...
> Who to himself is law, no law doth need,
> Offends no law, and is a king indeed.

He is trapped through his relationship with Tamyra, Countess of Montsurry. She is forced by her jealous husband to call Bussy to her, and he is then murdered. *The Revenge of Bussy D'Ambois* tells how Bussy's brother Clermont is induced by his brother's ghost to avenge the murder, and eventually kills Montsurry. There are again interesting similarities with *Hamlet*. Although Clermont is vowed to revenge, he is too reasonable and temperate a man for such a purpose. And indeed the fact that Bussy was killed by a wronged husband in revenge for adultery confuses the moral issue. But Chapman's pervading philosophic theme in both plays is the conflict between the worthy individual and members of a decadent courtly élite whose status and authority are unrelated to personal merit. Bussy is the aspiring isolate of dynamic energy, ready to introduce 'a new Fashion / And rise in Court for Virtue'. Clermont, stoical and undemonstrative, is proof against all the challenges of men and the chances of life. The Duke of Guise proclaims that the 'Senecal man is found in him'.

Chapman was a thinker. In each important situation his characters relate their behaviour and experience to a general philosophy of life. The characters are not so much psychologically developed as turned into mouthpieces of philosophical reflection. Nevertheless the central conflicts are powerfully articulated. In *The Revenge of Bussy D'Ambois* Baligny represents the king's party and directs his machiavellian villainy against Clermont and Clermont's friend, Guise.

> Treachery for kings is truest loyalty ...
> No authority should suffer censure
> But by a man of more authority.

Such is his position. Over against this, Clermont's utter disrespect for rank dissociated from merit is voiced in many a vivid phrase:

> Was not the wolf that nourished Romulus
> More humane than the man that did expose him?

Lest Chapman's thinking should be oversimplified, it is

desirable to add that in the two plays, *The Conspiracy, and Tragedy of Charles, Duke of Byron,* the pattern of reflection is reversed in that the king is good, indeed an ideal ruler. The hero, a man of ambitious nature with (like Macbeth) a great reputation for his former feats of valour in loyal service, is worked on by a machiavellian villain who suggests that he is not prized as he should be. Thus he involves himself in successive rebellious intrigues. The persisting conflict in the two plays is between machiavellian policy which is clever enough to enlist the aid of a great, valiant hero – tainted with inordinate pride and ambition – and honest, just, merciful authority vested in a good king. One must concede that the obsession with power-politics and the lack of human warmth (there is really no feminine element at all) make the plays inferior to *Bussy D'Ambois.* Even so, Chapman is an eminently quotable dramatist with a big mind and a powerful voice. It is surprising that his best work has not been revived on stage.

By contrast with Chapman, Thomas Heywood (*c.*1574–1641) did his best work in the field of private domestic tragedy, the genre of *Arden of Feversham* and Dekker's *The Witch of Edmonton.* Elsewhere his reputation is for competence rather than brilliance. For instance, *The Rape of Lucrece* is a dramatic rehash of Livy, including not only the Lucrece story but a potted history of the Tarquins that takes in the adventure of Scaevola and Horatius keeping the bridge. But in *A Woman Killed with Kindness* we find the perfect antithesis to the grandiose events and elaborate philosophical reflection of Chapman. The simple plot tells how Frankford, a country gentleman, generously helps Wendoll in whom he has absolute trust. The adultery of Wendoll and Mrs Frankford is discovered and Frankford banishes his wife to a country house, depriving her of no comfort but the company of their children and himself. There she repents and dies forgiven. Heywood's success in his characterization indicates a keen sensitivity and a disciplined control of material. Wendoll is convincingly sketched as a man conscious of the evil he does but mastered by passion. Frankford (surely the most testing problem for the dramatist) is authentic in his goodness and his trust. And it is impossible not to be moved by Mrs Frankford's reinstatement in wifehood and motherhood on her death-bed and by the direct simplicity of her husband's words:

> Though thy rash offence
> Divorced our bodies, thy repentant tears
> Unite our souls. ...
> My wife, the mother to my pretty babes!
> Both these lost names I do restore thee back,
> And with this kiss I wed thee once again.

The English Traveller is a dignified attempt to go over very similar ground again, but it is marred by an absurd and farcical subplot.

We return to the world of corrupt nobility in turning to the tragedies of Thomas Middleton (1580–1627), but if the social level is that of Chapman's tragedies rather than of Heywood's, the concern is with the personal emotional life of the characters, as in Heywood, not with the grand issues of *Bussy D'Ambois*. In *The Changeling*, the heroine, Beatrice-Joanna, is betrothed by her father, the governor of Alicant, to Alonzo de Piracquo; but she falls in love with Alsemero. She makes use of De Flores to murder Alonzo. De Flores is ugly and lustful: he was shunned as repulsive by Beatrice in her days of purity, and once the murder is accomplished she naturally wants to see the back of him. But she finds herself utterly in his power and he demands his price: her body. She recoils, ironically protesting, 'Why 'tis impossible thou canst be so wicked', but De Flores speaks home:

> You are the deed's creature, by that name
> You lost your first condition.

From this point Beatrice's progress in crime is rapid. Forni-cation with Flores marks her total surrender to the diabolical creature. She has to substitute Diaphanta in her bridal bed to deceive her husband, and then is involved in Diaphanta's murder. She begins to love the evil that was once so loathsome to her. In the end she dies of despair and self-disgust.

Middleton's interest in women, and their capacity for evil, is further illustrated in *Women beware Women*, where tragic passions culminate in slaughter. In the least impressive of its two interwoven plots Isabella is married to a simple-minded heir as a cover for an incestuous relationship with her uncle Hippolito, and the main agent in her corruption is Livia, Hippolito's sister. She deceives her niece with the fiction that Hippolito is not really her relation. The other plot is more subtly realized. Bianca, the wilful daughter of wealthy parents, has eloped with Leantio, a clerk of poor birth and circumstances. She takes the eye of the Duke of Florence. She is tempted and tricked into adultery with the Duke by Livia, and then becomes a partner in Leantio's murder, and is married to the Duke. Livia's postures as kind aunt and good neighbour to her respective victims are notable. So too is the psychological development in the study of Bianca. Her first taste for unambitious, lowly happiness is rooted in physical passion: it gives way as soon as her vanity and ambition are stirred, and she is made dissatisfied with Leantio's simple home. The play contains passages of great emotional power, including the famous scene where Livia occupies Leantio's mother in a game of chess while Bianca is tricked into the Duke's arms in a room above (on the balcony of the Elizabethan stage). A powerful irony is sustained in a dialogue about the game of chess which is full of double entendres (assisted by the fact that the 'rook' could be called a 'duke' at the time). This scene was in T. S. Eliot's mind in naming a section of *The Waste Land* 'A Game of Chess'.

The most famous dramatic collaboration of the period was that between Francis Beaumont (1584–1616) and John Fletcher (1579–1625). *The Knight of the Burning Pestle*, chiefly, and perhaps solely, the work of Beaumont, is a remarkable tour de force. A grocer, his wife and the apprentice

Ralph have come to watch a play. When the play ('The London Merchant') opens, they interrupt and demand a play representing the heroic achievements of a grocer, with Ralph in the lead part. From this point the grocer's grotesque adventures intertwine with the burlesque sentimental romance. The parody is hilarious; distinctive layers of dramatic reality are blended so as to undercut irony with double irony, and the audience's receptivity is goaded into responsiveness.

Fletcher was at work without Beaumont in *The Faithful Shepherdess*, a pastoral, highly stylized in the balancing of the characters, who represent differing attitudes to love, ranging from the platonic and the virginal to the cynical and the lecherous. The shepherds and shepherdesses are not seventeenth-century rustics but idealized figures (Perigot, Thenot, Daphnis, Clorin, Amoret and Amarillis) belonging to the classical tradition. The dignity of the treatment, the rich poetry, the faint religious overtones, and the celebration of chastity, make the play an apt and congenial precursor of Milton's *Comus*. In strong contrast, *Philaster*, in which Beaumont once more collaborated, represents the fashion served by Shakespeare's last romances. There is a tangle of usurpation, revenge, false accusation, disguise, rebellion and a mass of mischances, before hero and heroine are happily settled. The fitful charm of the play is matched by its persistent implausibility.

The Maid's Tragedy is generally accounted the best fruit of the collaboration: yet it is an uneven play whose powerful themes are again infected by a strain of implausibility such as tragedy can afford even less than tragicomedy. Amintor, engaged to Aspatia, is compelled by the king to marry Evadne, the sister of Amintor's friend, Melantius. Aspatia's pathetic lament in preparing the new bride in her bedroom ('This should have been / My night') helps to build up a scene highly charged with irony as the bridegroom discovers, step by step, that his bride is not for him; for she is the king's mistress and the marriage is a cover-up. When

Melantius learns the truth he brings about a sudden change of heart in the hitherto hardened Evadne, and induces her to kill the king who has ruined her. There is another impressive bedroom scene in which Evadne ties the sleeping king to the bed, then wakes him to murder him. The waking king, seeing his bonds, at first fancies that some new and perverse love-play is in store ('What pretty new device is this, Evadne?'). Aspatia meets her end, in male disguise, at Amintor's sword, Evadne at her own hand. The lack of a convincing hero is evident. Amintor's wrongs at the king's hands seem to require decisive action on his part, loyal monarchist though he is, and something more relevant than the slaughter of his own abandoned fiancée in disguise. Nevertheless the poetic power of intermittent scenes justifies tributes like that of Herrick in *Master Fletchers Incomparable Plays*: 'None writes loves passion in the world like Thee.'

'The author of *The Atheist's Tragedy* and *The Revenger's Tragedy*', T. S. Eliot has written, 'belongs critically among the earlier of the followers of Shakespeare. If Ford and Shirley represent the decadence, and Webster the late ripeness, then Tourneur belongs a little earlier than Webster.'[1] Though some might prefer to link Ford with Webster rather than with Shirley, we may justifiably conclude our survey of the drama of the period by considering Cyril Tourneur (c.1575–1626), Webster, Ford and Shirley in Eliot's order, and interposing a note on Massinger.

The Revenger's Tragedy is structurally the better of the two plays traditionally attributed to Tourneur, and there is now a school of thought that would attribute it to Middleton. It represents a rotten state and a revenge hero, Vendice, who cleans it up. The rottenness resides in the whole family of the Duke and his second wife. The family consists of the Duke's son by his first wife, Lussurio, and his bastard, Spurio, together with the Duchess's three sons by an earlier husband,

[1] T. S. Eliot, *Elizabethan Essays* (Faber & Faber, London, 1934).

Ambitioso, Supervacuo and the Youngest Son. The selfish intrigues of these five against one another, their treachery and murder and dissipation, superadded to the crimes of their parents, together build up a mass of extravagant incident culminating in slaughter. The profusion of crimes, machinations and counter-machinations, disguises and deceptions, makes it the busiest tragedy of its age. Prior to Act I the Duke has raped Gloriana (Vendice's mistress) and killed her, and caused the death of Vendice's father. Lussurio attempts the purity of Vendice's sister, Castiza, and corrupts their mother, Gratiana. Vendice is therefore in a situation comparable to Hamlet's, his father dead, his mistress raped and killed, and his mother corrupted. He begins to doubt the chastity of women, though Castiza's purity reinforces his faith. He indulges in cynical outbursts, adopts a disguise, feigns melancholy, bides his time, and eventually achieves the perfect revenge ('nine years vengeance crowd into a minute'). He prepares the skull of Gloriana with poison on its lips to receive the Duke's kisses when he is bent on a night assignation in the ducal grounds. The dying duke is made witness of his wife's adulterous tryst with his bastard Spurio. But when a new Duke is proclaimed, Vendice is executed for murder. His opposite number in *The Atheist's Tragedy* is a 'revenge hero' of different breed. Charlemont has his betrothed and his inheritance stolen and his father murdered, but the ghost who puts him in the picture tells him to 'leave revenge unto the king of kings'. So he suffers philosophically, learning the vanity of greatness and how to make his passions his subjects. His scheming enemy is his uncle, D'Amville, the atheist, who finally strikes out his own brains, inspired to the providential act of justice by the spectacle of Charlemont's courage.

John Webster (c.1580–?1638) wrote two of the most dynamic tragedies of the period, *The White Devil* and *The Duchess of Malfi*. In spite of defects in construction and in moral coherence, they have a tantalizing poetic power. In *The White Devil* the Duke of Brachiano is tired of his wife,

Isabella, and loves Vittoria, the wife of Camillo. Vittoria's brother, Flamineo, is the Duke's instrument in the seduction of Vittoria and the murder of Camillo. The Duchess Isabella too is poisoned; but she is sister of the Duke of Florence and he avenges her. Brachiano, Vittoria and Flamineo are all killed.

The villainy is novel. Camillo is murdered by having his neck broken while vaulting, Isabella by kissing her husband's portrait (poisoned) after her evening prayers. It is impossible to feel sympathy for Brachiano, and Vittoria is a woman of ill repute, ready to encourage her lover's crimes. Flamineo is a conscienceless self-seeker. His cunning and his quick-witted resourcefulness in the contrivance of villainy give him a vitality in action piquantly laced with sneering cynicism. He is the diabolical arch-plotter, tragedy's equivalent of comedy's Brainworm. Almost everyone is involved in lust, murder, hatrd and vengeance. The coherence of the play does not lie in its structural tidiness nor in the pattern of experience meted out to the characters individually: rather it lies in the generalized picture of depravity and corruption at large in the courts of the great and infecting those who serve there. The wholesale corruption is felt as symptomatic of the human situation. The poetry is vibrant with something deeper and more universal than events in an Italian dukedom can account for. The dying cries of Vittoria and Flamineo:

> My soul, like to a ship in a black storm
> Is driven, I know not whither –

> I am in the way to study a long silence:
> To prate were idle, I remember nothing.
> There's nothing of so infinite vexation
> As man's own thoughts –

spring *de profundis* from offended humanity's contact with evil and its dabbling in it. These are more adequate comments on Webster's panorama of wickedness than the limited and localized conclusion that Vittoria finally voices:

> O happy they that never saw the court
> Nor ever knew great men but by report!

The same note of poetic universality is heard in *The Duchess of Malfi*. It might fitly be called a 'persecution tragedy'. The Duchess, a widow, breaks through convention and declares her love for her steward, Antonio. The pair are married in secret. The Duchess's brothers, Duke Ferdinand and the Cardinal, keep a spy in her service, Bosola, who betrays her. Antonio and the Duchess are forced to flee, but the offended brothers pursue the Duchess remorselessly. She is mentally tortured and then strangled along with her children. The ostensible motivations for the retribution (social disdain, greed for an inheritance, and disapproval of second marriages) are inadequate to its ruthless cruelty; but Webster's poetic power conveys a sense of the persecution as a diabolical fury provoked in the evil by the spectacle of the good. However, the play is a tragedy of greater contrasts than *The White Devil*. The mellower tone evident in the touching scenes between the Duchess and Antonio casts a light through the action that is not to be found in the starkly rotten world of *The White Devil*. If death is the reward of good and evil alike, at least there are deaths and deaths, though it is the villainous, if chastened, Bosola who makes the point:

> Let worthy minds ne'er stagger in distrust
> To suffer death of shame for what is just.
> Mine is another voyage.

The two tragedies of John Ford (*c*.1586–1640) are generally regarded as the last two great tragedies of this great age of drama, though it must be conceded that one of them is patchily great. In a sense *Tis pity she's a whore* is another 'persecution tragedy' in that a loving couple persist fatally in their love against a hostile world. But this time, in spite of the fact that the love is at first the impetuous youthful abandon of a Romeo and a Juliet, the prohibition is one that touches the human nerve with revulsion, for Giovanni and Annabella are brother and sister. Annabella becomes pregnant, and she is married to Soranzo as a cover, but Soranzo discovers the truth and plans the murder of Giovanni. In the upshot Giovanni kills Annabella himself before killing Soranzo and being killed in turn.

T. S. Eliot has characterized the lovers succinctly: 'Giovanni is merely selfish and self-willed, of a temperament to want a thing the more because it is forbidden; Annabella is pliant, vacillating and negative: the one almost a monster of egotism, the other virtually a moral defective.'[2] Even so, Ford's poetry endows the guilty love with a flavour of passionate power and sincerity, and Giovanni argues for incest like a devotee of nature who would have no impulse fettered by convention ('Are we not therefore each to other bound / So much the more by nature?'). Over against this, the Friar's rehearsal of Christian doctrine and Annabella's tardy but clear sense of guilt when the net closes round her ('My conscience now stands up against my lust') play havoc with the audience's sympathies.

The Broken Heart is a more coherent study. It neatly blends two stories of love relationships blighted by opposition and hearts broken in consequence, and one story of love that comes to fruition in marriage. The correspondences between the love-marriage themes knit the various situations together, but Ford makes no attempt to rationalize his presentation into a problem play. He is content to represent life's tragic situations, knitting them into a unity, not by a clear moral pattern, but by their common thematic relationship with its definable emotional tone of melancholy, grief and frustration.

The long predominance of Philip Massinger (1583–1640) in the London theatre during the 1620s and 1630s is a measure of his competence and fluency, but he is a second-

[2] T. S. Eliot, *Elizabethan Essays* (Faber & Faber, London, 1934), p. 142.

rate writer, as a glance at *The Great Duke of Florence*, *The Maid of Honour*, *The Bondman* or *The Duke of Milan* (though the last is certainly the best of the four) will show. Massinger fails to preserve consistency in characterization and in emotional tone. He voices and re-voices established moral and philosophical generalities that are the tag-end of the Elizabethan conventions. Bombastic heroics and slogan-ized echoes of other people's thinking have a hollow ring. We look in vain for a single distinctive quality to match the emotional depth of Ford, the humanity of Dekker, the moral pathos of Heywood, the poetic power of Webster, the acrid bitterness of Tourneur. Yet an exception must be made in the case of the comedy, *A New Way to Pay Old Debts*, in which Sir Giles Overreach avariciously confiscates the prop-erty of his prodigal nephew, Frank Wellborn. At the same time he plans to marry his daughter Margaret to the wealthy Lord Lovell, though she is in love with Tom Allworth. He is frustrated in both schemes and goes mad. Bringing an extortioner down to the dust is a good recipe for comedy and Massinger had enough proficiency to make Overreach an attractive part for a leading actor.

With Massinger we have left the Jacobean Age for the Caroline Age, and with James Shirley (1596–1666) we come to the end of our period. Shirley's comedies have been seen as precursors of Restoration comedy and have been cited as interesting evidence that the comedy of manners was not just a foreign importation but had its native roots. It is true that Shirley's representation of social life, its preoccupations and its mode of discourse, gives him more affinity with Congreve than, say, with Jonson. But, in *The Lady of Pleasure* for instance, though the intrigue is neatly manipulated, the wit is very thinly spread, the character interest minimal, and the lack of either flair or inspiration so persistent that the general effect is flat and insipid. And the way Lady Bornwell, by using the services of a procuress, manages to copulate with a young gallant in the dark without his know-ing who she is, is unsavoury.

The two tragedies, *The Traitor* and *The Cardinal*, illustrate that Shirley is like Massinger in lacking originality, but he here excels Massinger in taste, skill and accomplishment. *The Cardinal* is the finer of the two plays because, though the action of *The Traitor* is well knit, it involves too many characters and themes of equal prominence, so that there is a dissipation of interest. No central tragic hero emerges, whereas in *The Cardinal* the Duchess (the widow-victim of the Cardinal's plot to marry her to his nephew) is the centre of interest throughout and all the action revolves around her. Correspondingly the play has its focus of evil, too, in the Cardinal. The Duchess is a spirited woman in the mould of the Duchess of Malfi, but when her chosen husband is murdered by the powerful suitor she has outwitted, she turns female Hamlet, feigning distraction while genuinely a little unhinged at the same time. The verse has dignity and fluency. One can accept Shirley's claim in the play's dedication that it was the best of his flock.

Shirley was an accomplished writer. 'Elizabethan' tragedy had solidified into an established literary form and Shirley, as a skilful craftsman, studied his predecessors, utilizing their ideas and material. There is a 'closet' quality about his work, an air of 'literary' self-consciousness which is to become a peculiar mark of later tragedy in the eighteenth century. There is a lack of spontaneity. Everything seems to be second-hand. Yet such is Shirley's skill that his best tragedies are more satisfying *as a whole* than those of many a genius-ridden predecessor. The fitful bursts of splendour have gone; but so have the moments of bad workmanship. Shirley's work is tidy, homogeneous, and lacks glaring faults: but it equally lacks the vitality and fiery originality of less equable and masterly predecessors. Perhaps a great age of drama fitly ends with that kind of tribute to its own past.

6
Elizabethan poetry

Sometimes the spirit of an age seems to be epitomized in the work and personality of one man. Such a man was Sir Philip Sidney (1554–86); one in whom the aristocratic virtues flowered in a life of study, travel, diplomacy and active service. When fatally wounded in the Netherlands, he handed to a dying soldier the cup of water brought for himself and spoke the famous words: 'Thy need is greater than mine.' The value that Sidney attached to literature may be judged from his *Apology for Poetry*, a serious critical work on the nature of poetry, the various categories of imaginative writing, and the current state of poetry in England. In it Sidney presents the poet as one who teaches more effectively than the philosopher. The philosopher 'teacheth, but he teacheth obscurely, so as the learned only can understand him, that is to say, he teacheth them that are already taught'. But the poet is 'the right popular philosopher'. He 'yieldeth to the powers of the mind an image of that whereof the philosopher bestoweth but a wordish description; which doth neither strike, pierce, nor possess the sight of the soul as much as the other doth'.

Sidney's *Arcadia*, whose first version was composed for his sister the Countess of Pembroke, is to modern eyes a remarkable extravaganza. It is a romance-epic in prose. It shows what are the effects of passions and vices on the individual, of bad rule and rebellious factions on the state, and it recommends private virtue and public duty. Its prose is interspersed with verse, and the prose itself is highly contrived, abounding in conceits and rhetorical devices, beautifully weighed and planted. Shipwreck, piracy, disguise, death sentences, imprisonment, magic potions – all the ingredients of the tragicomedy plot are interwoven with beautiful descriptions and fine speeches. The once fashionable tendency to criticize the mixture as capricious and unbridled fails to do justice to the polychromatic character of the Renaissance mind.

Sidney's great work as a pure poet is the sonnet sequence, *Astrophel and Stella*, whose basis is autobiographical. Sidney first met Penelope Devereux ('Stella') when she was a girl of twelve. She was married to Lord Rich very much against her will – though not, it would appear, because she loved Sidney. Sidney's affection seems to have grown in inverse ratio to her accessibility. The composition of sonnets continued after her marriage and even after his own (to Frances Walsingham). *Astrophel and Stella* contains poems very varied in mood and tone, and no attempt is made to present a fully coherent narrative. Rather it is a series of meditations on life and love – some intensely personal, others light-heartedly conventional. On the serious side, a conflict between love and virtue is represented with acuteness, as in Sonnet IV, where the poet begs Virtue to let him take some rest, for his mouth is too tender for her bit. The personal hunger sometimes breaks passionately across the dialogue:

> So while thy beauty draws the heart to love,
> As fast thy virtue bends that love to good:
> But, ah, Desire still cries, give me some food. (LXXI)

The sonnets are intermittently interrupted by lyrics, and one of the loveliest outbursts against Stella's chaste refusal of Astrophel's pressure is the Fourth Song, with its irresistible refrain:

> Take me to thee, and thee to me:
> No, no, no, no, my Dear, let be.

But equally charming are those sonnets in which the introspection and the analysis of Stella's responses are touched with a light irony. There is wry humour in Astrophel's contrast between Stella's lack of pity for his 'beclouded' face and her capacity to dissolve in tears on hearing a tragic love story about 'lovers never known'. If fancy can provoke more sympathy than her own 'servants wreck', he begs to be read as a tragedy:

> I am not I; pity the tale of me.

One of the first to pay tribute in verse to Sidney after his death was Edmund Spenser (?1552–99). Spenser's pastoral elegy, *Astrophel*, shows how immediate was the impact of the sonnet sequence on Sidney's acquaintances, for it dwells much on Stella's magnetism:

> To her he vowd the service of his daies,
> On her he spent the riches of his wit:
> For her he made the hymnes of immortall praise,
> Of only her he sung, he thought, he writ.

Spenser himself celebrated his own courtship of Elizabeth Boyle (his second wife) with a sonnet sequence, *Amoretti*.

Quieter in tone than Sidney's sonnets, they move steadily within the conventionalized literary idioms without becoming obvious. (One of the *Amoretti* has found its way into our hymn books – 'Most glorious Lord of life, that on this day'.) But the succeeding *Epithalamion*, in which Spenser celebrated his marriage, exhibits the mature range of a new and distinctive poetic voice. The poem is a magnificent blend of high religious dignity with rich sensuousness, and is vibrant with reverence and joy.

> Open the temple gates unto my love,
> Open them wide that she may enter in.

The scriptural overtones, reaching back to the Song of Solomon and the Psalms ('Wake, now my love, awake!' and the 'Damzels' with 'their tymbrels'), hymn a golden-mantled, green-garlanded, pearl-sprinkled maiden queen who yet has a breast 'like to a bowl of cream uncrudded' and 'paps like lillies budded'. This poem, and the famous *Prothalamion*, a 'spousal verse' made in another's honour ('Sweet Thames run softly, till I end my song'), represent some of Spenser's most delightful work outside *The Faerie Queene*.

Spenser's literary career had earlier started in earnest with the publication of his *Shepherds Calendar* in 1579. This is a collection of twelve eclogues, one for each month of the year; and they are mostly dialogues between shepherds, touching on love, religion, poetry and other matters, and figuring the author himself as 'Colin Clout'. The June eclogue is 'wholly vowed to the complayning of Colins ill successe in his love', but in the May eclogue 'under the persons of two shepheards Piers and Palinodie be represented two forms of pastoures or Ministers, or the protestant and the Catholique: whose chiefe talke standeth in reasoning, whether the life of the one must be like the other'. That Spenser, like Virgil and Milton, should have first tried his wings in pastoral verse, is appropriate. The versatility revealed in range of subject and of literary form gives the work vigour and freshness, for all its artifice. The sureness of Spenser's touch may be gauged from the moving elegy in the eleventh eclogue (November). Its stately pace and solemn cadences have touching authenticity as feeling and reflection move through grief to its conquest. The figure of Colin Clout was to appear again in *Colin Clouts come home again*, an allegorical representation of a visit to the court of Queen Elizabeth, but this came some twelve years later and meantime Spenser had lived in Ireland, where he went in the service of the Lord Deputy, and where he worked on *The Faerie Queene*. Though he paid intermittent visits to London, he was still in Ireland in 1598 when his home, Kilcolman Castle, was burnt in a rising of the O'Neills. Spenser and his family fled to Cork, and a year later he died in London.

'Virgil without the *Aeneid*, Milton without *Paradise Lost* ... would still rank as great poets',[1] C. S. Lewis observed, whereas Spenser's reputation is almost entirely dependent on *The Faerie Queene*. In a dedicatory letter to Sir Walter Ralegh, appended to the first edition of Books I to III (1590), Spenser explains that his book is a 'continued Allegory or darke conceit' of which the general purpose is 'to fashion a gentleman or noble person in vertuous and gently discipline'. He has chosen King Arthur as his epic hero, following the tradition, he claims, of Homer, Virgil and Tasso. In the person of Arthur he represents 'Magnificence', as being the perfection of all the virtues, and has made twelve other knights the 'patrons' of the twelve other virtues. The heroes of the first three books, the Redcross Knight, Sir Guyon and the Lady Britomartis, represent holiness, temperance and chastity respectively.

The poem plunges *in medias res* of course, but Spenser explains that if a historian had represented the events of the poem chronologically, the starting point would have been what was to occur in the twelfth and last book of his poem

[1] C. S. Lewis, *English Literature in the Sixteenth Century* (Clarendon Press, Oxford, 1954).

(it was never written). This was to show the Faerie Queene keeping her annual twelve-day feast, and on each day an adventurous cause would present itself, requiring the service of an heroic knight. Thus the real beginning of the action is when a 'clownish' young man arrives at the royal feast and desires a boon which, because of the feast, the queen cannot refuse. The request granted, he settles down on the floor, the only place befitting his 'rusticity'. A lady in mourning arrives, riding on a white ass, with a dwarf behind her, leading a warlike steed and a suit of armour. The lady falls before the queen, telling how her father and mother, themselves king and queen, are besieged in a castle by a huge dragon. She asks for a knight to champion the cause and the 'clownish person' claims his right. The queen is astonished: but the man persists, and the lady says he can go only if the armour fits him. (Spenser explains that it is the Christian's armour 'specified by St Paul' in the Epistle to the Ephesians.) Once fitted out in the armour, the man appears 'the goodliest man in al that company' and is forthwith 'well liked of the Lady'. So they sally forth: and we have arrived at the beginning of Book I and the adventures of the Redcross Knight. The lady is Una, symbol of truth, and their joint adventures involve encounters with Duessa (falsehood), Queen Lucifera in the House of Pride, the giant Orgoglio (arrogance) and Despair himself. Alongside the moral allegory there is a certain amount of topical allegory. That the Faerie Queene should be Gloriana, Queen Elizabeth, the perfect earthly beauty, is quite consistent with her spiritual significance as the symbol of heavenly beauty which is divine. Overtones of the Anglican-Catholic conflict accompany the Redcross Knight's struggle with Duessa (Mary Queen of Scots). But the political allegory flares up fitfully and is quickly forgotten, while the moral symbolism continuingly determines the character of the narrative. Book II is really a little epic in itself. Sir Guyon, the Knight of Temperance, comes upon the dying Amavia, widow of Sir Mordaunt, whose personality was destroyed by Acrasia, the enchantress, in her sensual and corrupting Bower of Bliss. Amavia has stabbed herself, and her baby, 'sad witness' of its 'fathers fall', is left with hands imbrued in her blood. This little miniature of the Fall and original sin is presented as 'the image of mortalitie', and from this point Sir Guyon's quest is to destroy humanity's corruptor, Acrasia, and tear her bower to pieces. But before achievement of this aim in Canto XII of the book, Guyon undergoes a series of testing adventures in which he is at grips with all the passions hostile to temperance. One of the tensest encounters occurs when we plunge with Guyon into the depths of the epic underworld, a miniature of those in Homer and Virgil, where Mammon, the symbol of covetousness and worldliness, dwells, his face tanned with smoke from his smelting furnaces, his eyes bleared, his head and beard covered in soot, his hands coal-black and his nails like claws. This formidable figure proclaims himself 'greatest god below the skye' and submits Guyon to a temptation that echoes Satan's temptation of Christ. But even at the very 'fountain of the worldes good' Guyon has strength to say, 'All that I need I have.'

The Faerie Queene is a monumental masterpiece, its magnificence lying so much in the fine texture of its detail, narrative and symbolic, that outline summary could do little to hint at its quality. Spenser did not finish the work, and it would appear, from the completed books, that he had deviated from his original scheme outlined in the letter to Sir Walter Ralegh. But Spenserian fragmentariness is perhaps less tantalizing than Chaucerian fragmentariness; and a secret of the poem's effectiveness is the stanza form which Spenser invented, the Spenserian stanza of nine lines, eight of them iambic pentameters and the ninth an Alexandrine. The stanza rhymes *ababbcbcc*. The cunning central couplet knits the two 'halves' of the stanza indissolubly, and, together with the final couplet, obviates any consciousness of quatrains strung together. The stanza proves a perfect vehicle for sustained use in a poem in which steadiness and discipline have to coexist with the maximum of flexibility for narrative, descriptive and reflective passages of all kinds and tones. The writer who creates a great world of his own asks you to submerge yourself in it, to make yourself at home there. The demand can be appropriately made provided that the prevailing atmosphere of that world is not too exhaustingly passionate or sensational, and yet that its inhabitants and events are immensely varied. Spenser's world is one you can settle down in. Moreover, having settled down and found yourself delighted by its ever-changing scenes, you can sense, through image and overtone and symbol, the movement of a mind that has patterned the moral and religious realities that face all men in all ages within the scope of its survey.

In speaking of the equable steadiness of Spenser's spirit, one naturally has in mind by contrast the explosive restlessness of contemporary dramatists like Marlowe, yet oddly enough Marlowe left behind fragments of a poem which are as mellow and untroubled as his tragedies are dynamic. He chose the story of Hero, a priestess of Aphrodite at Sestos on the northern shore of the Hellespont, who was loved by Leander. Leander lived at Abydos on the southern shore and used to swim across the Hellespont at night to be with Hero, until one night he was drowned in a storm. Then Hero drowned herself too. Marlowe wrote only two sestiads of *Hero and Leander*, but Chapman completed it after his death. Nevertheless Marlowe's fragment is a richly satisfying poem, drenched in direct sensuousness, uncomplicated by psychological analysis, but exuding the flavour of an imaginary classical world. Even as Leander dives into the sea the god Neptune follows and assails him with love, sliding between his arms to steal kisses, so that Leander has to remind him:

You are deceiv'd; I am no woman, I.

He arrives naked, dripping, and cold, at Hero's tower. Hero, in bed, hears his knock, jumps up, herself unclothed, and 'drunk with gladness', rushes to the door. His nakedness frightens her: she screams and runs back to bed, and Leander, shivering, begs to share its warmth.

> Herewith affrighted, Hero shrunk away,
> And in her lukewarm place Leander lay.

The poem is a riot for the senses, an idealized romp for the appetites, gloriously framed in an idiom that leaves day-to-day realities and moral issues out of sight.

Shakespeare's first published work was a poem of the same genre, *Venus and Adonis*, which tells how Venus pursues young Adonis with oppressive love, pulling him from his hunting horse, pushing him on to the ground, kissing him and netting him in her arms – but in vain. When finally she releases him, pressing for a meeting next day, she is told that he will be hunting the boar. In terror she flings her arms round him:

> She sinketh down, still hanging on his neck,
> He on her belly falls, she on her back.

Even so, she is compelled to let him go; and next day he is killed in the hunt, a 'wide wound' trenched by the boar 'in his soft flank'. The poem does not achieve the unity of tone evident in Marlowe's; and it is not easy to come to terms with Shakespeare's heavy-handed goddess of love whose 'face doth reek and smoke' with passion.

The Rape of Lucrece is a more approachable work. The description of Tarquin's stealthy approach to Lucrece's room in the darkness as the wind through 'little vents and crannies' blows the smoke of his torch in his face, of his grasp at Lucrece's glove – with the needle in it that pricks his finger, then of his guilty hand plucking at the latch while 'with his knee the door he opens wide'; these clear impressions accompany a mood of suspense that grows with the sight of the sleeping Lucrece and then of her waking ('Like to a new-kill'd bird she trembling lies') till the battery of Tarquin's ruthless demand and Lucrece's hopeless appeal to his conscience and compassion bring us to the edge of the horrifying climax.

> For with the nightly linen that she wears
> He pens her piteous clamours in her head,
> Cooling his hot face in the chastest tears
> That ever modest eyes with sorrow shed.

The descriptive power scarcely falters during this central passage till

> He like a thievish dog creeps sadly thence,
> She like a wearied lamb lies panting there;

and though there are artificial digressions and unnecessary elaborations elsewhere in the poem, the predominant memory for every reader must be of this tense and tragic episode.

Shakespeare's *Sonnets* represent the finest poetic craftsmanship of the age. They have the autobiographical content to be expected in such a sequence but the persons referred to defy identification. A large number of the poems express the writer's devotion to a handsome man of rank, though the precise character of the relationship cannot be determined. There is a dark lady, unfriendly but fascinating, whose unworthiness the poet recognizes, yet he cannot help loving her; and there is a stolen mistress. Not all the sonnets have the intensity of feeling which suggests immediate personal experience as the source, and it cannot be assumed that the sequence is a direct personal record. Nevertheless the authentic emotional power of the poems has lured critics into the probably vain attempt to read the sequence autobiographically and to reconstruct particular developments in the poet's intimate relationships.

It is inevitable that readers will continue to be teased into curious speculation by admissions like that which opens Sonnet CXLIV:

> Two loves I have of comfort and despair,
> Which like two spirits do suggest me still;

> The better angel is a man right fair,
> The worser spirit a woman colour'd ill.

But in the finest of the sonnets Shakespeare has involved whatever particularities they relate to in reflection upon illimitable issues – upon time's withering touch on love and beauty, upon love in absence and love in presence, upon the changing and the unchangeable, upon trust, upon resignation, and upon poetry's power to make the loved object live for ever,

> So long as men can breathe, or eyes can see,
> So long lives this, and this gives life to thee.

And indeed there is an undercurrent of hope that frequently rises to the surface and rings out in the final couplet of a sonnet after a sad or troubled beginning:

> For thy sweet love remembered such wealth brings
> That then I scorn to change my state with kings.

The sturdiness of outlook underlying much of the introspection, and undercutting the drift towards self-pity, represents a discipline of feeling and thought that matches the discipline of the compact sonnet form. Shakespeare achieves conciseness without angularity, clarity without sacrifice of colour or balance. However narrow the form, Shakespeare seems to move quite unfettered within it.

In this age so highly productive of poetry many poets tried their hand at a sonnet sequence. Barnabe Barnes (c.1569–1609) wrote an accomplished if unexciting *Divine Century of Sonnets* which, though they play with a ready-made religious idiom, do so with technical sensitivity:

> Ride on in glorie, on the morning's wings,
> Thrice puissant Conqueror, in glorie ride …

Even more accomplished is Samuel Daniel's (1562–1619) sonnet-sequence, *Delia* (1594). The control of idea and rhythm is sure and often subtle, the capacity to bring inti-

mately alive the relationship between himself and his beloved is sometimes unerringly acute:

> When men shall find thy flow'r, thy glory, pass,
> And thou with careful brow, sitting alone,
> Received hast this message from thy glass,
> That tells the truth and says that *All is gone*;
> Fresh shalt thou see in me the wounds thou mad'st.

The sequence includes the justly famous poem, 'Care-
charmer Sleep, son of the sable Night'. Daniel's next most
memorable work is his *Musophilus*, a remarkable dialogue
between two speakers, directed to the defence of poetry, more
particularly of the poet's dedication to his art.

Michael Drayton (1563–1631) wrote a sequence of sonnets
to Anne, the daughter of his patron, Sir Henry Goodere, but
she became the wife of another, while Drayton remained a
bachelor dependent on a series of patrons. The sequence, at
first called *Idea's Mirror*, but later revised and called *Idea*,
reflects a vigorous imagination. The style is extravagant yet
forceful; the impact of image and declamation such that
Drayton has been compared, at his best, with both Donne
and Marlowe:

> Whilst thus my pen strives to eternize thee,
> Age rules my lines with wrinkles in my face,
> Where, in the map of all my misery,
> Is modelled out the world of my disgrace.

The sequence includes the often anthologized sonnet, 'Since
there's no help, come let us kiss and part', which is justifiably popular. It is less easy to explain the apparent popularity of the Ballad of Agincourt, 'Fair stood the wind for
France', with its jog-trot dactyls and trochees. This is more
like the Drayton who wrote *The Song of Jonah in the
Whale's Bellie*: but Drayton was a professional poet and no
doubt tried to accommodate his public. Certainly he put a
good deal of energy into historical poems like *The Barons
Wars* and he created a massive poetic guide to England's

history and topography, *Poly-Olbion*, a work of over 10,000 rhyming hexameters:

> Of Albion's glorious isle the wonders whilst I write,
> The sundry varying soils, the pleasures infinite ...

Any anthology of Elizabethan or Jacobean lyrics will include poems taken from plays and masques. Some, like Lyly's 'Cupid and my Campaspe' (*Campaspe*) or Heywood's 'Pack clouds, away' (*The Rape of Lucrece*), stand out distinctly among their author's poems, but others, like those of Jonson and Fletcher, represent a generous vein of productivity. 'Queen and huntress, chaste and fair', from Jonson's *Cynthia's Revels*, and 'Come, my Celia, let us prove / While we may, the sports of love', from *Volpone*, are polished and compact poems, while *Her Triumph* ('See the chariot at hand here of Love'), from *The Celebration of Charis*, is a masterly blend of cunning rhythm and telling imagery with a rapturous lyrical climax ('O so white! O so soft! O so sweet is she!'). Such treasures are scattered about Jonson's prolific dramatic output. Similarly characteristic of their author are the hymns to Pan at the end of Fletcher's *The Faithful Shepherdess* ('All ye woods, and trees, and bowers') and in the first act of the play ('Sing his praises that doth keep/Our flocks from harm'). They are not great poetry, but they are recognizably the work of a poet. Beaumont is credited with the authorship of 'Come sleep, and with thy sweet deceiving' in *The Woman Hater*, and of course with the lyrics in *The Maid's Tragedy*, notably:

> Lay a garland on my hearse
> Of dismal yew;
> Maidens, willow branches bear;
> Say, I died true.

On a quite different level of philosophic generality, but nevertheless powerful in its rhetorical force and rhythmic dignity, is James Shirley's lament from *The Contention of Ajax and Achilles*:

> The glories of our blood and state
> Are shadows, not substantial things.

The poem rings with public rather than private grief and moralizes man's response to death's egalitarian dominion.

Not only plays but prose romances too were decorated with lyrics. Greene's romances are sprinkled with verses that move gracefully within the Elizabethan conventions, like the following from *Perimedes the Blacksmith*:

> Fair is my love, for April in her face,
> Her lovely breasts September claims his part ...

Better known is Sephesta's song to her child, from *Menaphon* ('Weep not, my wanton'), where form and idiom and tone are intimately blended in expressing the mother's tenderness. And Rosader's verses on his mistress's excellence from Lodge's romance, *Rosalynde* ('Like to the clear in highest sphere'), might stand as the pattern of the Elizabethan love-catalogue, the stanza-by-stanza glorification of the beloved's physical attributes – eyes ('sapphires'), cheeks ('blushing cloud'), lips ('budded roses'), neck ('stately tower') and breasts ('orbs of heavenly frame').

Among the less productive poets is Sir Walter Ralegh, whose long-standing devotion to Queen Elizabeth was rudely rebuffed when his marriage to her lady-in-waiting came to light. (Spenser represents Ralegh's relationship with the queen in the account of Timias's love for Belphoebe in Book III of *The Faerie Queene*.) Ralegh wrote commendatory verses on *The Faerie Queene*, a lively parodic reply to Marlowe's 'Come live with me and be my love', and the expression of religious commitment, 'Give me my scallop shell of quiet'. Another religious poem, of rare distinction, is *The Burning Babe*, a Christmas vision by the Roman Catholic priest, Robert Southwell (1561–95) who was imprisoned, tortured and executed for his faith. Ben Jonson paid generous tribute to Southwell in the *Conversations*: 'That Southwell was hanged yett so he had written that piece of his, the Burning Babe, he would have been content to destroy many of his.'

Jonson was less generous towards Sir John Davies (1569–1626), whose poem, *Orchestra*, he mocked on more than one occasion. Its opening lines tickled him:

> Where lives the man that never yet did hear
> Of chaste Penelope, Ulysses's Queen?

Jonson described how a gentleman called his cook to ask him if he had ever heard of Penelope, and on receiving a negative response exclaimed:

> Lo, there the man that never yet did hear
> Of chaste Penelope, Ulysses's Queen.

Davies's poem is in fact a competent treatment, in rhyme royal, of the theme of the dancing, ordered universe, in which Elizabeth's court provides the image of perfect concord. The philosophical study, *Nosce Teipsum*, is well-organized argumentative verse but scarcely achieves the status of poetry. A more successful philosophical poem, though not strictly 'Elizabethan', is *Ode upon a Question moved Whether Love should continue for ever* by Lord Herbert of Cherbury (1583–1648). It anticipates the stanza of Tennyson's *In Memoriam*. Lord Herbert, the elder brother of George Herbert, was a man who distinguished himself in so many fields, as philosopher, diplomatist, soldier and autobiographer, that Jonson declared:

> If man get name for some one virtue, then
> What man art thou, that art so many men.

7
Metaphysical and Cavalier poetry

Some writers leave behind them a biographical legend entwined inseparably with what they have written. John Donne (1572–1631) was one such. He came of a Roman Catholic family, and his mother, as the daughter of John Heywood, was great grand-daughter of Sir Thomas More. His father died before John was four, but the boy studied at Oxford and the Inns of Court and, after travel and foreign service, he became secretary to Sir Thomas Egerton, the Lord Keeper. But in December 1601 his prospects were ruined by his secret marriage to Lady Egerton's niece, Ann More, whose father had him dismissed and, for a time, imprisoned. 'John Donne – Ann Donne – Un-done', the young husband wrote in a letter to his wife, and though he managed to make his peace with his father-in-law, he was not reinstated, and he and Ann brought up a rapidly increasing family in very straitened circumstances. Donne, who had early become critical of the Roman Church, joined in the polemical writing of the time and was pressed to take Anglican orders, but declined until pressure from James I, together with developments in his own thinking, brought him to the view that it was God's will that he should do so, and he was ordained in 1615. The death of his wife in 1617 was the end of a most loving partnership. Izaak Walton, in his *Life of John Donne,* tells how Donne was now 'the careful father of seven children then living, to whom he gave a voluntary assurance never to bring them under the subjection of a step-mother; which promise he kept most faithfully, burying with his tears, all his earthly joys in his most dear and deserving wife's grave ...' And indeed Donne's sonnet on his wife's death ('Since she whom I lov'd') is one of his loveliest:

> Here the admyring her my mind did whett
> To seeke thee God; so streames do shew their head ...

It was in 1621 that Donne was made Dean of St Paul's, where he achieved a great reputation for his sermons and his piety.

The contrast between the young Jack Donne, a great visitor of ladies, who circulated witty mockeries in verse, recommending promiscuity, like *Communitie* (women are ours 'as fruits are ours', to be tasted or devoured at will) and *Confined Love* ('Good is not good, unlesse / A thousand it possesse ...') and the Dean renowned for his piety can easily be overdramatized. One needs to see the element of fashionable charade in the literary postures of the young libertine. Moreover, like St Augustine and other converts, Donne tends to over-emphasize his past sinfulness. Nevertheless the contrast remains, an aspect of that life-long tension in which the man's whole work is involved.

Donne's importance is enhanced for us today by his influence upon twentieth-century poetry. T. S. Eliot found in his work a blend of emotional and intellectual quality which was an example and an inspiration in the revivification of the poetic tradition. For Donne's poems put us into immediate contact, not just with a sensitively feeling heart, but with a vigorously active mind; and the two move in concert:

> Yesternight the Sunne went hence,
>   And yet is here to day,
> He hath no desire nor sense,
>   Nor halfe so short a way:
>   Then feare not mee,
> But beleeve that I shall make
> Speedier journeyes, since I take
>   More wings and spurres than hee.

Thus Donne transmutes the emotional experience of parting into intellectual terms in 'Sweetest love, I do not goe'. There is an argument; and it moves. The tone of the argument is such that it does not disinfect the emotion; rather it clarifies and intensifies it.

As well as an argument, there is a situation. The speaker confronts another and, though she does not directly speak, we are aware of her presence and of the movement of her responses through the express movement of the speaker's own. In *The Sunne Rising*, the voice of the lover, wakened by the morning sun from a night of love, is alive with the joy and pride of possession as he pours scorn on the monarch of the sky – an interfering busybody, a peeping Tom at the window. The glorious all-regulating king of the planets is rebuked as 'Busie old foole, unruly Sunne'. So the lover's voice pours derision on sun, king, court, and everything subject to the 'rags of time'; and we sense that the white-hot activity of the poet's brain is the perfect expression of the lover's abounding zest of superiority to all that till this moment passed as grand and magnificent. For now the beloved is the epitome of all kingdoms, himself the epitome of all kingship, and the world's statesmanship but a charade imitative of the reality of honour and wealth that is with him in the bed:

> She'is all States, and all Princes, I,
> Nothing else is.
> Princes doe but play us; compar'd to this,
> All honour's mimique; All wealth alchimie.

What earned Donne and his fellows the label 'metaphysical poets' was the habit of philosophical argument of the kind just illustrated, and the use of extravagant and far-fetched imagery, sometimes technical in substance. In *The Flea*, for instance, the lover playfully builds a persuasive argument for feminine surrender on the basis of the fact that a flea has sucked the blood of speaker and lady alike, thereby already mingling their bloods. Donne is at his finest in his short poems, but he worked on a more extended scale in the *Satyres* – busy commentaries on topical affairs and current types, harsh in tone, and in the *Elegies*, a series of extremely diverse poems on various aspects of love. Satyre III, serious in tone, voices the indignant resolution of a searcher after truth in an age of violent strife between religious bodies, while Satyre IV is a devastating representation of being pinned at court by a pretentious social bore. Correspondingly there is an earnest simplicity in Elegy XVI, *On his Mistris*, while Elegy XIX, *To His Mistris Going to Bed*, is a frank yet mannered prologue to coition:

> Licence my roaving hands, and let them go
> Before, behind, between, above, below.

Even more extensive in scale are the two *Anniversaries* written in memory of Elizabeth Drury. Donne did not personally know her: he made the poems reflective studies of the human soul's pilgrimage and destiny.

In the *Holy Sonnets* the urgent voice of the lover is heard again in tortuous dialogue with his beloved: but now the beloved is God. The reluctance of the beloved has become the reluctance of God to sweep away the reluctance of the poet. He calls upon God to show the full force of his love by taking him from the grip of his rival, the Devil. 'Except thou rise and for thine own work fight', I shall be left in the possession of the Satan who hates me, he proclaims (Sonnet II). And he invites God to batter his heart, overthrow him, break and burn him, indeed to divorce him from betrothal to the diabolical enemy and imprison him:

> for I
> Except you'enthrall mee, never shall be free,
> Nor ever chaste, except you ravish me.   (XIV)

Never have the paradoxes of Christian vocation and surrender been more forcefully expressed than in the recapitulation of this loving contest with God. To have transposed the mock-hostilities of erotic dialogue onto this level of spiritual truth was a fine and sensitive achievement. But perhaps the high point of Donne's poetic exploration is reached in *Good Friday 1613 Riding Westward*, where the paradoxical theme of rising by dying is handled with subtlety of image and intensity of personal devotion.

Among Donne's complimentary verse letters is one to Lady Magdalen Herbert, the mother of George Herbert (1593–1633), the next most important poet of the metaphysical school, and a friend of Donne, of Bishop Andrewes and of Nicholas Ferrar of Little Gidding. It was into Nicholas Ferrar's hands that Herbert entrusted the manuscript of his poems at death, leaving him the option of publication or incineration, so it was Ferrar's wise decision that gave us *The Temple*, a collection of religious poems of extraordinary power and sincerity. Herbert came of an aristocratic family, but after early ambitions in the way of public office, he eventually found his vocation in the Anglican priesthood and spent his last years as rector of Bemerton in Wiltshire. He died at the age of forty, a loved and saintly parish priest. That he knew the value and delight of what he sacrificed in entering the priesthood is made evident in *The*

Pearl. 'I know the wayes of Learning.... I know the wayes of Honour.... I know the ways of Pleasure ...'

> My stuffe is flesh, not brasse; my senses live,
> And grumble oft that they have more in me
> Than He that curbs them, being but one to five:
>   Yet I love Thee.

The two poems called *Jordan* make it clear that Herbert thought carefully about the use of poetry in expressing love for God, and the character it should have.

There is in *The Temple* the maximum technical variety in rhythmic suppleness and in stanza form. The intellectual content is less obtrusive than in Donne, and the disconcerting restlessness of Donne is evident only where restlessness is appropriate. In *The Sacrifice* Herbert sustains a reflective sequence on the Passion through sixty three stanzas of cumulative meditation which has its paradoxes and its shocks, yet avoids the twistings and turnings that mark Donne's thinking. There is no lashing and flailing of the intellectual tail in Herbert. Even when the opening mood of a poem is one of intense rebellion ('I struck the board, and cry'd, No more'), the movement of thought rises steadily without tergiversation to its climax, and then lapses as suddenly to a magnificent peace:

> But as I rav'd and grew more fierce and wilde
>   At every word,
> Me thought I heard one calling, *Child*!
>   And I reply'd, *My Lord*.

A number of the poems give expression to Herbert's own spiritual experience and the conflicts he underwent. The sense of need and the hunger for peace are conveyed without histrionics yet with no dearth of bold imagery. 'Kill me not ev'ry day', one prayer (*Affliction*) begins, and 'Throw away Thy Rod', another (*Discipline*). 'Take the gentle path', the latter continues, a far cry from Donne's demand for divine violence. But over against anguished appeals *de profundis* one must set the steady consolatory poise revealed in the well-known poem to *Vertue* ('Sweet day, so cool, so calm, so bright') and the outbursts of triumphant joy in such poems as *Praise* ('King of glorie, King of peace'). Like Donne, Herbert indulges in controversy with God, but less heated and, it is fair to say, less one-sided. In *Love* the poet is Love's reluctant guest, guiltily conscious of 'dust and sin'. Love draws near. Does he lack anything?

> 'A guest,' I answer'd, 'worthy to be here.'
>   Love said, 'You shall be he.'
> 'I, the unkind, ungrateful? Ah, my dear,
>   I cannot look on Thee.'
> Love took my hand, and smiling did reply,
>   'Who made the eyes but I?'

The poet does not just speak. He listens; and Love gets the better of the argument. There is more to follow: but God is given the last word:

> 'You must sit down,' says Love, 'and taste My meat.'
>   So I did sit and eat.

Richard Crashaw (1612–49) too belonged to the circle of Nicholas Ferrar's friends, but he became a Roman Catholic. His poetry is drenched in colour and he has rare imaginative sensitivity:

> Not in the evening's eyes
> When they red with weeping are
> For the Sun that dyes,
> Sitts sorrow with a face so fair ...

So he writes of St Mary Magdalene in *The Weeper*. It is in the same poem that Crashaw's taste for hyperbole leads him to describe the eyes of the tearful woman following Christ not only as 'two faithfull fountains' but even as:

> Two walking baths; two weeping motions;
> Portable & compendious oceans,

There are too many tears in Crashaw and too many lavishly pictured wounds. The lack of restraint ('Upwards thou dost weep', he writes in *The Weeper*) combined with his mellifluousness and his taste for fragrant eloquence sometimes produces a cloying sweetness. Nevertheless, where the dignity of restraint is preserved, the rich texture of the verse shows up as something precious: it is jewel-studded poetry.

Crashaw paid Herbert the tribute of calling his own volume of poems *Steps to the Temple*. Henry Vaughan (?1622–95) was even more indebted to Herbert, whose influence is reflected in detailed echoes in many poems. Vaughan's volume *Silex Scintillans* was published in 1650. His poetic vein is altogether chaster than Crashaw's. Its texture sometimes has an uncluttered lucidity and limpidity highly appropriate to the mystical strain. There is much spiritual self-criticism in his earlier work and that sense of the world's dreariness in its alienation from God that is the reverse side of the coin of mystical insight. Vaughan's brightest lines are those in which the mystic's glimpse of the divine brings joy to himself, light and life to the whole of creation:

> I saw Eternity the other night
> Like a great Ring of pure and endless light.
>
> (*The World*)

Many a poem contrasts the vision or hope of the beyond with the sad dimness of man's life in a clouded world, shut off from God's brightness.

> They are all gone into a world of Light,
> And I alone sit lingering here,

he begins a celebrated poem, and ends by praying either that the mists blotting his vision may be dispersed, or that he shall be removed away to that hill 'Where I shall need no glass'. In *Night*, however, a fine piece of ruminative artistry inspired by Nicodemus's visit to Jesus by night, the blackness of night is 'this worlds defeat'. The contrast is between 'this worlds ill-guiding light' and the 'deep, but dazzling darkness' of God. There is anticipation of Wordsworth in *The Retreate*, a reminiscent poem of those early days of 'Angell-infancy' when heaven was about him and, seeing the 'weaker glories' of a gilded cloud or a flower he could spy 'Some shadows of eternity'. This is the authentic Wordsworthian experience. He feels through all his 'fleshly dresse / Bright *shootes* of everlastingness'.

There is the same theme of childhood insight and innocence in the poetry of Thomas Traherne (1637–74), a parish priest, and later a household chaplain, whose prose work *Centuries of Meditations* is full of Christian joy in creation and in the love of God. There is an infectious freshness and urgency in his work. 'Shall Dumpish Melancholy spoil my Joys?' he begins his ode *On Christmas Day*, a paean of unclouded praise. But the same urgency runs through *Solitude*, a poem vastly different in tone, in which he laments the absence in the world around him, and even in the Church's rites, of that 'Eden fair', that 'Soul of Holy Joy' which he is vainly seeking to ease his mind. The poems in praise of infancy, however, like *The Rapture* and *The Salutation*, represent the more constant mood of delight and wonder. That the child is 'A Stranger here' means that he meets strange things, sees strange glories, finds strange treasures 'in this fair World'. And strangest of all is the fact that 'they *mine* should be who Nothing was'. It is difficult not to like the man who wrote thus. More so than Vaughan's, Traherne's raptures are earthed in wonder at things as they are. Correspondingly his style has a clarity and sturdiness that compels the reader from stanza to stanza. If it is true that there is nothing in Traherne to match Vaughan's finest lines, we must remember that there is not a lot in Vaughan to match Vaughan's finest lines. Traherne's style is reliable.

Robert Herrick (1591–1674), though another priest, is sharply distinct from the religious poets we have just dealt with. Although he wrote some religious poems, they have not the mystical reach nor the spiritual depth of Vaughan's and Traherne's: they do not reveal grave inner tensions nor reflect any grappling with the conflict between divine vocation and human weakness. Poems like *A Thanksgiving to God for his House* ('Thou mak'st my teeming Hen to lay / Her egg each day') and the justly admired *Letanie to the Holy Spirit*:

> When (God knowes) I'm tost about,
> Either with despaire, or doubt,
> Yet before the glasse be out,
>   Sweet Spirit comfort me,

are religious only in the sense that they are addressed to God. The poet's concern is with the earthly pleasures he delights in and the earthly pains he fears. The prayers are sincerely directed, but they are not outbursts of love for God, still less of impatience to know Him more closely. In this, no doubt, Herrick is nearer to most of us than either Donne or Herbert is. Herrick demands of us no entry into pieties beyond our reach.

Similarly Herrick's lyrics expressing a sense of life's brevity, and the quick fleeting away of beauty and love and youth, make no intellectual demand but call out a quick response by their apt phrasing ('Gather ye Rose-buds while ye may' and 'Fair Daffadills, we weep to see / You haste away so soone'), phrasing with the semi-proverbial flavour that derives from voicing the commonplace human reaction without being commonplace in utterance. Sometimes (as in 'Bid me to live, and I will live / Thy Protestant to be') fine feelings are unpretentiously embodied in shaped and fluent stanzas that defy criticism; and sensuous experience of touch or sight may be neatly recaptured in images of unpremeditated felicity. The voluptuous quality of silk is subtly verbalized in:

> When as in silks my *Julia* goes,
> Why, then (me thinks) how sweetly flowes
> That liquefaction of her clothes.

Herrick wrote much bad and mediocre verse, and he could be guilty of indecent bad taste, but an idealized world of great charm is freshly and frankly reconstituted in his best lyrics. Faultlessly patterned stanzas shape it, and it is sprinkled with the lore of a well-stocked, if wanton, mind.

In reading Herrick we note a decisive shift from the centre of poetic interest evident in the work of Donne and his school. We leave the poets who struggle with themselves, struggle with love and struggle with words, for a poet who comments with an air of facility. The group of poets known as the 'Cavalier poets' are akin to Herrick in this respect. Poetry does not seem to be an essential business of their lives. This does not merely mean that they were not professional poets: neither were Donne and Herbert. But poetry seemed to *matter* to Donne and Herbert precisely because what they were using it for mattered enormously. Much of the poetry of the Cavalier poets is, we feel, so peripheral to their true inner and active lives as to represent a fashionable accomplishment rather than an art. Thomas Carew (?1594–1640), in *Disdain returned*, explains to Celia why, having learned her arts, he will never return to her. Wordsworth spoke of poetry as 'emotion recollected in tranquillity', but this is emotion dissipated in tranquillity. So is the poem *Ingratefull beauty threatned*. 'Let fools thy mystique forms adore', says the poet, explaining that his verse created Celia's image and he himself cannot be taken in by it. This is the poetry of disengagement, even, very often, of disenchantment.

What is said of Carew applies even more surely to Sir John Suckling (1609–42), another royalist man about town. The one or two polished lyrics that creep into anthologies are really all that are worth preserving. The amusing conclusive outburst ('The divel take her') in 'Why so pale and wan, fond lover?' and the jaunty 'Out upon it, I have loved / Three whole days together' are entertaining stuff but when, at times, Suckling's disenchantment is applied to what is nauseating or obscene, the note of cynicism is struck where humour was intended.

There is a crucial difference between Carew and Suckling on the one hand and Richard Lovelace (1618–c. 1657) on the other, for Lovelace's work reveals a wide range of feelings rather than a set of postures. It is notable that when Carew writes in praise he seems to be posing, whereas Lovelace is obviously posing when he writes in mockery:

> Why should you sweare I am forsworne,
> Since thine I vow'd to be?
> Lady it is already Morn,
> And 'twas last night I swore to thee
> That fond impossibility.

This tongue-in-the-cheek testimony to the joy of variety in love is much in the vein of Donne's light-hearted mockeries. But when Lovelace writes seriously of fidelity and duty, as in the poems to Lucasta ('If to be absent were to be / Away from thee' and 'Tell me not (Sweet) I am unkinde') the note, though not deeply passionate, is authentic. And Lovelace's finest lyric, *To Althea from Prison* ('Stone Walls doe not a Prison make / Nor iron bars a Cage'), was written while he was paying the penalty for signing a petition on behalf of Church and episcopacy in 1642. Even here, however, there is a courtly polish which seems to distance tribulation – and such distancing of what might disturb with passion or anguish is a mark of Cavalier poetry in general – but to rise in scorn above the confinement of prison is to be distinguished from rising in scorn above commitment to the female sex.

In the end it must be remembered that the poets of this period had grave issues to face. Carew died too young to suffer under the Commonwealth; but Herrick lost his living for over twelve years, Suckling, an ardent royalist but not a hardliner, had to flee abroad after supporting Strafford, and Lovelace was in prison more than once. It may be that the posture of libertinism and the devil-may-care stance were roles played out defensively when passion and anguish were about them in action too immediate for transmutation into literature.

A royalist whose quality sets him a little apart from this group is John Cleveland (1613–58). His contemporary literary success was immense, but his extravagant metaphysical conceits appealed to his own age more than they have appealed to posterity:

> I am not Poet here; my pen's the spout
> Where the rain water of my eyes run out.

So he writes in his elegy to Edward King, published in the same volume that contained *Lycidas*, for Cleveland was Milton's contemporary at Christ's College, Cambridge. His elegy on Ben Jonson is more restrained and tasteful; and there is a charming tribute, *Upon Phillis walking in a morning before Sun-rising*. The roses mix amicably in her cheeks – 'no Civil War / Between her *Yorke* and *Lancaster*'. Probably Cleveland's liveliest vein is the satirical vituperation with which he baits the Scots in heroic couplets in *The Rebell Scot*:

> Had *Cain* be *Scot*, God would have chang'd his doom,
> Not forc't him wander, but confin'd him home.

This kind of thing links Cleveland with his friend, Samuel Butler.

Abraham Cowley (1618–67) too stands apart from the group by the fact that writing was a more dominant interest in his life. He was a fellow of Trinity College, Cambridge until the Civil War, and then, having moved to France, became cipher-secretary to Queen Henrietta Maria. In this post he coded and decoded letters between the queen and the king. His status as a poet was at its peak in his own day. His technical gifts were immense and he had a lasting influence in establishing the Pindaric ode, with its freedom for irregular patterning of line length, rhyme and stanza, as an English form. (See the ode 'To Mr Hobbes'.) The Pindaric and other odes illustrate the diversity of his interests and his poetic expertise. We find mastery of the heroic couplet in the massive biblical epic, *Davideis*, but as often with Cowley, the work shows him occupied energetically with interests he fails to communicate to the modern reader. More approachable is *The Mistress*, a cycle of love poems in which familiar themes of Cavalier poetry are handled with fine artistry. Nevertheless the works smacks of the study, for a vein of dispassionate analytical objectivity runs through its reflections on the dilemmas of love. Cowley sometimes has an obviousness of phrasing that, in an age of startling lines, clamours to pass unnoticed. 'It was a dismal, and a fearful night', the elegy on Mr William Hervey begins, and later we have 'He was my *Friend*, the truest *Friend* on earth'. This intermittent pedestrianism is one aspect of that lack of passion and intensity which have ensured neglect of his work in the past. For all his technical brilliance, and indeed his graceful directness, he fails to compel attention. But his essays are delightful, combining ingredients of humour, engaging self-revelation, social observation and philosophical reflection in a most appetizing blend. The prose of the essays is interspersed with poetry. The essay, *Of Myself*, includes a lively visionary dialogue in which the royalist sets the record straight against Cromwell. It also includes verses on himself written when he was only thirteen:

> This only grant me, that my means may lie
> Too low for envy, for contempt too high.

It is odd that, historically, his poetic reputation should have achieved just such a status.

Where Edmund Waller (1606–87) matches Cowley is first in the shared professionalism of his approach to poetry. That does not mean that he was a full-time writer; but his poems were not the easy throwaways of Cavalier spiritedness; rather they were conscious attempts to make progress in the techniques of versification. Waller matches Cowley too in the achievement of a high contemporary reputation. He left us one or two lyrics in which the mannered graces of the Cavaliers are recaptured without their air of disenchantment. In the well-known lyrics, 'Goe, lovely Rose' and *On a Girdle*:

> That which her slender waist confin'd
> Shall now my joyfull temples bind;
> No Monarch but would give his Crowne
> His armes might do what this has done,

the feeling is no doubt carefully posed, but it is neither nerveless nor insipid. The mastery of smoothness and lucidity is evident in Waller's (unsuccessful) poetic courtship of 'Sacharissa' (Lady Dorothy Sidney, of the celebrated family). Her portrait is claimed to exalt her above the ladies in Sir Philip Sidney's *Arcadia*:

> This glorious piece transcends what he could think,
> So much his blood is nobler than his ink.

The cultivated neatness of thought and style was highly regarded, and indeed, along with Denham, Waller helped to bring the heroic couplet to that degree of polish and flexibility which was to make it such a fine instrument in Dryden's hands, and later in Pope's. He experimented with the balancing of line against line, and half-line against half-line, while at the same time preserving a smooth sequence; so he played his part in establishing that contrapuntal relationship between form and flow which is the secret of the best eighteenth-century work in the couplet. Thus he addresses Cromwell in *A Panegyric to my Lord Protector*:

> If *Romes* great Senate could not wield that Sword,
> Which of the Conquer'd world had made them Lord,
> What hope had ours, while yet their power was new,
> To rule victorious Armies but by you?

It is customary to link Waller's name with that of Sir John Denham (1615–69). Denham's most significant work is

Cooper's Hill, a long topographical poem in which descriptions of scenery are mingled with reflective consideration of subjects brought to mind by what is pictured. The description of Runnymede leads to reflections on kingship, for instance. On the strength of his achievement in this poem Johnson claims Denham as the originator of the genre of 'local poetry' to which later works like Pope's *Windsor Forest* and Dyer's *Grongar Hill* belong. Denham's close affinity with Waller is shown in his skilful heroic couplets: they have a simple directness of idiom and an easy syntactical naturalness. Economy and concentration of expression are combined with impressive architectural symmetry. His most quoted lines come in the description of the view of the Thames from Cooper's Hill:

> O could I flow like thee and make thy stream
> My great example, as it is my theme!
> Though deep, yet clear, though gentle, yet not dull,
> Strong without rage, without o'erflowing full.

To Denham goes the credit for paying an immediate tribute to *Paradise Lost* in the House of Commons when it was first published.

Lesser poets of the period who deserve to be mentioned include Francis Quarles (1592–1644), who is still remembered for his *Emblems*, a book highly rated by his contemporaries. It consists of symbolic engravings illustrated by biblical texts, quotations from the Fathers, and verses in various metres. Thus Quarles comments in verse on, 'My beloved is mine, and I am his; He feedeth among the lillies':

> Ev'n like two little bank-dividing brooks,
> That wash the pebbles with their wanton streams,
> And having rang'd and search'd a thousand nooks,
> Meet both at length in silver-breasted Thames,
> Where in a greater current they conjoyn:
> So I my best-beloved's am; so he is mine.

Soon after the publication of this work there appeared *A*

Collection of Emblemes by George Wither (1588–1667). Its character may be judged from *The Marigold,* beginning:

> When, with a serious musing, I behold
> The gratefull, and obsequious *Marigold,*

and leading to the prayer that, as the flower bends to the sun in total dependence on its light, so the poet may aspire, though grovelling on the ground, to the Sun of Righteousness. Wither became a Puritan and exercised his powers on didactic and satiric poetry. His famous lyric, 'Shall I wasting in Dispaire / Dye because a *Womans* faire?' was included in the pastoral epistle, *Fidelia.* Wither collaborated with William Browne (1591–1643) in *Shepherds Pipe,* but Browne is chiefly remembered for his *Britannia's Pastorals,* a long narrative poem in couplets, treating of the loves of shepherds and shepherdesses and interspersed with lyrics.

Two brothers, Giles Fletcher (1585–1623) and Phineas Fletcher (1582–1650) call for attention if only because they exercised some influence on Milton. Giles Fletcher's *Christs Victorie and Triumph in Heaven and Earth* deals fluently and readably with the Fall, the Incarnation, the Redemption, the Ascension, and ends with a vision of the marriage of the divine Spouse and his mystical Bride, the Church. It is effective descriptively, yet not because there is much inventiveness: rather there is much that is recognizably derivative, harking back to standard prescriptions:

> About the holy Cittie rolls a flood
> Of molten chrystall, like a sea of glasse ...

Its section dealing with the temptation of Christ influenced Milton in *Paradise Regained.* Phineas Fletcher's influence on Milton may be gauged from *The Locusts,* a harsh attack on the Jesuits, who are involved in a diabolical conspiracy against healthy religion, originating in Hell:

> The Porter to th'infernall gate is Sin,
> A shapeless shape, a foule deformed thing,
> Nor nothing, nor a substance ...

Phineas's imaginative range is bigger than Giles's, but he too has limited resources of imagery so that the poetic instrument at his disposal often seems an impoverished one.

There is an enigmatic quality about the character and work of Andrew Marvell (1621–78). Though he seems to have been in royalist circles in his twenties, he became Cromwell's admirer. He lived for a time in the household of Lord Fairfax, the Parliamentarian commander, at Nun Appleton in Yorkshire, acting as tutor to Fairfax's daughter Mary; and it was here that he wrote *Upon Appleton House*, a descriptive and reflective poem in stanzas made up of octosyllabic rhyming couplets. Later Marvell was tutor to Cromwell's ward, William Dutton, and eventually he had a post in the Latin secretaryship under Milton. He became a member of Parliament in 1659.

Marvell's admiration for Cromwell can be measured from his three poetic tributes, *An Horatian Ode upon Cromwell's Return from Ireland*, *The First Anniversarie of the Government under O.C.*, and *A Poem upon the Death of O.C.* The famous *Horatian Ode* exalts Cromwell as the mighty man of destiny, picked out from his 'private Gardens' to 'cast the Kingdome old / Into another Mold'; yet it also speaks with respect of Charles's dignity at his execution:

> He nothing common did or mean
> Upon that memorable Scene ...

In *The First Anniversarie* foreign ambassadors are moved to question where Cromwell can have learned the arts of rule:

> He seems a King by long succession born,
> And yet the same to be a king does scorn.

The poem on Cromwell's death includes a note of more private and personal sorrow which indicates how Marvell's appreciation of the Protector grew.

Marvell is linked to the metaphysical poets by his fanciful conceits which achieve a vitality of their own. In *Upon*

Appleton House a correspondence is drawn between England and a garden: the flowers become soldiers displaying silken ensigns, drying their 'pans' (of the muskets), then firing 'fragrant Vollyes':

> Well shot ye Firemen! Oh how sweet,
> And round your equal Fires do meet;
> Whose shrill report no ear can tell,
> But echoes to the Eye and smell.

The imaginative theme is explored through several stanzas, but the eventual sober reflection:

> But War all this doth overgrow:
> We Ord'nance Plant and Powder sow.

leaves the reader feeling that the gravity of the couplet is out of key with the less earnest character of the conceit it interrupts: and this in itself is a serious problem for the student of Marvell – that it is by no means always clear in what tone of voice he is speaking, and therefore how he is to be understood.

At its best Marvell's poetry has the shapeliness of conception and the living tension within it which are the marks of the metaphysicals. Crisp couplets are taut with such tension in the *Dialogue between the Soul and Body*. Moreover the implicit dialogue threaded through *To his Coy Mistress* is more than a confrontation between lover and beloved, for the plea to seize the moment is given the dimensions of man's outcry against finitude:

> But at my back I alwaies hear
> Times winged Carriot hurrying near:
> And yonder all before us lye
> Desarts of vast Eternity.

Marvell's best-loved poem, *The Garden*, is at once richly sensuous and packed with thought. The implicit contrast between the beauty of women and the beauty of the garden leads to an emphasis on the paradisal purity and sweetness of the place so intense that it seems to predate even the creation of Eve. The idea that an Eveless Paradise would be two Paradises in one, and a delight beyond the lot of mortal man, matches the idea that the mind finds greater pleasure within itself than in the loveliest garden. The familiar contemporary theme of disengagement acquires a mystical dimension.

8
Elizabethan and seventeenth-century prose

Quite apart from books which directly contributed to the development of the novel and which we shall consider later, there were many influential prose works written in this period that must necessarily interest us if only for the fact that they fed the minds of the reading public that included the great poets and dramatists we have been considering. As in all ages, some of the most successful books were much less than masterpieces. John Lyly's *Euphues, the Anatomy of Wit* (1578), and its sequel, *Euphues and His England* (1580), achieved great notoriety. Though they were ostensibly prose romances, the narrative element is a thin skeleton clothed with dialogue, discourses and didactic letters. Succeeding sections have such titles as 'How the lyfe of a young man should be ledde' and 'Of the education of youth'; but the moralizing is shallow, and Lyly has no claim to be considered a serious thinker. It was his style that 'caught on', and gave us the words *euphuism* and *euphuistic*. It is highly artificial, abounding in balanced antitheses or pseudo-antitheses, and it is cluttered with pretentious allusions, mythological and pseudo-scientific:

> The Spider weaveth a fine web to hang the Fly, the Wolfe weareth a faire face to devour the Lambe, the Mirlin striketh at the Partridge, the Eagle often snappeth at the Fly, men are always laying baites for women, which are the weaker vessels: but as yet I could never heare man by such snares to entrappe man: For true it is that men themselves have by use observed, yat it must be a harde Winter when one wolfe eateth another.

The style was widely taken up by the gallants and provoked both appreciative and parodic imitation in literature.

Among the books which give a first-hand account of Elizabethan England is the *Survey of London* by John Stow (?1525–1605), 'Conteyning the Originall, Antiquity, Increase, Moderne estate, and description of that City', The survey breaks the city down ward by ward for detailed treatment, and contains many sections too on buildings, customs, pastimes and city government. A wider survey of the country was made by William Harrison (1534–93) in his *Description of England*, which has chapters 'Of Degrees of People in the Commonwealth of England', 'Of Cities and Towns in England', 'Of Gardens and Orchards' and so on. This material was incorporated by Raphael Holinshed in his *Chronicles* (1577). Shakespeare's sometimes detailed indebtedness to Holinshed in the history plays, in *Macbeth, King Lear* and *Cymbeline,* can be gauged from these lines in Holinshed's account of Macbeth:

> Malcome, following hastilie after Macbeth, came the night before the battell unto Birnane wood; and, when

his armie had rested a while there to refresh them, he commanded everie man to get a bough of some tree or other of that wood in his hand, as big as he might beare, and to march foorth therewith in such wise, that on the next morrow they might come closelie and without sight in this manner within view of his enimies.

An even more remarkable influence on Shakespeare is that of Sir Thomas North (?1535–?1601) who published his translation of Plutarch's *Lives of the Noble Grecians and Romans* in 1579. Shakespeare was indebted to North not only for basic historical material in the Roman plays but also for the way in which the plots were fashioned and the characters conceived. Moreover Shakespeare borrowed from him many a turn of phrase. The famous description by Enobarbus in *Antony and Cleopatra* of Cleopatra in her barge on the river Cydnus illustrates the verbal indebtedness at its closest. North's phrases so appealed to Shakespeare the artist that they were transmuted with deceptive ease into rich blank verse.

A chronicler of a different breed from the historians was Richard Hakluyt (1553–1616) who published his *Principall Navigations, Voiages, and Discoveries of the English Nation* in 1589 and issued a much enlarged version in three volumes in 1598–1600. It is a compendious collection of narratives based both on research and on oral interviews, and including eye-witness accounts of adventures, battles and discoveries. The voyages of the Cabots, of Drake, of Frobisher and Sir John Hawkins are included in this vast record of English navigation and discovery, a patriotic tribute that had an infectious effect on adventurous spirits. It would be absurd to try to particularize about the effect on contemporary literature of the travel and exploration Hakluyt recorded, for the themes it inspired are threaded into the imagery of the age's poetry ubiquitously.

We have already referred to the War of the Theatres, and this was only one manifestation of the polemical and satirical pamphleteering which flourished at this time. Many writers important for their work in other fields also wrote prose works of social or controversial interest, like Robert Greene's pamphlets on 'Coney-catching', which picture the low life of London. Thomas Nashe (1567–1601) stands out among the pamphleteers. C. S. Lewis called him 'the perfect literary showman, the juggler with words who can keep a crowd spell-bound by sheer virtuosity'.[1] His *Pierce Pennilesse his Supplication to the Divell* contains within the framework of an appeal to the Devil a satirical survey of the vices of the time. His hearty, hectoring style flows vigorously on with little discipline or restraint and the zestful invective demolishes enemies ruthlessly. Nashe, in his anti-Puritan pamphlet, *An Almond for a Parrot*, also contributed to the most famous of all Elizabethan wars of words, the 'Martin Marprelate' controversy, so called after the pseudonym adopted by the anonymous author who issued his pamphlets from a secret press in the years 1588–9. The pamphlets were Puritan attacks against episcopacy: they had a serious theological basis in that they were provoked by episcopal legislation to suppress Puritan publications; but the personal attacks on individual bishops are scurrilous, and the racy, railing idiom is not the vehicle for grave controversy.

A more sombre vein runs through Dekker's pamphlets on the plague, such as *The Wonderfull Yeare*, *A Rod for Runawaies* and *London looke backe*, in which descriptions and anecdotes of the London plague are interspersed with moral criticism and with some religious exhortation. Prosaic descriptions of sudden deaths as people arise from a meal, or prepare to set out to market, or pause in a walk in the street, are made telling by Dekker's homely, economic style. There is even a case of a bride seized with the last sickness before the altar at the words 'in sickness and in health'. And there are scarifying tales like that of a man who guaranteed to

[1] *English Literature in the Sixteenth Century* (Clarendon Press, Oxford, 1954).

his fellow drinkers at an inn that he could get them away
without paying, however big the bill. He aroused the landlady's curiosity by talk of the plague tokens. She had never
seen them, she said. Whereupon the fellow ripped open his
doublet to reveal a chest peppered with the blue marks 'received by Haile-shot out of a Birding-piece through mis-
chance'. Within seconds the landlady was on her knees
begging them to take the 'spotted man' away without waiting for any reckoning.

In turning to the theological and religious prose of the
seventeenth century we turn to a rich inheritance, and no
figure stands out more attractively than Richard Hooker
(c.1554–1600), a priest who became the formidable defender
of the Anglican *via media* between Puritanism and Rome. In
reading Hooker's sermons, one finds oneself in contact with
a man deeply and sensitively aware of human need, especially of the pressure of doubt, yet full of warm personal assurance for those he addresses. A person of evident charity and
devoted to truth, he gave himself to the composition of the
monumental study, *Of the Laws of Ecclesiastical Politie*,
published in 1594 (the first four books) and 1597 (the fifth
and much the biggest book). The power of the book lies in
the massive structure of its argument, steadily and system-
atically developed, rather than in any passages of singular
striking force. It begins by laying philosophical foundations
in a survey of a natural law in the universe as representative
of divine reason, and of the operation of reason in the ordering of society. Within his system, under the dominion of
divine reason and, ideally, of human reason, sin is a disturbance of universal order and an offence against the fitness
and beauty of creation. (We are near to the spirit of Shakespearian tragedy here.)

> For there was never sin committed, wherein a less
> good was not preferred before a greater, and that wil-
> fully; which cannot be done without the singular dis-
> grace of Nature, and the utter disturbance of that divine

order, whereby the pre-eminence of chiefest acceptation is by the best things worthily challenged.

On such foundations, calmly laid, Hooker proceeds step by step to erect his vast but tightly knit argument in defence of the Church of England's position against Puritan bibliolatry and hostility to ceremony, and leading, in the last book, to a full-scale examination of Anglican practice as represented in the Book of Common Prayer.

Donne's best religious prose lends itself much more readily to immediate appreciation, for his arguments are contained within the smaller compass of his reflective *Devotions upon Emergent Occasions* and of his sermons. Moreover Donne's prose abounds in 'punch lines':

> When *God* and wee were *alone*, in *Adam*, that was not enough; when the *Devill* and wee were *alone*, in *Eve*, it was enough.

He sprinkles his argument with imagery which sometimes repetitively and cumulatively hammers a point home, as when he presses the need, in illness, to wait patiently for convalescence:

> Yet we cannot awake the *July-flowers* in *January*, nor retard the *flowers* of the *spring* to *autumne*. We cannot bid the fruits come in *May*, nor the *leaves* to sticke on in *December*. A *woman* that is weake cannot put off her *ninth month* to a *tenth*, for her *deliverie*, and say shee will stay till shee bee *stronger;* nor a *Queene* cannot hasten it to a *seventh*, that shee may be ready for some other pleasure.

Donne's rhetoric can be lavish: he can sustain the rhythm of uninterrupted thought and utterance as he mounts through clause after clause in some tremendous paragraph of Ciceronian proportions, especially when he is dwelling on human wickedness or the horrors of damnation. But he can also be economical in thought and concise in expression, turning an antithesis or a paradox deftly so that it bites. In his sermon on the conversion of Saint Paul he dwells on the relevance of Paul's experience to our own, at one point touching on Paul's experience of blindness, and adding, 'not darknesse, but a greater light, must make us blinde'. And in his last sermon he probes his congregation audaciously:

> About midnight he was *taken* and *bound with a kisse*. Art thou *too conformable* to him in that? Is that not *too literally*, too exactly *thy case*? at *midnight* to have been *taken and bound with a kisse*?

This last, most famous sermon, was preached not many days before his death. It came to be called 'Death's Duell'. Walton tells us how Donne presented himself in the pulpit with a 'decayed body and a dying face' and took the text 'And unto God the Lord belong the issues from death'. His faint and hollow voice persuaded many that he 'had preach't his own Funeral Sermon'.

Lancelot Andrewes (1555–1626), who was in turn Bishop of Chichester, Ely and Winchester, left a number of sermons that were posthumously published. His is a packed, concentrated style abounding in parentheses and Latin quotations, clearly directed at an intellectual audience. Andrewes was a great scholar and though he never matched Donne's theatricality or his surge of rhetoric, he does not lack imaginative touches, and there is a note of deep sincerity and piety in his prose. Oral delivery alone can do justice to Andrewes's way of pressing his points home in short, probing phrases. We cite the lines from a sermon 'Of the Nativitie' which had an infectious influence on T. S. Eliot's *Journey of the Magi*:

> A cold coming they had of it, at this time of the year; just the worst time of the year, to take a journey, and specially a long journey, in. The waies deep, the weather sharp, the daies short, the sun farthest off, *in solstitio brumali*, the very dead of *Winter*.

Another Anglican divine, Jeremy Taylor (1613–67), who

became Bishop of Down and Connor, and later of Dromore, wrote books of sermons and prayers, but is best known for *Holy Living* and *Holy Dying*. The former is a book of guidance for living the Christian life and deals comprehensively with religious duties, personal morality, civic, domestic and educational responsibilities. *Holy Dying* is a work of advice and comfort in sickness and in dying, all the more moving in that it sprang from Taylor's loss of his wife. Taylor's prose is more musical than Andrewes's. There is a liturgical splendour about his cadences. It lacks Donne's extravagance but not his warmth.

It is a far cry from the cultured prose of the Anglican divines to the homespun idiom of the tinker of Bedford, John Bunyan (1628–88). He soldiered in the Parliamentary army in his youth and later, after his first wife's death, experienced a profound religious conversion which transformed his life and set him on his course as a nonconformist preacher. He suffered twelve years' imprisonment from 1660 for unlicensed preaching. It was during a briefer, second imprisonment that he wrote *The Pilgrim's Progress* (1678). This allegorical story traces Christian's arduous pilgrimage from the City of Destruction to the Celestial City. The journey takes him through the Slough of Despond, the Valley of Humiliation, the Valley of the Shadow of Death (with the mouth of Hell in the middle of it) and Vanity Fair. There are places of refreshment and encouragement *en route* too, like the House Beautiful, where the lovely damsel Discretion introduces Christian to the spiritually nourishing discourse of Piety, Prudence and Charity, and the Delectable Mountains, where the shepherds, Knowledge, Experience, Watchful and Sincere, provide hospitality, point out the topographical pitfalls ahead (from the Mountain of Error and Mount Caution), and give the pilgrims (Christian and Hopeful) a note of the route to be followed. In the Valley of Humiliation Christian endures sore combat for half a day with the fiend Apollyon, clothed with scales like a fish, winged like a dragon, footed like a bear, with fire and smoke issuing from his belly. At Vanity Fair, the symbolic metropolis of worldliness, Christian and Faithful are mocked, besmeared with dirt, caged, chained in irons, and put on trial simply for their honest attachment to a truth which is a maximum irritant to the dominant inhabitants. A careless diversion through By-path Meadow leads to imprisonment in Doubting Castle and gross brutality at the hands of its owner, Giant Despair. The book is busy with people. Helpful and inspiring guides, directors and fellow travellers include Evangelist, Interpreter and the two pilgrims, Faithful and Hopeful, who in turn share Christian's trials at his side. There are countless encounters with hypocrites, half-believers, backsliders, worldlings and self-deceivers, like Hypocrisy and Formalist, Talkative, Ignorance, Mr By-ends, Mr Money-love, Little-faith and Vain-hope. Bunyan's style is direct and unpretentious, but tough and compelling in its impact:

> I saw then in my dream so far as this valley reached, there was on the right hand a very deep ditch; that ditch is it into which the blind have led the blind in all ages, and have both there miserably perished.

That thirty-seven of the forty-three words in this sentence are monosyllables is a mark of Bunyan's simplicity and his power. Biblical echoes and homiletic fervour enrich the colloquial sturdiness; they add dignity to a style that is vital and urgent in both narrative and dialogue. The reader is in touch throughout with a mind acutely responsive to the spiritual and moral condition of the world around him and able to realize it feelingly in words. Bunyan added a second part to the *Pilgrim's Progress*, tracing the pilgrimage of Christian's wife, Christiana, and her children. They follow the same route and Mr Great-heart is their guide. An inspiring figure is Mr Valiant-for-truth, who recites 'Who would true valour see', and who, when summoned, passes unflinchingly over the river of Death – 'and all the trumpets sounded for him on the other side'.

Among Bunyan's other works are *Grace Abounding to the Chief of Sinners*, an autobiographical record of 'the exceeding mercy of God in Christ, to his poor servant, John Bunyan', and *The Life and Death of Mr Badman*, in the form of a dialogue between Mr Wiseman and Mr Attentive. This book hangs much preaching on the history of Mr Badman, who from being a liar and thief as a child, hating the Lord's Day and all it stands for, becomes an adult fraud and hypocrite. The preaching is interspersed with incidental anecdotes such as that of Dorothy Mately, swearer, curser, liar and thief. She was taxed with stealing twopence, denied it, 'wishing the ground might swallow her up' if she had done so, and then, before the eyes of one George Hodgkinson, sank along with her washtub into the ground. Yet Bunyan's attack on bourgeois vice is gravely weighed and his finger is always on the pulse of real life. Mr Badman is unwarily trapped into a second marriage in spite of his boast that whoring is cheaper ('Who would keep a cow of their own that can have a quart of milk for a penny?'). His debaucheries finish him off, and his deathbed behaviour towards companions in vice and genuine if pious well-wishers, respectively, is vividly portrayed.

The astonishing variety of the religious literature of this period may be savoured by turning from Bunyan to Sir Thomas Browne (1605–82). 'Savoured' is an apt word to be applied to the reader's experience of Browne's style in *Religio Medici*, a defence of Christian belief very different in tone from Bunyan's strict simplicity and commitment. Browne was a scholar and a doctor, and he elaborated his thesis with curious fruits of his erudition. His prose is a delicately fashioned instrument, abounding in symmetry and graceful rhythms. His faith is a faith in revelation as a mystery distinct from what can be scientifically established. He can warm the heart with his spirited declamations: he can also amuse by the oddity of his fancies, as when he wishes that 'we might procreate like trees, without conjunction, or that there were any way to perpetuate the world without this trivial and vulgar way of union ...' He adds beguilingly that he has no aversion to the sweet sex but is rather 'naturally amorous of all that is beautiful', so much so that he could spend a day looking at a picture, even the picture of a horse. Browne also wrote *Vulgar Errors* (Pseudo-doxia Epidemica) in which popular delusions and mis-conceptions are surveyed and examined.

With Browne we have entered the borderland between philosophy and theology. Two deeply influential philosophi-cal thinkers stand out in the age we are concerned with, Bacon and Hobbes. Francis Bacon (1561–1626) combined a career of scholarship and writing with a career in public life in which he rose to be Lord Chancellor. His philosophi-cal treatise, *The Advancement of Learning*, examines the current state of knowledge and the means of advancing it. The *New Atlantis* is an unfinished fable recounting a visit to an imaginary island, Bensalem. It has an institution for scientific study, Salomon's House, whose activities are ex-plained to the visitors by one of its 'fathers'. But the *Essays* are of chief concern to the student of literature. They are polished set pieces dealing with personal and public themes, giving judicious advice under such headings as 'Of Parents and Children', 'Of Marriage and the Single Life', 'Of Envy', 'Of Ceremonies and Respect'. Bacon draws on wide reading for his illustrations and the essays display sharpness of mind and a gift for aphoristic expression. The essay on 'Delays' (XXI) begins:

> Fortune is like the market, where many times, if you can stay a little, the price will fall ...

and that on 'Suspicion' (XXXI) begins:

> Suspicions amongst thoughts are like bats among birds, they ever fly by twilight ...

A magisterial air is inevitable at times in the act of so consciously disseminating wisdom, and one needs to take the weighted propositional certainties in limited doses, for they can overpower. Nevertheless the fruits of perceptive reflection are often memorably capsulated: 'Reading maketh a full man; conference a ready man; and writing an exact man ...' (*Of Studies*, L).

Thomas Hobbes (1588–1679) was for a time in touch with Bacon and acted as his secretary. Hobbes's work as a philosopher scarcely falls within the scope of this survey, but his book *Leviathan* is a forceful attack on the notion of divine and derived sovereignty, and builds a theory of society ordered by contractual limitation of liberty and contractual concentration of authority. Such organized control is necessary to combat natural human self-interest which otherwise militates against civilizational stability. The doctrine of authority would justify claims upon a subject's obedience from a *de facto* ruler like Cromwell, as from a *de jure* one. Hobbes's presuppositions are materialist, and his dismissive treatment of theology offended many; but the influence of his work was immense.

Our last concern in this period is with the public and private chroniclers of life, that is to say, those historians, biographers and diarists who left a peculiarly rich picture of their age. Edward Hyde, Earl of Clarendon (1609–74), after first sympathizing with Parliament, supported the king decisively from 1641 and became Lord Chancellor under Charles II. His *History of the Rebellion and Civil Wars in England* is a massive work in a carefully structured style that has both dignity and fluency. Clarendon's treatment of events does not allow of great narrative excitement, but the steady record is enlivened by fascinating personal studies of important participants. His study of Charles I ends thus:

To conclude, he was the worthyest gentleman, the best master, the best frende, the best husbande, the best father, the best Christian, that the Age in which he lyved had produced, and if he was not the best kinge, if he was without some parts and qualityes which have made some kings great and happy, no other Prince

was ever unhappy, who was possessed of half his virtues and indowments, and so much without any kinde
of vice.

There is a rather niggling portrait of Clarendon himself by
a much younger contemporary, Gilbert Burnet (1643–1715),
a Scottish divine. He wrote not only a *History of the Reformation in England* but also a *History of My Own Times*, that
was published after his death. Clarendon 'had too much
levity in his wit, and did not always observe the decorum of
his post', Burnet says. 'He was high, and was apt to reject
those who addressed themselves to him with too much
contempt.' But Burnet has neither Clarendon's penetration nor his masterful periodic style. Sometimes the
clauses follow each other with quick-fire rapidity: he
seems to spill sentences onto the page with a lively lack of
restraint.

There is a good deal more contrivance in the style of
Thomas Fuller (1608–61) who wrote a *History of the Holy
War* (the Crusades) and *The Worthies of England*, a survey
of topographical and antiquarian interest which includes a
memorable reference to the numerous 'wit-combats' between
Shakespeare and Ben Jonson. Jonson was 'a Spanish great
Galleon ... far higher in learning, solid, but slow in his
performance'; Shakespeare was 'the English man-of-war,
lesser in bulk, but lighter in sailing, could turn with all tides,
tack about and take advantage of all winds by the quickness
of his wit and invention'.

Though it is not strictly history, Earle's *Microcosmo-
graphie* may fitly be mentioned here, for it certainly chronicles the age, if in imaginative form. For John Earle (*c.*1600–
65), who eventually became Bishop of Worcester, put together in this collection a series of portraits of contemporary
types under such headings as 'A meer Alderman', 'A Serv-
ing Man', 'An Insolent Man' and 'An upstart Knight'.
They are pleasing, tolerant studies by a keen observer who
has a sense of humour. He has, too, considerable literary

skill in planting his ironies and giving dramatic life to his portraits. Thus, of 'A She precise Hypocrite', he writes:

> She doubts of the Virgin *Mary's* salvation, and dares not saint her, but knows her own place in heaven as perfectly as the pew she has a key to. She is so taken up with Faith she has no room for Charity, and understands no good Works but what are wrought on the sampler.

The genre to which these vivid sketches belong is known as the Theophrastian character (after Theophrastus, a pupil of Aristotle's, who practised the form). Other seventeenth-century writers who produced comparable sketches were Joseph Hall (1574–1656) in his *Character of Virtues and Vices* (1608) and Sir Thomas Overbury (1581–1613).

There is liveliness again in the biographical pieces (mostly notes and memoranda) left by the antiquary John Aubrey (1626–97) among his papers and published last century as *Brief Lives of Contemporaries*. Aubrey is meaty, informative and gossipy, and he is capable of deft descriptive touches. His idiom and his mode of jotting down material are nearer to the homely chatter of the diarists than to the controlled formality of Clarendon and Fuller.

The *Lives* which Izaak Walton (1593–1683) wrote are more edifying, but they contain descriptive and anecdotal material that brings their subjects warmly to life. We have quoted already from the *Life of Dr John Donne*; there are also lives of Richard Hooker, Sir Henry Wotton and George Herbert. A famous glimpse of Hooker's domestic life shows pupils visiting a somewhat hen-pecked Richard who has been assigned to the duties of tending the sheep and rocking the cradle. And a glimpse of George Herbert shows him arriving dirty at a musical gathering at Salisbury because he has helped a poor man to unload and reload a fallen horse *en route*. Rebuked for demeaning himself, he replied that the thought of what he had done 'would prove Musick to him at

Midnight', whereas the omission would have disturbed his conscience for ever after when he passed the place in question. Better known is Walton's guide for fishermen, *The Compleat Angler, or the Contemplative Man's Recreation*, though it is perhaps successfully recreational for the contemplative rather than completely instructive for the angler. Written in dialogue form, and beginning with competitive claims for their respective recreations by a fisherman, a fowler and a hunter, it proceeds to give instruction in the art of fishing. It is the book of an open-hearted, equable personality who loves musing and reading, and is quaintly self-revealing. Walton is a writer who can illustrate a point by reference to Pliny, Du Bartas or Bacon, and who will turn from his theme to introduce an entertaining anecdote of gypsies and beggars or to describe an encounter with milkmaids singing verses by Marlowe and Ralegh. A country scene inspires him to the praise of the simple life and to pity of the over-affluent, or provokes the grateful recitation of Herbert's 'Sweet day, so cool, so calm, so bright'; for the text is sprinkled with poetry.

The two great diarists of the age were John Evelyn (1620–1706) and Samuel Pepys (1633–1703). Evelyn began to keep a regular diary in 1641 (though he added a brief survey of his earlier life) and continued till just before his death. It was written up at intervals, and not daily like Pepys's. Evelyn's record covers such a vast area of public and private experience that it seems pointless to particularize. He was abroad for much of the troubled time of the war and the Commonwealth, and his informative account of travel is enriched by his keen eye for oddities and curiosities. Back at home he had public appointments that kept him close to the centre of affairs in London, but though his record is therefore an inexhaustible mine of information, it does not bring great events like the Plague and the Fire to life as Pepys's diary does. There is little drama about Evelyn's presentation of events even when those events have obviously moved him. Witness the entry in January 1649:

The Villanie of the Rebells proceeding now so far as to Trie, Condemne & *Murder* our excellent King, the 30 of this Moneth, struck me with such horror that I kept the day of his *Martyrdom* a fast, & would not be present, at that execrable wickednesse; receiving that sad account of it from my Bro. Geo ...

About Cromwell's death in 1658 he is even briefer:

September 3. Died that archrebell *Oliver Cromwell*, cal'd Protector.

Pepys's *Diary* is much more a work of art both in its fine, sustained descriptions of events like the coronation of Charles II, the Plague (during which Pepys stayed at his post) and the Fire of London, and in its divertingly rich reportage of life's daily minutiae. Pepys, the son of a London tailor, had to make his own way in life, but with the help of Sir Edward Montagu, a cousin of his father's, he obtained a clerkship in the public service and rose by his zeal and industry to become Secretary to the Admiralty and an MP. He was in touch with both Charles II and James II, and exercised great influence on naval policy. The *Diary* gives a minute picture of public and personal life between 1660 and 1669, when he laid it aside because of failing eyesight. The record gives a completely uninhibited revelation of Pepys's private interests and pursuits. Pepys's amiable candour was not meant for the public. He wrote in shorthand, sometimes breaking into code for such intimate concerns as his own erotic adventures. The diary itself was left in manuscript in Pepys's library. The library was bequeathed to Magdalene College, Cambridge, and the code was deciphered over 100 years later by the Reverend John Smith. This led to the first publication in 1825.

Pepys overflows with information about what he eats and what he wears, the books he has read and the music he has heard. He was an avid theatregoer and an equally avid churchgoer. We hear that he thought Webster's *The White*

Devil 'a very poor play' and never had so little pleasure in a play in his life, and that he thought one experience of *A Midsummer Night's Dream* enough, 'for it is the most insipid ridiculous play that I ever saw in my life'. Jonson's comedy got higher marks: he thought *The Silent Woman* 'an excellent play' and *Bartholomew Fair* 'most admirable ... but too much prophane and abusive'. He enjoyed Betterton in *Hamlet* and learned 'To be or not to be' by heart. Pepys's touching pride in mingling with the great emerges time after time in remembered details like the way the Lord Chancellor (Clarendon), passing by, stroked him on the head in approval of a letter about the treatment of watermen. And the domestic scene is intimately recorded: Pepys frankly takes us through the quarrels with his wife. Sometimes they lead to violence; but he is sorry afterwards and does his best to make things up. Elizabeth was sorely tested on occasions, and he tells once of her coming to the side of his bed at 1.00 a.m. with red hot tongs, intending to pinch him with them – for he had been out without telling her 'which did vex her, poor wretch'. Fortunately she was soon appeased.

9
Milton to Dryden

For John Milton (1608–74) poetry was a vocation, and such is the personal and public importance of his masterpiece *Paradise Lost* that one can fitly measure the other activities of his life up to its composition according to how they prepared the ground for it or delayed it. Milton's father was a well-to-do scrivener who gave him a good education and every encouragement to steep himself in literary and musical culture. Before he completed his studies at Cambridge by taking the MA degree in 1632, Milton had already written his first significant poem, the ode *On the Morning of Christ's Nativity* (1629). *L'Allegro* and *Il Penseroso* followed not long after. For five years Milton lived at Horton in

Buckinghamshire, preparing himself mentally and spiritually for his chosen vocation. The masque *Comus* was written for performance at Ludlow Castle in 1634 and *Lycidas*, the elegy for his fellow student, Edward King, in 1637. Milton's next phase of self-preparation was a tour on the Continent on which he met Italian men of letters.

It was the Civil War that brought him back, and he threw himself into polemical writing on the anti-episcopal front, laer on behalf of Cromwell's government and even in justification of Charles's execution. Meanwhile sudden marriage in 1642 to Mary Powell, a young girl of sixteen, had been so unsuccessful that Mary returned to her royalist parents within a few weeks and did not come back to her husband until 1645; and Milton had by then written pamphlets in defence of divorce. Distaste for censorship provoked his *Areopagitica*, a stout defence of the freedom of the press. Milton's appointment as Latin Secretary in 1649 committed him more officially to the Commonwealth so that when the Restoration came it put an end to his cherished endeavours. His eyesight had completely failed as early as 1652, and his first wife had died in the same year, leaving three daughters. His second wife, whom he married in 1656, lived only two years. Milton's retirement to private life at the Restoration brought his life's work to a climax in the composition of *Paradise Lost*, which was published in 1667. *Paradise Regained* and *Samson Agonistes* were published in 1671.

Milton's years of work for the Parliament deflected him from the pursuit of his prime work as a poet: yet the years of active controversy in the heat of fierce conflict, superimposed on the years of disciplined intellectual self-preparation, perhaps provided the exact nourishment needed for poetic endeavour on the scale of the epic. Certainly, though the substance of Milton's prose output removes much of it from the sphere of what is lastingly interesting except to specialist scholars, the long discipline of developing a style apt for all the purposes of heated current controversy must have operated towards the achievement of that mature periodic fluency which marks the style of *Paradise Lost*. Be that as it may, no English writer's career is so memorably, even dramatically, shaped as that which leads from Cambridge and the *Nativity* ode, through Whitehall and political pamphleteering, to the cottage at Chalfont St Giles, and the portrait of the lone and broken and blinded Samson.

L'Allegro is the cheerful spirit's cry for laughter and jollity, mirth and pleasure, while its companion piece, *Il Penseroso*, calls for pensive musing melancholy, peace and quiet, and retirement to silent contemplation. Each explores scenes and activities proper to its mood in the most accomplished octosyllabic couplets in our literature. These two poems with *Lycidas* would have made Milton's name as a front-rank poet had he written nothing more. *Lycidas* is an elegy contributed to a collection of memorial tributes on the occasion of the death of a fellow student, Edward King, who was drowned *en route* for Ireland. The elegy seems to effect the impossible by giving emotional authenticity and moral gravity to the pastoral convention with its stylized machinery of shepherds and swains. King was destined for the priesthood, and lament for lost youthful talent and promise is the keynote. The threat of being cut off in the prime of life leads to meditation on the motive that fame provides to 'scorn delights, and live laborious days'. The grief of King's loss is shared even by Saint Peter: he could better have spared the many worldly and ignorant priests under whom the 'hungry sheep look up, and are not fed'. There is a final triumphant cry of faith in Lycidas's rising in Christ. In introducing his tribute, the poet insists that he is plucking fruit prematurely 'with forc'd fingers rude': he is writing before his self-preparation is complete. 'Bitter constraint and sad occasion drear' compel this untimely anticipation. The apology is for writing prematurely 'once more' because in 1634 Milton fulfilled a commission to supply a masque for presentation at Ludlow Castle before the Earl of Bridgewater, and wrote *Comus* for the occasion. Comus is an enchanter, descended from Bacchus and Circe, who lures travellers to his 'palace' and transforms them into half-monsters. A Lady loses her two brothers in a forest and Comus deceptively takes her to his 'palace', there to press his corrupting drink upon her. Her resistance is the resistance of chastity to self-indulgence. There are interesting anticipations of *Paradise Lost* in the discussion between the brothers about whether virtue in itself is proof against assault and in the cunningly persuasive arguments by which Comus tries to seduce the Lady. He is an amateur Satan confronted by an incorruptible Eve. Unblushing delight in innocence and cheerful praise of chastity give the play its appealing warmth. It is Milton's 'Paradise Preserved'.

His *Paradise Lost* sets out to 'justifie the wayes of God to men' by rehearsing the high argument of man's fall and redemption. We are taken first to Hell to see the plight of the fallen angels and to hear them debating whether to renew active warfare or to try to make the best of things in Hell. A notable feature of the debate is the total diabolical irrationality brilliantly registered by Milton in sequence after sequence of illogicality and self-contradiction that is conveyed with all the emotive blur and sleight of intellect characteristic of cosmic media-men. The debate is rigged so that Satan is chosen to set out and seek God's new world with the intention to alienate His new creature from Him and thus damage Him indirectly.

Book III takes us to Heaven where we listen to a council at which the fall of man is foreseen. The Son of God offers self-sacrificially to save man by ransom as Satan offered himself to destroy man by seduction, and we recognize that as Hell travestied Heaven by its grotesque parody of rational discourse in irrationality, so the movements of Satan are parodic negativities burlesquing the acts of the divine. Meantime Satan has found his way to earth, and we go to Eden to see Adam and Eve, erect and godlike creatures in whom the 'image of their glorious Maker' shines. In the idyll of their innocent converse and their connubial delights Milton's poetic range reaches levels of sensuous wonder that are at once deeply personal and sublime. The metaphorical overtones and allusions add a symbolic dimension, so that we recognize Paradise as Heaven's image just as Hell was Heaven's parody: correspondingly the human family with its offspring-to-be is as clearly an image of the heavenly Trinity as the satanic family (Satan, Sin and Death) is its parody.

In the central books of the poem we are taken back to the beginning of things, for Raphael is sent by God to Adam, and the War in Heaven, the Creation of the World, and the waking to life of Adam and Eve, are covered in their converse. Book IX brings the drama to its climax, for Eve encounters Satan in the body of a serpent marvellously able to speak, to flatter, to indicate how a being can rise above its own nature. A serpent, he claims, may become virtually human, a human being virtually divine: the secret is the fruit of a certain tree. Eve is taken to see it, knows it for the forbidden tree, but nevertheless accepts the diabolical guarantee of its virtue:

> So saying, her rash hand in evil hour
> Forth reaching to the fruit, she pluck'd, she eat:
> Earth felt the wound, and Nature from her seat
> Sighing through all her Works gave signs of woe,
> That all was lost.

Returning to Adam, she induces him against his better judgement to eat as well. Shame, lust and quarrelsomeness overtake them.

The concluding books not only trace the judgement upon Adam and Eve but also include a vision of the future of the human race, presented for the consolation of our first parents by the Archangel Michael. The vision, by its inclusive summary of the pattern of redemption in Christ, completes the original intention to justify God's ways to men.

Our greatest poem is a masterpiece of organization in

which blank verse is employed to enable words to stand out with the force which in rhymed verse only rhyming words have. Thus key words, employed time after time ('fruit', 'death', 'woe', 'seat', 'mute', and many more) are so planted (using all feet of the pentameter) as to resoundingly pull together far scattered but related passages in a pattern of sound and meaning musical in shape, associative and symbolic in texture. The pattern of interconnections is so subtle and complex that the poem offers the delights of unlimited exploration and discovery on a scale rare in literature. It is a masterpiece too by virtue of the universality of its substance, psychological and emotional, mythic and religious. The blending of deeply felt personal interest in the lot of Adam and Eve with a profound theological estimate of the human predicament and destiny is delicately sustained. The balance is preserved by the presence of the humble, prayerful poetic persona, drawing the reader into involvement with himself and with Adam and Eve.

Paradise Regained is a remarkably superfluous poem in view of the vision of human redemption and the endless ages of new Heaven and new Earth prefigured at the conclusion of *Paradise Lost*. It concentrates on the temptation of Christ by Satan, which is not in fact capable of bearing the weight of a central significance shifted from the events of the Passion. The static interchange of dialogue is not inspired. It is difficult to understand Milton's lapse from the poetic level sustained elsewhere. One inevitably feels, on reading, that the magnificent flow of *Paradise Lost*, to which Milton's muse had geared itself, just had to be allowed to run out.

Samson Agonistes is a tragedy in the Greek mould, presenting Samson's final act of retribution after his imprisonment by the Philistines. He is visited by a series of people while a Chorus keeps up an intermittent commentary, recalling the past, musing in prayer and exhortation on the ways of God to men, consoling Samson and blessing his resolve. The first visitor, Samson's old father Manoa, brings the tempting hope of release. Samson's response is that his evils are remediless and that death alone can close his miseries. The second visitor, Samson's wife Dalila, who betrayed him by cutting off the hair in which his strength lay, offers the tempting lure that even for a blind and broken man life 'yet hath many solaces, enjoy'd / Where other senses want not their delights / At home in leisure and domestic ease'. Samson resists with a ferocity that testifies to the seductive power of the temptation. The third visitor, Harapha the Philistine, comes to taunt and mock the beaten champion and receives a dignified rebuke. Samson has sustained the battery of confrontation and he is spiritually ready now to fulfil his destiny. The Philistines call him to entertain them at their feast and his first refusal is quickly retracted as he senses a divinely offered opportunity in the invitation. He goes, assuring the Chorus that they will hear nothing dishonourable of him, nothing unworthy. After Manoa has returned to stimulate a last shallow hope of escape by ransom, the news comes that Samson has pulled down the theatre on the audience and himself.

The free verse which Milton adopts is an instrument of power and flexibility. Of the four Miltonic figures who have to wrestle with temptation – the Lady (*Comus*), Eve, Christ and Samson – there is most of Milton in Samson, the blind old warrior who has lived to see himself bereft of power and influence under an alien dispensation. Though Milton's self-projection is never obtrusive, the pathos of the obviously felt correspondences comes through in the voice of suffering and the voice of faith.

The reaction at the Restoration against the austerities of the Commonwealth gave a tone of licentiousness to the life of the court and of London society. To turn from the poetry of Milton to the poetry of fashionable Restoration society is to bridge a chasm.

> Grace was in all her steps, Heav'n in her Eye,
> In every gesture dignitie and love.

That is Adam's praise of Eve.

> She's plump, yet with ease you may span her round
>   Waste,
> But her round swelling Thighs can scarce be embrac'd;
> Her Belly is soft, not a word of the rest;
> But I know what I think when I drink to the best.

So the court poet, Sackville, hymns his Bess. Charles Sackville (1638–1706), better known as the Earl of Dorset, was
one of the group of Court Wits surrounding Charles II and
sharing in the gay dissipations that marked his reign. They
were not of course mere crude debauchees, but men of culture who patronized the arts. Nor was the vein of satirical
bawdy presented above their predominant idiom; but certainly the group sought to shock sensitivities by outrageous
exhibitionism as well as by cultivated raillery, and their practice of permissiveness is near in psychological origin to
the movements towards decadence in our own post-war
society.

Sir Charles Sedley (?1639–1701), the dramatist, was another
member of the group. His graceful versification achieves
a lyrical ease whose rhythmical distinctiveness lifts it well
above banality, as in the well-known *Song to Celia*:

> All that in Woman is ador'd
> In thy dear self I find,
> For the whole Sex can but afford
> The Handsome and the Kind.

Another dramatist, Sir George Etherege (?1635–91), though
deriving from a humbler social background, skilfully
assumed the poses of the circle with an air of unaffectedness
that can briefly charm in spite of its obviousness:

> Then since we mortal lovers are,
> Let's question not how long 'twill last;
> But while we love let us take care,
> Each minute be with pleasure past:

> It were a madness, to deny
> To live, because w'are sure to die.

Yet this unforced flow of phrase, masterfully contrived, somehow frames word and pose alike in isolation from reality. The point may be made even in relation to some of the poetry of John Wilmot, Earl of Rochester (1647–80), the best of the group. He dramatizes the paradox of constancy and inconstancy in 'Absent from thee', where the lover demands freedom to leave his mistress so that his 'fantastick Mind' can 'prove' the torments of separation. Then let him return 'wearied with a World of Woe' to her safe bosom and expire there contented:

> Lest once more wand'ring from that Heav'n,
> I fall on some base Heart unblest;
> Faithless to thee, false, unforgiven,
> And lose my everlasting Rest.

Stance and stanza alike are beautifully fashioned, so neatly indeed that the awareness of toying with life as well as with words is the impression left on the sensitive reader. Yet Rochester's lyrics ('All my past life is mine no more', for instance) often touch deeper levels, levels on which the realities of adoration, change and inconstancy are at once metaphysically formulated and keenly felt. Moreover Rochester is a satirist, deftly characterizing contemporary poets in *An Allusion to Horace*, and achieving a philosophic dimension in *A Satyr against Mankind*. In the latter, and in the gravely devastating cadences of *Upon Nothing*, the new 'Augustan' spirit is decisively with us:

> The great Man's Gratitude to his best Friend,
> King's Promises, Whores' Vows, tow'rds thee they bend,
> Flow swiftly into thee, and in thee ever end.

A poet of a different breed, but no less representative of Restoration reaction, was Samuel Butler (1612–80), author of *Hudibras*, a lengthy mock-heroic poem immensely successful in its day. Its targets are bigotry and hypocrisy. It ridicules the Puritans and Independents by describing the adventures of Hudibras and his squire Ralpho, absurd figures derivative from Cervantes's *Don Quixote*. If the satire is sometimes heavy-handed and the octosyllabic metre heavy-footed, Butler can be dexterous in word-play, and many a shaft has shrewd epigrammatic force:

> What makes all Doctrines plain and clear?
> About two Hundred Pounds a Year.
> And that which was prov'd true before,
> Prove false again? – Two Hundred more.

The literature of the last quarter of this century was dominated by the massive figure of John Dryden (1631–1700). He was a literary giant of a kind very different from Milton, and his claims are always more difficult to demonstrate than to recognize. He was a superb professional craftsman. His career was a writer's career; and the turbulent events that rendered it a life of conflicts, of failures and successes, were many of them literary events arising from the rivalries of competing dramatists and poets. Because he was a professional, consciously devoting himself to the refinement of English prose and verse, he was prepared to turn his hand to a great variety of forms and purposes; and Dryden's greatness lies in a total achievement comprising plays, prose and poems of varying character rather than in this or that masterpiece. There is no single work that brings all his immense gifts to fruition, no single work on which all those gifts are brought to bear. It would be idle to pretend that his best poem, *Absalom and Achitophel,* in any way represents the fullness of his genius as *Paradise Lost* represents Milton's. And the satirical voice which gives such brilliance to *Absalom and Achitophel* never breathes a sound in his best play, *All for Love.*

Dryden came of a Puritan family, but moved in stages through royalism and Anglicanism to Roman Catholicism. The changing nature of his allegiances indicates the serious search for stability and truth that occupied him mentally and spiritually during years of experience which taught him to see through the postures of successive ruling parties. Dryden's first successes were in the theatre, but we reserve consideration of his plays to the next chapter. In *Annus Mirabilis, The Year of Wonders*, 1666, he celebrated the national achievements against the Dutch and also paid tribute to London's ordeal in the Fire:

> Methinks already, from this chymic flame,
> I see a city of more precious mould:
> Rich as the town which gives the Indies name,
> With silver pav'd, and all divine with gold.

The characteristic energy and fluency are already apparent, though the tautness and concentration of Dryden's maturity are yet to be achieved. After a decade of immersion in the theatre, the full flowering of Dryden's satiric wit was marked by the publication of *Absalom and Achitophel* in 1681. It is a topical poem intended to sway people's minds about immediate events. Charles II's illegitimate son, the Duke of Monmouth, became involved in an attempt to exclude the Catholic Duke of York from succession to the throne. Dryden represents the Earl of Shaftesbury as Achitophel and the Duke of Monmouth as Absalom. Absalom is lured by Achitophel to join the rebellious action. The first description of Achitophel is devastating in its impact:

> Of these the false Achitophel was first;
> A name to all succeeding ages curst:
> For close designs, and crooked councils fit;
> Sagacious, bold, and turbulent of wit;
> Restless, unfix'd in principles and place;
> In power unpleas'd, impatient of disgrace.

Achitophel's cunning appeal to Absalom to make himself 'champion of the public good' touches the spirit of a youth 'too covetous of fame, / Too full of angel's metal in his frame'; and in spite of loyal devotion to his father, the burden of his illegitimacy weighs heavily upon him. 'Desire of greatness is a godlike sin', he cries and Achitophel diabolically pours poison into this wound in his virtue. But the memorable force of the poem lies in its gallery of portraits, scathingly sketched with an adroitness of stroke that flaunts Dryden's consummate mastery of the couplet. No one is polished off more deftly and ironically than Zimri, the Duke of Buckingham:

> A man so various, that he seem'd to be
> Not one, but all mankind's epitome:
> Stiff in opinions, always in the wrong;
> Was everything by starts, and nothing long ...

In view of the numerous identifiable portraits it is not surprising that the popularity of the poem was immediate, and Nahum Tate wrote a second part a year later to which Dryden contributed some 200 lines.

There is comparable polish and humour in the satire, *Mac Flecknoe*, an attack on the poet Shadwell, who is selected to succeed the retiring arch-poet of nonsense, as being supreme in that sphere:

> Shadwell alone, of all my sons, is he
> Who stands confirmed in full stupidity.
> The rest to some faint meaning make pretence,
> But Shadwell never deviates into sense.

Dryden's use of the heroic couplet for the very different purpose of philosophical and theological reasoning is, considering the superficial unattractiveness of such a project, remarkably successful. His *Religio Laici* is ostensibly a defence of the established religion against the extremes of Roman traditionalism and dissenting individualism. On the one hand the 'partial Papists' have claimed infallibility for their Church and abused the claim. On the other hand the loudest dissenting bawler becomes the most inspired interpreter of biblical truth. 'The spirit gave the doctoral degree.' The conclusion is rather a philosophical plea for a middle way between institutional arrogance and individual ignorance than a doctrinal defence of the claims of *Ecclesia Anglicana*. But there is a decisive theological emphasis earlier in the poem where Dryden defends orthodox Christianity against the Deists, laying great stress on the doctrine of the Incarnation and the Atonement. This firm theological base, considered alongside the poet's urgent quest for authority, makes his subsequent conversion to Rome readily understandable.

Hence, after his conversion in 1685, the instrument of argument here perfected is applied to a full-scale defence of the Roman Church in *The Hind and the Panther*. Dryden shows remarkable skill in modifying the sharp, biting couplet of the satirical poems to an instrument for sustaining the flow of logic so that the reader is carried easily yet wakefully, and not bounced from shaft to shaft, from tirade to tirade. The 'milk-white hind, immortal and unchang'd' represents the Roman Church. There is also a 'bloody Bear' representing the Independents, a 'buffoon Ape' for the atheists, the 'bristled Baptist Boar', and various other brutes. The Church of England is represented by the Panther, 'sure the noblest, next the Hind, / And fairest creature of the spotted kind'. As 'mistress of a monarch's bed', she wields the crosier and wears the mitre; her upper part reveals 'decent discipline' but Calvin's brands mark her too so that, 'like a creature of a double kind', she is confined in her own labyrinth and cannot be exported. When such creatures argue about the religious issues of the day the animal allegory is inevitably ornamental rather than essential to the dialogue, and when in the last book the Panther and the Hind resort to animal fables to make their points, one finds oneself reading a fable within a fable.

Dryden's odes are technically brilliant. There is one 'To the Pious Memory of Anne Killigrew, excellent in the two sister arts of poesy and painting', which Dr Johnson described as 'undoubtedly the noblest ode that our language has produced'. It includes an interesting lament on the 'steaming ordures' of the contemporary theatre, produced by prostitution of the Muse in a 'lubrique and adulterate age'. Two odes were written for St Cecilia's Day in 1687 and 1697 respectively. There is an element of bravura about both of them ('From harmony, from heavenly harmony' and *Alexander's Feast*). It is as though the craftsman is showing off the full scope of his virtuosity. One feels that Dryden has flexed his poetic muscles for a demonstrative work-out, as perhaps a solo instrumentalist might display the range of his expertise in the cadenza of a concerto. It is all done with splendid ease and consummate skill. And there is monumental evidence of Dryden's mastery of the couplet in his translation of Virgil. Wherever one opens the text of his *Aeneid* one finds it astonishingly readable. The vitality is sustained through action, description and dialogue alike, and diverse moods are caught in phrase and rhythm with unerring aptness. There are many good things, too, scattered about the numerous prologues and epilogues which Dryden wrote for performances of his plays and other special occasions. One might cite the incisive comments on Shakespeare, Fletcher and Jonson in his *Prologue to the Tempest*. For sheer polish there is little to match the beautifully modulated couplets in which Dryden pays touching tribute to John Oldham, a gifted poet cut off at the age of thirty (*To the Memory of Mr. Oldham*):

> For sure our souls were near allied, and thine
> Cast in the same poetic mould with mine.

Dryden wrote a great number of prefaces and dedications, and in many of them he discussed literary subjects and defended his own practice. In addition he wrote the *Essay of Dramatic Poesy* in the form of a platonic dialogue. It was in this essay that he paid his famous tribute to Shakespeare:

> To begin, then, with Shakespeare. He was the man who of all modern, and perhaps ancient, poets had the largest and most comprehensive soul.

It is only necessary to quote one such sentence to indicate what Dryden did for English prose. The readiest way to sum up his achievement is to admit that of all seventeenth-century writers he is the only one to write sentences which, we feel, might almost have been written yesterday. Dryden's recognition of Shakespeare's outstanding quality, at a time when it was far from generally appreciated, is a mark of his critical acumen. Nor was it exceptional, as his appreciation of Milton and Spenser would show. Chaucer he called 'the father of English poetry'. It was highly appropriate that Dr Johnson should have called Dryden himself 'the father of English criticism'.

10
Restoration drama

Dryden's work for the theatre is uneven in quality. His comedies have neither the naturalness nor the wit of those Restoration dramatists whose plays can still hold the stage. His tragedies for the most part exemplify those artificialities of style that are especially associated with Restoration tragedy. *The Indian Emperor, The Conquest of Granada* (in two parts) and *Aureng-Zebe* are carefully structured extravaganzas, in rhyming couplets, whose central themes are those of honour and love. Service to honour is represented in a series of super heroes, performing gigantic military feats and exalting their own prowess in bombastic rhetoric. Love, the other value, is an overpowering force, fatal and irresistible. Dryden manufactures a series of situations in which love and honour clash. Perhaps the hero finds himself in battle on the opposite side to his beloved. Such dilemmas recur. The hero must either renounce love or see his beloved slain; the hero can save himself only by renouncing love; the heroine can save the hero only by forsaking him for ever or giving herself to a 'vllain'; the hero can save the heroine only by also saving his bitterest rival (possibly the heroine's husband, as in *The Conquest of Granada*).

Plots are complicated excessively in order to produce such situations. When one such situation is cleared up, a further development (often a battle) produces a different one. Events serve to fabricate situations of emotional tension according to standardized formulas. The consequence of using battles as background machinery to produce dramatic situations is of events from the emotional patterns: the one is engineered to produce the other: there is a lack of that inevitability by which plot and emotional sequence are all of a piece. Thus the heroic drama of this period too often sacrifices naturalness and artistic discipline to supposed force of impact; and it fails to purchase sympathy through over-selling astonishment. Restoration writers position their tragic characters on a lofty plane of contrived situational improbability and emotional extravagance. Having created realms of remote make-believe, succeeding dramatists, like Lee, Otway and Rowe, attempt frontal assaults on their audience's tear-ducts. Lavish verbal resources are expended especially on the passion of unhappy love. The reliance upon love, in arousing pity, bypasses tragedy's interest in man's conflict with destiny.

The flamboyant idiom in which Dryden's heroes expound their emotional dilemmas may be illustrated by Almanzor's reaction to the unveiling of Almahide's beauty (in *The Conquest of Granada*):

> I'm pleas'd and pain'd, since first her Eyes I saw,
> As I were stung with some *Tarantula*:

> Arms and the dusty field I less admire,
> And soften strangely in some new Desire.
> Honour burns in me not so fiercely bright,
> But pale as Fires when master'd by the Light.
> Ev'n while I speak and look, I change yet more;
> And now am nothing that I was before.
> I'm numb'd, and fix'd, and scarce my Eye balls move;
> I fear it is the Lethargy of Love!

That the greatest poetic craftsman of his age should have devoted so much energy to the portrayal of dramatic postures like this is astonishing. But then it is the same Dryden who polished up Chaucer's 'rough' original into smooth couplets and who turned *Paradise Lost* into a spectacular musical, with an Adam who, at the beginning of Act II, awakes 'as newly created' on a bed of moss and flowers with a Cartesianism on his lips:

> What am I? or from whence? For that I am
> I know, because I think; but whence I came,
> Or how this frame of mine began to be,
> What other Being can disclose to me?
> I move, I see, I speak, discourse, and know,
> Though now I am, I was not always so.

In one case, that of *All for Love, or the World Well Lost*, Dryden brought an artistic discipline to bear that put it in a category of its own. The recipe for heroic drama is not jettisoned. We find the familiar dilemmas: Antony's men demand that he forsake Cleopatra: Cleopatra is offered the kingdom of Syria as well as Egypt by Caesar if she will forsake Antony. But Dryden has avoided excess. He takes the story of Shakespeare's *Antony and Cleopatra* and pares it down to the size of a personal drama in which Antony is poised between the claims of Cleopatra and those of Octavia and his own loyal followers. The tension is powerful, the emotional tone unforced, and the blank verse alive with dignity, sometimes with rare simplicity, even in those last scenes which inevitably invite comparison with Shakespeare:

> But grieve not, while thou stay'st
> My last disastrous Times:
> Think we have had a clear and glorious day;
> And Heav'n did kindly to delay the Storm
> Just till our close of Ev'ning.

All for Love stands alone among Dryden's tragedies, and
it is easy to appreciate why George Villiers (1628–87), the
Duke of Buckingham (and the Zimri of *Absalom and
Achitophel*), should have parodied passages from Dryden
in his burlesque of the heroic drama, *The Rehearsal*. Yet the
extravagances of the form were even more excessive in the
works of Nathaniel Lee (*c.* 1649–92) than in those of Dryden.
The blank-verse tragedy, *The Rival Queens*, explores the
triangular relationship between Alexander the Great, his
wife Statira and a former wife Roxana, who finally stabs
her successor to death. The dying queen begs the life of her
murderess:

> And, O sometimes amidst your Revels think
> Of your poor Queen, and e'er the chearful Bowl
> Salute your lips, crown it with one rich Tear,
> And I am happy. (*Dies*)

An even more uplifting resilience in death is displayed by
Titus in *Lucius Junius Brutus*, when Valerius has run him
through:

> O bravely struck! thou hast hit me to the Earth
> So nobly, that I shall rebound to Heav'n,
> Where I will thank thee for this gallant Wound.

Dryden collaborated with Lee in *Oedipus* and *The Duke of
Guise*: he also collaborated with Sir William D'Avenant
(1606–68) in making an adaptation of Shakespeare's *The
Tempest*. D'Avenant, who had been active as a dramatist
before the revolution, returned to the theatre after the
Restoration and became a great 'improver' of Shakespeare.
Rumour had it that he was Shakespeare's illegitimate son.

Some of the most successful tragedies of the period were those of Thomas Otway (1652–85); though the reason why is not always self-evident. In *The Orphan* (1680) the devoted twin brothers, Castalio and Polydore, have been brought up with the orphan girl, Monimia. Both love Monimia but she loves Castalio, who secretly marries her. Polydore, unaware of the marriage, pretends to be Castalio and goes to her bed in the darkness, leaving Castalio locked out. There are powerful scenes of crisis. Castalio is bitterly cruel to Monimia and she is pathetically unable to understand, since she thinks she has spent the night in his arms: but the tension seems to result from trickery more appropriate to comedy than to tragedy.

Otway's finest tragedy is *Venice Preserv'd* (1682). Jaffeir has married Belvidera to the disgust of her father, the senator Priuli; and Priuli has cast her off. Borne down by poverty and rejection, Jaffeir vengefully joins a group of rebels bent on destroying the republic. Jaffeir's friend, Pierre, introduces him to the conspirators, and Jaffeir hands over Belvidera to the care of their leader, Renault, as a pledge of his trustworthiness. Renault tries to ravish her, and her horrified husband reveals the conspiracy to her; whereupon she induces Jaffeir to betray the plotters to the Senate in exchange for a guarantee of their lives. The senators break their pledge and execute the rebels. Jaffeir stabs Pierre to death, at his own request, to save him from the agony and indignity of death on the wheel. Then he kills himself while Belvidera goes mad and dies.

So far as the political plot is concerned, the audience's sympathies are somewhat confusingly appealed to. What we see of the Venetian senators is almost wholly bad: Priuli is cruel, Antonio a pervert. Yet Belvidera involves our feelings on the side of law and order and evasion of bloodshed. Even so, Pierre the rebel dies a martyr's death. The ultimate conflict at the core of the hero's dilemma has no ideological content: the interest is personal and domestic. It is love that draws Jaffeir to turn traitor on the rebels while his honour is pledged to them. Yet the clash between love and honour is enigmatically produced by Jaffeir's questionable act in pawning Belvidera, an act which seems to presuppose that genuine rebels must be at least temporarily celibate. It is *Julius Caesar* with a Brutus whose motive for rebellion is hatred of his father-in-law, and a Portia who drags her husband to the Capitol to give the game away to the Senate. The blank verse is technically easy on the ear but gives way to rant. The action proceeds on a level of almost unrelieved crisis in which characters are always inviting their fellows to kill them. The dialogue is frequently conducted in highly charged obliquities, implicitly indicative of the danger everyone is always in. There is a prevailing atmosphere of ubiquitous suspicion.

Heroic tragedy persists into the Augustan Age in the work of Nicholas Rowe (1674–1718). His play, *Tamerlane* (1702), achieved its reputation because of the resemblance of Tamerlane to William III and of Bajazet, his foe, to Louis XIV. In fact a practice was established of reviving the play annually on 5 November, the anniversary of William's landing. One recognizes a similar topicality in the treatment of the struggle between Roman Catholics and Protestants in a much later play, *Lady Jane Grey* (1715). But in both these plays the public action is only a background used to produce interesting situations for the participants in a love plot. Tamerlane is a nominal hero only, standing above most of the action (like Cato in Addison's play). Too often, in Rowe, the main characters do little: things happen to them. This is so even in Rowe's finest play, *The Fair Penitent* (1703), which Rowe based on Massinger's play, *The Fatal Dowry*. The villain, Lothario, a pitiless seducer exulting in the pride of conquest, gave his name archetypally to the polished eighteenth-century philanderer and provided one of the models for Richardson's Lovelace in *Clarissa Harlowe*. He has basely had his will of Calista, the heroine, before the play opens. She is powerless under the passion awakened by the skilful seducer. The young hero, Altamont, has been brought up by Calista's father, Sciolto, who loves him for his virtue. The play opens on a note of rapturous joy as the hopes of Sciolto and Altamont are to be blissfully realized in the marriage of Altamont and Calista. Horatio, husband of Altamont's sister, Lavinia, stumbles on evidence of Calista's liaison with Lothario. The action traces the awaking of Altamont's awareness, the movement of Calista's thoughts and feelings, through rebellious passion for Lothario and rejection of her new husband, to penitence and genuine sympathy for her injured father and bridegroom. She kills herself at the end. The male lead's role is that of a victim: it is Calista who holds the centre of the stage.

The theatrical qualities of the play kept it fitfully on the stage for 100 years, but the literary recipe to which it is compounded will not stand up to scrutiny. The rhetoric is sustained by familiar current devices. Characters indulge in mutual congratulation on an inordinate scale: near relations address each other (and refer to themselves) in the third person. There is a peculiar heroic device of extended hypothesis. The heroic dramatist would not be content to say, 'If I forget thee let my right hand forget its cunning'. He would have to mention his left foot too, and indeed would be unable to drop the subject until he had pictured an epidemic of paralysis:

ALTAMONT: When I forget the vast Debt I owe thee,
    Forget! (but 'tis impossible) then let me
    Forget the Use and Privilege of Reason,
    Be driven from the Commerce of Mankind,
    To wander in the Desart among Brutes,
    To bear the various Fury of the Seasons,
    The Night's unwholesome Dew and Noon-day's Heat,
    To be the Scorn of Earth and Curse of Heav'n.

Nor does the extravagance depend only on excess. Brevity has its hazards too. Witness Calista's famous question:

    Is it the Voice of Thunder, or my Father?

There is one more tragedy deserving of attention, and it

had topical significance because it was published at a time when Queen Anne was failing in health and there was concern about the succession. This was *Cato* (1713) by Joseph Addison (1672–1719). It shows Cato holding out at Utica against the victorious Caesar and making very fine speeches in praise of liberty. But Cato does little else: the main interest centres in love themes that have no inevitable connection with his story. Two sons of Cato are rivals in love for Lucia, while Cato's daughter, Marcia, is coveted, romantically and lustfully, by a noble Numidian prince and a treacherous senator respectively. Thus the austere republican's dying gesture is to preside over the distribution of brides.

Byron, in *English Bards and Scotch Reviewers*, looks back enviously to the great literary age of Pope and Dryden, when 'Congreve's scenes could cheer, or Otway's melt'. If Otway's tragic power is less esteemed today, Congreve's mastery in comedy remains unchallenged. William Congreve (1670–1729) brought to perfection the form which we call the comedy of manners. Its concern is rather with the social postures adopted by human beings than with their native endowments. Men and women are measured according to their capacity to adjust graciously and intelligently to the social code of the day, and this gives the plays a decisive topicality. But Congreve does not accept the social code of the day as an absolute. Though it is the mark of a civilized man to live at ease with it, the intelligent man will see its absurdities. Congreve's ironical detachment gives his work lasting qualities. The squire who is up from the country may cut a poor figure in the drawing room, but what he has to say about the values of polite society carries its sting nonetheless. Witwoud is an acclimatized townsman and his former guardian, Sir Wilful, comes up from Shropshire. 'This fellow would have bound me to a maker of felts,' Witwoud says in horror. 'S'heart,' says Sir Wilful, 'and better than to be bound to a maker of fops; where I suppose you have served your turn' (*The Way of the World*).

The Way of the World is certainly the finest comedy of

the period. Its felicitous phrasing and polished wit give it an air of sophistication perfectly in tune with the mores depicted. Mirabell's aim is to win Lady Wishfort's niece, Millamant, without sacrifice of that half of her inheritance over which Lady Wishfort has control. And it has already been put at risk by Mirabell's device of 'wooing' Lady Wishfort in order to cover his love for her niece. Lady Wishfort's susceptibility to be wooed is not weakened by her fifty-five years, and Mirabell's plot to get her into his power involves subjecting her to another false suit by a disguised servant, Waitwell. Waitwell has been hurriedly married to a fellow servant, Foible, just to make sure that the tables are not turned by a real wedding between servant and lady that could put everything into the servant's hands. Lady Wishfort is a great comic study and, when roused, a fluent fount of what has been called 'boudoir Billingsgate'. Her preparation for receiving her bogus suitor, 'Sir Rowland', prefigures the humour of Sheridan:

> Well, and how shall I receive him? in what figure shall I give his heart the first impression? ... yes, yes, I'll give the first impression on a couch. – I won't lie neither, but loll and lean upon one elbow: with one foot a little dangling off, jogging in a thoughtful way ... yes – O, nothing is more alluring than a levee from a couch in some confusion: – it shows the foot to advantage, and furnishes with blushing and recomposing airs beyond comparison.

Over against this devastating mockery of middle-aged pretensions to charm and allure, Congreve's young lovers, Mirabell and Millamant, are partners in wit and discrimination whose brittle phrases and shared ironies suggest an inner contract deep below the level of their banter. 'I won't be called names after I'm married', says Millamant in the famous bargaining scene:

MIRABELL: Names!
MILLAMANT: Ay, as wife, spouse, my dear, joy, jewel, love,

sweetheart, and the rest of that nauseous cant, in which
men and their wives are so fulsomely familiar.... Let us
never visit together nor go to a play together; but let
us be very strange and well-bred; let us be as strange as
if we had been married a great while; and as well-bred
as if we were not married at all!

The Way of the World (1700) brought Congreve's literary
career almost to completion at the age of thirty. Of his earlier
comedies *Love for Love* is the most memorable. The pursuit
of love and money is again at issue, and there is thematic
unity in the spectacle of true love requited by true love and
spurious love meeting with spurious requitals. The astro-
loger, Foresight, reminds us of Jonson's quacks, while Sailor
Ben Sampson brings a breath of the seven seas that
anticipates Smollett. But there is less subtlety in the
play than in *The Way of the World*, and there is a hardness
in the wit of Angelica, the heroine, which compels one
to ask whether Congreve's women do not too often talk like
men.

The precarious balance Congreve preserves in his relish of
that social scene which his deeper shafts undermine gives his
work a faintly amoral charm. We would not wish Mirabell
and Millamant different from what they are, and with varying degrees of sympathy we warm to them and to their
companions. This reaction marks the gulf between Congreve's comedies and those of William Wycherley (1640–
1716). In *The Country Wife* (1675) almost all the characters
are dislikeable. If Congreve's comedies have a somewhat
amoral power to attract, Wycherley's have a deeply moral
power to repel. In place of Congreve's polish and wit,
Wycherley's plays abound in coarseness and indecency. The
delicacy with which physical sexuality can be distanced in
Congreve has no parallel in Wycherley:

MIRABELL: ... Item, when you shall be breeding –
MILLAMANT: Ah! name it not.

MIRABELL: Which may be presumed with a blessing on our endeavours.

MILLAMANT: Odious endeavours!

For Wycherley, at least in his last two (and most important) plays, is a savage critic of contemporary licentiousness and tears the veil of sophistication away to reveal animality and cynicism at large in Restoration permissiveness.

The control of three related themes in *The Country Wife* shows skilful dramatic craftsmanship. Mr Pinchwife, with his new 'country wife', is absurdly possessive and jealous, and as a result suffers what he is most desperate to avoid: his wife begins to love another. Mr Sparkish is absurdly confident of Alithea's devotion, and as a result she becomes the wife of another. (These complementary excesses of suspicion and credulity seem to hark back to the comedy of humours.) Mr Horner has a false medical report circulated, testifying to his impotence, and as a result becomes for the husbands of the town the favourite companion of their womenfolk. He makes the most of the opportunities they shower upon him. The satire is at its fiercest in the development of this theme: we find ourselves in a society whose women have no time for a man sexually incapable and whose men will cheerfully closet their wives with him behind locked doors, sniggering at the irony of it. The audience has a different irony to snigger at; and when the gentlemen push their wives into Horner's hands Wycherley's use of double entendres presses the irony home. Wycherley presents a sex-obsessed society in which the young fellows' complaint is that in the pursuit of women they

> lose more time, like huntsmen in starting the game, than in running it down. One knows not where to find 'em; who will or who will not. Women of quality are so civil, you can hardly distinguish love from good breeding, and a man is often mistaken . . .

The Plain Dealer (1677) presents Manly, a frank, honest sea captain who is disillusioned with the world. He has lost trust in all except his friend, Vernish, and his mistress, Olivia. On going to sea, he has entrusted his fortune into Olivia's hands. In his absence Vernish has married Olivia and they plan to keep Manly's money. An oddly romantic theme complements this one in that Fidelia, who loves Manly, has been at sea with him disguised as a young man. Manly uses her as a go-between in the attempt to soften Olivia, and Olivia falls in love with the supposed young man. Point for point at this stage the relationships are what they are in *Twelfth Night* between Duke Orsino, Viola ('Cesario') and Olivia: but the two Olivias are women of different breed. In a tangle of assignations and contrived eavesdroppings the full treachery and sensuality of Wycherley's Olivia and Vernish is brought to light. Manly's surly disgust with the world enables Wycherley to voice his sour condemnation of current hypocrisy, and the seaman's rugged sarcasms largely determine the tone of the play. (Dryden fitly praises 'manly Wycherley' for his 'satire, wit, and strength' in the laudatory *Epistle to Mr Congreve*.) The development of sub-sidiary material (the affairs of the litigious widow Blackacre) prevents the play from having the structural tidiness of *The Country Wife*, but it is more varied in interest and has a more human appeal. A dedicatory preface addressed to 'My Lady B——' (Mother Bennet, a well-known London bawd and former prostitute) is a scathingly witty pseudo-eulogy to set beside dedicatory addresses to 'great ladies' of the day:

> Your house has been the house of the people; and when you arose, 'twas that others might lie down, and you waked that others might rest; the good you have done is unspeakable.

Of writers we meet in other fields who turned their hands to comedy in the Restoration period, the novelist Aphra Behn was notably prolific, but the coarseness of her work restricts its appeal. The same complaint can be laid against Sir Charles Sedley's *Bellamira*, a comedy based on Terence's

Eunuchus. Sir George Etherege's comedies, however, have earned him the claim to be classed with Congreve and Wycherley. The lightness of touch evident in the dialogue of *She Would If She Could* (1668) becomes something scintillating eight years later in *The Man of Mode.* Here a sequence of comic scenes of fashionable life is loosely framed in a frail plot. The arch-fop, Sir Fopling Flutter, is a vivid comic study; and the rake, Dorimant, is said to be a portrait of Rochester. The wit may be unfailing, but Dorimant's devastating treatment of disposable mistresses indulges a vein of cruelty ('next to the coming to a good understanding with a new mistress, I love a quarrel with an old one'). The character of Young Bellair in this play was one of those acted by George Farquhar (1678–1707) in his brief career on the stage, a career which was terminated when he fought a duel too realistically in the last act of Dryden's *The Indian Emperor* and seriously wounded his opponent. Thereafter Farquhar gave himself to writing comedies. Farquhar came from Londonderry, was educated at Trinity College, Dublin, and brought a new Irish warmth into the hard world of satirical comedy. The tone of *The Constant Couple* (1700) is more heartily humorous than that of Congreve's and Wycherley's plays, and in Sir Harry Wildair he created the first of a series of frank, impetuous young heroes whose sexual zest and social vivacity is matched by warm-heartedness and good humour.

But it is in his last two plays, *The Recruiting Officer* (1706) and *The Beaux' Stratagem* (1707) that Farquhar really comes into his own, and completes the transformation of Restoration comedy by replacing its cynicism with rollicking humour, its barbed wit with easy fun, its hot-house London atmosphere with a breath of fresh air from the country. The scene of *The Recruiting Officer* is Shrewsbury, where Captain Plume, Captain Brazen and Serjeant Pike are recruiting. Plume is Sir Harry Wildair's successor, and Sylvia, daughter of Justice Balance, who is in love with him, has disguised herself as a young man and manages to get herself arrested, tried by her own father and consigned to Captain Plume as a new recruit. This situational sequence, the bread-and-butter stuff of comedy, is characteristic of Farquhar who handles the stock devices of disguise, deception and discovery with a smooth naturalness that keeps them fresh as ever.

Sunniest and most wholesome of all his comedies is the last, *The Beaux' Stratagem*. It is scarcely credible that he wrote it during his final illness and had death in sight as he worked. Not only so, but he had been living in poverty, burdened by debts, and started work on it only because his old friend, Wilks, who had acted with him in the former Dublin days, found him and generously gave him the means and encouragement to write again. Just over two months after the play's opening success at the Queen's Theatre, Farquhar was dead. Yet the play has the bright, unforced humour and liveliness that we find again in the best comic work of Goldsmith and Sheridan. Two young gentlemen, Aimwell and Archer, arrive at an inn in Lichfield, looking for marriage to put an end to their financial worries. Aimwell pretends to be a lord (as indeed his elder brother actually is) and Archer his servant. The ideal heiress appears, Dorinda, daughter of Lady Bountiful, and it is love at first sight with Aimwell, as it is between Archer and Dorinda's sister-in-law. The latter frets in miserable marital bondage to Dorinda's half-brother, Squire Sullen, a blockhead and an alcoholic. Visiting highwaymen complicate matters, and their attempt to burgle the manor house gives Aimwell and Archer the chance to protect their ladies heroically. The prevailing high-spiritedness, distributed among a bunch of deftly differentiated personalities, keeps the play alive from the first word to the last. There is no sag: and to be in the company of men and women who are not straining after wit is relaxing. There is an obviousness about Farquhar's technique that makes one want to ask: how does he get away with it? The answer, perhaps, is that a personal warmth permeates his comedies. It is not just that all his characters are clearly felt and likeable. He himself, shadowily known historically, is vividly felt in the plays as intensely likeable.

A less gifted writer, but one who exercised an immense influence on the theatre of the day, was Colley Cibber (1671–1757). His autobiography, *Apology for the Life of Mr Colley Cibber Comedian*, is full of information about theatrical events and personalities of the time, for Cibber was actor and manager at Drury Lane and his skill as a playwright gained him such reputation that he was made Poet Laureate in 1730. To read his plays is to feel sympathy for a man whose flair was so slight and whose competence could never quite bridge the gap between mediocrity and artistry. He is generally considered to be at his best in *The Careless Husband*. The dialogue trembles intermittently on the edge of real wit. Sometimes one feels that it misses by a hair's breath. Nevertheless it misses.

It was however the success of Cibber's *Love's Last Shift* that prompted Sir John Vanbrugh (1664–1726) to turn his hand to comedy. In Cibber's play the libertine Loveless has left his wife and his debts and gone abroad. When he returns, he finds Amanda, his wife, both faithful and enriched by inheritance. A convenient reformation follows. Vanbrugh's sequel, *The Relapse, or Virtue in Danger*, traces Loveless's subsequent relapse with an attractive young widow Berinthia. And a subsidiary plot traces how Young Fashion, younger brother of Lord Foppington, impersonates his brother and marries Miss Hoyden, daughter of Sir Tunbelly Clumsey, thus forestalling Foppington's own intention. Vanbrugh's dialogue is conversationally easy on the ear, but the moral tone is more questionable than Farquhar's. Hear Berinthia comparing how men treat women with how girls treat their dolls:

> For nature has made them Children, and as Babies. Now, Amanda, how we used our Babies, you may remember. We were mad to have 'em, as soon as we saw em; kist 'em to pieces, as soon as we got 'em; then

> pull'd off their Cloaths, saw 'em naked, and so threw
> 'em away.

It does not surprise us that Vanbrugh, along with Congreve,
was a main target in Jeremy Collier's attack on the contemporary theatre: *A Short View of the Immorality and
Profaneness of the English Stage*, published in 1698, a work
which aroused a good deal of controversy, though its immediate effect on stage practice was not remarkable. Cibber
had a double share of reflected glory from *The Relapse*, for
Vanbrugh, he tells us,[1] 'not only did me the honour, as an
author, by writing his *Relapse*, as a sequel, or second part,
to *Love's Last Shift*; but as an actor too, by preferring me
to the chief character in his own play' – Lord Foppington of
course.

Vanbrugh was fertile in invention. *The Provok'd Wife*,
another comedy, is packed with incident. Lady Brute, a virtuous wife, is under provocation from her drunken and de-
bauched husband from the moment the curtain rises. Sir
John Brute curses his marriage and rejects all his wife's
approaches with mockery:

LADY BRUTE: What is it, that disturbs you?
SIR JOHN: A parson.
LADY BRUTE: Why, what has he done to you?
SIR JOHN: He has married me. (*Exit* Sir John)

His acquaintances get the same sort of treatment when they
ask after his good lady, apprehensive of her lot:

HEARTFREE: Why, there's no division, I hope.
SIR JOHN: No; but there's a conjunction, and that's worse.

Lady Brute's second provocation is the earnest devotion of
Constant, who presses persistently for a response to his
approaches. His friend, Heartfree, falls in love with Lady
Brute's niece, Belinda, to make a foursome. After much
frolicsome intrigue, the final dénouement begins when Sir

[1] Cibber, *An Apology for the Life of Mr Colley Cibber Comedian.*

John opens a closet door at home to find the two wooers hiding there. There is inventive abundance and an ease of expression in Vanbrugh's own work that conveys a sense of the man's immense giftedness. We feel that the architect of Blenheim Palace and Castle Howard is relaxing when he takes up his pen.

11
Origins of the novel

The word 'novel' is scarcely applicable to anything written
during the Elizabethan period, but it was from the prose
fiction of the period that the English novel was born. A fictional framework is used in Lyly's *Euphues* as a basis for the
somewhat undisciplined display of supposed worldly wisdom,
in Sidney's *Arcadia* a complex aggregation of fictional incident is decorated with poetry, but no less relevant than either
of these works to the development of the novel is *Rosalynde*
(1590) by Thomas Lodge (?1558–1625), which has some resemblance to both. To Lyly Lodge is indebted for the
euphuistic patterning of sentences:

> Let time be the touchstone of friendship, and the friends found faithful lay them up for jewels.

However, this level of euphuistic artifice is preserved but fitfully, and the story is ably told at a time when mastery of presentation in prose narrative, as we now understand it, was scarcely to be found. The plot is that used by Shakespeare in *As You Like It*, with Sir John of Bordeaux for Shakespeare's Sir Rowland de Boys, Rosader for Orlando, and Alinda for Celia.

Lodge's narrative is interspersed with set pieces, distinguished by subtitles. When Sir John is at the point of death he delivers a rhetorical exhibition piece moulded of stock didactic themes. Fate and fortune are bowed to: then systematic advice is rehearsed on the subject of thrift, honour, prudence, friendship, appearance ('The outward show makes not the inner man, nor are dimples in the face the calendars of truth'), love, women ('women are wantons, and yet one cannot want one'), human folly and life's transience. Sometimes such set pieces fulfil the function of soliloquies in which characters tend to address themselves by name in the second person ('Now, Rosader, Fortune ... presents thee with the brightness of her favours'). There are also carefully posed dialogues like Alinda's 'Comfort to Perplexed Rosalynde' after their banishment by the king. Such passages abound in rhetorical flourishes ('Why, how now, Rosalynde, dismayed with a frown of contrary fortune?'), not to mention pedantic allusions ('But perchance thou wilt say, *Consulenti nunquam caput doluit*'). In addition the story is peppered with lyrics and even includes passages of dialogue in verse. When 'Ganymede' comforts Rosader in Arden, the make-believe is formally framed in an eclogue. But for all the artifices and formalities the management of the narrative, as it shifts from thread to thread in the carefully woven fabric, is extremely smooth.

Greene's stories have their delights, but they are almost submerged under the luxurious rhetorical formalities of rhythm, balance and alliteration. His *Pandosto* has special interest because it provided Shakespeare with the plot of *The Winter's Tale*. (Among Shakespeare's close verbal echoes of Greene is the oracle's formal rebuke of the jealous king: its terse sentences repeat Greene's almost verbatim.) An extended romance by Emanuel Ford, *Ornatus and Artesia* (1595), further illustrates the close link between prose fiction and drama, and also exemplifies the apparent lack of interest, at this stage, in building out a single plot over a story of some length. Extension is achieved by accretion. In this 'novel' of some 150 pages there is enough plot material to furnish a dozen Elizabethan plays, and the reader is continually reminded of parallel situations in *As You Like It*, *Hamlet*, *The Winter's Tale*, *Romeo and Juliet*, *Measure for Measure* and even *King Lear*, to mention Shakespeare alone. The story is a set of separate episodes strung together. Many a brief episode has in itself a tolerable dramatic shapeliness, but the method of extended construction by aggregation seems to evidence the necessity for the novel to be invented.

Nashe's *The Unfortunate Traveller* (1594) is a work of a different genre. The subtitle is *The Life of Jack Wilton* and it introduces an autobiographical record of travel and adventure that is the precursor of Defoe's stories and of the picaresque novel. There is no need for an organized plot in this literary form: the material is bound together by the continuing presence and personality of the storyteller. At the beginning of the story Jack Wilton is a page at the court of Henry VIII. His early adventures are elaborate practical jokes, his first victim being a camp victualler whom he deceives with the tale that he is suspected of being a spy, thereby inducing him to distribute his provisions among the soldiers. Plainly we are in a world remote from Lodge's Forest of Arden. The gusto of the book is astonishing. It moves at a heady pace and Wilton travels about Europe, taking in an execution, a theological disputation and an escapade with an Italian courtesan. The tone changes appropriately, and later episodes, especially those in plague-stricken Rome, are horrific at times. The account of the rape of Heraclide is an exercise in verbal violence:

> He graspt her by the yvorie throat, and shooke her as a mastiffe would shake a young beare, swearing and staring he would tear out her weasand if she refused .... On the hard boords he threw her, and used his knee as an yron ramme to beat ope the two leavd gate of her chastitie. Her husbands dead bodie he made a pillow to his abhomination.

Heraclide's outbursts of prayer and protest, then of shame and horror, are moving declamations.

The exploits of Thomas Deloney's heroes are centred in the homelier field of industry. Deloney (c. 1543–?1600) directed his stories at the Elizabethan tradesmen, telling how hardworking apprentices get to the top. *The Gentle Craft* deals with shoemakers, and the Simon Eyre of Dekker's *The Shoemaker's Holiday* figures in it. Perhaps *Jack of Newbury* is the best known. It is dedicated 'To all Famous Cloth workers in England' and tells how Jack Winchcombe, an extremely assiduous apprentice, is wooed by his master's widow. The vitality and humour with which the Dame contrives the marriage makes this the most entertaining part of the book. Successes in the field of matrimony and commerce are followed by a taste of military glory as Jack musters 250 men for Queen Katherine, all 'prepared for the warre at his own cost against the King of Scots at *Floden Field*'. It is a small step from this to entertaining the king at a banquet in his own house. Once this peak has been reached, the story 'runs down', losing its impetus in a rather disconnected sequence of public events and domestic anecdotes. The style is never so distinctive as Nashe's: it is aptly utilitarian, though sometimes the dialogue sparkles.

Our glance at Elizabethan prose fiction has been for the most part directed at works which would deserve very little attention from students of literature, were we not searching for the origins of the great new form added to imaginative literature in the modern age. Of course these origins to some extent lie quite outside the field of prose fiction that we are now examining. The pamphlets of the Elizabethan period which gave first-hand pictures of low life, and satirically portrayed the follies and vices of the day, fed a taste which later the novel satisfied. Greene, in his *Cony-Catching* pamphlets, Dekker, in his *Gull's Hornbook*, and Nashe, in works like *Pierce Penniless*, have an indirect importance in the story of the development of the novel, just as later the journalism of Addison and Steele does. And indeed because of its overall design and compelling human interest, Bunyan's *Pilgrim's Progress* foreshadows the achievements of future novelists more surely than the embryonic efforts we have so far considered. An interesting literary oddity on a much slighter scale is Congreve's *Incognita* (1692), a skit on the prose romance, equipped with a light-hearted preface (in which Congreve claims at least to have 'gratified the Bookseller'), and then presented to the accompaniment of jocular asides from author to reader. It is a highly artificial story of complicated intrigue similar to the contrivances of Restoration comedy. The high-life setting gives us a world of fashionable gallantry, balls, duels and quarrels. There is, as one would expect, some brilliance in the dialogue, and there is some subtle, though sly and light-hearted, analysis of feminine psychology. The satirical flavour is sharp. A competition in sighing is provoked between the friends Aurelian and Hippolito at the mere utterance of the 'name of Love'. One plies the other close till they are both 'out of Breath'.

Another Restoration dramatist turned to prose fiction with far more serious intent. Mrs Aphra Behn (1640–89) is a writer whose own story is tantalizingly wrapped in mystery: her autobiography has come to be regarded as probably no less fictional than her tales. We can no longer assume that her best story, *Oroonoko* (1688), is based on any first-hand experience. But its quality is unquestioned. Mrs Behn knew how to restrict her material and brought her dramatist's

talent to its organization. *Oroonoko* is a speedy, vital ~~~
of adventure, battle, grand passion and tragic death. It is in
some ways very unlike the work of a woman. As a background to the passionate story there is a deep conflict of
ideology between the lofty, natural pagan morality of the
African natives, and the selfish, unprincipled shiftiness of
the European settlers.

Oroonoko, a negro prince of fascinating natural beauty
and grace, an accomplished, humane and generous hero,
loves Imoinda, a general's daughter. She is sought for the
king's harem, and sold into slavery by the king when he discovers her love for Oroonoko. Oroonoko, captured by English
sailors, finds himself, as a slave, reunited to Imoinda in the
West Indies. He raises a revolt, but surrenders on receiving
a promise of pardon from Byam, the English governor. The
promise is cruelly and treacherously broken: Oroonoko
plans to sacrifice himself in vengeance on Byam, but first
kills Imoinda to save her from the slave-drivers. She dies
happy; but his suicide is forestalled, and he is barbarously
executed.

The story moves excitingly: the female characterization is
sympathetic and convincing, and the study of Oroonoko is
heroically idealized without losing authenticity. No doubt
Mrs Behn has an axe to grind: the simplicity of pagan faith
is contrasted with the complexities of Christian dogma: the
treachery of Europeans, their humiliating and dishonourable oppression of generous-hearted and high-souled natives,
is brought home with passion that bespeaks an outraged
sense of justice and decency. Thomas Southerne (1659–1746)
turned the story into a heroic tragedy, and sentimentalized
it in the process.

Though Oroonoko is perhaps long enough to be called
a short novel, Mrs Behn's other stories are definitely 'short
stories'. *The Fair Jilt* is a tale of uncontrolled passion, vanity
and selfishness leading through extravagance and deception
to criminality. The plot is carefully constructed, involving
even a story within the story. A persuasive personal touch

the device of passing events off as truth
eye-witness:

etend to entertain you here with a feigned
story, . . . ything pieced together with romantic accidents; but every circumstance to a tittle, is truth. To a
great part of the main I myself was an eye-witness . . .

Two other stories, *The Nun* and *Agnes de Castro*, are fatalistic tragedies. *The Nun* has a complicated intrigue, involving the loves of Sebastian, Ardelia, Elvira and Henrique in
an entanglement like that of a Restoration comedy; but
there is a tragic conflict in Henrique between friendship and
love which harks back to the tragedy of Shakespeare's day.
In *Agnes de Castro* the characters exist rather on the grandiose ideal level of Restoration tragedy.

It becomes proper to use the word 'novel' when we reach
the work of Daniel Defoe (1660–1731), a writer whose extraordinary career involved various failures in business, service as a government agent and counteragent, and prolific
activity as journalist, pamphleteer and author of books.
Defoe's satirical poem in support of William III, *The True
Born Englishman*, made its point popularly:

> Thus from a mixture of all kinds began,
> That heterogeneous thing, an Englishman,

but Defoe's fluent versification does not make him a poet.
His famous exercise in irony, *The Shortest Way with the
Dissenters* (he was himself an enthusiastic dissenter), was
misunderstood and landed him in the pillory. The ironical
argument that dissenters should be destroyed in the interests
of charity to one's neighbours 'not for the Evil they have
done, but for the Evil they may do' was apparently too near
the bone.

The full list of Defoe's published works would include such
diverse titles as *The Complete English Tradesman*, *A Plan
of the English Commerce*, *Tour through the Whole Island
of Great Britain*, *Religious Courtship* and *The History of*

Peter the Great. The novels date from his last fifteen years. They have the stamp of life upon them, even the stamp of life's disorder, its inconsistencies and confusions. Their form is autobiographical. There is no overall plot and little feeling for built-up situations. There is no unified pattern of relationships embracing a number of characters, only a sequence of unilateral relationships between the hero and successive partners or contacts. *Robinson Crusoe* succeeds partly because the very story itself precludes the development of a pattern of relationships: one does not miss something which the story could not possibly have.

Crusoe's story was based on the experience of Alexander Selkirk, who spent five years on an uninhabited island after being put ashore there in 1704. Crusoe is shipwrecked but is able to salvage basic tools and materials from the wreck and thus uses his ingenuity to manufacture the means of shelter and livelihood. Danger from visiting cannibals adds excitement, and the acquisition of a companion, the savage Man Friday whom he saves from the cannibals, adds human interest. But the fundamental appeal of the book depends on the patience and self-reliance with which Crusoe copes with his difficulties and constructs an oasis of individual civilization such as every child dreams of in his desert island fantasies. Moreover the situation is such that the urgent pieties of the dissenter – always on the tip of Defoe's tongue – have a depth and relevance which they lack in his studies of the bustling life of pleasant vice and profitable dishonesty, *Roxana* and *Moll Flanders*. The isolated Crusoe's reflections on man's frailty and God's mercy, on the need for prayer and repentance, and on the valuelessness of most earthly possessions, are the logical artistic outgrowth of the moving story of man's struggle to dominate his own natural surroundings and find inner peace. There is no comparable quality in Part II, *The Farther Adventures of Robinson Crusoe*, in which Crusoe revisits his island years later.

Moll Flanders (1772) is a fascinatingly vital fictional autobiography of a woman 'born in Newgate ... twelve years a whore, five times a wife (whereof once to her own brother), twelve years a thief, eight years a transported felon in Virginia, at last grew rich, liv'd honest, and died a penitent ...' The artistic and moral difficulties involved in the simultaneous access to riches, honesty and penitence add piquancy if not polish to Defoe's study. He tells us in the preface (a superb blurb directed at virtuous and curious readers alike) that one cannot unfortunately prevent 'vicious readers' from misrepresenting the aim of the author who allows his subject to recount her career of vice. Nevertheless his principle throughout is that 'there is not a wicked action in any part of it (the book), but is first and last rendered unhappy and unfortunate'.

It is not true. Moll's zestful career of promiscuity and theft is so frankly and spiritedly recounted that her intermittent bouts of penitential moralizing sound hollow and incongruous. The quality of the book resides in its heart-to-heart directness and its unsophisticated delight in the world of street and warehouse, goal and shop and brothel; a world humming with people and packed with commodities. Successive liaisons and successive bouts of thieving follow each other episodically, interspersed with outbursts of remorse and apostrophes to human weakness. But Moll is left at the end living on what are really the profits of crime.

Defoe was at least fitfully troubled by this problem. *Captain Singleton* (1720) is the autobiography of an adventurer who goes to sea, turns mutineer, amasses a fortune, spends it, turns pirate and makes a second fortune. Before returning home, he and his companion, William, have heart-to-heart talks on the combined topic of repentance and settling down on their profits. As the idea of repentance engrosses the Captain's thoughts his great wealth begins to seem like dirt under his feet. He opens up the subject with William (who has been his spiritual mentor). Will they be able to smuggle their wealth safely home? William is reassuring. Will God allow them 'if he be a righteous judge' to get away with the plunder of 'so many innocent people'?

William dwells on God's double attributes of justice and mercy, emphasizing the latter at the expense of the former. The Captain reminds William that he taught the nature of repentance as including reformation. Caught on the hook, William pronounces judgement. They *cannot* return what they have stolen, having no knowledge of the owners. They must stick to it, watching for opportunities put into their hands by providence to do justice at least to some of the injured. 'Captain Bob' finds his conscience satisfied. They return to England very rich and he marries William's sister.

The businessman is never far away in Defoe. Moll Flander's stage-by-stage reckonings of how she stands at each turning point are financial as well as spiritual. Her body is a commodity. The same can be said of the heroine of *Roxana or the Fortunate Mistress* (1724), a delightful auto-biographical record of a French refugee brought up in England, who is deserted by her husband and reduced to poverty. Her maid and companion, Amy, encourages her not to be squeamish when a man of substance is attracted by her beauty. After his death she moves to France to become the mistress of a prince. Her attachments are at once genuinely affectionate and highly convenient. Defoe's representation of her moods, her thoughts and her talk is winningly frank. She emerges as lovable and faithful in her fashion, yet in the back of her mind her common sense, bred of hard experience, sometimes reduces the most personal issues to their commercial essentials:

> In all this affluence of my good fortune I did not forget that I had been rich and poor once already, alternately, and that I ought to know that the circumstances I was now in were not to be expected to last always; that I had one child and expected another, and if I bred too often it would something impair me in the great article that supported my interest, I mean what he called my beauty ...

For all the unshapeliness of Defoe's fictional biographies,

each puts us in touch with a personality and throws us into the stream of life in another age. An undeniable air of truth is produced by Defoe's directness and by his conversational readiness to be specific in reference to facts and figures at one moment and vaguely unsure about causes and identities at the next moment. It is notable that in his fictional record, the *Journal of the Plague Year*, the apparent authenticity is no less convincing than it is in books whose events fall within the range of his own experience. This supposedly first-hand record of the London outbreak of 1665 is of course based on factual documentary accounts. Nothing could be more seemingly authoritative than its sober, direct reportage, packed with descriptive and anecdotal detail, and threaded through with the reflections of common sense as well as of piety.

12
The age of Swift and Pope

We have already trespassed into the reign of Queen Anne
in following the course of post-Restoration drama as far as
the tragedies of Rowe; and in pursuing the growth of the
novel we considered works by Defoe which were published
in the reign of George I. Nevertheless the dividing lines we
have adopted are useful. There is a fading out of post-Restoration drama in the work of Rowe, and the early eighteenth
century adds little else of significance to English dramatic
literature. Moreover, by taking the account of the novel as
far as Defoe we have prepared the ground for the decisive
breakthrough in this new literary form which came in the
1740s with the work of Fielding and Richardson. In short

the years 1700 to 1740 write only an epilogue to the Restoration drama and only a prologue to the eighteenth-century novel. Yet so impressive is the character of this period that it has been called the 'Augustan Age'; and the phrase makes an implicit correspondence with the classical age of outstanding literary productivity under Caesar Augustus, when Virgil, Horace and Ovid were at work. If we have already set foot in the Augustan Age chronologically in our study of the drama and the novel, we have done so culturally in our attention to Dryden with whom the spirit of the Augustan Age is born. He established the heroic couplet which became the norm of Augustan Poetry.

We tend to associate the Augustan Age with the technical polish and intellectual poise exemplified in the work of Pope, yet the period is also represented by Jonathan Swift (1667–1745), a writer whose immense talent exploded in works that seem to erupt from some centre of strange, sometimes demonic power. Swift, of course, laboured under a double frustration, professional and personal. He served the Whigs and then the Tories with his pen, yet never attained the preferment which his labour and his gifts merited – though he eventually became Dean of St Patrick's Cathedral, Dublin, in 1713. (He was Dublin-born, and had a prebend there already.) His personal frustration is a more mysterious matter. While in the service of Sir William Temple at Moor Park in Surrey, he became the great friend of Esther Johnson (Stella), a girl who fell in love with him and to whom he was attached for the rest of his life, so much so that he persuaded her, with her companion, Rebecca Dingley, to take up residence in Dublin where they could be in daily contact. It has been suggested that he may eventually have been induced to marry her in secret and without consummation. To what extent Swift's strange course was affected by his concern for Esther Vanhomrigh (Vanessa), who had also fallen in love with him, is not known. The latter relationship is celebrated in the poem, *Cadenus and Vanessa*. The attachment to Stella can be judged not only from the massive journal he wrote for her day by day between September 1710 and June 1713, while he served the Tory ministry in London and the ladies were in Dublin, but also from the moving tribute he paid when she died (*On the Death of Mrs Johnson*), the touching little collection, *Bons Mots de Stella*, and the prayers he wrote for use in her 'last sickness'.

Swift's *The Tale of a Tub* (1704) is a humorous satire. The author's preface explains 'that seamen have a custom when they meet a whale, to fling him out an empty tub by way of amusement, to divert him from laying violent hands upon the ship'. This parable is mythologized. The ship of state is in danger from Hobbes's *Leviathan* ('the whale') which 'tosses and plays with all schemes of religion and government'. Hence this new diversion: and after numerous mock-preliminaries we reach the story of three sons, to each of whom their father has bequeathed a coat to be kept in good order. The three sons, Peter (the Roman Catholic Church), Martin (the Church of England) and John (the dissenters), quarrel: they disobey their father's injunction by tampering with their coats; for when the fashion changes they 'rummage the will' to find clauses that can be twisted into support for making alterations. Late in life when Swift reread the tale, he exclaimed, 'Good God! What a genius I had when I wrote that book', and indeed the work establishes the character of Swift's satire, which is so rich in humour and so large-minded in the reach of its application, that the particular allegorical intention (in this case directed towards support of the Church of England) is subsumed under the wider sweep of a wisdom that passes judgement on mankind's littleness and self-deception in the round. This extensive range it is which produces in the reader that sense of Swift's immense, almost superhuman stature, upon which many have commented.

It was in support of Sir William Temple, who had been involved in literary controversy, that Swift wrote *The Battle of the Books*, and pictured the ancients at war with the moderns. The mutinous moderns have difficulty in organizing leadership, especially among the horse, 'where every private trooper pretended to the chief command, from Tasso and Milton to Dryden and Withers'. The army of the ancients is different: 'Homer led the horse, and Pindar the light horse; Euclid was chief engineer; Plato and Aristotle commanded the bowmen; Herodotus and Livy the foot ...' This is Swift's lighter satirical vein. Some of his harshest satire was written in indignant and scathing indictment of English policy towards the Irish. In *The Drapier's Letters*, posing as a Dublin draper, Swift so devastatingly assailed the policy of selling the right to supply copper coinage to the Irish that the government dropped the plan. Even sharper was the *Modest Proposal for Preventing the Children of the Poor People from Becoming a Burthen to their Parents or Country, and for Making them Beneficial to the Public*, a proposal which recommended the profitable edibility of Irish children, and listed six major advantages to be drawn from their consumption (including reduction in the number of papists). Swift did not spare his readers' sensibilities:

> A child will make two dishes at an entertainment for friends; and when the family dines alone, the fore or hind quarter will make a reasonable dish, and seasoned with a little pepper or salt will be very good boiled on the fourth day, especially in winter.

Infant's flesh will be in season throughout the year, and plentiful in spring, for in Roman Catholic countries a peak period for births is nine months after Lent. A year is allowed for fattening on inexpensive breast-milk.

Swift's satirical masterpiece is *Gulliver's Travels* (1726). Part I tells of Gulliver's shipwreck on the island of Lilliput, an island inhabited by diminutive beings whose controversies, traditions and wars seem so trivial and petty that their English equivalents are correspondingly made to look silly by reflection. Part II takes Gulliver to Brobdingnag, whose gigantic inhabitants question Gulliver about his homeland, and English practices again look ludicrous and pretentious when defended by a virtual human midget. Hearing Gulliver's account of recent English history, the king of Brobdingnag concludes that the natives of England are a 'pernicious race of little odious vermin'. In Part III the satire is more direct, for Gulliver visits Laputa, where the learned are abstracted from the realm of common sense. Indeed they have to be attended by 'flappers'. A flapper is a servant equipped with 'a blown bladder fastened like a flail to the end of a short stick'. With this instrument the mouth or ears of a Laputan can be flapped and in this way his mind can be brought to bear on the conversation he is supposed to be conducting. The flapper must also attend his master on his walks to prevent him from falling down a precipice or bumping into a post while wrapped in cogitation. Laputa is a flying island from which the king can brutally suppress potential rebellion in his dominion beneath. Thus England's oppression of Ireland is again under condemnation. At Lagado, capital of the continent below (Balnibarbi), scientists are occupied in absurd experiments like curing colic by inserting a bellows up the anus. The intensest satire comes in Part IV. Gulliver visits the land of the Houyhnhnms, virtuous beings with the bodies of horses, who cherish their power of reason and are wholly governed by it. They have at their disposal a filthy race of man-shaped beasts called Yahoos. On his return home, Gulliver finds it impossible to stomach fellow Yahoos again: even his wife stinks of Yahoohood.

Swift writes so much obliquely and ironically that it is worth while to look at his sermons, where he speaks in his own voice, for there we find an earnest directness and a deep concern genuinely religious in their roots, whether he is giving moral instruction, or analysing the 'causes of the wretched condition of Ireland', or paying due anniversary tribute 'on the martyrdom of King Charles I'. Such material makes it all the harder to understand the man whose poems like *Strephon and Chloe* reveal an obsession with the contrast between the charms of the fair sex and their need to make water and excrete. In *The Lady's Dressing Room* Strephon stumbles on evidence of Celia's evacuations and steals away disgusted:

> Repeating in his amorous fits,
> 'Oh Celia, Celia, Celia –!'

Yet this is part of Swift, as is the little language of baby-talk scattered tenderly about the *Journal to Stella*, the touching verse tributes on Stella's birthdays, the moving sermons, the passionate anger for Ireland, and the savage misanthropy of the 'Voyage to the Houyhnhnms'. Swift's mental powers declined and he was declared legally irresponsible some years before his death. He had given vastly to charity during his lifetime, and he left money to found a hospital for imbeciles. Even this was wryly forecast in his uncannily cheerful and suggestive verses *On the Death of Dr. Swift*, written in 1731:

> He gave what little wealth he had
> To build a house for fools and mad;
> And show'd by one satiric touch
> No nation wanted it so much.

One of the most famous friendships of literary history is that between Swift and Pope, who admired each other's talents and kept up a correspondence for many years. Alexander Pope (1688–1744) suffered his own frustrations, as a Roman Catholic, as a man of diminutive stature, and as a victim of life-long ill-health involving curvature of the spine. He early and consciously devoted himself to poetry, and his prodigious gifts and disciplined application enabled him to reach a level of technical virtuosity in the arrangement of words that appeals to the subtlest sensibilities. *Windsor Forest* (1713) recalls *Cooper's Hill* in its blend of scenic description with reflections on associated historical and literary figures. The indebtedness is made explicit:

(On Cooper's Hill eternal wreaths shall grow,
While lasts the mountain, or while Thames shall
flow) . . .
Here his first lays majestic Denham sung;
There the last numbers flow'd from Cowley's tongue.

In only two important poems is passionate love the theme.
The *Elegy to the Memory of an Unfortunate Lady* pays
tribute to a victim of suicide in couplets handled with delicacy and feeling. The poor woman may not lie in con-
secrated earth:

Yet shall thy grave with rising flow'rs be drest,
And the green turf lie lightly on thy breast!

Eloisa to Abelard versifies the appeal in the tender letter of
the abbess Eloisa to her former teacher and lover, Abelard.
She has come across his own record of their long-past relationship and it stirs her to a moving expression of her continuing devotion.

Pope's gifts reach their full maturity in *The Rape of the
Lock*. His good offices were sought to submerge in good
humour a quarrel between two families. The occasion of
dispute was the theft of a young lady's curl. Pope brought
the full panoply of epic grandeur to bear upon this event.
The account of Belinda at her toilet has the ceremonial
splendour of a sacred rite; in her sail to Hampton Court she
is girt about with lucid squadrons of Sylphs and Sylphids,
charged with the protection of her hair, her complexion,
her petticoat and the like. But a game of cards, followed by
coffee, leads up to the fatal climax: the scissors are drawn,
the glittering Forfex is spread wide; and as the fatal engine
closes to detach the lock, it cuts a too dutiful Sylph in twain.
('But airy substance soon unites again.') Shrieks rend the
affrighted skies: then a dusky, melancholy sprite dives
down to the middle of the earth to the Cave of Spleen, to
beg the wayward queen (who rules the sex 'to fifty from
fifteen') to touch Belinda with chagrin. It is done. Belinda
burns with more than mortal ire.

> 'O wretched maid!' she spread her hands, and cry'd,
> (While Hampton's echoes, 'Wretched maid!' reply'd)

The wrath is not readily appeased. But the lock is carried up aloft to become a new star in the firmament and Belinda is urged to cease mourning the ravished hair, for it 'adds new glory to the shining sphere'. The poem is a masterpiece of light, satirical wit and delicate contrivance, abounding in those qualities of tact, sensitivity and good humour which it was once fashionable to deny to Pope.

The Dunciad, Pope's most ambitious original work, is a satire after the model of Dryden's *Mac Flecknoe*. The first three books were published in 1728 with Theobald as the chief target (Theobald had criticized Pope's edition of Shakespeare). In 1742 a fourth book was added and Colley Cibber was substituted for Theobald in the recasting of the whole. By simulating the devices and echoing the events of classical epic – of Homer, Virgil and Milton – for comic effect, Pope is extending the experiment of *The Rape of the Lock*: but his purpose here is the more earnest and aggressive one of holding literary incompetence up to ridicule in the name of intelligence and good sense. Book I introduces us to the empire of the goddess Dulness, who claims Cibber for the throne in succession to Eusden (he was poet laureate before Cibber). Book II shows Cibber throned Miltonically (like Satan in *Paradise Lost* Book II):

> High on a gorgeous seat, that far out-shone
> Henley's gilt tub, or Fleckno's Irish throne,

and, after the fashion of Homer and Virgil, heroic games celebrate the solemnity. Booksellers, poets and critics fail to stand up to a gruelling test of their ability to keep awake while authors' works are read aloud. Ultimately (in Book IV) the goddess Dulness comes into her own on earth, leading the Sciences captive and silencing the Muses. The final consummation is the restoration of Night and Chaos. So grave is the danger menacing culture; and to enter with full sympathy into Pope's vast work of protest, the modern reader must sense the serious concern for civilized values which underlies the poet's assault upon the spurious literature that threatens them.

Much can be learned from Pope's didactic poem, *An Essay on Criticism* (1711), of how seriously he thought out his critical principles and poetic practice. 'Nature' is proposed as the standard of judgement, and traditional rules deserve respect as being 'but Nature methodiz'd.' It is necessary to approach literature without pride and to judge a work as a whole. The dangers of excessive concern with conceits, with style, with regular rhythm, are contrasted with the true appreciation of variety and appropriateness. Reduced to prose, the instruction is perhaps platitudinous, if sound, but the memorable couplets give it freshness and bite. Simple home truths acquire dignity and forcefulness from the epigrammatic versification and indeed perfectly illustrate the character of wit as summed up in Pope's own definition:

> True Wit is Nature to advantage dress'd,
> What oft was thought, but ne'er so well express'd.

Pope's *Essay on Man* (1733–4) is a serious philosophical work consisting of four epistles in couplets, and addressed to Henry St John Bolingbroke. The first epistle establishes that 'Whatever is, is right' by displaying man's finely adjusted place in the scale of creation:

> All are but parts of one stupendous whole
> Whose body Nature is, and God the soul.

Individual man is then analysed as a creature in whom two principles, self-love and reason, reign. The passions (modes of self-love) must enlist under reason and reason must 'keep to Nature's road'. Pope then turns to picture the ordered human society living in harmony with nature. The confident location of individual and social happiness in the operation of reason and enlightened self-love is given a Deistic

basis in all-pervasive divine benevolence. There are beautifully lucid and sensitive passages in the work. 'God loves
from Whole to Parts', Pope avers: but it is not easy, in
reading his poem, to extend one's love of its parts to its
whole.

It would be wrong to leave Pope without acknowledging
the immensity of his achievement in translating Homer's
Iliad and his *Odyssey* into heroic couplets. The versions are
eminently readable still and have an exciting vigour. But
perhaps some of the sharpest and, conversely, the most
genial things he did are passages of portraiture and criticism to be found in his epistles, like the delightful *Epistle
to Miss Blount, on her leaving the town after the Coronation*, with its neatly voiced contrast between urban and rural
life:

> She went from Op'ra, Park, Assembly, Play,
> To morning-walks, and pray'rs three hours a day.

Indeed, if one seeks evidence of the many-sidedness of
Pope's talent and his personality, it is to be found in the
Epistle to Dr Arbuthnot, with its frank reflections on his
own past experience as a writer, its warm words for his
father and mother, and its praise of Gay. The same poem
contains the well-known portrait of Addison ('Atticus').
There is nothing more devastating in literature than the
cool packaging-up of the vain author's devious characteristics – a man who could

> Damn with faint praise, assent with civil leer,
> And without sneering, teach the rest to sneer...
> Who but must laugh, if such a man there be?
> Who would not weep, if ATTICUS were he?

Joseph Addison (1672–1719) is firmly linked with Sir
Richard Steele (1672–1729), for though both writers have
achievements in other literary forms, their collaboration in
journalism produced their best work. The sudden flowering
of the periodical essay in the Augustan Age is a remarkable

phenomenon. To some extent Defoe anticipated the achievements of Steele and Addison in his *Review* that ran for nine years from 1704, treating of current affairs, political, commercial, religious and moral. But Defoe's aggressive fervour gave the journal a very different tone from that of the *Tatler* (1709–11) and its successor, the *Spectator* (1711–12 and 1714). In these Steele and Addison managed to combine entertainment with enlightenment at a level of literary accomplishment and cultural sensitivity that fills the modern reader with envy. The secret of the popular appeal is the imaginative inventiveness with which topics are handled so as to keep the pages alive with personalities involved in the familiar activities of social life. A piece of abstract advice or a generalization is quickly rendered vital by a concrete instance – a journey in a coach, a visit to a theatre, or an encounter with an eccentric. The authors do not hesitate to advise their generation. Women are warned of the unhappy consequences of their love of finery ('Many a lady has fetched a sigh at the toss of a wig, and been ruined by the tapping of a snuff-box'), and ladies are, after some ironical raillery, gently but firmly admonished that their attendance at trials for rape is not consistent with female modesty.

Letters are a great standby. There is one from a father protesting at the pernicious consequence of reading the *Tatler* for his daughter Winifred, who has been encouraged to fall in love of her own accord: 'For my part, I think that where man and woman come together by their good liking, there is so much fondling and fooling that it hinders young people from minding their business.' There is a brief billet from Chloe:

> Dear Mr Bickerstaff,
> Are you quite as good as you seem to be?

and the editor's cogent reply:

> Dear Chloe,
> Are you quite as ignorant as you seem to be?

And there is a query to the editor from a lady, protesting that she has 'lived a pure and undefiled virgin these twenty-seven years' and is sick of being called an old maid. Ought she to be 'prevailed upon by the impertinency of my own sex, to give way to the importunities of yours?'

More serious is the vein of domestic sentiment with which Steele touches the hearts of his readers. The famous essays, *Mr Bickerstaff Visits a Friend*, successively picture a family home alive with warmth and happiness, and the same home transformed by the death of the mother. Steele recreates parental joy in children and the loving banter between husband and wife as unerringly as he lays his finger on the helpless sorrow of the newly bereaved husband:

> His condition is like that of one who has lately lost his right arm, and is every moment offering to help himself with it.

Indeed it is the character portraits that are most unforgettable. Nothing is funnier in the *Tatler* than the account of Ned Softly, amateur poet, presenting the fruits of his Muse to Mr Bickerstaff with much appreciative elucidation (and being gently but deftly managed in reply):

> For, Ah! it wounds me like his dart.
> Pray how do you like that 'Ah!' – .... My friend Dick Easy assured me, he would rather have written that 'Ah!' than to have been the author of the *Aeneid*.

The *Spectator* brings the character portraiture to a fine fruition in the accounts of the club led by Sir Roger de Coverley, good-humoured country squire, who has his fair share of prejudices and idiosyncrasies, but whose singularities create him 'no Enemies, for he does nothing with Sourness or Obstinacy'. The company includes Sir Andrew Freeport, an industrious, strong-minded city merchant, Captain Sentry, the soldier, and Will Honeycomb, an honest worthy man 'where Women are not concerned'. Some papers take the reader to Sir Roger's country seat, so the life of the town is balanced by that of the country. The De Coverley papers were Addison's work: so too were the papers of serious literary criticism like those on *Paradise Lost*. These extremes indicate the range of interests catered for. The commercial institutions of the day, the inns, the clubs, the theatres, the churches, the courts – all these centres of human interest are fitfully before us, the fashionable world is under scrutiny, and there is philosophy and theology for everyman too. Much has been said about the civilizing influence of the *Spectator*'s urbanity, good sense, good temper and recommendation of virtue. There was an important literary influence too; for the accomplished representation of contemporary types, genially alive and articulate, both stimulated the appetite for imaginative prose and hastened its coming satisfaction in the novel.

Of the minor poets of the period one, Matthew Prior (1664–1721), has a distinctiveness that exudes the spirit of a lively and likeable personality. Few minor writers have so ably combined concentration with spontaneity, epigrammatic wit with freshness of appeal. The engaging blend of personal sincerity with lightness of touch, the hint of self-mockery, the undercurrent of good humour – these ingredients give a memorable flavour to Prior's best work. In it we feel that Cavalier disenchantment has mellowed into rueful resignation, and Augustan clarity is tempered by self-knowledge. It is in the short poems and in outstanding passages of the longer ones (like *Alma, or the Progress of the Mind* or *Solomon on the Vanity of Human Wishes*) that Prior's gifts emerge, rather than in sustained achievement throughout the big poems. Stanzaic lyrics (like the well-known 'The Merchant, to secure his treasure') represent him at his most engaging. He can realize a situation feelingly and fills it out in nicely balanced stanzas without a wasted word. A favourite stance is that of the no-nonsense suitor who wants to get down to brass tacks without loss of poise for either party. Prior has been compared to Swift (Swift in his lighter moods) in his use of the octosyllabic couplet, and certainly some of Prior's comic verse has a crisp vernacular vigour, but however rollickingly it runs, it stops short of coarseness. The three-line stanzas of *Jinny the Just* have enough unexpectedness in vocabulary and rhythm to keep alive one's sense that a craftsman is at work:

> With a just trim of Virtue her Soul was endu'd,
> Not affectedly Pious nor secretly lewd
> She cut even between the Cocquet and the Prude.

In his 'Essay supplementary to the Preface' to the *Lyrical Ballads* Wordsworth excepted one writer from his condemnation of Augustan poetry for not producing new images of external nature: the exception was Anne, Countess of Winchilsea (1661–1720). The countess had indeed that observant eye and ear that Wordsworth looked for; and in the *Nocturnal Reverie* the night scene is alive with a clutter of detail that almost overfeeds the hungriest sensitivities:

> When the loos'd *Horse* now, as his Pasture leads,
> Comes slowly grazing through th'adjoining Meads,
> Whose stealing Pace, and lengthen'd Shade we fear,
> Till torn up Forage in his Teeth we hear.

The countess's famous *Petition for an Absolute Retreat* is plainly in the tradition of Marvell's *The Garden*, and as plainly differentiates itself from Marvell's ideal. The retreat is to be free of intruders, of vain, purposeless visitors, and of the world's news; it is to abound in all the fruits of Eden except the Forbidden Tree; its cherries and peaches and strawberries are to offer themselves within easy reach, but Marvell's mystical yearning for solitude is replaced by a more human desire:

> Give me there (since Heaven has shown
> It was not Good to be alone)
> A *Partner* suited to my Mind,

> Solitary, pleas'd and kind;
> Who, partially, may something see
> Preferr'd to all the World in me...

Her more ambitious work, *The Spleen,* which treats of the eighteenth-century malady with some seriousness and with some satirical force, is less likely to find avid modern readers.

A marked contrast in poetic temperament emerges if we compare the countess's night-piece with *A Night-Piece on Death* by Thomas Parnell (1679–1718), a Dublin-born cleric who was the subject of a sympathetic biography by Goldsmith. Goldsmith observes that Parnell managed to keep the friendship of the 'Whig wits' (Addison, Steele and Congreve) as well as the 'Tory wits' (Pope, Swift, Arbuthnot and Gay). Parnell was much given to elation and depression, and while the countess's poem on night is rich in direct delight and 'sedate Content', Parnell's picture is of graves and tombs, of funereal yew and charnel house. Under the fading moon the bursting earth unveils the shades:

> All slow, and wan, and wrap'd with Shrouds,
> They rise in visionary Crouds,
> And all with sober Accent cry,
> *Think, Mortal, what it is to die.*

For the countess the breaking of morning means the return of confusion, the renewal of cares and toils and clamours; for Parnell, as death is a 'Path that must be trod / If Man wou'd ever press to God', so the rising of souls to life again is to:

> Clap the glad Wing and tow'r away
> And mingle with the blaze of Day.

Parnell's adroitness and fluency in the use of octosyllabic couplets is equally evident in his *Hymn to Contentment,* a cry for peace of mind from one who knows that it cannot be found in the pursuit of power, wealth, adventure or knowledge, and that 'Solitude's the Nurse of Woe'. His answer comes in the quietness of a wood where he feels the 'Presence of the Grace' and hears the call to rule his will, know God and learn the 'Joys which from Religion flow'.

Among the more cheerful poetic spirits of the period should be mentioned John Philips (1676–1709). His poem *Blenheim*, Dr Johnson complained, is the work of a scholar 'all inexpert of war', of a man 'who writes books from books, and studies the world in a college'. His Miltonic burlesque, *The Splendid Shilling* (1705), is a very different kettle of fish. The possessor of the splendid shilling is contrasted with the hapless and penniless poet:

> Me lonely sitting, nor the glimmering Light
> Of Make-weight Candle, nor the joyous Talk
> Of loving Friend delights.

Inditing mournful verse, he meanwhile struggles 'with eternal Drought', sometimes falling into a slumber, only in his dreams to tipple 'imaginary Pots of Ale'. His blank-verse poem *Cyder* (1708) is imitative of Virgil's *Georgics* and cheerfully informative about all the stages of apple-growing and cider-making.

In the same year (1708) John Gay (1685–1732) started his poetic career with a similar but less successful poem, *Wine*. The first effective realization of his gifts, however, came in the six mock-pastorals, *The Shepherd's Week* (1714). In these the machinery of classical pastoralism is comically blended with the realities of eighteenth-century country life, satirically exaggerated of course. Thus, in the lines on Blouzelinda's funeral, the neighbours follow the bier, throw flowers on the grave, listen to an hour-long sermon from the parson, then, having fenced off the tomb to keep at bay the parson's horse and cow, they trudge home to the deceased's mother's farm for new cider and ginger. 'Excessive sorrow is exceeding dry.' The louts wail out the immortal memory of Blouzelinda until bonny Susan catches their eye and turns their thoughts to the living present. Soon the willing maid is repairing the loss of Blouzelinda with her kisses. Gay's amusing urban guide in three books, *Trivia, or the Art of Walking the Streets of London,* escorts the reader through London streets, introducing him to the characters, desirable and undesirable, that throng them; and so doing, may be said to extend the range of material fit for poetry in something like the way in which Lillo extended the range of tragedy. Gay's *Fables* were more popular, however, and though the moral direction is often platitudinous, yet Gay's native tendency is to entertain, and good humour prevails. The dying fox penitently warns his gathered sons against gluttony and the forfeiting of the foxes' good name. The grieving sons observe that it's a bit too late to retrieve the good name of foxes after their long ancestral heritage of disgrace and infamy. Even if they reformed, they would be blamed anyway for every plundered henroost.

> Nay then, replys the feeble Fox,
> (But, hark! I hear a hen that clocks)
> Go, but be mod'rate in your food;
> A chicken too might do me good.

There is obvious accomplishment in such work, yet we feel that Gay's poetic spirit does not really catch fire until we reach the songs and ballads of the operas, *The Beggar's Opera* (1728) and *Polly* (1729). Here at last flair is added to Gay's talent, and the novel mixture in *The Beggar's Opera* (inspired by a suggestion from Swift) took the theatrical world by storm. It involves burlesque of the fashionable Italian opera, a keen vein of social satire, and skilful interweaving in the action of tuneful popular airs that have been fitted with eminently singable verses. The stage is graced by Peachum, an informer and receiver of stolen goods, and his daughter Polly, who falls in love with Captain Macheath the highwayman; by a Newgate warder and his daughter; by Macheath's gang (such as Nimming Ned, Mat of the Mint, and Crook-fingered Jack, and by Women of the Town (like Dolly Trull, Betty Doxy, and Molly Brazen). The whole thing contrives to be at one and the same time a high-spirited romp, a down-to-earth social documentary and a delicious musical entertainment. The saying was that it made Gay rich and Rich (his impresario) gay.

A far, far less subtle outburst of high spirits is the burlesque of contemporary tragedy, *Chrononhotonthologos*, by Henry Carey (?1687–1743), the author of *Sally in our Alley*. Chrononhotonthologos is king of Queerummania, and his queen Fadladinida, is tragically attracted by the captive king of the Antipodes. Hear Aldiborontiphoscophornio addressing Rigdum-Funnidos:

> But lo! the King, his Footsteps this Way bending,
> His *cogitative* Faculties immers'd
> In *Cogibundity* of *Cogitation* ...

The burlesque, it will be observed, is heavy-handed but not unfunny. It is interesting that Carey and Gay (as well as Pope) shared a common satirical target in Ambrose Philips (?1675–1749) whose Pastorals were mocked in Gay's *The Shepherd's Week* and whose rather twee verses to little children inspired Carey's attack in *Namby Pamby*:

> Namby Pamby Pilli-pis, is
> Rhimy pim'd on missy-mis,

and earned him his nickname, 'Namby Pamby Philips'. Actually the child poems are not contemptible but sometimes observant and sensitive.

Two writers whose earlier tragedies no doubt helped to call out Carey's ridicule, Edward Young (1683–1765) and James Thomson (1700–48), were both primarily important in the field of poetry. Young's life spanned many reigns and his poem *Night Thoughts* came after his tragedies, being published between 1742 and 1745. It is an immense work in blank verse containing some 10,000 lines disposed in nine books with such titles as *On Life, Death, and Immortality* and *On Time, Death, and Friendship*. Much of it is ruminative rhetoric bespattered with exclamation marks. The consciously exalted idiom that delivers semi-conversationalized philosophy in ornate garb is not *always* turgid ('Time wasted is existence, used is life') but the strain tells on the reader:

> We thwart the Deity …
> Hence our unnatural quarrels with ourselves;
> Our thoughts at enmity; our bosom-broils:
> We push time from us, and we wish him back;
> Lavish of lustrums, and yet fond of life …

In the last book, *The Consolation*, the poet is granted a vision in which he sets out from earth 'in ardent contemplation's rapid car' and mounts swiftly past the moon to 'pierce heaven's blue curtain'. He pauses at every planet on the road to 'ask for Him who gives their orbs to roll' and learns that love, not reason, 'keeps the door of heaven'.

Thomson's *Seasons* (1730) will bring us down to earth. In *Spring* the season is described at work in nature, then in man, for the book concludes 'with a dissuasive from the wild and irregular passion of Love, opposed to that of a pure and happy kind'. The literary recipe is a blend of descriptive writing, reflection, exhortation and anecdote. Thus *Summer*, after its celebration of sunrise and its episodes on haymaking, sheep-shearing and the like, eventually tells the tale of Damon. Seeking Musidora in her favourite retreat, he finds her undressing to bathe:

> What shall he do? …
>   Ye Prudes in virtue say,
> Say, ye severest, what would you have done?

Damon lingers to watch 'th'inverted silk' drawn from snowy leg and slender foot, indeed to see 'th'alternate breast' on his lawless gaze in 'full luxuriance' rise. Soon Musidora is the lovely guest of the closing waves. Damon's heady rapture is eventually checked by 'love's respectful modesty', and he goes, leaving a note for Musidora, gently intimating what has happened. Musidora, on reading it, soon recovers from her shock, and rewards him for his restraint with an encouraging answer – 'the time may come you need not fly'.

The tone of lofty passages is affected by the stilted artifices that afflicted eighteenth-century poetic diction where it lay under the supposed Miltonic impress. Yet the poem is not without its observant glimpses of the living countryside, like the falling of the leaves in *Autumn*. First they slowly circle down through the waving air:

> But should a quicker breeze amid the boughs
> Sob, o'er the sky the leafy deluge streams;
> Till choak'd, and matted with the dreary shower,
> The forest-walks, at every rising gale,
> Roll wide the wither'd waste, and whistle bleak.

The Castle of Indolence (1748) is a curious poem less easy to place. In it Thomson adopts the stanza and style of Spenser's *Faerie Queene*. He mimics the Spenserian voice impressively, indeed parodically; but in the account of those inhabiting the castle and drugged by its 'slumbrous influence' Thomson caricatures himself and some of his contemporaries.

Both Thomson and Young wrote for the stage. Young's tragedies are exercises in tangled extravagance. The entanglements produce dramatic situations of irony and tension but Young overplays them. In *The Brothers* King Philip of Macedon is consumed with hatred for Rome and love for his two sons. Demetrius, the younger son, is framed by Perseus, the elder, on a charge of treacherous collusion with the Romans. Philip faces the question whether to execute his son for political good or spare him as a father. Demetrius is offered the chance to clear himself by marrying the daughter of Dymas, a Roman-hater. Demetrius expresses forced compliance ('Pardon, ye gods! an artifice forc'd on me') and loses his own beloved to Perseus.

Thomson's tragedies exploit the established formalities left behind by Restoration drama and fossilized in pseudo-Miltonic rhetoric. *Sophonisba* (1730) and *Agamemnon* (1738) put on display familiar devices of pompous self-projection, syntactical distortion, and high-flown apostrophe, such as Cassandra's cry of distress in *Agamemnon*:

O country! freedom! friends! relations!

In *Sophonisba*, Masinissa, throwing himself beside the dead heroine, cries:

> Why to that pallid sweetness
> Cannot I, Nature, lay my lips and die!

while in *Agamemnon* Egisthus declares:

> On the bank of ruin
> We, tottering, stand.

The parenthetic directives and elucidations ('Nature' and 'tottering') make the heroic figures sound to us as though they are dictating their agonies to shorthand typists. In *Tancred and Sigismunda* (published 1745, acted 1752), the best of Thomson's plays, the theme of public duty and private passion is worked through to the final moral condemnation of parentally imposed unions:

> Ne'er with your children act a tyrant's part:
> 'Tis yours to guide, not violate the heart.

In an interesting epilogue to the play Thomson deals a blow at the practice of tacking a flippant epilogue onto the end of a tragedy. His second lady enters and begins to speak just such a sly, sniggering piece; but the Tragic Muse appears, advancing slowly to music, and indignantly dismisses the kind of epilogue 'that tries / To wipe the virtuous tear from British eyes'.

Early eighteenth-century comedy suffered the stylistic artifices that disfigured tragedy. In Mrs Centilivre's comedy *The Busy Body* (1709), at a moment of crisis for Isabinda, when it becomes necessary to explain away a letter that has come into her father's hands, Isabinda's maid, Patch, exclaims, 'Oh, Invention! Thou chambermaid's best friend, assist me!' (This is not the first such characterization of her profession. She has already observed to herself that 'a dexterous chambermaid is the ladies' best utensil'.) And in Mrs Centilivre's *The Wonder; A Woman Keeps a Secret!* (1714), when the heroine's maid Flora is discovered hiding in a cupboard, she shrieks:

> Discovered! nay, then, legs befriend me. (*Runs out*)

Susannah Centlivre (1667–1723), the wife of Queen Anne's cook, wrote a number of proficient and entertaining plays. Along with Colley Cibber she fed the appetite for situational comedy, bereft of Restoration sharpness and sophistication, and increasingly sentimentalized. We have already referred to the decay of wit in Cibber. Just as Thomson preserves a shell of pseudo-Miltonic utterance sometimes enclosing little but vacuity, so in Cibber's comedy one finds syntax parading as substance, and the devalued counters of Restoration discourse strike the ear hollowly.

Steele alone perhaps does something to comedy to compensate for what it has lost. He injects into it an earnestness of sentiment and even of social concern that is in tune with his own personal sympathy and warmth of temperament. When, in *The Conscious Lovers* (1722), Sir Bevil says, 'To be a father, is to be in care for one, whom you oftener disoblige than please by that very care – Oh! that sons could know the duty to a father before themselves are fathers!' we are suddenly reminded that there are deeply felt natural human relationships which, in their homelier character, Restoration comedy simply forgot.

There is one writer who stands apart from all his fellow dramatists, and that is George Lillo (1693–1739) who broke with fashion so far as to write a prose tragedy with a homely London setting, *The London Merchant* or *George Barnwell*. The story is derived from an old ballad and tells how George Barnwell is seduced by Millwood, then at her instigation robs his employer, Thorowgood, and murders his uncle. Lillo's moral purpose is made too explicit, too obtrusive, and it gives the play the tone of a sermon. It is patchily effective nonetheless. Thorowgood is the virtuous, benevolent businessman whose heart and soul are in his work: he is a generous, charitable and forgiving Christian.

A vague sense of conflict emerges between the honest, hard-working life of business and the life of the dissipated, impecunious 'society' as represented by Millwood. The virtues of hard work, honesty and loyalty are pressed on the apprentice, and the implication is that such virtues lead not only to moral peace but also to material prosperity, so that there is an almost 'Victorian' air about the ethos. George Barnwell has only to be honest and hardworking and he can step right into his master's shoes and marry his daughter too. Lillo seems to be taking up where Deloney left off.

On the moral side Lillo shifts responsibility from the erring hero. Millwood's scheming wickedness is responsible for corrupting Barnwell, and Lillo attempts to maintain sympathy for him throughout. Thus in the very course of committing his crimes, he is eloquent about the despicable horrors he has descended to. He does not spare himself verbally, and can plead only the irresistible commands of Millwood. This spoils the play artistically, turning the murder of Uncle Barnwell into something like a burlesque. George dies on the gallows a sanctified, almost a martyr's, death.

In *The Fatal Curiosity* (1736) there is a similar attempt to shift responsibility for crime from the guilty one. Old Wilmot and his wife, hounded by poverty, murder a stranger for the casket of wealth he has entrusted to them, and learn that he is their long-lost son who had returned to succour them but indulged the 'fatal curiosity' of being received first in disguise. The play is short, has three acts only, and is written in blank verse. The dramatic power is unquestionable, but Lillo does not show men and women urged to crime by their passions; rather they are ostensibly trapped by circumstances.

It would not be appropriate to end this chapter without some reference to the distinguished thinkers who, though they were not writers of imaginative literature, produced books that profoundly influenced their contemporaries and successors. George Berkeley (1685-1753), who eventually became Bishop of Cloyne, was another Irish product of Trinity

College, Dublin, who became acquainted with Pope, Swift and Addison. His important philosophical books belong to his earlier years. *A New Theory of Vision* was published in 1709 and his *Principles of Human Knowledge* in 1710. Berkeley's metaphysical position is represented by his doctrine of idealism. The objects of human knowledge are ideas. The essence of reality is that it is perceived. Particular things are collections of ideas imprinted on our senses. Indeed the things that surround us, even the fabric of the universe, are such that their *being* consists in their being perceived or known. Objects exist continuingly when we are not perceiving them because they are within the thought of God. To some extent Berkeley's thought countered that of John Locke (1632–1704), whose *Essay concerning Human Understanding* had been published in 1690. Locke was an opponent of Platonic idealism. His aim in the *Essay* is to inquire into the nature of human understanding, and his position is the empirical one that our ideas derive from experience via sensation or reflection.

Locke, like Berkeley, was concerned for the defence of Christianity, and they both pursue their philosophical inquiries to the point at which belief in the existence of God is justified, though Berkeley's insistence on the primacy of mind is perhaps a more obvious obstacle to unbelief than Locke's emphasis on material reality. But a more formidable defender of Christianity was Joseph Butler (1692–1752), Bishop of Bristol and later of Durham, whose *Analogy of Religion* (1736) moves in a tightly-locked argumentative sequence from consideration of the world we know, under the apparent guidance of a divine Author, to the step-by-step justification of revealed religion. More generally influential, however, than these scholarly treatises was the very widely read work by William Law (1686–1761), *A Serious Call to a Devout and Holy Life*, whose simple, direct teaching on living the Christian life made an important personal impact on many people, as, for instance, John Wesley and Dr Johnson themselves testified.

13
The age of Johnson

No personality in the history of English literature is more powerful than Samuel Johnson (1709–84). The magnetism of the man reaches us through two channels, that of his own work, and that of the greatest biography in our language by James Boswell (1740–95). The *Life of Johnson* is strictly outside our immediate period in that it was not published until 1791, well after Johnson's death. But we cannot ignore it in looking at Johnson; and the fidelity of Boswell's reportage is such that one can allow it to fill out the picture as naturally as one allows Keats's letters to colour one's reading of his poems. Even so one must remember that Boswell's first meeting with Johnson, in 1763, occurred when Johnson was already fifty-four and had acquired the eminence and free-dom from financial cares which it had taken him over thirty years to purchase.

Johnson survives in verbal and visual portraiture at the centre of the famous club which included Sir Joshua Reynolds, Burke and Goldsmith. These, and men of the quality of Garrick, Dr Burney and Boswell, gathered round the table to leave behind them a mythology of conversational brilliance in which theme after theme is crowned by the master's sage and spontaneous virtuosity. The mythology lives because it is genuine; because the famous epigrammatic ripostes enshrine not only superlative common sense but also a fine sense of humour. Ponderous wisdom is made palatable by ironic overstatement, or crisp rhetorical elegance is lavished on a leg-pull. Thus Johnson reacted with unpredictable acuteness to praise of a violinist's performance. 'Difficult do you call it, Sir? I wish it were impossible.' And when Boswell told of attending a Quaker meeting where a woman preached, he said, 'Sir, a womans' preaching is like a dog walking on his hind legs. It is not well done; but you are surprised to find it done at all.' Johnson's brief *dicta* enchant because they are charged with personality, because even in print they acquire a tone of voice for the reader's ear and a lifting of lip or brow for his eye.

The son of a provincial bookseller, ex-schoolmaster, and married to a widow twenty years his senior, Johnson came from Lichfield with his former pupil, David Garrick, both of them to impose themselves on the capital's cultural and social scene. Garrick (1717–79) was the quicker in attaining success. He was soon recognized as the greatest actor of the day, and his immense achievements as actor-manager at Drury Lane Theatre included many Shakespearian as well as contemporary productions. Meantime Johnson first worked for Edward Cave on his *Gentleman's Magazine*, and under his influence the journal became more serious in tone, even pioneering the publication of parliamentary reports. His poem *London* was published in 1738. It is a farewell to the corruptions of the town (in imitation of Juvenal). It contains a deeply felt outburst against poverty, in which the strains of Johnson's struggle become evident:

> This mournful truth is ev'rywhere confess'd,
> SLOW RISES WORTH, BY POVERTY DEPRESS'D.

The companion piece, *The Vanity of Human Wishes* (also after Juvenal), followed some ten years later in 1749. Here the poet reflects on the vain pursuit of power, of learning and of military prowess; and then the issue is widened to a judgement on the precarious character of life in time, subject to all the accidents of nature. The concluding advice is to submit prayerfully to the will of God:

> Still raise for good the supplicating voice,
> But leave to Heav'n the measure and the choice,
> Safe in his pow'r whose eyes discern afar
> The secret ambush of a specious prayer;
> Implore his aid, in his decisions rest,
> Secure whate'er he gives, he gives the best.

Fine and supple as is Johnson's control of the couplet, his blank verse in the tragedy *Irene* is, like Addison's, too obviously the blank verse of a couplet-writer, firmly carved up into single and double lines. The rhythmic finality achieved at the line-end is often in open conflict with the continuing flow of sense and syntax. Garrick generously put the play on in 1749, but it is a work dominated by moral reflection rather than by dramatic action: this was not Johnson's medium.

Rather his biography of Richard Savage (1744) and his *Plan* for the *Dictionary* (1747) indicated where the fruition of his vast gifts was to be. Savage, illegitimate aristocratic pretender, had been Johnson's 'intimate companion', Boswell tells us, though his character was an astonishing blend of 'profligacy, insolence, and ingratitude' with a 'warm and vigorous, though unregulated mind'.[1] Savage, Johnson ob-

[1] *Life of Johnson.*

served, was one who 'by imputing none of his miseries to himself ... was never made wiser by his sufferings, nor preserved by one misfortune from falling into another'. His poem, *The Bastard*, ironically enumerates 'the imaginary advantages of base birth':

> He lives to build, not boast a generous Race:
> No Tenth Transmitter of a foolish Face.

The Johnsonian humour as well as the Johnsonian acumen and generous-heartedness are evident in the biography. The same magisterial eloquence and shrewdness pervade the essays that Johnson wrote twice weekly for the *Rambler* between 1750 and 1752, and again those he wrote under the title, *Idler*, for the weekly *Universal Chronicle* between 1758 and 1760. Weighty as the moralizing is in Johnson's essays, entertaining anecdotes lighten the tone, and a rich vein of humour is tapped in such pieces as the solemn inquiry into the tendency of writers and thinkers to dwell in garrets. Johnson develops the theory that we cannot know a man's capacities until he has been tested in operation at every degree of elevation from cellar to garret. It is not just a question of the change of atmospheric pressure, but of the increased speed with which the dweller aloft is whirled through space. Research into the applicability of this principle to education is recommended.

The *Dictionary* was published in 1755 and won Johnson academic renown – first an honorary MA from Oxford, and later doctorates from both Dublin and Oxford. The work was not a dry word list but an attempt to do full justice to subtle variations of meaning and to show, by the use of illustrative quotation, how connotation changes and develops. Even the much-quoted absurdities are the fruit of ingenuity and smell as much of self-parody as of pomposity:

> network. Any thing reticulated or decussated, at equal
> distances, with interstices between the inter-
> sections,

and the frankly satiric shafts are a delight:

> pension. An allowance made to anyone without an equivalent. In England it is generally understood to mean pay given to a state hireling for treason to his country.

The publication brought belated support from Lord Chesterfield, who had failed to respond when Johnson addressed his *Plan of an English Dictionary* to him nine years earlier. This tardy recognition provoked Johnson's famous and dignified rebuke of the man from whose door he had been repulsed:

> Is not a Patron, my Lord, one who looks with unconcern on a man struggling for life in the water, and, when he has reached ground, encumbers him with help?

Lord Chesterfield (1694–1773), it seems, would never willingly have had Johnson turned from his door, but Johnson was not to be mollified. He condemned Chesterfield's *Letters to His Son* (1774), in which worldly advice is given, as teaching 'the morals of a whore, and the manners of a dancing-master'. Indeed superficial social sophistication seems to be valued in the letters more than moral virtue, and the advantage of education is advertised by reference to Shakespeare's lack of it:

> If Shakespeare's genius had been cultivated, those beauties, which we so justly admire in him, would have been undisguised by those extravagances and that nonsense with which they are frequently accompanied.

It is clear that there was more than personal resentment separating the two proud minds.

The 'novel', *Rasselas*, was written within eight days out of urgent need for money. Rasselas, Prince of Abyssinia, and Imlac, the philosopher, escape from imprisonment in the Happy Valley where stands the palace for the royal children, where life is a succession of delights and every desire is granted. Accompanied by Princess Nekayah and Pekuah, they travel about inquiring into the possibility of happiness, and learning by personal encounter that thinkers and rulers, men of wealth and simple shepherds, all have their discontents. The conversations are couched in Johnson's shapely prose at its most insinuating. A lightly ironic smile lingers over many a polished phrase. There is the eloquent philosopher who, when he had finished disseminating wisdom, 'looked round him with a placid air and enjoyed the consciousness of his own beneficence'. Such sly touches abound. There is a weighty dissertation upon poetry and a perceptive debate on marriage. And the temporary loss of Pekuah involves the princess in a deep grief whose phases are subtly and feelingly probed. At the end of it all she finds that 'the choice of life is become less important; I hope hereafter to think only on the choice of eternity'.

Johnson's plan to edit Shakespeare, mooted in the *Proposals* he issued in 1745, eventually came to fruition in 1765. The *Preface* lays emphasis upon the universality of Shakespeare's sympathetic reading of human nature. Johnson maintains firmly that 'every man finds his mind more strongly seized by the tragedies of *Shakespeare* than of any other writer', and though he criticizes Shakespeare for the lack of a clear 'moral purpose', he will have nothing to do with the pseudo-classical bias by which Voltaire could exalt Addison's *Cato* above Shakespeare's 'extravagances'. 'Let him be answered that *Addison* speaks the language of poets, and *Shakespeare*, of men.'

Boswell called *The Lives of the English Poets* (1779–81) 'the richest, most beautiful, and indeed most perfect, production of Johnson's pen'. The *Lives* arose from a project initiated in 1777 by London booksellers to issue a uniform edition of English poets with a concise account of each poet's life by Johnson. Johnson accepted the proposal readily, but such was his interest and enthusiasm that in many cases the 'concise account' was expanded into a full scale biographical and critical study. Thus the lives of Milton, Dryden, Pope and others became major critical works. Of course there are lapses into prejudice. But the notorious attack on Milton's character as a republican and the devastating dismissal of *Lycidas* ('of which the diction is harsh, the rhymes uncertain, and the numbers unpleasing') must be offset by the high estimate of *Paradise Lost*. The *Lives* are peppered with illuminating judgements, crisply voiced and imaginatively conceived.

An interesting opportunity to compare the personalities of Johnson and his biographer is provided by the two products of their joint Scottish tour of 1773, Johnson's *A Journey to the Western Islands* (1775) and Boswell's *The Journal of the Tour of the Hebrides* (1785). Johnson's account is an orderly narrative, observant and informative, and when he is stimulated by experience to develop his thinking, it tends to be in the direction of a scholar's generalizations:

> Man is by the use of fire-arms made so much an over-match for other animals, that in all countries, where they are in use, the wild part of the creation sensibly diminishes.

Such a vein seems flat and dimensionless when put beside the imaginative vitality of Boswell's journal in which the never-failing sensitivity to human personality is continually stimulated by his experience of travel. Boswell's alert perceptiveness, his zest for encountering interesting personalities, and his indefatigable assiduity in putting experience onto paper are evidenced in the immense mass of journals and papers he left behind him. To these qualities, in writing his great biography, he added those of meticulousness in organizing his material and real artistic insight in the fashioning of the central persona.

Johnson's friendly jibe at Oliver Goldsmith (1730–74) was that he wrote 'like an angel' and talked like a parrot. Goldsmith's literary output was highly professional in its diversity. His prose works included an eight-volume *History of the Earth and Animated Nature* (1774) as well as a Roman history, a Grecian history, and a history of the Fathers.

There were also biographies of Lord Bolingbroke, Dr Parnell, Richard Nash and Voltaire; and Goldsmith's journalistic essays included the series of letters supposedly written by a Chinese philosopher living in London to explain English life to his friends in the East (*The Citizen of the World*). The opportunity this device provided for satire on the absurdities, superficialities and hypocrisies of contemporary society were fully exploited, and Goldsmith also probed the graver evils and abuses of politics, the law, drink, gambling, and the like.

Goldsmith's achievements in poetry, the drama and the novel are among the best of the century. In *The Traveller* (1764) the poet contrasts settled domestic contentment with his own wandering search for 'some spot to real happiness consigned'. Reviewing conditions in Switzerland, France, Holland and Britain, he turns at last to the praise of freedom and an attack on the inequalities that produce the grandeur of opulence on the one hand and stern depopulation on the other. It is this theme which is fully expanded in *The Deserted Village* (1770), a poem in which the couplet is so dexterously handled to serve a diversity of descriptive and emotional purposes that one can only marvel at Goldsmith's meticulous mastery of word and rhythm. The poet goes back to the village of his childhood, Auburn, to find it depopulated through enforced emigration. The affluence of the aristocracy has destroyed the 'bold peasantry'. The poet's thoughts go back to the village as it was, and he sketches human portraits from the past. There is fervent moral indignation in the contrast between the lost simplicities of village life and the sickening pleasures of wanton wealth and 'midnight masquerade', between the glittering brocade of the courtier and the toil of the pale worker, between the blaze and tumult of expensive nightlife and that cost in human suffering which Goldsmith symbolizes in a picture of a seduced and betrayed country girl lying in the cold and the wet near the door of her betrayer.

Goldsmith's comedy, *The Good Natur'd Man*, only faintly

anticipates the brilliance of *She Stoops to Conquer*. In his essay on *Sentimental Comedy* Goldsmith repeats the classic view that tragedy should display the 'calamities of the great' and comedy exhibit 'the follies of the lower part of mankind'. Current sentimental comedy 'in which the virtues of private life are exhibited, rather than the vices exposed' is really a 'species of bastard tragedy'. It is easy to write, but morally questionable in that it asks us to applaud people's 'faults and foibles' on account of the 'goodness of their hearts'. So Goldsmith turns back to the comedy of incident like that of Vanbrugh and Farquhar. The plot of *She Stoops to Conquer* is said to have been based on Goldsmith's own experience when, as a boy in Ireland, he was directed to a private house as to an inn and did not discover the joke until he asked for the bill next morning. On this basis Goldsmith developed the story of the young hero, Marlow, who is similiarly misdirected by the winningly mischievous Tony Lumpkin, and mistakenly makes love to Kate Hardcastle as to a barmaid. He is bold enough at this, but when he meets the same young lady (but unrecognized) as Miss Hardcastle herself, and a possible bride, he is all bashfulness. This is but one thread in a network of misunderstandings and conscious deceptions that produce a series of divertingly ironic and farcical situations. Characterization is clear and sharp, but thought and action skate smoothly above that level of psychological reality or social seriousness at which the manipulation of stage types would be queered by probing inquiry into feelings and motivations. In short, it is not a 'bastard tragedy'.

One must read Goldsmith's tale, *The Vicar of Wakefield*, too in the light of his attack on the sentimental vein in comedy. The vicar, the Reverend Dr Primrose, and the various members of his family are conducted through a series of dire misfortunes – loss of money, seduction, elopement, imprisonment and even apparent death – only to be restored to happiness by a highly contrived dénouement. The tale is not a 'bastard tragedy'. Goldsmith's Irish tongue gently probes his cheek as the kind, gullible and unworldly vicar is subjected to the stock disasters of contemporary literature like an eighteenth-century Job. We soon detect that the vicar attracts catastrophes too readily, especially at moments when he is dwelling on the blessings of his lot. But the irony is not depreciative. Dr Primrose, who responds to unjust imprisonment by preaching to his fellow convicts, is no moral lightweight. Melodramatic villainy and coincidental tergiversations of fortune may be sportively handled, but the direly tested fortitude, family love, and faith are all real enough.

Johnson's admiration for Goldsmith as a writer is interestingly counterbalanced by his dislike of Thomas Gray (1716–71). He mocks the verbal artifices of Gray's *Ode on a Distant Prospect of Eton College*, a nostalgic poem about his old school. In all Gray's odes, Johnson says, 'there is a kind of cumbrous splendour that we wish away'; indeed they are 'marked by glittering accumulations of ungraceful ornaments'[2] Such is the Johnsonian response to the meticulously fashioned verbal splendours and lofty cadences of those odes like *The Progress of Poesy* and *Ode for Music* that are as packed with learning as they are with technical expertise. All the paraphernalia of personification and allusive symbolism are at Gray's disposal in presenting Milton (in *The Progress of Poesy*) as riding 'on the seraph-wings of Extasy' beyond the 'flaming bounds of Place and Time', while 'Dryden's less presumptuous car' is drawn by two coursers 'with necks in thunder clothed, and long-resounding pace'.

For all the admitted finish of Gray's versification and construction, and in spite of the powerfully felt verbal response to life which sometimes surges musically above the formal artifices of the odes –

> How vain the ardour of the Crowd,
> How low, how little are the Proud,
> How indigent the Great!　　　(*Ode on the Spring*)

[2] *Life of Gray.*

– Johnson's implicit verdict that he was a one-poem poet, unjust as it may be, has never been popularly dislodged. Indeed there grew up a habit of citing Gray to exemplify those defects of eighteenth-century poetic diction which Romantic ardour and sincerity rejected. But critics are now less happy to oversimplify this issue by submitting eighteenth-century artifices of diction to a negative scrutiny more rigorous than would be applied to the verbal artifices of other periods such as the fourteenth century or the Elizabethan Age. Gray, a wifeless scholar, was busy year after year at Cambridge studying in preparation for books he never wrote and lectures he failed to give. He was given to melancholy, noted for effeminacy, and deeply moved by the sight of grand and picturesque scenery. Certainly his temperamental and technical endowments caught fire in the *Elegy written in a Country Churchyard*. Johnson himself put his finger on its quality when he said that it 'abounds with images which find a mirror in every mind, and with sentiments to which every bosom returns an echo'. There is finely modulated music in its intricately disciplined musings. They probe the deep emotional universalities of man's confrontation with finitude. The obviousness of contrasting life's simple activities and happinesses with death's undifferentiating dominion, or of questioning whether there is among the unlettered poor potential human greatness that never comes to light, is the wholesome, bread-and-butter obviousness on which profound speculative thought as well as honest emotional responsiveness to the human situation is nourished:

> The boast of heraldry, the pomp of pow'r,
> And all that beauty, all that wealth e'er gave,
> Awaits alike th'inevitable hour.
> The paths of glory lead but to the grave.

Gray's enthusiasm for Celtic studies and Norse literature, like his sensitivity to scenery and his susceptibility to *angst*, seems to anticipate the Romantic movement as surely as his pindarics and his ornate diction fasten him in his period; but the *Elegy* rises above history to speak now with the same immediacy of impact that called out eleven quick editions on its first appearance in 1751.

In a memorable comparison, Swinburne praised Gray as an elegiac poet and then added that 'as a lyric poet, he is simply unworthy to sit at the feet of Collins'. William Collins (1721–59) had a short and tragic life that culminated in insanity. Johnson's warm sympathy for the indolent, thriftless and dissipated but vigorously gifted poet does credit to his heart and his head. 'By degrees I gained his confidence', Johnson tells us, 'and one day was admitted to him when he was immured by a bailiff that was prowling in the street.'[3] The ode, *The Manners*, autobiographically records Collins's decision to leave Oxford, where he had failed to get a fellowship, to forsake the 'prattling Page', to 'read in Man the native Heart' and to learn from living nature. This seems to have meant plunging into the fashionable sociabilities of the town, where Collins developed Gray's penchant for not writing the books he planned – and even, in one case, the book (a translation of Aristotle's *Poetics*) he had been paid for.

There are pre-Romantic leanings in the oriental interest revealed in his *Persian Eclogues* as in the response to nature and the emphasis laid on the emotions in the *Ode to Pity* and the *Ode to Fear*. The former plea is invested with artifices of diction like 'Youth's soft Notes' and the 'Buskin'd Muse', but urgency of pulse and image gives a feverous, indeed ominous vitality at times:

> Ah *Fear*! Ah frantic *Fear*!
> I see, I see Thee near.
> I know thy hurried Step, thy haggard Eye!

There is exaltation of the inspired poetic imagination in the *Ode on the Poetical Character* and a vein of patriotic sensi-

[3] *Life of Collins.*

tivity in the *Ode to Mercy* and *Ode to Liberty*. The former, written in 1746, touches on the Jacobite rebellion of 1745. A finer note of simplicity is sounded by Collins when he forsakes the stilted flourishes and strophic grandeurs of the concert ode to hymn the fallen in battle in the stanzaic directness of 'How sleep the Brave, who sink to rest, / By all their Country's Wishes blest' and to hymn the dead personal friend and fellow poet in *On the Death of Mr Thomson*. 'In yonder grave a Druid lies', Collins exclaims, standing on the bank of the Thames, and just forty years after the publication of the poem in 1749, Wordsworth, in his *Remembrance of Collins*, floats by on the river and pauses momentarily to pray:

> that never child of song
> May know that Poet's sorrows more.

It is a touching tribute indicative of the affection won by the poet both in life and in his work. The finest thing he did was his *Ode to Evening*, a poem drenched in atmosphere – the hushed tranquillity of evening as it returns gently and genially to the musing poet. The vocabulary is alive with a sensuous responsiveness to what is felt and seen.

Arbitrary dividing lines have to be drawn in literary histories, and John Dyer (1700–58), the Welsh poet from Carmarthenshire, is not the only writer under consideration whose early work falls in the age of Pope and later work in the age of Johnson. The poem *Grongar Hill* (1726) describes the scenery round the river Towy in octosyllabic couplets, and the influence of Milton's *L'Allegro* and *Il Penseroso* is evident. It belongs to the genre of 'local poetry' represented by *Cooper's Hill* and *Windsor Forest*. Wide panoramic glimpses of meads, woods, houses, castles and spires are animated by sharper vignettes etched with clarity. Then the human note is heard increasingly as the sight of ruins leads to reflections on the levelling power of time, the transient smile of fate, and the riverlike flow of human life on its journey to the sea of endless deep. Dyer ends on the theme of finding tranquil and temperate contentment in the country as against the vanity of seeking peace on the marble floors of courts. Didactic themes like those of 'all-devouring Time' and the 'pride of Pomp' are illustrated on a more extensive scale in *The Ruins of Rome* (1740), but Dyer's blend of earnest moralizing and description achieves its fullest expression in *The Fleece*, a long blank-verse poem about sheep-raising and the woollen industry. It is engaging to see Dyer moving from the busy account of the construction of Carthage in the *Aeneid* to its contemporary parallel:

> Such was the scene
> Of hurrying Carthage, when the Trojan chief
> First view'd her growing turrets. So appear
> Th'increasing walls of busy Manchester,
> Sheffield, and Birmingham, whose redd'ning fields
> Rise and enlarge their suburbs.

To Boswell Johnson spoke slightingly of *The Fleece*. 'The subject, Sir, cannot be made poetical. How can a man write poetically of serges and druggets!'

But, in his *Life of Dyer*, Johnson fairly reports the view of Akenside that capacity to appreciate *The Fleece* was a mark of poetic judgement, and that the poem's standing was a criterion by which the soundness of the 'reigning taste' could be gauged. Akenside's judgement on *The Fleece* neatly pinpoints his own poetic character. His odes are unexciting exercises in the use of over-used and vague vocabulary. In the *Ode to the Evening Star* for instance he is quick to involve Hesper and Hymen, and to roam in quest of 'Philomela's bower'. Music has 'healing charm', the stream is 'silver', the shade 'solemn' and 'awful', there is a 'golden ray', a 'level mead', a 'melting note' and a 'sequester'd spot'. Of course it is not difficult, with most minor eighteenth-century poets, to rummage out epithets which, when listed *en masse*, make it sound as though their verses have been put together from standard pre-fabricated units supplied in a poetic do-it-yourself kit; but there are generally compensatory peaks of inspiration too. The modern reader will need patience to seek out those in Akenside's long, blank-verse study in aesthetics, *The Pleasures of Imagination* (1744). Mark Akenside (1721–70) was only twenty-three when he published it. Remarkable as an achievement in the sustained flow of verse, it is far too unrestrained and diffuse. Simple reflections that would be crystallized in a deft couplet in Gray or Dyer are expanded by intolerably repetitious illustrations. The prolixity leads to a blurred vagueness in which the line of argument gets lost.

James Grainger (1721–66), like Dyer, was the object of Johnson's ridicule – for his poem, *The Sugar Cane* (1764). His Periphrastic style is illustrated by Boswell,[4] who refers to a passage dealing with the havoc caused by rats and mice:

> Nor with less waste the whisker'd vermin race,
> A countless clan despoil the lowland cane.

But Johnson had a word of praise for the 'noble' octosyllabic couplets of the *Ode to Solitude*, where at least the standard figures like 'Halcyon Peace' and 'Blushing artless Modesty' are accompanied by a truly animated picture of 'Health that snuffs the morning air'. The indefatigability of eighteenth-century writers in dignifying the most unlikely topics with the full blank-verse treatment may be savoured also by reference to the work of John Armstrong (1709–79), a doctor-poet from Roxburghshire, whose *The Art of Preserving Health* (1744) David Hume described to Boswell as 'the most classical poem in the English language'.[5] Another Scot, William Falconer (1732–69), maintained a readable if unexciting level of competence in the heroic couplets of *Shipwreck* (1762). The mariner-poet had his own personal experience to work on and a technical nautical vocabulary at his disposal. Indeed he later devised a dictionary of nautical terms.

[4] *Life of Johnson*.
[5] Boswell, *The Ominous Years, 1774–6*, ed. Ryskamp and Pottle, (Heinemann, London, 1963), p. 200.

A more exclusively and self-consciously 'poetic' personality was William Shenstone (1714–63), who spent more than he could afford in the fabrication of an elaborately picturesque mini-estate, with its dingles, precipices, cascades, streams, bridges, grots and alcoves, not to mention thickets, Gothic seats, rustic buildings, terraces, and the like, all littered with poetic inscriptions. Shenstone's interests took in ballads as well as landscape gardening, though his own *Jemmy Dawson*, lamenting the tragic execution of a young Jacobite and his sweetheart's death from shock, is a somewhat uncomfortable envelopment of the pathetic and the gruesome in stanzaic jog-trot. Some of his songs have a neat, unforced charm, like 'When bright Roxana treads the green'; but *The Schoolmistress* (1737) is his most celebrated poem. It is direct imitation of Spenser and begins in a delightfully parodic vein:

> One ancient hen she took delight to feed,
> The plodding pattern of the busy dame,
> Which ever and anon, impell'd by need,
> Into her school, begirt with chickens came,
> Such favour did her past deportment claim …

But the tone is less happy, less certain, when corporal punishment is administered on a schoolboy and he is left painfully 'bum y-galled. The child's indignant distress breaks right out of the jocular irony that seems intended to distance and contain it.

A writer of vastly greater skill and fertility was Charles Churchill (1731–64). The character of his poetry is for the most part aggressively satirical. His control of intense invective and of taunting irony gave him power to savage opponents ruthlessly. Actors were the target in *The Rosciad*, Bute and his fellow Scots in *The Prophecy of Famine*, Hogarth in *An Epistle to William Hogarth* and Smollet in *The Author*. The wit and force of his best work is undeniable, but when Johnson said that Churchill's poetry 'being filled with living names, would sink into oblivion',[6] he hit the nail on the head. We can sense the injurious power of his personal attacks, but to get at their real significance we need an apparatus of explanatory notes.

We have already looked at several Scottish writers whose work flowed into the mainstream of English literature. Among the more distinctively and self-consciously Scottish was Allan Ramsay (1686–1758). Chronologically he could have been more fitly included among the Augustans; indeed he established the 'Easy Club' in Edinburgh in 1712 after the pattern of the *Spectator* Club; but some of his work points forward clearly to Burns, and his *Tea Table Miscellany*, issued between 1724 and 1732, stimulated the pre-Romantic taste for ballads. Sir Walter Scott said of his *Hardiknute*, 'It was the first poem I ever learnt – the last I shall ever forget.'[7] The cultivation of vernacular verse gave Ramsay some permanent importance. The flavour of it may be gauged from a *Song* in Act I of his dramatic pastoral, *The Gentle Shepherd*:

> My Peggy is a young thing,
> And I'm not very auld,
> Yet well I like to meet her at
> The wawking of the fauld.

David Mallet (born Malloch, 1705–65) was a Scot of different breed. Johnson tells us how in England he 'cleared his tongue from his native pronunciation so as to be no longer distinguished as a Scot',[8] and changed his name. He worked his way into London literary life and collaborated with Thomson in the masque *Alfred* (containing the song, 'Rule Britannia'). His blank-verse narrative, *Amyntor and Theodora*, was cited by Warton as finely illustrating the 'nauseous affectation of expressing everything

---

[6] Boswell, *Life of Johnson*.
[7] Lockhart, *Life of Sir Walter Scott*.
[8] *Life of Mallett*.

pompously and poetically'.[9] Mrs Cibber drew copious tears when she played in Mallet's tragedy *Elvira* in 1763, but Garrick was compelled to take it off after a few nights. Mallet is now chiefly remembered for his *William and Margaret*, in which wild balladry is tamed and domesticated, if not yet emasculated:

> 'Twas at the silent, solemn hour,
> When night and morning meet.
> In glided Margaret's grimly ghost,
> And stood at William's feet.

Faithless William is upbraided and invited to visit her grave. He does so, lays his cheek to it, and never speaks again.

The cult of the ballad was a sign of literary change as notable as Gray's interest in Old Norse legends. A complementary attempt to popularize the taste for primitive epic was made by James Macpherson (1736–96), a farmer's son from Kingussie, who published works purporting to be translations of Gaelic poems by a legendary third-century bard called 'Ossian'. The two epics, *Fingal* (1762) and *Temora* (1763), along with shorter fragments like *The Death of Cuthullin* and *The Battle of Lora*, aroused immense enthusiasm. At its best the style has a certain rhetorical sublimity and a rhythmic urgency. The blending of the human and the natural is an element in the technique:

> Who fell on Carun's sounding banks, son of the cloudy night? Was he white as the snow of Arvden? Blooming as the bow of the shower?[10]

Repetitive variation is as important as it is in the psalms:

> Selma, thy halls are silent. There is no sound in the woods of Morven. The wave tumbles alone on the coast. The silent beam of the sun is on the field.[11]

[9] Joseph Warton, *Essay on the Writings and Genius of Pope.*
[10] *Comala.*
[11] *Lathmon.*

It must not be forgotten that, far as this taste for the pseudo-primitive seems at first sight to be from the elaborately postured idiom of, say, eighteenth-century tragedy, in fact the reader is just as much involved in a world of grandiose description and pompous speechifying in the one as in the other:

> Raise my standards on high; spread them on Lena's wind, like the flames of an hundred hills ... Ye sons of the roaring streams, that pour from a thousand hills, be near the king of Morven! attend to the words of his power! ... O, Oscar, of the future fights! Connal, son of the blue shields of Sora! ...[12]

One cannot, of course, live at this level for long; and some may think the most useful thing Macpherson did was to hand on to Scott a recipe for flavouring the speech of Highland chieftains with a dash of Celtic spice. Dr Johnson, for one, was quick to question the authenticity of Macpherson's 'translations'. A controversy on the subject has raged ever since. It seems clear that Macpherson was not translating; but we do not know how far he invented and how far he utilized legendary romances and folk tales surviving in oral tradition.

Among Macpherson's friends whose faith in 'Ossian' remained firm was John Home (1722–1808), a Presbyterian minister who was compelled to resign his parish at Athelstoneford because of Calvinistic disapproval of the theatre. Home's tragedy, *Douglas* (1756), brought him into ecclesiastical disgrace. Home, who had been out with volunteers against the Jacobites at Prestonpans, was a man of some spirit, and made himself another career. There is a syntactical directness in the blank verse of *Douglas* but phrasing stays unyieldingly aloft. The villain Glenalvon practises his deceits with well-advertised satanic cunning. 'Thy virtue awes me. First of womankind', he says, and Lady Randolph's rebuke is no less stagy: 'Reserve these accents for some

[12] *Fingal, Book IV.*

other ear.' In short, too often again we feel that characters are addressing each other in propositional headlines. Nevertheless Mrs Siddons was later to move audiences deeply in the pathetic role of Lady Randolph, whose first husband Douglas was killed in feud with her own family, and whose son by Douglas, long believed lost, turns up under the unlikely name of 'Norval' on the Grampian hills, only to be killed by her second husband. In succeeding tragedies Home never repeated the success of *Douglas*, though he came near to repeating the plot identically in *Alonzo* (1773).

The decade that saw the first production of *Douglas* saw also the first production of a tragedy in utter contrast to it, *The Gamester* (1753) by Edward Moore (1712–57). It picks up the thread of moralistic domestic tragedy twenty-two years after Lillo's *George Barnwell*. It is a prose drama tracing the last stages of a gambler's descent from wealth to poverty and finally to suicide by poisoning. The pathetic emphasis on the sufferings of the gamester's wife, and on the desperately ineffective unselfishness of others who try to help, gives the play a moving power. Mrs Beverley's protective and self-sacrificial devotion is in the mould of Otway's Belvidera in *Venice Preserv'd*. Her sister-in-law Charlotte's share in the distress as her marriage is postponed presses home the moral of how the misery caused by the gaming table ripples out in widening circles among the victim's friends and relations. No doubt the villainous Stukeley is an overdrawn study in malevolence, but Moore can still make us feel that the evils were real and the social problem a crippling one. This tragedy cuts near the bone. An eighteenth-century gentleman was much more likely to ruin himself at gaming than to have his posthumous son reared on the Grampian hills by a frugal swain called Norval.

There is a poet of this period whom no classificatory system could accommodate, and it seems that the eighteenth-century social system had difficulty in accommodating him too, for he was put away more than once in a lunatic asylum. This was Christopher Smart (1722–71), a victim of religious

manìa. His great poem, *A Song to David* (1763), is one of
the finest of the century. After contacts with lunatics in an
asylum, Samuel Beckett's Murphy (in the novel *Murphy*) is
inclined to 'call sanctuary what the psychiatrists call exile'.
Certainly Smart dwelt in a 'sanctuary' of the mind when he
voiced his magnificent praise of God and of the created
world in the *Song to David*. There is a riotous profusion of
rich and exact imagery, a spirit of bounding joy, an overflowing abundance of inspired responsiveness to what is
good, beautiful and deserving of praise: yet all is powerfully disciplined in ordered sequences in which form is subtly
fused with substance. David's virtues, his achievements, and
his psalmody are treated in turn:

> He sung of God – the mighty source
> Of all things – the stupendous force
> On which all strength depends;
> From whose right arm, beneath whose eyes,
> All period, pow'r, and enterprize
> Commences, reigns, and ends.

The sinewy grandeur of the whole is compelling.

There are one or two significant members of Johnson's
circle whom we have not touched on. Joseph Warton (1722–
1800) illustrates a trend that is to grow, in his praise of the
natural as against the 'luxury and pomp' that 'proudly ban-
ish Nature's simple charms'. Such are his phrases in *The Enthusiast: or the Lover of Nature* (1744) whose title itself is a
sign of the trend. Augustan literary fashion is subject to
criticism on a comparable basis in his *Essay on the Writings
and Genius of Pope* as well as in *The Enthusiast*:

> What are the lays of artful Addison,
> Coldly correct, to Shakespeare's warblings wild?

His younger brother, Thomas Warton (1728–90), moves in a
similar literary direction in *The Pleasures of Melancholy*
(1747), derivative in its use of the standard epithets, but
luxuriating in 'aweful solitude', dew-drenched 'drooping

temples' and the lonesome night in which 'religious horror wraps / My soul in dread repose'. More important is his pioneer critical work such as *Observations on Spenser's Faery Queen* (1754) and the *History of English Poetry* (1774), both scholarly studies by a man sensitive to the past.

Of the writers of the period whose work is strictly outside the field of imaginative literature, but whose influence on other grounds was vast, David Hume (1711–76), the Scottish philosopher, worked in the empirical tradition of Locke and Berkeley. His scepticism reduces objects to impressions or ideas, and the human being to a perceiver whose beliefs and value-judgements are based on feelings. His *History of England* (1754–61) has been less influential than the series of philosophical books which began with the *Treatise on Human Nature* in 1739–40. Such was Hume's character that Boswell told him he was better than his books. The social stigma attached to anti-Christian views in the mid-eighteenth century may be judged from a letter by one of the fascinating letter-writers of the age, Lady Mary Wortley Montagu (1689–1762). Lady Mary censures the folly of Lady Orford, whose character is held 'in universal horror':

> I do not mean from her gallantries, which nobody trouble their heads with, but she had a collection of free-thinkers that met weekly at her house, to the scandal of all good Christians.[13]

Hume's fellow sceptic, Edward Gibbon (1737–94), was less warmly treated by Boswell, who describes him as speaking 'with his usual sneer'.[14] It must be admitted that Gibbon's massively comprehensive work, *The Decline and Fall of the Roman Empire*, is a little marred by the anti-Christian prejudice which colours his account of Rome's decline, matchless as the whole is for the dignity of its style and the flow of its narrative.

Master of stately and sonorous prose in others fields was

[13] Letter to Mr Wortley Montagu, 20 June 1751.
[14] *Life of Johnson.*

the Dublin-born orator Edmund Burke (1729–97), the great parliamentarian whose eloquence in the House of Commons was complemented by eloquence on paper – in the philosophical field with such works as *A Vindication of Natural Society*, in the field of political theory with *Thoughts on the Causes of the Recent Discontents* (1770) and in his attack on the revolting French masses in *Reflections on the Revolution* (1790). And if we may end this glance at the age of Johnson by turning from the prose of world history and public affairs to that of quiet private life, a mention may be made of Gilbert White (1720–93) who recorded his observations of the natural life around him in the Hampshire village of Selborne, writing a series of informative and reflective letters that were later gathered and published as *The Natural History of Selborne* (1789).

14
The eighteenth-century novel

At the beginning of the year 1740 the English Novel was in
its infancy: fifteen years later three great novelists, Richardson, Fielding and Smollett, had published almost all their
major works. This transformation is remarkable in that the
novel as it took shape in those years was virtually a new form,
yet was extremely diverse in character. In particular the
contrast between Richardson and Fielding, as exponents of
what imaginative literature is about, matches the contrast
in our own century between Lawrence and Joyce.

Samuel Richardson (1689–1761), a successful printer, took
to novel-writing by accident when two booksellers invited
him to compile a volume of letters for the guidance of people

inexperienced with their pens. In working on this project, Richardson's imagination was caught by the idea of using the epistolary technique to tell a story he had once heard of a young servant girl who resisted the seductive assaults of her young master, much as she liked him, and thus won not only his respect but also his person in marriage. *Pamela: or Virtue Rewarded* (1740) was an immediate success. Pamela's letters to her parents at home tell how her master, Mr B, forcefully presses his advances upon her with such energy and ingenuity that she has to flee the house. Mr B pursues her and ultimately makes amends by marrying her. The vitality of the book resides in Pamela's strength of character, her bold self-defence, and her rigorous distinction between those areas in which a maid owes dutiful obedience to her master and those in which personal integrity demands an equality of relationship between individuals whatever their respective social status. The fine vigour of Pamela's moral certitude and her ingenuity in resistance blend spicily with the undercurrent of real affection for her master and of tacit sexual sensitivity.

The formula thus stumbled upon was to produce a masterpiece when given the full treatment in *Clarissa Harlowe* (1748). The epistolary style is chosen for its immediacy, we are told in the preface. In the letters we have a day-by-day, minute-by-minute record of the heroine's persecution at the hands of her own family, who would marry her advantageously to the hateful Mr Solmes. Rejection by her own family throws her into the hands of the unscrupulous arch-rake, Lovelace, whose trickeries culminate in her being drugged and violated. The proud refusal of Clarissa to marry the man who has forfeited all her respect is a tragic transmutation of Pamela's pert rebuffs of the ardent Mr B. Clarissa has been physically sullied: she will not spiritually sully herself: it is better to die. And die she does. The approach of her demise she records with unflagging literary assiduity, and the reader's grief is his edification. It is easy to make fun of the book, yet its intensity and power are undeniable. 'This Richardson is a strange fellow,' writes Lady Mary Wortley Montague, 'I heartily despise him, and eagerly read him, nay sob over his books in a scandalous manner.'[1] The pressurized naturalism of the book is such that a felt intimacy between Clarissa and the reader involves one in her agonies and frustrations. The closeness of contact has its disadvantages. If you know Richardson's characters as you know your own acquaintances, they can bore you in the same way, being intolerably repetitious and oppressively predictable.

Yet Richardson has surgical skill in the subtle exploration of human motive, pretence and subterfuge, as well as in the presentation of troubled conscience, conflicting obligations and torn emotions. 'Sir,' said Dr Johnson to Boswell, 'there is more knowledge of the heart in one letter of Richardson's than in all *Tom Jones*.'[2] As the story came out, volume by volume, the public demand for a happy ending expressed itself in a mass appeal from reader to writer. 'On this subject also,' says Scott, 'Cibber ranted and the ladies implored, with an earnestness that seems to imply at once a belief that the persons in whom they interested themselves had an existence, and that it was in the power of the writer of their memoirs to turn their destiny which way he pleased ...'[3] Scott's neat phrasing of the self-contradictory demand reinforces our gratitude that Richardson was a big enough artist to resist popular clamour.

But he gave way to popular feminine clamour in another instance – by agreeing to display a thoroughly good man. *Sir Charles Grandison* (1754) fulfilled this solemn purpose. The heroine, Harriett Byron, has given a true Richardsonian rebuff to the proposal of marriage pressed by the wealthy but arrogant Sir Hargrave Pollexfen. His subsequent attempt to carry her off is foiled by Sir Charles. An obligation to an Italian lady, scrupulously adhered to, hinders Sir Charles

[1] Letter to the Countess of Bute, 22 September 1755.
[2] Boswell, *Life of Johnson*.
[3] Scott, *Lives of the Novelists*.

from allowing his delightful relationship to ripen into marriage – until the obligation is conveniently removed at the eleventh hour.

Sir Charles, 'the best of men', is an oppressive study in propriety. Didactic purpose increasingly dominates the book. One cannot but sense, when one comes to the end of Richardson's output, that there is a cultural aridity about his work. His literary taste can perhaps be measured by Sir Charles's comment when he has occasion to quote a rather undistinguished couplet by Addison, and takes the opportunity to address the ladies on its merits:

> I see with great pleasure, said he, the happy understanding that there is between you three ladies: It is demonstration, to me, of surpassing goodness in you all. To express myself in the words of an ingenious man, to whose works your Sex, and if *yours*, *ours*, are more obliged, than to those of any single man in the British world,

> > Great souls by instinct to each other turn,
> > Demand alliance, and in friendship burn.

Henry Fielding (1707–54) was a man of letters to his fingertips. Fielding discusses his own work in the successive introductory chapters to the eighteen books of *Tom Jones* – whose action proceeds under the eye of a good-humoured if somewhat magisterial authorial presence. Fielding sees himself as an innovator ('for as I am, in reality, the founder of a new province of writing'), but an innovator in the tradition of the great poets and dramatists of the past. When he lists the qualifications of the novelist ('historian', he calls himself), illustrative references reach out to Homer, Milton, Horace, Shakespeare and Jonson. Indeed he explicitly claims that 'Homer and Milton, though they added the ornament of numbers to their works, were both historians of our order'. Eighteenth-century and subsequent criticism dwelt on the parallel. Lord Monboddo, in *The*

Origin and Progress of Language, regards *Tom Jones* as 'a legitimate kind of poem'. Arthur Murphy, Fielding's first biographer, spoke of *Amelia* as Fielding's *Odyssey* and of *Tom Jones* as his *Iliad*. Later Byron was to call Fielding 'the prose Homer'.[4] And indeed the stories of *Joseph Andrews*, *Tom Jones* and *Amelia* are structured so as to parallel the patterning of adventures in both Homeric and Virgilian epic. The eighteen books of *Tom Jones* fall into three groups of six each, centred respectively at home, on the road and in London. That Fielding sought also the universality of epic in characterization is evident from the discussion in Book III, chapter 1 of *Joseph Andrews*: 'I declare here, once and for all, that I describe not men, but manners; not an individual, but a species.' Two papers (Nos. 55 and 56) which Fielding wrote for his periodical *The Covent Garden Journal*, that came out twice a week in 1752, show him thinking out the theory of character with reference to Jonson's doctrine of humours. Fielding was a dramatist before he turned to prose fiction. His comedies are now forgotten, but his burlesque, *The Tragedy of Tragedies or Tom Thumb the Great* (1730), remains highly entertaining:

KING: Let nothing but a face of joy appear;
   The man who frowns this day shall lose his head,
   That he may have no face to frown withal.

The fruits of his experience as playwright can be seen in the narrative technique of the novels, more particularly in the liveliness of the dialogue, the sharpness of the characterization and the fondness for stage-like situations.

It was Richardson's *Pamela* that drove Fielding to burlesque fiction, first in *Shamela* (1741) where Mr B emerges as Mr Booby and Pamela becomes a calculating minx, and then in *Joseph Andrews* (1742) where Pamela's brother, Joseph, suffers assaults on his virtue from Lady Booby, and is sacked for resisting them. But when, after an attack by

---

[4] Quoted by Scott, *Lives of the Novelists*.

robbers, Joseph is aided by Parson Adams, the story quickly outgrows the initial burlesque impulse. The study of the parson, a robust, good-hearted Christian who is ingenuous and unsuspecting to the point of naïveté is delightfully sustained. In the 'Author's Preface' to *Joseph Andrews* Fielding defines his novel as 'a comic epic poem in prose; differing from comedy, as the serious epic from tragedy: its action being more extended and comprehensive; containing a much larger circle of incidents, and introducing a greater variety of characters'. This concept is fully realized in *The History of Tom Jones, A Foundling* (1749). Tom Jones is brought up by Squire Allworthy who is unaware that the foundling is his sister Bridget's son. Bridget's legitimate son, Blifil, a mean cad, becomes Tom's rival for the love of Sophia Western and cunningly discredits him in Allworthy's eyes, not without some assistance from Tom's erratic if generous-hearted impetuosities, such as the liaison with Molly Seagrim. After a series of elaborately contrived adventures, the beautifully articulated plot is deftly monitored to a happy ending. The themes from which the plot is woven are the stuff of drama – the sinister villain's conspiracy against the hero, the hero's uncertain origin, and the alienation of the hero from his friends by misunderstanding and deception. Sudden discoveries, timely rescues, a deathbed confession and startling near-misses by people chasing each other all play their part. And to this theatrical display the author acts as chorus, curtain-puller and fellow member of the audience, digging his elbow into the reader's ribs at points when detached comment might enrich the irony ('I ask pardon for this short appearance, by way of chorus, on the stage'). The participants live vividly through the vigour of their self-presentation and the sharp outlines of their portraiture.

An endearing aspect of Fielding is the righteous moral indignation that lies at the back of his ironical glorification of delinquency, cruelty and crime in *Jonathan Wild the Great* (1743). Fielding hates cant and hypocrisy, cruelty and arrogance. Only a man of great humanity could have crowned his literary career with a book so inspired with social passion as *Amelia* (1751), which opens in Newgate Prison with an impressive picture of the squalid indignities and corruptions of the place. Through the trials of the feckless William Booth and his suffering wife, Amelia, we explore a world of rottenness, and Fielding's judgement on it implicitly comments on the wider human scene it miniatures. Acquaintance with Fielding is a rich relationship for a sensitive reader, and the last picture we have of him, the posthumously published *Journal of a Voyage to Lisbon* (1755), is movingly expressive of his humanity and fortitude in his last illness.

The third (and lesser) member of the great mid-century triumvirate in the history of the novel was Tobias Smollett (1721–71), a Scotsman who failed with his first literary effort (the tragedy, *The Regicide*), then served in the navy as a surgeon's mate before settling down to journalism, translation (he translated *Gil Blas* in 1749), history (his *Complete History of England* came out in four volumes in 1757–8) and fiction. The first novel, *Roderick Random* (1748), established Smollett's chosen form, the picaresque, in which a series of separate adventures is loosely connected in the continuing life story of the hero. There is but the frail shadow of a plot, yet the book has immense vitality. A handful of memorable characters surrounds the hero; Lieutenant Tom Bowling, the sailor ('Avast, brother, avast! sheer off!'), the Welsh surgeon, Morgan ('Got and my Reteemer!'), and the warm-hearted Strap. The hero's adventures as a naval surgeon's mate allow Smollett to give a vigorous picture of seamen in action and to spotlight evil conditions and bad leadership in the navy. There is some progress in plotting between *Roderick Random* and Smollett's last novel, *Humphry Clinker* (1771), but Smollett's passion for packing into the novel anything that comes into his head, especially if it stirs his wrath or provokes his ridicule, gathers strength. In *Humphry Clinker* twenty-one contemporary celebrities are actually introduced (many more are referred to) and none of them has any connection with the 'plot'. In the same novel there are guidebook descriptions of Bath, London, Harrogate, Scarborough, York, Durham, Edinburgh, Glasgow, Dumfries and Carlisle. Plot or no plot, if Smollett wants to let off steam about electioneering, the tobacco trade, education, sanitation, the British Museum, Scottish dialect or Parliament and press, he does so without restraint.

In *Peregrine Pickle* (1751) the plot is a little stronger than in *Roderick Random*. Peregrine is alienated from his parents, as Tom Jones is, and young Gamaliel's machinations against his brother are parallel to Blifil's. Peregrine's protector is Commodore Hawser Trunnion, a sailor who has spent so long aboard and remains so nautical in habit and in the conduct of his 'garrison' that his bride, Mrs Grizzle, has to share a hammock with him on the nuptial night. After falling in love at the university and finding the relationship obstructed by misunderstandings, the hero goes off for a foreign tour – a sequence of scrapes, attempted seductions, practical jokes and dissipations that culminate in poverty and imprisonment. There is a massive digression (the 'Memoirs of a Lady of Quality') before the plot raises its head again, Peregrine's father dies intestate, a fortune and the relenting Emilia are his. Smollett nursed the delusion that practical jokes are as funny on paper as they are in real life. One tires of them, and of the insensibility that assumes Mr Jumble, the university tutor, to be a fit object of youthful cruelty because his father was a bricklayer and his mother sold pies. One tires too of the nocturnal attempts to enjoy the favours of strange ladies in awkwardly positioned bedrooms in country inns, and of the frequency with which such efforts terminate in uproar.

Ferdinand Count Fathom (1753) is superior in organization, and Smollett's preface shows his thinking on the matter:

> A novel is a large diffused picture, comprehending the characters of life, disposed in different groups, and

> exhibited in various attitudes, for the purpose of a
> uniform plan, and general occurrence, to which every
> individual figure is subservient.

There is a rich man with a real son (Renaldo) and an adopted
son (Fathom). Fathom villainously ruins Renaldo's reputation with his father (Blifil and Tom Jones again). He persuades Renaldo and his mistress, Monimia, each that the
other is unfaithful, then attempts to seduce Monimia.
There is much more to it in the way of intrigue, battles,
duels, card-sharping and gaming: there are also incongruous anticipations of the 'Gothick' – a vigil at Monimia's
tomb, a clock striking twelve, an owl screeching from a
ruined battlement, an opening door, and a sexton with a
glimmering light to take us to the dreary aisle under which
the lady is interred. It is a strange episode in a book that
begins with a rollicking, mock-heroic account of Fathom's
infancy that is rich in irony.

Sir Launcelot Greaves (1762) does not quite come off. Sir
Launcelot, temporarily disappointed in love, turns Don
Quixote and crusades about the eighteenth-century countryside punishing corrupt justices and freeing innocent
prisoners. So quixotic is the study that it is not clear
whether Sir Launcelot is a noble knight putting the world
to rights (Sir Charles Grandison on tour) or a sentimental
lover in a state of temporary derangement. But in *Humphry
Clinker* (1771) Smollett recaptures the exciting vitality of
his earlier picaresque style. He manages to sustain a fairly
tightly knit scheme in spite of the problems of the picaresque
form in which changes of scene continually lead to new
faces and new situations; for instead of taking a hero across
the Continent, he drags a family around England and Scotland. This is virtually a plot on wheels. Smollett has already
delighted us by making his sailors talk like sailors, his
squires like squires and his lawyers like lawyers: now, using
the epistolary technique, he allows diverse members of a
family to characterize themselves by their own pens. Hence

the vigorous, no-nonsense style of irascible but benevolent Matthew Bramble, the lady's idiom in which Lydia delicately veils and unveils her heart, and the comic output of servant Win Jenkins's pen as she overflows with feelings and ideas beyond her power to express.

It is difficult to grade Smollett's novels *as novels*, but they are entertaining books, in part because of the lively, if inartistic, flow of comment upon anything and everything. The quality of Smollett's characterization (caricatured eccentrics especially) is undeniable, and its influence on Scott and Dickens notable. His *Travels in France and Italy* (1766), like Fielding's *Voyage to Lisbon,* is an invalid's record of a roaming search for health, but nothing like so good-tempered as Fielding's.

There is a case for turning our great triumvirate into a quadrumvirate by adding the name of Laurence Sterne (1713–68), Irish-born Yorkshire parson who published *The Life and Opinions of Tristram Shandy* two volumes at a time between 1759 and 1765, with a ninth volume added in 1767. The book exploits typographical tricks like asterisks, dashes, expurgations, catalogues, blank chapters and even a blank page. Its content is no less whimsical than its format. The hero is not born until Book IV: digressions outnumber relevancies; interrupted dialogue allows free rein to the associative flow of thought in the midst of such connected immediacies as the author sees fit to provide. Book I takes us straight into the household of Tristram's parents. There are two duties which Mr Shandy performs on the first Sunday night in each month, and one of them is to wind up the grandfather clock. The 'other little family concernments' which he conveniently associates with it (so as 'to get them out of the way at one time, and be no more plagued and pestered with them the rest of the month') are of such a personal nature that his wife has established a comparable association of ideas. Hence her disastrous question at the moment of Tristram's conception: 'Pray my dear ... have you forgot to wind up the clock?' 'Did ever woman, since

the creation of the world, interrupt a man with such a silly
question?' Mr Shandy rejoins. With this kind of progress in
biography it is not difficult to spend four books in coming
at the hero. And if the accident at his begetting deprives him
of vital spirits, a later accident deprives him of something
else. When Susannah finds the expected chamber pot missing from under the bed and holds her little charge out of
the window to relieve himself, the sash slaps down and
Tristram suffers the indignity of instant circumcision. But
'thousands suffer by choice, what I did by accident', Tristram consoles himself, while his father observes that he
'comes very hardly by his religious rites'. Never was anyone
initiated 'in so oblique and slovenly a manner'.

The Shandian world is buzzing with innuendoes, ambiguities and double entendres. Indecency is pervasive. Widow
Wadman's wooing of Uncle Toby is all the richer for the
equivocal interchanges in connection with the miniature
fortifications and the wound in his groin that are both the
products of his military zeal. Sterne's subtlety plays on our
sentiment as well as our sense of humour: his characters
are lovable as well as funny. The cheerful inconsequentiality that blends mischievous trifling with half indulged compassion is uniquely touching at its finest. *A Sentimental
Journey through France and Italy* (1768) develops this vein,
and the traveller's delight in what he encounters is contrasted with the peevishness of Smollett in his *Travels in
France and Italy*. Calling Smollett 'Smelfungus', Sterne
mocks his petulant grumbles about the discomforts of
travel:

> 'I'll tell it,' cried Smelfungus, 'to the world.' – 'You
> had better tell it,' said I, 'to your physician.'

Among the minor novelists who deserve mention, Robert
Paltock (1697–1767) published *Peter Wilkins* (1751), an autobiographical adventure story that takes us to a new world
inhabited by flying men and women. It has charm and
artistry, even if it lacks the immediacy of Defoe. Fanny

Burney (1752–1840), daughter of the musician, Dr Burney, scored a success when her novel, *Evelina, or The History of a Young Lady's Entry into the World*, was published anonymously in 1778. The epistolary style and the setting of contemporary life are in the Richardsonian tradition, though the plot culminates in the heroine's accession to heiressdom. Fanny Burney's later novels, *Cecilia* (1782) and *Camilla* (1796) are now unread; but not so her lively *Diary and Letters* which records events in a life so long that at the beginning she is being praised by Dr Johnson and at the end by Sir Walter Scott.

Another writer who published even before Fanny Burney, yet lived to be cherished by Scott (who dedicated *Waverley* to him) was Henry Mackenzie (1745–1831). His book *The Man of Feeling* (1771) exhibits the cult of sensibility. It is as much a collection of linked essays as a novel. The slender scheme of action can scarcely be called a plot. Harley, the man of feeling, is a country gentleman of decayed but still adequate means. He goes to town in the hope of getting a grant of land through an influential contact, fails by virtue of his delicacy and unselfishness; returns to his home and, after planning to marry Miss Walton, quickly falls ill and dies. The 'story' is presented as an incomplete manuscript that has accidentally come into the hands of the curate, who is introduced with the author at the beginning. The first chapter is headed 'Chapter XI' and opens in the middle of a conversation. We keep leaping over chapters 'missing' from the manuscript. For the most part we stroll about London and the countryside, meeting moral and social upsets which shock the heart – the over-sensitive girl reduced to prostitution, the peasant ruined by a rapacious landlord, and scholarly materialists who have gone insane. In the person of Harley, the gentler, tenderer virtues are cherished, not as principles or duties, but as the natural expression of a benevolent soul, fraught with pity and overflowing with sensibility. This promising experiment in a form halfway between the periodical essay and the fully plotted novel was followed in *The Man of the World* (1773) by a melodramatic study in villainy and degeneracy; for Sir Thomas Sindall is a blacker version of Goldsmith's Squire Thornhill (*The Vicar of Wakefield*) and the Annesley family's sufferings surpass those of the Primroses. But the moral stance is unequivocal: it involves a violent attack on indulgence currently extended to excesses on the part of the gentry. It was perhaps in reaction to this study in hair-raising malevolence that Mackenzie's next novel, *Julia de Roubigné* (1777), showed heart-rending tragedy overtaking characters who are led astray by their feelings. Mackenzie's later work as an essayist earned him the title, 'the Addison of the North'. The *Mirror* came out in 1779–80 and the *Lounger* from 1785 to 1787. It was in the latter in 1786 (No. 97, 9 December) that Mackenzie gave a warm welcome to Burns's first published poems.

Before we turn to the new movement represented by the 'Gothick Novel', mention may be made of Richard Cumberland (1732–1811) who, as a novelist, was content to keep the mid-century model ticking over in the eighties and nineties with *Arundel* (1789) and *Henry* (1795). Cumberland harks back conservatively to Fielding, Smollett and Richardson. *Henry* is a cross between Tom Jones and Joseph Andrews. Perilously handsome and engaging, he is assailed by attempts on his virtue from the gin-sodden reprobate, Jemima Cawdle, the pretty, naïve servant girl, Susan May, and the voluptuous Fanny Claypole. Their wiles are laughable. Susan's strategy is to bring her breasts into close proximity with the resolute hero's hands and eyes. Fanny Claypole, a more ingenious vamp, ambushes the hero in organized undress in a dark corridor during a thunderstorm. After this we have difficulty in accepting that Henry is morally obliged to marry her and in entering into his agonies over the dilemma. The *deus ex machina* is medical testimony that she was not *virgo intacta* to begin with.

The aristocratic dilettante Horace Walpole (1717–97) was one of the great letter-writers of his age. In his correspondence we get occasional reminders of the literary tensions that separated some of the great. Friend and admirer of Gray, he praises Milton, but Fielding is 'perpetually disgusting',[5] Boswell 'contemptible'[6] for his gross flattery of Johnson, and Johnson himself condemned for the 'fustian of his style' and 'the meanness of his spirit'.[7] This is the sensitive voice of the man whose tragedy of double incest, *The Mysterious Mother* (1768), provoked a less aristocratic brand of 'disgust'. His gothick villa, Strawberry Hill, betrayed the same taste for the antique as his gothick novel, *The Castle of Otranto* (1764). In this pseudo-medieval extravaganza Manfred holds the domain of Otranto through the villainy of his grandfather, who murdered Alphonso the Good. He rules in defiance of Frederick – apparently a nearer heir – and both are ignorant of the existence of Theodore, direct heir of the supposedly childless Alphonso. The unknown 'peasant' Theodore falls in love with Manfred's daughter Matilda, while Manfred wickedly persecutes Frederick's daughter Isabella with determination to marry her. He tries to hold her prisoner in the castle, which is linked happily to the nearby monastery by a mysterious underground passage, replete with trapdoors and by-ways. The fortress stands near rocky, cavernous fastnesses of terrifying gloom. With trumpet and tempestuous roar a cavalcade of chivalrous knighthood rides challengingly up to the gate, for far off in the Holy Land a lonely hermit, gaunt with emaciation, muttered deathbed directives that led to the exhuming of relevant prophetic instructions in verse. Fate eventually executes vengeance and the doom is provocatively advertised from the start. A mammoth helmet falls from the heavens in the courtyard and the companion spear is buried hundreds of miles away in Palestine: there is a statue whose nose bleeds, a portrait walks out of its frame, the hermit's skeleton puts in a return visit of exhortation like the Ghost in *Hamlet*,

[5] Letter to John Pinkerton, Esq., 26 June 1785.
[6] Letter to Miss Berry, 26 May 1791.
[7] Letter to the Reverend William Mann, 1774?

and there is the clash of celestial armour above the clouds. Ultimately the gigantic figure of Alphonso bursts the walls of Otranto with its magnitude before joining the form of Saint Nicholas in the firmament.

'The machinery is so violent that it destroys the effect it is intended to excite', wrote Clara Reeve (1729–1807), one of Walpole's disciples. She freely admits, however, that her own novel, *The Old English Baron* (first called *The Champion of Virtue: a Gothick Story*, 1777), 'is the literary offspring of the Castle of Otranto'. She is determined to 'unite the most attractive and interesting circumstances of the ancient Romance and the modern Novel' (preface to *The Old English Baron*). 'Unite' is the wrong word. The mixture is compounded of *Hamlet*, *The Castle of Otranto*, *Tom Jones* and *Clarissa Harlowe*, and it is highly indigestible. The Richardsonian standard of conversation and deportment, which envelops even the most perilous expeditions among the departed spirits, is absurdly incongruous. The haunted east wing of the family mansion, shut up from year's end to year's end, visited by no living soul, has no artistic connection with the day-to-day life of a polite eighteenth-century household that proceeds with disarming unconcern in other sections of the establishment. Moreover, the pervading vein of sensibility is embarrassing. This is hero Edmund being happily grateful:

> Edmund threw himself at their feet, and embraced their knees, but could not utter a word. They raised him between them, and strove to encourage him; but he threw himself into the arms of Sir Philip Harclay, deprived of strength and almost life. They supported him to a seat ...

Mrs Reeve's critical work in dialogue form, *The Progress of Romance* (1785), contains some interesting comments on contemporaries ('To praise the works of Mr *Richardson* is to hold a candle to the sun'). Her story, *The History of Charoba, Queen of Egypt*, published alongside it, is an adaptation of an ancient Egyptian tale that was later to be used in Landor's *Gebir*. As an exercise in the oriental it is scarcely to be compared with *Vathek* (1786) by William Beckford (1759–1844), which is steeped in the colour and magic of the Arabian Nights. Beckford too built his gothick mansion, Fonthill, and the Caliph Vathek's visit to the sub-terranean Hall of Eblis owes its magnificent atmosphere to the lofty, loud-echoing hall of Old Fonthill. So Beckford tells us in a letter to the Reverend Samuel Henley in 1782. The 'idea of the hall' was 'generated from my own. My imagination magnified it and coloured it with the Eastern character.'

Another writer whose imagination enabled her to drench her work in the poetry of atmosphere was Mrs Ann Radcliffe (1764–1823). Mrs Radcliffe's powers developed rapidly. In *The Castles of Athlin and Dunbayne* (1789) there is but slight promise of what was to follow, and *A Sicilian Romance* (1790) is excessively packed with action calculated to excite agitation and suspense; but *The Romance of the Forest* (1791) shows real gain in restraint and in the power to invest a tale with the perturbing atmosphere of mystery. In this book it is observed that 'ignorance of true pleasure more frequently than temptation to what is false, leads to vice'. Thus Mrs Radcliffe brings to the gothick novel a strain of sensibility that links her with Henry Mackenzie. She sees culture as the best security against vice. Her piety is en-tangled with sensitivity to natural beauty and the cultiva-tion of the affections. Her greatest work is *The Mysteries of Udolpho* (1794): her last novel, *The Italian* (1797), has the Inquisition, with all its sinister paraphernalia, as the basis of its dark and dire events.

The Mysteries of Udolpho is the story of Emily St Aubert. Bereft of her parents, she is carried off from the proximity of her loved friend, Valancourt, by the sinister Signor Mon-toni who has married her aunt. His castle in the Apennines is alive with dim figures in the moonlight and echoing groans where no man is. Equipped with trapdoors and secret corridors, 'its mouldering walls of dark grey stone' render it a 'gloomy and sublime object'. We first see its battlements 'tipped with splendour' above the purple-tinted walls as the sun fades to leave 'the whole edifice invested with the solemn duskiness of evening. Silent, lonely, and sublime ...' Mrs Radcliffe's landscapes are tremendous. Scott claimed for her the title, 'the first poetess of romantic fiction'.[8] Her scenes are shot through with a vein of exalted mysticism or melancholy nostalgia. Childhood memories, recollections of the lost hopes of early youth, the sense of time's transience, infuse her scenes with a flavour of bitter-sweet regret. And as scenery acquires emotional ambience, so do the characters. Montoni is haughty, grave, reserved, discontented, fiery; yet these adjectives convey little of what he means to us until we add the word 'fearful'. He fore-shadows the Byronic hero. Mrs Radcliffe fastens the reader's attention by mysteries that tease his curiosity and play on his imaginative sensitivities. Of the hundred and nine mysteries in the book many lead nowhere and are feebly related to the central plot. Others reside in hints and sus-picions so nebulous that it is a mystery to know what the mystery is. There is a let-down at the end when mysteries are cleared up and preternatural possibilities are eliminated with hygienic thoroughness.

It is said that a reading of *The Mysteries of Udolpho* spurred Matthew Gregory Lewis (1775–1818) to take up again the manuscript of his novel, *The Monk*, that he had put aside, and to finish it for publication (1796). Of Mrs Rad-cliffe's many imitators he was the most original and powerful. He also published collections of ballads, *Tales of Terror* (1799) and *Tales of Wonder* (1801), and to the latter Sir Walter Scott contributed original work (e.g. *The Fire-King* and *Glenfilas*) as well as translated verse (*The Wild Hunts-man* from the German of Bürger). *The Monk* gained the admiration of Shelley and Byron too. Its power is as unques-

---

[8] *Lives of the Novelists.*

tionable as its extravagance. Ambrosio is a Capuchin abbot in Madrid, renowned for his ascetic saintliness. Matilda, a fiend in human form (we do not know this until the end), disguises herself as a boy to gain admittance to the monastery. There she plays on Ambrosio's weakness and vanity, and gradually seduces him. She drives him from crime to crime: he seduces his penitent, Antonia, kills her mother, Elvira, and later Antonia herself. Incest is added to his sins, for he proves to be the long-lost son of Antonia's mother. The psychological sequence is valid. Ambrosio's monastic career has been an unnatural repression of a vigorous, sensitive personality under the impetus of the very vanity that Matilda plays on. At the end, faced by the Inquisition, he makes a last desperate bid to buy safety by the sale of his soul; but the powers of darkness seize him.

While Lewis's control of atmosphere and exploitation of suspense owe much to Mrs Radcliffe, his attitude to the preternatural is very different. He uses the paraphernalia of sorcery – magic mirrors, charmed herbs and conjuration of evil spirits – and takes it seriously. The technique is the reverse of Mrs Radcliffe's in that, in the celebrated story of the 'Bleeding Nun', initial scepticism gives place to mystery and belief and not *vice versa*. The preternaturalism runs riot: there is little finesse in Lewis's assault upon nerve and sensibility. An ice-cold phantom breathes on our faces; spirits rise in thunder and fire from the bowels of the earth; moans echo through the murky, damp ruins of subterranean charnel vaults. There is Lucifer before us, naked and beautiful, a bright star sparkling on his forehead and fires playing around his hair; there is Raymond under the ruined moonlit towers of Lindenberg receiving into his arms the shadowy figure of a nun, a white veil shrouding her features and her dress dripping blood; there is Ambrosio with his knee on Elvira's stomach, her face black with the agony of strangulation. The polysyllabic verbosity is often bad, yet the story compels quick reading and consequent connivance. Lewis wrote for the stage too. *The Castle Spectre* was put on at Drury Lane in 1797 and *Adelgitha* was published in 1807.

We may conclude our survey of this period by reference to a few novels that carry a message. Charles Johnstone's (?1719–?1800) sharply satirical tale, *Chrysal, or the Adventures of a Guinea*, published in the 1760s (the manuscript had been read and recommended by Dr Johnson), was a highly successful though bitter and sarcastic assault on the public and political scene of his day. The scurrility to which Johnstone descended, the lack of humour and of magnanimity, and the sheer topicality of its detail, have prevented the book from keeping its appeal. Robert Bage (1728–1801) wrote *Mount Henneth* (1781) and *Barham Downs* (1784), but is chiefly remembered for *Man as he is* (1792) and *Hermsprong, or Man as he is not* (1796). He was a sceptical materialist with a revolutionary philosophy and his books were written with a propagandist purpose. They were criticized for the laxity of his views on female behaviour and marriage, as well as for idealization of the poorer classes and crude satire on the rich. Hermsprong, the perfect man, is wholly a creature of reason. And in this respect Bage's work touches that of William Godwin (1756–1836), author of *Political Justice*. Godwin's two propaganda novels were *Caleb Williams* (1794) and *St Leon* (1799). Caleb Williams is a young man of humble birth who becomes secretary to Falkland and discovers that his master has a murder on his conscience. Falkland thereafter persecutes Williams with persistent cunning without destroying his loyalty. Williams's nobility of character eventually causes Falkland to throw himself into his arms and confess. 'Williams, said he, you have conquered! I see too late the greatness and elevation of your mind.' Williams at the last recognizes the quality of Falkland, whose 'crime' had been to get rid of an arrogant tyrant; and the Godwinian message is pressed home: 'But of what use are talents and sentiments in the corrupt wilderness of human society?'

15
The close of the eighteenth century

We reach the 'Eve of Romanticism', yet the phrase must be used as the label of a period, not of a literary movement. There were writers productive contemporaneously who could scarcely be bracketed together except by the calendar (Sheridan and Cowper, for instance). Moreover anticipations of the Romantic reaction against the predominant tastes of eighteenth-century culture were not confined to the last quarter of the century. The passion for the primitive in the 'Ossianic' literature is closely related to the taste for the archaic in Mrs Radcliffe and Keats. There was an enthusiast for genuine archaism in Dr Johnson's own circle: Bishop Thomas Percy (1729–1811) issued his *Reliques of Ancient English*

Poetry in 1765. Percy's versions of old ballads and metrical romances (like *Chevy Chase* and *The Rising of the North*) nourished the reviving cult of the past. The power of its grip may be measured by the tragic career of Thomas Chatterton (1752–70) who passed off his fabricated 'medieval' poems as the work of 'Thomas Rowley'. What Chatterton read in the library of St Mary Redcliffe, Bristol, fused with an astonishing gift for the reproduction of an idealized verbal antiquity:

> In Virgyne the sweltrie sun gan sheene,
> And hotte upon the mees did caste his raie;
> The apple rodded from its palie greene,
> And the mole peare did bende the leafy spraie ...
> *(An Excelente Balade of Charitie)*

Chatterton's suicide, in despair and poverty, at the age of eighteen turned him into a legend of the sensitive young poet at loggerheads with the world.

A career vastly different from Chatterton's began almost simultaneously and will illustrate the diversity of the current literary scene. Richard Brinsley Sheridan (1751–1816) was as fervent a devotee of the living world of society about him as Chatterton was of an idealized past. His own story too is a romantic drama. When Elizabeth Linley, famous soprano and delight of Bath society, was under menacing pressure from a persistent and unwanted lover, Major Matthews – and was even driven to the stage of considering suicide – Richard carried her off to France, married her secretly in Calais simply to safeguard her reputation, then deposited her in a convent. Her family brought her back; Sheridan humiliated Matthews at sword point by breaking his sword in pieces; then, in a formal duel which turned into a scuffle, was himself seriously wounded. Hearing the news, Elizabeth involuntarily cried out, 'My husband!' and would have made her secret public had it not been assumed that she was overwrought; but in fact opposition was eventually overcome and the couple were officially married in 1773, just about a year after the ceremony at Calais.

Sheridan's comedy, *The Rivals* (1775), carries echoes of this romantic story. Though the play was a failure on the first night, Sheridan quickly revised it and it became an instant success. The delightful posture of Lydia Languish, whose romantic sensibilities demand that she marry without her aunt's consent and thus forfeit most of her fortune, is balanced by the shrewd contrivances of Captain Absolute, the officially acceptable suitor, who pretends to be a half-pay ensign 'Beverley' in order to match up to Lydia's dreams of disadvantageous passion. The ironies and situational topsy-turvydoms latent in the contrast are fully exploited in a plot of polished perfection. The high comedy has the verve and clean-cut theatricality of Farquhar and Vanbrugh, yet it is free of indecent innuendo. The tone is fresh, youthful and unsophisticated. We are not involved much in psychological sympathy, but we are vastly amused by the neat human caricatures – the fiery Irishman, Sir Lucius O'Trigger, the unheroic country suitor, Bob Acres, and the wordy Mrs Malaprop, who thinks her niece not wholly 'illegible' as a bride for the Captain.

Sheridan's success with Sir Lucius encouraged him to follow up *The Rivals* with a short Irish study, *St Patrick's Day; or the Scheming Lieutenant*. A more venturesome and profitable project followed when he collaborated with his father-in-law in the opera *The Duenna* (1775). Sheridan succeeded Garrick as manager of Drury Lane Theatre in 1776 and adapted Vanbrugh's *The Relapse* to the more refined taste of the day as *A Trip to Scarborough* (1777). The same year saw the production of the comic masterpiece, *The School for Scandal*. The ingredients of this comedy combine into a gilt-edged guarantee of success. Charles Surface is the good-hearted but reckless hero, and Joseph, his elder brother, the hypocritical apparent pillar of rectitude. They are rivals for Maria, one wanting her heart, the other her fortune, and become competitors too for the inheritance from their rich

uncle, who arrives home from India and puts their respective
characters to the test. The upshot is hilarious.

Sheridan's last original play was the burlesque, *The Critic;
or a Tragedy Rehearsed* (1779), in which the target is the
contemporary theatre. It includes the rehearsing, under critical and authorial commentary, of a play within the play,
'The Spanish Armada'. At a memorable point in this tragedy
the Governor of Tilbury Port has to check the flow of his
unhappy daughter's Cassandra-like prevision of cumulative
doom. 'Hold, daughter,' he interrupts:

> The Spanish fleet thou canst not see – because
> – It is not yet in sight.

The tragedy also contains a standard discovery scene, which
reveals to a Justice and his Lady that a prisoner is their long-
lost son. His name is Tom Jenkins; his father lived in
Rochester and was a fishmonger: the accumulation of such
factual detail confirms a gipsy's prophecy. 'Prepare!' cries
the Justice. 'I do', says the prisoner. And the news is
broken:

> I am thy father; here's thy mother; there
> Thy uncle – this thy first cousin, and those
> Are all your near relations.

Sir Fretful Plagiary in *The Critic* is a caricature of Richard
Cumberland (author of *Henry*) whose serio-comedies *The
Brothers* (1769), *The West Indian* (1771), *The Fashionable
Lover* (1772) and *The Choleric Man* (1775) competently illustrate the unexciting mediocrity of the late eighteenth-
century theatre, Sheridan excepted. The mixture of melodramatic events and virtuous sermonizing is a long way
from the effervescent sparkle of wit and action in Sheridan.
At the end of *The Brothers* Belfield senior, who has victim-
ized his younger brother, is suddenly faced by his faithful
and forsaken wife, and collapses in penitence: 'How shall
I look upon you? ... Oh! take me to your arms, and, in that
soft shelter, let me find forgiveness and protection.' 'Be this

your only punishment! and this!' says his wife Violetta. He comes out of it much better than Joseph Surface. 'My whole life shall be employed in acts of justice and atonement', he concludes. And we ascend to a similar moral plane at the end of *The Choleric Man*:

> If marriage ever shall regain its dignity in this degenerate age, it must be by the union of such hearts as these.

There is an interesting comment on this taste for serio-comedy at the end of *The School for Wives* (1774) by Hugh Kelly (1739–77) when Lady Mildew says, 'Why, the modern critics say, that the only business of comedy is to make people laugh', and Belville replies, 'That is degrading the dignity of letters exceedingly, as well as lessening the utility of the stage. A good comedy ... should be directed to the noblest purpose.'

A comparable desire to instruct is found in the work of Thomas Holcroft (1745–1809), but his message is social and revolutionary rather than moral. His novel, *Hugh Trevor* (1794), bears comparison with Godwin's *Caleb Williams*. His play, *The Road to Ruin* (1792), is a sentimental study of a young man, Harry Dornton, who is finally prevented from sacrificing himself in marriage to a rich widow out of altruistic desire to obtain money needed by his father:

> You have a generous and a noble nature! But your generosity would have proved more pernicious than even your dissipation. No misfortune, no not the beggary and ruin of a father, could justify so unprincipled a marriage.

The closing decades of the century had something more substantial than these platitudinous solemnities to offset the wit of Sheridan and the extravagance of gothick novelists. While Sheridan forsook play-writing for a parliamentary career, William Cowper (1731–1800) turned his back on a career in law to shelter his sensitivities in a life of simple domestic routine. The loss of his mother in childhood, the sufferings he endured at a boarding school, and the failure of his love for his cousin Theodora had together contributed to a depression in which he attempted suicide. On recovery, he settled in the home of Morley and Mary Unwin in Huntingdon. When Mrs Unwin was left a widow, Cowper moved with her to Olney, where the evangelical clergyman, John Newton, exercised an influence that perhaps contributed to the return of his mania, a mania that involved the notion that he was damned. Mary Unwin wisely encouraged him to write: so too did another lady who befriended him, Lady Austen; and he knew some years of comparative tranquillity and fruitfulness before Mary's death, in 1794, plunged him into a black silence from which he never recovered.

The hymns Cowper contributed to *Olney Hymns* were composed in 1771 and 1772. Some of them have that fine blend of sparseness, dignity and simplicity that makes for the best in hymn-writing. The volume includes 'Oh! for a closer walk with God' and 'There is a fountain fill'd with blood'. In 'Hark, my soul! it is the Lord' the lucid use of dialogue, image and frank self-exposure represents a rare vein of controlled evangelical fervour. The rhetoric ('Higher than the heights above, Deeper than the depths beneath'), as in 'Jesus, where'er thy people meet':

> Lord, we are few, but thou art near;
> Nor short thine arm, nor deaf thine ear,

has an Anglo-Saxon sturdiness that resists submergence in sentimental singability. The sixteen successive monosyllables in the two lines above point to Cowper's conscious craftsmanship as surely as does the fine counterpoint of rhythm with metre. There is a rich literary culture at the back of Cowper's simplicities of image and rhythm.

It is to Lady Austen's happy suggestion that we owe our delight in Cowper's ballad, *John Gilpin* (1782), and in *The Task* (1785). In a burst of fun the ballad tells how Gilpin, a London tradesman, borrows a horse so that he can have an anniversary wedding lunch with his wife at 'The Bell' at Edmonton. Mrs Gilpin goes ahead in a coach. Her husband follows on the borrowed mare, but it is obstinately determined to go to its own master's house at Ware, and is then equally determined to race back to London. On the outward and return journeys alike Gilpin flashes past his waiting wife.

Asked by Lady Austen to write about the sofa in blank verse, Cowper obliged to the tune of some 5,000 lines disposed in six books. *The Task* is a discursive exercise in which the poet mingles descriptive writing with reflections on the world around him and on the human lot, under the successive titles *The Sofa, The Time-Piece, The Garden, The Winter Evening, The Winter Morning Walk* and *The Winter Walk at Noon*. The meandering poetic garrulity is finely relaxed and insinuating at its best, flaccid or prosy at its worst. The poem is sprinkled with memorable lines, many a one summing up an important theme in the fabric of its reflections:

> God made the country, and man made the town ...
> (I. 749)
> England, with all thy faults, I love thee still ...
> (II. 206)

These are the more obvious expressions of simple attachments; but there are more indignant humanitarian convictions:

> I would not have a slave to till my ground ...   (II. 29)

and more eclectic delights:

> There is a pleasure in poetic pains
> Which only poets know ...
> (II. 285–6)

There is a devastating attack on vain and affected clergy, a passage on the limitations of human knowledge, and a deeply personal picture of himself as the 'stricken deer, that left the herd'. Wounded, he was found by the divine archer, himself scarred in hands and side, and restored by the drawing out of the darts.

The mood shifts and veers delightfully. The garden, the fireside and the teapot get the same poetic attention as do the external world of nature and the larger themes of political freedom, divine creation and the problem of evil. In the last book there is much about discerning the face of God in nature, much too about cruelty to animals, and finally a Christian vision of the restoration of all things with a cry of invocation and acclamation to Christ the King:

> Come then, and added to thy many crowns,
> Receive yet one, the crown of all the earth ...
>
> (VI. 855–6)

Cowper's lyric gift flared into excellence once or twice in poems like *The Poplar Field* and *To Mary*; but otherwise what most commands attention is the cry *de profundis*, *The Castaway*, a cry springing from despair not long before his death. The poem draws a dreadful parallel between a man washed overboard at sea and his own spiritual case, perishing alone 'whelm'd in deeper gulphs' than the drowning castaway.

A famous phrase in *The Task* extols 'the cups that cheer / But not inebriate', and Cowper's contemporary, George Crabbe (1754–1832), began his poetic career with a poem called *Inebriety* (1775). It was a flat and prosaic beginning for a writer from that ostensibly flat and prosaic town of Aldeburgh on the Suffolk coast. Leaving for London, Crabbe managed to interest Edmund Burke in some samples of his poetry. Through Burke's kindness the contact brought him an introduction to Sir Joshua Reynolds, then to Dr Johnson, who read the manuscript of *The Village*, praised it and made a few improvements to the text. It was published in 1783, but in the meantime Crabbe had been ordained, had married, had obtained a living in Lincolnshire and had published *The Library* (1781) anonymously. *The Village* is a discursive poem in two short books, mingling description and reflection in the manner of Cowper but in sturdy heroic couplets. Crabbe pictures country life with an unromantic awareness of its harshness and its evils:

> I paint the Cot
> As Truth will paint it and as Bards will not.

He has sought the simple life of nature and found that:

> Rapine and Wrong and Fear usurp'd her place
> And a bold, artful, surly, savage race.

There was a gap of twenty years between *The Village* and *The Newspaper* (1785) and the publication of the volume containing *The Parish Register* in 1807. In this the priest-poet surveys the 'simple Annals' of his parish poor, the year's baptisms, weddings and funerals providing his starting points. Thus we are launched on a series of records that do full justice to life's ironies and frustrations, with an adequate quota of girls seduced and prostituted, couples ill-matched, cruelties indulged and careers awry. The sad tale of 'Phoebe Dawson' is masterly. We see her in the full pride of maidenhood and are jolted without pause into sharing her forsakenness and poverty as mother and wife. Fox had this story read to him on his deathbed.

Three large poems followed, *The Borough* (1810), *Tales in Verse* (1812) and *Tales of the Hall* (1819). *The Borough* consists of twenty-four 'Letters' that picture the life and personalities of the township. In *Prisons* (Letter XXIII) the account of the damp, noisome and sunless place is characteristic of Crabbe's unblinking confrontation with the real world, a confrontation that marks his work with a sombre undertone of melancholy. He will not play down life's bitterness for the common man:

> 'Tis well – that Man to all the varying states
> Of good and ill his mind accommodates;
> He not alone progressive grief sustains,
> But soon submits to unexperienced pains.

The biographical sketches touch the most sensitive nerves of pessimism by revealing suffering that is little modified by compassion. Some, like the *Life of Blaney* (Letter XIV), a rake's progress, have the high colouring of melodrama. But in others, like *The Parish Clerk* (Letter XIX), subtlety matches relentlessness and intensifies the sombre commentary. For Jachin is a grave, upright detester of Satan, conscious of his virtues; but 'desire of gain' corrupts the virtue which the stratagems of the villagers have failed to seduce, and he begins to steal from the collection plate. The tale moves to a grim climax of public unmasking. Even more tense and profound is the famous story of Peter Grimes (Letter XXII), son of a strict father, youthful rebel turned surly neurotic by the combination of remorse (for knocking down his now dead father), shame and discomfiture with self and society. He hires poor boys to work for him as a fisherman, ill-treats them, and is virtually made a murderer by their deaths. The local inhabitants turn on him, and his destiny is worked out with terrifying retributive thoroughness as he is hounded into solitude and driven mad by hallucinatory visitations. Montagu Slater used the poem to make the text of Benjamin Britten's opera.

The *Tales in Verse* show Crabbe's technical powers at their height. Their strength lies in narrative technique, management of dialogue, exploitation of the dramatic and rhetorical possibilities of the couplet, and above all in the deftly economic concentration on lively incident and verbal interchange. There is variety of tone too: a free rein is given to mellow humour in *The Frank Courtship*. Sybil Kindred's strict Puritan father destines her for the earnest, upright son of a co-religionist. Sybil bridles at the threat, determined that the man who aspires to her shall love with awesome devotion. The mother can see no prospect of good Josiah filling this role:

> 'He kneel and tremble at a thing of dust!
> 'He cannot, child:' the Child replied, 'He must.'

This comic potential of the crisp couplet is something Crabbe hands on to Byron. *Tales of the Hall* (1819) repeats the mixture as before: there is tragedy and bitterness, comedy and pathos.

By the time we take leave of Crabbe he has become a nineteenth-century poet; yet a poet with whom it is natural to compare him was born five years after him and died nearly forty years before him. Robert Burns (1759–96) was rooted in Ayrshire as firmly as Crabbe was rooted in Suffolk, and his knowledge of the life of the poor was even more intimate in that he never attained security himself. The struggle against poverty, by unsuccessful farming and by working for the Excise, ultimately broke his health. In *The Life of George Crabbe By His Son* (1834) we are told, 'Of Burns he was ever as enthusiastic an admirer as the warmest of his own countrymen.' But John Gibson Lockhart (in his *Life of Robert Burns*, 1828) asserts firmly that Crabbe's unflattering portrait of *Edward Shore* (Tale XI of *Tales in Verse*), the genius who runs to seed, is coloured by knowledge of Burns's career.

Myths woven round the figure of Burns make it important to try to disentangle the man and the poet from the cartoonery of offended moralists and from the idolatry of the 'Ploughman Poet' cult. Admittedly Burns himself by his poetic stance encouraged the legend of the unlettered spokesman of natural passion. In the *Epistle to J. Lapraik* (1785) he lambasts superior critics and adds:

> Give me ae spark o' Nature's fire!
> That's a' the learning I desire;
> Then though I trudge, through dub an' mire
> > At pleugh or cart,
> My Muse, though hamely in attire,
> > May touch the heart.

But the 'simple, untutored Bard' legend will not do. In the letter to Dr Moore of 2 August 1787, Burns explains how the

son of a struggling cottar came to find his 'highest enjoy-
ment' in 'love and poetry'. It was meeting with Fergusson's
Scottish poems that moved him to emulation. In his progress
through poverty, illness, misfortune and insanity to death
at the age of twenty-four, and in the enormous promise held
out by his work, Robert Fergusson (1750–74) had been something of a Scottish Chatterton. The satiric vein, the social
criticism and the moral bite in Fergusson's powerful vernacular verses proved a heady diet for Burns:

> Ye wha are fain to hae your name
> Wrote i' the bonny book o' Fame,
> Let Merit nae pretension claim
>   To laurel'd wreath,
> But hap ye weel, baith back and wame,
>   In gude Braid Claith.

> (Fergusson's Braid Claith)

The volume that won Burns fame in Scotland and acceptance in Edinburgh, *Poems Chiefly in the Scottish Dialect*
(1786), contained that sentimental if highly sensitive picture
of the homely, pious, peasant family, *The Cottar's Saturday
Night*. Though we are reminded of Henryson by the sight of
the 'miry beasts' and 'blackening trains o' craws' on a winter
evening when 'November chill blaws loud wi' angry sough',
we are soon going home with the toil-worn cottar, to be
greeted by gleeful toddlers, clean hearth-stone, bonnily
blinking ingle and 'thriftie wifie's smile'. There is every
prescribed ingredient of sentimentality from beautiful bash-
ful daughter Jenny in the first flush of love, to Scotch por-
ridge for supper, paternal Bible-reading and family worship, yet Burns's genius infuses it all with a genuine fervour
for what is good and happy, with love for his native soil
and with prayer for the blessing of sweet content on the
'hardy sons of rustic toil'.

By contrast the fierce ironies that make *Holy Willie's
Prayer* such a devastating attack on pious hypocrisy are
those of a scathing satirist. Self-condemned by his own

thanksgiving for the grace that makes him a 'shinin' light', Holy Willie rejoices in his elect status and calls down divine wrath on his own and the Lord's enemies. The liturgical tone adds bitter force to the irony. *The Holy Fair* makes its point at the expense of ecclesiastical rigorism and orthodoxy in a mellower vein by setting Hell-fire preaching in the context of holiday junketing and those preoccupations that make up the spirit and colour of life. Obsessive religiosity is deflated by the company it is made to keep. Burns weakens the power he attacks by implicitly downgrading it. And when he flays the wealthy and the pious in poems like 'Is there for honest poverty?' and *Address to the Unco Guid*, he does not snipe from below but blisters from above. But Burns's emotional assault upon the comforts of religion, wealth and social status is contained among the responses of a writer whose large humanity cannot be grafted onto a radical cause. Poems like *To A Mountain Daisy* and *To a Mouse* lead direct from finely observed wonder at the bonnie gem and the timorous beastie to reflections on the precariousness of human happiness. We are at grips with the human, not the social, situation.

Finally Burns is the spontaneous singer of tender love, voicing its irrepressible raptures, its heart-catching vicissitudes, and also its tender homely stabilities when it survives the bread-and-butter years of marriage. 'Oh, my luve's like a red, red rose', *Highland Mary*, 'Ye flowery banks o' bonnie Doon', 'John Anderson my jo, John' and the many, many Scots songs he collected and rewrote represent him as a lyric poet able to catch in unforgettable words such moments and moods as belong to all men, and of which they will sing if they sing at all.

The most revolutionary of the poets of the period, William Blake (1757–1827), was revolutionary over such a wide field – social, artistic and philosophical – that he scarcely gained a public at all during his lifetime. The Ossianic poems influenced him and so too did the revived interest in the ballad, but his innovations in the use of rhythms and symbolism separate him sharply from the central eighteenth-century literary tradition. With the publication of *Songs of Innocence* (1789) the new and powerful poetic voice was unmistakable, and Blake illustrated the volume himself. Wonder and delight, simplicity and deep compassion – these qualities are caught in lines that glitter with flashes of insight. Poems like *The Lamb* ('Little Lamb, who made thee?'), *The Little Black Boy* (' ... And I am black, but O! my soul is white') and *The Chimney Sweeper* have a potency that transcends sentimentality. The boy sweeper dreams of thousands of sweepers locked up in black coffins:

> And by came an Angel who had a bright key,
> And he opened the coffins & set them all free.

The *Songs of Experience* (1794) counterbalance the *Songs of Innocence*. Into similar (and sometimes parallel) lyrical forms intrudes a note of evil – especially the evil of selfishness, poverty and insensitively rigidified religiosity.

> Love seeketh only Self to please,
> To bend another to Its delight,
> Joys in another's loss of ease,
> And builds a Hell in Heaven's despight.

Such is the Pebble's reply to the converse acclaim of unselfish love voiced by the Clod in *The Clod and the Pebble*. Not that unsullied wonder is absent from this collection, for it includes the magnificent poem *The Tyger* ('Tyger! Tyger! burning bright') in which there is dichotomy, but positive not negative ('Did he who made the Lamb make thee?')

The poems in this volume indicate the direction of Blake's thinking that is developed in his prophetic books like *The Marriage of Heaven and Hell* (1790), *Visions of the Daughters of Albion* (1793), *The Book of Urizen* (1794) and *The Book of Los* (1795). Blake's poetry is not a record of men and women studied and of nature observed: it is a vision registered and affirmed. The idiom is that of a visionary. 'He stammers into a speech of angels, as if just awakening out of Paradise', says Arthur Symons.[1] *The Marriage of Heaven and Hell* was published by Blake's own method of engraving the text and illustrations, and colouring the copies by hand. It overturns orthodoxies of religion and morality with startling oracular aphorisms:

> Prisons are built with stones of Law, Brothels with bricks of Religion.
>
> The nakedness of woman is the work of God.
>
> The tygers of wrath are wiser than the horses of instruction.
>
> Sooner murder an infant in its cradle than nurse un-acted desires.

Such are the proverbs of Hell collected by the poet as he walks 'among the fires of hell, delighted with the enjoyments of Genius, which to Angels look like torment and insanity'. Blake's mystical insight coexists with a passion for freedom and a conviction of the sacredness of instinct. His rapturous sense of life's wonder and delight is offset by harsh criticism of social institutions and human selfishness for their corruption of the spirit and for the cruelty of poverty. The combination in Blake himself of an extraordinary innocence and a fierce creative energy is closely related to that strain in his philosophy which determined him to link the beauty and purity of the heavenly with the dynamic power that is too readily associated with Hell. The cherished (if apocryphal) picture of Blake and his wife sitting naked in their garden, reading *Paradise Lost* aloud under their vine ('Come in, it is only Adam and Eve', he is reputed to have said in greeting a caller) does justice to his unapologetic idealism.

The difficulty of Blake resides in his invention of a new symbolism by which he gave personification and voice not

[1] Arthur Symons, *William Blake* (Archibald Constable, London, 1904).

only to abstract concepts like energy and prophecy, and to natural agencies like the spirit of water or of the earth, but also to forces representative of current thinking and contemporary civilization – hence his nymphs of the mills caught up in the bitter pains of mechanization. The fabrication of this symbolic scheme reaches labyrinthine proportions as Blake works through to the last great poems in this vein, *Milton* (1804) and *Jerusalem* (1804). The fascination the occult systems have for fervent disciples is undeniable, but critical opinion is divided as to whether his work surpasses that of almost all English writers except the few greatest, or whether his genius suffered, in T. S. Eliot's words, from the lack of 'a framework of accepted and traditional ideas which would have prevented him from indulging in a philosophy of his own'.

The question does not belittle Blake's immense imaginative power, though the repetitiousness of his energetic rhetoric is no recipe for clarity or for neatness of design. Of course Blake's oppositions between the native goodness of man and the corruptions of society, between the full range of imaginative and emotional expressiveness and the inhibiting effects of the rational and the institutional, intensify familiar late eighteenth-century drifts towards the cultivation of sensibility and feeling. But Blake's sense of man's nature as being dismembered by conventional religious and social codes, especially his protest against the severance of the spiritual from the physical, the energic from the rational, is perceptively diagnostic of the human condition. Blake's religion of the imagination cherishes a human wholeness comprehensive enough to embrace forces that reason and tradition have regarded as irreconcilable. The question remains: to what extent are the missing restraints of economy, discipline and submission to the common mind of our culture damaging to its poetic exposition?

16
Wordsworth and the Romantics

Our survey of the literature of the second half of the eighteenth century has touched on many a tendency anticipatory of the Romantic Movement. Much that was new and distinctive in the work of Burns and Crabbe, Cowper and Chatterton, Radcliffe and Walpole, marked them as precursors of Romanticism. Extensions of literary concern in the direction of passion and mystery, imagination and creativity, and towards the fuller exploration of man and nature, may be subsumed under the label 'Romantic'. So too may movements away from the conventionalized forms of eighteenth-century literary expression. The concept 'Romantic' is wide because the movement was a rich one, involving some of the most exciting literary personalities of our history.

William Wordsworth (1770–1850) was born in Cockermouth and educated at Hawkshead near Esthwaite Water. After studying at Cambridge, he visited France, was infected with revolutionary fervour ('Bliss was it in that dawn to be alive') and fell in love with a royalist surgeon's daughter, Annette Vallon, by whom he had a child. (Some impression of the tensions caused by this liaison can be gathered from the poem, *Vaudracour and Julia*.) The Terror that succeeded the Revolution reinforced private distresses and unhinged the young poet for a time. He toyed with the philosophy of reason expounded in Godwin's *Political Justice*, and vented his pessimism in *Guilt and Sorrow*, a narrative of suffering, and *The Borderers*, a tragedy of treachery, but he recovered his balance fully under the influence of nature and with the help of his sister, Dorothy, whose *Journals* prove how indebted he was to her sensitivity and perceptiveness ('She gave me eyes, she gave me ears', he said in *The Sparrow's Nest*). Friendship with Coleridge strengthened his inspiration, while a bequest from a friend, Raisley Calvert, freed him from financial worry. Intimacy with Coleridge bore fruit in their publication of *Lyrical Ballads* (1798). Later, in his work of philosophical and literary criticism, *Biographia Literaria* (1817), Coleridge was to recall how the two poets decided to collaborate, the one to deal convincingly with incidents and agents 'in part at least supernatural', the other with subjects 'chosen from ordinary life'. It was for an enlarged edition of the joint volume, published in 1800, that Wordsworth wrote the famous preface to the *Lyrical Ballads* in which he attacked the 'gaudiness and inane phraseology' of much current poetic diction, pressed for use in poetry of 'a selection of the language really spoken by men', asserted that 'all good poetry is the spontaneous overflow of powerful feelings', and made the climactic claim that 'Poetry is the breath and spirit of all knowledge ... the first and last of all knowledge ... immortal as the heart of man'.

In earnest realization of his grandiose conception of the poet's role, Wordsworth started work on *The Prelude* in 1798. Intended to be the introductory portion of a long work, *The Recluse*, it undertook a preliminary survey of the growth of the poet's mind and powers. As such, it became itself a full-length study and, together with *The Excursion* (1814), represents what the whole project eventually came to. In the first two books of *The Prelude* Wordsworth traces the nourishing of the poetic spirit in childhood as he was 'fostered alike by beauty and by fear' at the hands of Nature herself. Nature educated him by awe and fear, for 'low breathings' and 'sounds of undistinguishable motion' pursued him after he had poached someone else's trapped bird at night, and a huge peak 'upreared its head', towering between him and the stars, when he rowed in a stolen boat. Nature, first a background of delight to boyish games, is eventually loved 'for her own sake' and becomes a means of spiritual exaltation. It is 'bliss ineffable' to feel the 'sentiment of Being' spread over all that moves and all that seems still, and to commune in love and adoration with 'every form of creature'. Philosophical reflection is sparked off by recorded instances of Nature's touch upon him in boyhood, and they are some of the finest things in our poetry. In later books Wordsworth pursues the story of his life at Cambridge, his reading, his travels on the Continent, his residence in London and then in France at the time of the Revolution. Here, we are told, his heart and love were given to the people. Back in England, when France became an enemy country, he found himself rejoicing in military reverses suffered by his own countrymen. But the Terror changed all that, and the subsequent disillusionment and spiritual rootlessness was healed only when 'Nature's self, / By all varieties of human love / Assisted', led him back to the peace and understanding found in reconciliation between heart and head. In Books XII and XIII Wordsworth records the full recovery of spiritual poise and strength and he dedicates himself to sing of the heart of man as 'found among the best of those who live' ... 'In Nature's presence', deeply aware that Nature has the power 'to breathe / Grandeur upon the very humblest face / Of human life'.

It must be accepted that Wordsworth's best poetry revolves around himself, but then his deepest personal concerns reach out to the whole body of Nature and to his fellow creatures contained within her embrace. The *Lines composed a few miles above Tintern Abbey*, included in *Lyrical Ballads*, track in fine summary the autobiographical development surveyed in *The Prelude*. The mastery of blank verse in these two poems is something unmatched since Milton for individuality and flexibility. A work of comparable distinction, the *Ode: Intimations of Immortality* (1807), is a subtle fabric of rhymed and rhythmic architecture connecting 'the glory and the dream' of childhood with the notion of human pre-existence elsewhere, and presenting the child's uncertainty of footing in this life as evidence of an otherworldly affiliation. We come from God, our home: we come 'trailing clouds of glory' with 'shadowy recollections' that illuminate our lives. And our early joy in natural beauty is movingly enriched by passing experiences of man's mortal lot.

Wordsworth, at his finest, has a sturdy simplicity of idiom that matches the profound solemnities of country life he so feelingly recaptures. *Michael* (1800) tells the story of a shepherd and his wife who part with their dear son Luke at a time of financial stress, for Michael cannot bear that his fields should pass into a stranger's hands, and there is hope that Luke will make money in the town. The boy goes to the bad there. The sheepfold father and son were building together remains symbolically unfinished, while the parents die, the estate is sold and the cottage ploughed over. There can be few more moving poems in our literature. But Wordsworth's studies of man in nature are less often complete narratives than records of personal encounters that have provoked the poet to reflections on the human situation. In *Resolution and Independence* (1802), suddenly overcome with the sadness of the poet's destiny, as seen in the lives of Chatterton and Burns, Wordsworth meets with an aged leech-gatherer sustained by his perseverance in spite of a dwindling supply of leeches, and the poet laughs his own worries to scorn at the contrast with the old man's cheerfulness and firmness of mind. *The Old Cumberland Beggar* (1800) is a comparably sympathetic study, and there is no more compelling passage in *The Excursion* than the disturbing record in Book I of the cheerful and devoted wife Margaret, gradually borne down by sufferings – her husband's sickness, his embitterment, his disappearance and the death of her baby. Again the steady, unadorned blank verse is quietly compulsive.

The same skill with pentameters, more rigorously patterned yet none the less easy and natural, is displayed in the best of Wordsworth's sonnets. 'Earth hath not anything to show more fair' (*Composed upon Westminster Bridge*) and 'It is a beauteous evening, calm and free' are evocative descriptive sonnets, while 'The World is too much with us' and 'Milton! thou shouldst be living at this hour' are weighty moral exhortations issued with unchallengeable prophetic authority. Wordsworth's range is far-reaching. Exercises in the simple treatment of simplicity, like *The Last of the Flock*, are balanced by impressive ventures into revelatory vision: 'types and symbols of Eternity' are traced in the immeasurable grandeurs of the Simplon Pass (*The Simplon Pass*). Homely tributes like 'She was a Phantom of delight' are balanced by public declamations like 'I grieved for Buonaparte'; yet the voice that recurs most hauntingly to our minds is the one that sings in brief lyrics of love between man and earth on the first mild day of March, of the wandering voice which is the cuckoo, or of Lucy growing like a flower in sun and rain, lovely in her silence and calm and grace, and the same Lucy bereft of motion and force, rolled round with the rocks and trees in death.

Samuel Taylor Coleridge (1772–1834), son of a Devon parson, was gifted with a scholarly and inquiring mind, but lacked the tough moral fibre of Wordsworth; his prescribed use of opium led to addiction. In his early twenties he shared his revolutionary ardour with Southey, and the two of them planned a communistic community in North America called a 'Pantisocracy'. The immediate result of this collaboration was marriage to the two Fricker sisters, marriage which in Coleridge's case proved unfortunate. The Coleridges were living at Nether Stowey in Somerset when Wordsworth came to the district and the remarkable friendship, rooted in intense mutual admiration, began. Coleridge's contribution to *Lyrical Ballads* included *The Rime of the Ancient Mariner*, on which his high poetic status very largely, and justly, depends. The old mariner detains a wedding guest at the very doors of the bridegroom's home and pins him with his compulsive tale. And so the ballad, hauntingly urgent in rhythm, eerily bold in image, unfolds the story of how the mariner's ship was tossed towards the South Pole and locked in a desolation of ice till an Albatross came through the fog and ate at the sailors' hands. Then the ice split and they steered through it; but the mariner shot the bird that had brought them luck, and a terrible price was paid. Becalmed on the Equator, one after another of the crew died of thirst, each one cursing the mariner. Back home after his ghastly adventure, the mariner is shriven, but a lifetime's penance periodically compels him by a renewal of his agony to retell his tale. Unforgettable pictorial horrors are stamped on the reader's mind by its telling, yet one can scarcely ask why Coleridge never produced another ballad of such power when our entire literature could not provide one. He managed at least to match its archaic and haunting mystery in *Christabel* (1816). In this lovely fragment the Lady Christabel finds in the forest one who claims to be a forlorn maiden, 'Geraldine', and takes her home to the castle to succour her. But 'Geraldine' is an evil being in disguise and at night she takes Christabel in her arms to lay a spell on her. The plot scarcely develops in the two sections which were all that Coleridge's indolence and, no doubt, flagging inspiration, allowed him to complete. The four-stress lines contain widely differing numbers of syllables and embody repetitive rhetorical devices that, together with the bold, suggestive images, give a strange incantatory eeriness to the work:

> And what can ail the mastiff bitch?
> Never till now she uttered yell
> Beneath the eye of Christabel.

Nebulous preternaturalism makes the gothick background convincing. The spell of insistent and insinuating versification falls on the reader, suspending disbelief.

How far drugs contributed to the calling up of dreamlike and nightmarish atmospheres is a question brought sharply into focus by the remarkable opium-product, *Kubla Khan*, a fragment which Coleridge was pouring spontaneously onto paper when he was interrupted by a 'person from Porlock'. There is rare beauty and colour in the rich, exotic flood of sensuous image and symbol. It seems to well up from some deep source of verbal magic that is tapped only rarely in the history of literature. The brevity and incompleteness are tantalizing. Outside these three poems Coleridge's inspiration flared but fitfully. *France* and *Fears in Solitude* express reactions to the Revolution and to the threat of invasion. *To a Young Ass* has exacted an understandable ridicule of its bold greeting, 'I hail thee brother!' ('the bard who soars to elegise an ass'[1] Byron called him). *Dejection: An Ode*, like these, represents the secondary level of Coleridge's achievement, though, knowing his hopeless passion for Wordsworth's sister-in-law, Sarah Hutchinson, one cannot read without emotion the stark analysis of joylessness it contains.

There is a pathos about any writer whose fame, while he lives, is immense and, when he is dead, all but obliterated. Robert Southey (1774–1843) suffered such an eclipse. Revolu-

[1] *English Bards and Scotch Reviewers.*

tionary ardour in youth produced controversial works like the anti-English *Joan of Arc*. The full tide of his productivity was represented by vast epics like *Thalaba the Destroyer* (1801), an Arabian tale told in uncomfortably formal yet varied stanzas that weary the eye and dizzy the head, and *Madoc* (1805), a more readable, blank-verse tale of a twelfth-century Welsh prince who sails to America and is involved in heroic conflict with the Aztecs. Southey's very successful prose *Life of Nelson* (1813) is still read, and he has entered our anthologies with his anti-war poem, *After Blenheim* (it has the memorable ironic refrain, 'It was a famous victory'), and with 'My days among the Dead are past' (*His Books*), more subtly ironic for us now in that Southey's work smacks all too much of the library. His gifts of ease and fluency are not matched by intensity of emotional or imaginative expression. His cautious sensibility is evident in his letter to Charlotte Brontë, who had submitted her early poems for his judgement. He writes as one apprehensive of what the plunge into poetic activity may cost. 'The day-dreams in which you habitually indulge are likely to induce a distempered state of mind', he argues, warning against seeking for excitement in the life of the imagination.[2] It is odd that Southey is now known to us chiefly through his delightful children's tale, 'The Story of the Three Bears',[3] while his greatest notoriety attaches to the poem that Byron mercilessly burlesqued, *A Vision of Judgment*. Southey was Poet Laureate and wrote the poem, an exercise in hexameters, on the death of George III. The poet has a vision of the arrival of the king at the Gate of Heaven, where he drinks from the Well of Life and is transformed, the corruptible putting on the incorruptible. George Gordon Lord Byron (1788–1824) reacted to this extravagance under a double provocation, for in the preface to the poem Southey had attacked the 'horror and mockery, lewdness and im-

[2] Mrs Gaskell, *Life of Charlotte Brontë*.
[3] It occurs in Volume IV of his miscellany, *The Doctor*, seven volumes of which came out between 1834 and 1847.

piety' polluting contemporary poetry, and made a special target of the 'Satanic school'. Byron's *A Vision of Judgment* reconstituted the heavenly reception of George III in comic mockery and derisively added the Poet Laureate to the company above. There he causes consternation and hubbub by trying to recite his own poetic tribute.

Byron's career was near its end when *A Vision of Judgment* was published. His first entry on the poetic scene can best be understood if one recalls that Sir Walter Scott (1771–1832) dominated that scene after 1805 with his fluent, vivid and racy narrative poems. *The Lay of the Last Minstrel* (1805) established the popular taste. An old minstrel recites the tale. It has a ballad-like intermixture of three-stress lines with the standard four-stress base. The metrical effect is like that of *Christabel* which Scott greatly admired. The ingredients of the tale include lovers divided by a family feud, disguise and challenge, and emergency recourse to a magic book from a wizard's tomb. The setting is the Border Country in the sixteenth century. The appeal to actual topographical, historical and legendary interests in an easily assimilated but none the less accomplished verse form was an aesthetic and commercial success. (The ballad of 'Rosabelle' is included in the minstrelsy.) Scott followed it up with *Marmion, A Tale of Flodden Field* (1808), highly distinguished in its descriptions of battle, and spiced with the tale of Constance de Beverley, a nun who has broken her vows and disguised herself as a page to be with Marmion, and who is doomed to be walled up alive in punishment. 'O, young Lochinvar is come out of the west' occurs in the text. A third success came with *The Lady of the Lake* (1810), a story in steady octosyllabic couplets, centred in the area around Loch Katrine. One of its immediate effects was to put an end to the seclusion of the district. Holiday sightseers thereafter flocked to the Trossachs. For his next venture Scott turned south, setting *Rokeby* (1813) in the area around Barnard Castle; but the reception was disappointing (by Scott's extraordinarily high standards). Even genial Tom

Moore poked fun at the border minstrel's decision to come by quarto stages to town, beginning with Rokeby ('the job's sure to pay') and doing 'all the gentlemen's seats by the way' (*The Twopenny Post-Bag*, Letter VII). Not that Moore had anything to complain about in the appetite Scott created, for he was to feed it happily himself in *Lalla Rookh* (1817). However, though Scott added further to his list of romantic narratives, his supremacy was lost to Byron.

The publication of the first two cantos of Byron's *Childe Harold's Pilgrimage* in 1812 took the literary and social world by storm, and the succession of verse romances that quickly followed (*The Bride of Abydos*, *The Giaour*, *The Corsair* and *Lara*) proved that Byron could beat Scott, if not artistically, yet commercially, at his own game. The new ingredients that gave added spice to the Wizard of the North's original recipe were first the more exotic oriental settings, secondly Byron's greater command of the voluptuous and the erotic, thirdly his capacity to hint at hidden, unspeakable deeds, and lastly, of course, the cultivation of the Byronic hero. Conrad in *The Corsair* is such a one. He has an indefinable magnetism, a 'rising lip', a half-concealed arrogance, an air of things hidden:

> As if within that murkiness of mind
> Work'd feelings fearful, and yet undefined.

He is 'warp'd by the world', a man of unyielding pride who is feared and shunned yet has the measure of those who detest him. Lone, wild, strange and remote as he is, there is yet one soft feeling in him – for the gentle Medora. Oriental pirate lairs and Turkish harems are standard Byronic backgrounds. Suddenly Loch Katrine sounds like the right venue for a school outing.

Lockhart (in his *Life of Sir Walter Scott*) frankly cites Byronism as the cause of *Rokeby*'s failure. The 'darker passion of Childe Harold, the audacity of its morbid voluptuousness, and the melancholy majesty of the numbers in which it defied the world, had taken the general imagination by storm'. The Byronic posture is more fully developed in the third and fourth cantos of *Childe Harold* (1816 and 1818), as the guise of the 'pilgrim' is gradually discarded. The hero seeks escape from the hollow world of society, whose pleasures and dissipations he has drunk to the dregs. He travels about Europe, responding with conscious sensibility to the great monuments of the past, the scenic beauties and the artistic treasures awaiting the tourist. Harold broods on the battlefield of Waterloo and the downfall of Napoleon, and expatiates in the first person on his quarrel with the world. In canto IV he escorts us through Italy, extracting personal philosophic torment from the massive wreck of time, the Coliseum, and vicarious agony from recapturing the last moments of a dying gladiator. And he hymns the pleasure of pathless woods and lonely shores where the soul can mingle with the universe. There is sustained rhetorical dignity and fervour in Byron's clean-cut Spenserian stanzas. In spite of its fitful grandiose excesses, the work has undeniable poetic authority.

Byron's turbulent ancestry, his unsympathetic mother ('a vulgar, violent woman', Tom Moore called her),[4] and his club foot have been cited as contributory causes of that unique personality that gained him the 'Satanic' label and that formed the base of the poetic posture which overpowered Europe. The projection of this figure – sombre, brooding and defiant, locking within himself the stormy secrets of a mysteriously black past – is successful because it suspends over the human character a nebulous anti-halo evidencing the forbidden and the unspeakable. A great burden of remorse hangs over the hero of the dramatic poem, *Manfred* (1817). There is a power upon him which makes it his fatality to live. He 'could not tame' his nature down. He is of the 'brotherhood of Cain' and he is his own destroyer. What the hero's crime is we do not know. In the tragedies, *Cain* (1821) and *Werner* (1823), we do. But in

[4] *The Journal of Thomas Moore, 1818–1841*, ed. Peter Quennell (Batsford, London, 1964) (10 July 1827).

all of them we are in a world of ready-made poetic gloom in which such differences matter little. The gloom's the thing.

Yet the Byronic hero and the Byronic gloom are refreshingly rejected from *Don Juan*, the long comic epic which was published between 1819 and 1824, and represents the peak of Byron's achievement. In sixteen cantos there are over 1,900 stanzas of fluent *ottava rima*, flexibly adjusted to a diversity of emotional, narrative, descriptive and satiric purposes. Don Juan's youthful affair with his mother's friend, Donna Julia, leads to his being sent off on his travels. After shipwreck, near starvation, and cannibalism at sea, Juan is thrown up on land to awake in the tender care of Haidée, a maiden of seventeen whose father, Lambro, a Greek pirate, sails conveniently away on business. The love which follows is voluptuously and idyllically registered from its birth to its consummation:

> And now 'twas done – on the lone shore were plighted
> Their hearts; the stars, their nuptial torches, shed
> Beauty upon the beautiful they lighted;
> Ocean their witness, and the cave their bed ...

Lambro returns by surprise. Juan is bound and despatched on a pirate ship, while Haidée wilts and dies. Juan is sold as a slave, and there are bedroom antics in harems and violent military adventures before Juan finishes up in England, and Byron has him where he wants him for six cantos of satire on the English social scene. Approaching the capital, the hero waxes eloquent in praise of England. Here is Freedom's chosen station:

> 'Here laws are all inviolate; none lay
> Traps for the traveller; every highway's clear;
> Here' – he was interrupted by a knife,
> With – 'Damn your eyes! your money or your life!'

Byron exploits this trick time after time, the final couplet of a stanza biting ironically home in bathetic contrast to what has come before. With such weapons Byron lays about him, settling old scores with social, political and literary victims of his scorn. The sheer virtuosity is astonishing. It seems likely now that Byron's fame will rest in the future on *Don Juan* rather than on the poems that created the Byronic legend; though one should not forget those lyrics and short poems in which his love of rhetoric and rhythm flowered in outbursts of solemn or surging music – 'When we two parted', 'There be none of Beauty's daughters' and 'The Assyrian came down like the wolf on the fold'.

The age was rich in lyrical output of this kind, and no poet made a greater success of song-writing than Byron's friend and biographer, Thomas Moore (1779–1852). 'I have you by rote and by heart', Byron wrote to him,[5] telling him how his songs ran in his mind. The friendship is recorded in many lively letters from Byron; and indeed Byron's published *Letters*, coming from outside the country, complement the genial and gossipy picture of England's literary life given in *The Journal of Thomas Moore, 1818–1841*. Moore's *Irish Melodies* were published in series between 1808 and 1834. In these his musical sense and his gift for purveying an authentic Irish flavour produced lilting and singable verses guaranteed to fuse uncompetitively with the melodic line. Easy as it may be to depreciate the art which fed English appetite for a romanticized Emerald Isle, the significance of achieving universal memorability for verses like 'The Minstrel Boy', 'The Harp that once through Tara's Halls', 'Believe me, if all those endearing young charms' and 'Oft in the stilly night' cannot be whittled away.

According to Mary Shelley, her husband too was among the fervent admirers of Moore's lyric gift. He 'was too true a poet not to feel your unrivalled merit' she wrote to Moore, as he recorded in his journal.[6] Percy Bysshe Shelley (1792–1822) had himself a fertile lyrical gift. The verses that first

[5] Thomas Moore, *Letters and Journals of Lord Byron and Notices of his Life* (1830) (Letter of 8 December 1813).
[6] 18 to 19 January 1839.

spring to mind from the anthologies are urgent in rhythm and rich in metaphor – 'When the lamp is shattered', 'One word is too often profaned' and 'I arise from dreams of thee' (*Lines to an Indian Air*). They belong in the mind alongside the Shelleyan image of the archetypal young poet, handsome, fervently passionate and sincere, incorrigibly rebellious. Thomas Jefferson Hogg, his companion at Oxford and his biographer (*The Life of Percy Bysshe Shelley*) helped to create an image that one relishes like a work of art, yet with which one can never be quite at ease:

> As his port had the meekness of a maiden, so the heart of the young virgin who has never crossed her father's threshold to encounter the rude world, could not be more susceptible of all the sweet domestic charities than his ...

Such was Shelley's virginal innocence, we are told, that he once entered company at his home in Italy, fresh from bathing and quite forgetful of his own nudity. This was the disconcerting young man, son of a baronet, who was sent down from Oxford for publishing an atheistical pamphlet, married the sixteen year old Harriet Westbrook in 1811, left her three years later (she committed suicide), eloped with Mary, daughter of William Godwin and Mary Wollstonecraft (author of *The Rights of Woman*), and lived in Italy, readily cherishing idealized passions for other young ladies (the lyrics to 'Jane' – Jane Williams – indicate what such relationships inspired), to die by drowning at the age of thirty while sailing near Spezzia. The tragic end is vividly recorded by E. J. Trelawny in his *Recollections of the Last Days of Shelley and Byron*.

Shelley's status as a poet is a matter of controversy. The list of his big works includes poems that are not much read. *Queen Mab* (1813) is the work of a boy; but the boy is keen on fairies as well as on lambasting institutions, civil, religious and marital. *Alastor* (1816) tells how 'a youth of uncorrupted feelings and adventurous genius' idealistically seeks – and seeks in vain – for a prototype of his conception of what combines the wonderful, the wise and the beautiful. 'Blasted by his disappointment, he descends to an untimely grave.' So the poet tells us in his preface to the blank-verse poem, a poem that suffers from Shelley's nebulous intangibility, which dilutes the impact of image and event alike. The same complaint could be made against *The Revolt of Islam* (1818). There are over 500 Spenserian stanzas in the twelve cantos of this symbolic account of two lovers, Laon and Cythna, who lead a revolt against Islamic tyranny and are burnt at the stake after a counter-revolution has desolated the land.

Prometheus Unbound (1820), a poetic drama, is less imprecise and elusive. In the person of Prometheus, sustained by his mother Earth and his beloved, Asia (a symbol of natural beauty and love), mankind stands firm against the hatred of Jupiter. When Demogorgon deposes Jupiter and Prometheus is freed, there follows a reign of bliss and love – and a sustained outburst of lyrical rapture celebrates it. Indeed the poem contains many lyrical passages of great energy and beauty in which the modulations of tone and rhythm indicate the versatile range of Shelley's orchestration. The Furies that torment Prometheus in Act I are ministers of pain, fear, hate and crime:

> From wide cities, famine-wasted;
> Groans half heard, and blood untasted;
> Kingly conclaves stern and cold,
> Where blood with gold is bought and sold ...

By contrast in Act II Asia and Panthea hear the voices of spirits singing the rapturous, iridescent stanzas of 'Life of Life! thy lips enkindle'. *Epipsychidion* (1821) celebrates the poet's passionate idealization of the nun, Emilia Viviani, as a partner, soul with soul, in a relationship freed from the crude particularities of monogamy:

> True Love in this differs from gold and clay,
> That to divide is not to take away.

The Cenci is a powerful, if flawed, tragedy based on a six-teenth-century record of a Count Cenci whose evil life culminated in an incestuous passion for his daughter, Beatrice. She conspired with her brother and stepmother to have him murdered. The subject made it unstageable.

Shelley's fluency calls for a discipline which the chosen metrical pattern does not always impose; but there is clarity and economy in the reflective octosyllabics of the *Lines Written Among the Euganean Hills*, and the images contained within the *terza rima* of the *Ode to the West Wind* have an intensity sometimes hard to find in his work. It is all the more interesting that he should have chosen *terza rima* for the allegorical poem he was working on at the time of his death, *The Triumph of Life*. *Adonais*, Shelley's elegy on the death of Keats, also achieves an emotional thrust and some firmness of expression that make its images and cadences memorable.

John Keats's (1795–1821) short life of rich productiveness, terminated by consumption at the age of twenty-four, added another facet to the figure of Romantic poethood personified. Wordsworth's solitary spiritual grandeur, Coleridge's drug-fed exoticism, Byron's volcanic emotional lawlessness, Shelley's rapturous idealism, Keats's poetic priesthood of beauty – these traits coalesce with an immense cult of revolutionary ardour on behalf of the uncorruptedly natural and human, to form the image of the Romantic poet.

> O for ten years, that I may overwhelm
> Myself in poesy; so I may do the deed
> That my own soul has to itself decreed.

So Keats voiced his self-dedication in *Sleep and Poetry*, one of the poems in the volume, *Poems by John Keats*, published in 1817. A month after its publication we find him writing to John Reynolds: 'I find I cannot exist without Poetry – half the day will not do – the whole of it ...' What gave surest promise of the future in the 1817 volume was the group of sonnets. Some of them voiced the young poet's delight in poetry: 'Great spirits now on earth are sojourning' pays tribute to Wordsworth; 'Keen, fitful gusts are whispering here and there' praises Milton and Petrarch; and there is also the famous *On First Looking into Chapman's Homer*.

Endymion deals allegorically with the love of Cynthia, the moon goddess, for the shepherd Endymion and with his wandering search for her (as for ideal beauty) that it inspires. 'A thing of beauty is a joy for ever', the poem begins, but the four books of overwritten and underprecise couplets, though drenched in lush imagery ('O he had swoon'd / Drunken from pleasure's nipple') lack coherence and restraint. Yet the 'Ode to Sorrow', sung in Book IV by the forsaken Indian maiden (who turns out finally to be Cynthia herself) has disciplined artistry as well as Keatsian profusion. The savaging of *Endymion* in the *Quarterly Review* became romantically associated, for the pain it caused, with Keats's physical decline.

The simplicity and restraint evidenced in the *ottava rima* of the narrative poem, *Isabella; or the Pot of Basil*, mark a big development. There is a Websterian grimness about the murder of Isabella's lover by her brothers, her discovery of the body, and her cherishing of the head in a flowerpot. But, good as it is, the achievement is eclipsed by that of *The Eve of Saint Agnes*. Its rich Spenserian stanzas are alive from beginning to end with some of the most potently orchestrated language of atmosphere and sensuous description in our literature. Whether it is the chill of winter evening or the heraldic colour and blare of medieval sight and sound; whether it is the urgent devotion of Porphyro or the magical loveliness of Madeline – whatever Keats touches in this rapturous idyll of love against a background of felt menace, he transmutes into the rarest poetry. Louis MacNeice called Keats a 'sensuous mystic'[7] The unnerving mastery of timbre and tint, of verbal cajoleries felt on the tips of finger and tongue, makes the phrase an apt one.

In the epic fragment, *Hyperion*, the subject is the de-

[7] *Fifteen Poets* (Clarendon Press, Oxford, 1941).

thronement of the old sun god by his successor, young Apollo. In the first of the two versions Keats made, the Miltonic opening represents Saturn lamenting his lost power and considering with the other Titans how he may restore it. The second version, *The Fall of Hyperion*, attempts to escape the Miltonic pattern and stylistic influence. This time the poet has a visionary encounter with the goddess Moneta who, before opening to him the spectacle of the fallen Saturn, chides him as one of that dreaming tribe who do no benefit to the world and are unfit to be placed among 'those to whom the miseries of the world/Are misery, and will not let them rest'. Both fragments mark the high peak of Keats's technical expertise, but one has to turn to the odes to find this expertise employed on material less remote, thus setting the crown on Keats's short but packed poetic career.

The transience of earthly beauty, joy and love is the theme of *Ode to a Nightingale*, *Ode on a Grecian Urn* and *Ode on Melancholy*. Over against the 'weariness, the fever, and the fret' of human ageing and suffering, the song of the nightingale outlasts the 'hungry generations' and lifts the poet out of himself momentarily to share its ecstasy. The Greek urn, 'unravish'd bride of quietness', has a frieze on which men and women are immortalized at their time of beauty and love, lifted thus above the tormenting and cloying experience of human passion. The generations waste away, but the work of art will remain, a permanent 'friend to man', testifying that 'Beauty is truth, truth beauty'. And the *Melancholy* ode shows melancholy present at the heart of all joy in the knowledge that beauty must die and happiness pass. A less philosophical vein enables the poet to create a rich texture of sensuous awareness in the ode *To Autumn* and to give himself acceptingly to the mood of the scene and the season so potently evoked. Here, and in the haunting verses, *La Belle Dame Sans Merci*, Keats's strangely concentrated talent races to a breathtaking level of maturity.

A poet of the period who has not weathered well is Thomas Campbell (1777–1844), and in so far as he is remembered, it is not for his reflective study, *The Pleasures of Hope* (except for the single line, 'Tis distance lends enchantment to the view'), but for a handful of ballads and rolling songs of battle. *Lord Ullin's Daughter* is competent balladry, *The Soldier's Dream* an accomplished piece of narrative sentimentality, *Ye Mariners of England* ('the battle and the breeze') is rousing and rollicking rodomontade, and *The Battle of the Baltic* is a rhythmically more sophisticated, if scarcely more subtle, glorification of the 'might of England'. No doubt the generation is dying out that learned to recite these verses at school. So too with the verses of Samuel Rogers (1763–1855), like 'Mine be a cot beside the hill' and 'Sleep on, and dream of Heaven awhile'.

A more gifted poet than either of these was Thomas Hood (1799–1845), a bookseller's son who made a somewhat precarious living by editing periodicals and by freelance journalism. Hood's facility often leaves the impression of haste, and the accomplishment sometimes outruns the inspiration; but his incantatory power can overwhelm the reader with gloom, bitterness or compassion. In sombre gloom *The Dream of Eugene Aram, the Murderer* recreates the agony and remorse consequent on murder through the murderer's own voice: for he tells his story compulsively to a boy (he himself is an usher), pretending it a dream. For bitterness in the cry of the sweated labourer there is nothing to match *The Song of the Shirt* sung by a poor woman at her stitching. And *The Bridge of Sighs* laments the suicide by drowning of a forsaken woman. It is done in terse, clipped phrases of distilled suffering and sympathy. The facility with rhyme and rhythm, when neatly controlled and charged with wit, serves Hood well in comic verse too. The *Ode on a Distant Prospect of Clapham Academy* is a well-sustained blend of burlesque and wry sentiment. But one must admit that there is much writing in Hood's lighter verse that trembles uncomfortably on the edge of true humour, even when the wit is evident. The puns are notorious. They embellish the sick humour of the ballad of amputation and suicide, *Faithless Nelly Gray*:

> Ben Battle was a soldier bold,
> And used to war's alarms:
> But a cannon-ball took off his legs,
> So he laid down his arms!

It is impossible to read deeply in this period without coming across heartfelt tributes to Charles Lamb (1775–1834). 'O, he was good, if e'er a good Man lived!', Wordsworth wrote in his lines *Written after the Death of Charles Lamb*. And such were the feelings of many writers who enjoyed his literary evenings. Something of their flavour, perhaps, can be caught from Hazlitt's essay, *Of Persons one would wish to have seen* (*Literary Remains*). 'A clever fellow certainly', Tom Moore wrote of Lamb, 'but full of villainous and abortive puns, which he miscarries of every minute.'[8] The lively and amiable sociability of the man earned him the company and friendship of Coleridge, Wordsworth, Southey, Rogers, Hazlitt, De Quincey and others. His clerical post at East India House kept him for thirty-three years reluctantly but an amateur of letters until the pension came which he celebrated in the charming essay, *The Superannuated Man*:

> A man can never have too much Time to himself, nor too little to do ... Man, I verily believe, is out of his element as long as he is operative. I am all together for the life contemplative ... I am Retired Leisure. I am to be met with in the trim gardens ... I walk about; not to and from.

The persona is amiably insinuating, but it has a battery of literary devices at its disposal and a vast reservoir of literary knowledge to be readily drawn upon. Familiarity with seventeenth-century writers helped to mould the elaborate style,

[8] *Journal*, 4 April 1823.

and current fashion finds some of his prose overwritten, but essays like *Old China, Grace before Meat* and *A Dissertation Upon Roast Pig* bring the spell of an alertly and cheerfully ruminative imagination to bear upon the reader who is not impatient of allusive ramification and verbal coloratura. In *Mrs Battle's Opinions on Whist* a redoubtable personality is evoked in the shape of Sarah Battle, one of the breed who believes in the rigour of the game. She will have no truck with those who treat its wars less gravely than international conflicts. One mentions Lamb's essays first because it is through his collections, *Essays of Elia* (1823) and *The Last Essays of Elia* (1833), that he is best known. 'Elia' was the pseudonym Lamb used for his contributions to the *London Magazine*. It is perhaps especially difficult now to do full justice to a literary form that has been devalued by a century of watered-down journalistic imitation and which, precisely because of its civilized graces, long provided the model for classroom initiation into the art of wielding the discursive pen.

Lamb collaborated with his sister Mary in the *Tales from Shakespeare* and followed this with another effort at educative popularization in *The Adventures of Ulysses*. His critical work included papers, *The Tragedies of Shakespeare* and *On the Genius and Character of Hogarth*, contributed to the *Reflector*, a journal edited by Leigh Hunt that ran to only four issues.

No tribute to Lamb should ignore the burden he gladly undertook when a temporary fit of madness drove his sister Mary to stab their mother to death. He took over the care of his sister, who remained subject to periodic fits of insanity. His own less serious susceptibility to mental instability seems also to have stood in the way of marriage. He had his share of personal and literary disappointments: his attempts to turn playwright were not successful, but his interest in Elizabethan drama bore fruit in his *Specimens of English Dramatic Poets contemporary with Shakespeare, with Notes* (1808), an influential aid to the developing recognition of writers like Webster and Middleton. As a poet, Lamb is remembered for one or two exercises in limpid sentiment, like *The Old Familiar Faces* ('All, all are gone, the old familiar faces'), and for the lighter touch exemplified in the versified love-hate for the weed ('For thy sake, Tobacco, I / Would do anything but die') in *A Farewell to Tobacco*.

In contrast to the manifest likeableness of Lamb, the edginess of William Hazlitt (1778–1830), whom he befriended, is evidenced by many a personal relationship gone wrong. He was the angry young man of the age, passionately persistent in revolutionary enthusiasm and bitterly critical of the changing attitude to France represented by Wordsworth, Southey and Coleridge. His wild 'consistency' drove him to long years of apologetic for Napoleon in the four-volume *Life of Napoleon Buonaparte*. Hazlitt wrote and lectured in philosophy, contributed political articles to the *Morning Chronicle*, and wrote miscellaneous essays for journals like the *Examiner* and the *London Magazine*. These later found their way into his published collections, *The Round Table* (1817), *Table Talk* (1821–2) and *The Plain Speaker* (1826). Hazlitt's reflective and descriptive essays are charged with insatiable zest for life. They are not studied and polished set pieces, but forays of an alert imagination among tumbling ideas. Hazlitt draws you into his company with a compulsive autobiographical frankness in reflective essays like *On Going a Journey* and *On the Fear of Death* (both from *Table Talk*). When his scene is fully peopled, as in *The Fight* (*Literary Remains*), where Bill Neate makes a sorry mess of Tom Hickman, the Gas-man, at Hungerford, the text reads like a fragment from a vibrant, rolling novel. But we prize Hazlitt equally as a literary critic, for the penetrating insight he revealed in getting at the heart of great literature, past and contemporary. He was never content to fall back on literary history or biography. Rather he chose to subject imaginative literature to the searching and illuminating scrutiny of his own keen judgement and generous appreciation. His *Characters of Shakespeare's Plays* shows him touched at heart by the poetry and pouring out his own romantic rhetoric; and his reputation was enhanced by the *Lectures on the English Comic Writers* (1819) and the *Dramatic Literature of the Age of Elizabeth* (1820).

On his contemporaries Hazlitt's judgements were discerning, provocative, courageous, full of the meat of his own brain and the thrust of his own personality:

> If Mr Coleridge had not been the most impressive talker of his age, he would probably have been the finest writer; but he lays down his pen to make sure of an auditor, and mortgages the admiration of posterity for the stare of an idler.

> Lord Byron makes man after his own image, woman after his own heart ...

> To the author of *Lyrical Ballad*s, nature is a kind of home; and he may be said to take a personal interest in the universe.

> Mr Crabbe's Helicon is choked up with weeds and corruption; it reflects no light from heaven, it emits no cheerful sound ...

Such brilliant shafts recur throughout *The Spirit of the Age* (1825) and there is no less fire and fervour in the treatment of earlier writers in the *Lectures on the English Poets*.

We have quoted snippets from Hazlitt: it is not inappropriate to cite the criticism of Hazlitt made by his contemporary, Thomas De Quincey (1785–1859):

> Hazlitt was not eloquent, because he was discontinuous. No man can be eloquent whose thoughts are abrupt, insulated, capricious, and (to borrow an impressive word from Coleridge) non-sequacious.[9]

He made the same charge against Lamb, that he 'shrank from the continuous, from the sustained, from the elabor-

[9] *De Quincey's Literary Criticism*, ed. H. Darbishire (OUP, London, 1909).

ate'. De Quincey was enough of a scholar and philosopher to sense the fitfulness of the creative moods and moments that make up the best of Lamb and Hazlitt. Yet his own work flared but fitfully into glowing brilliance too. The opium habit weakened him, though it enabled him to write his finest book, *Confessions of an English Opium Eater* (1822), a book none the less compelling for De Quincey's glorious abandon in his own illimitable sequaciousness. There is great lyrical beauty and descriptive power, especially in the accounts of opium dreams, where De Quincey's gift for highly decorative rhetoric serves him well:

> Thousands of years I lived and was buried in stone coffins, with mummies and sphinxes, in narrow chambers at the heart of eternal pyramids. I was kissed, with cancerous kisses by crocodiles, and was laid, confounded with all unutterable abortions, amongst reeds and Nilotic mud.

Neither logical system nor critical acumen is the mainspring of De Quincey's literary criticism, whose quality is essentially poetic, imaginative and personal. There are memorable moments of intuitive enlightenment like the distinction between the literature of *knowledge* and the literature of *power* in his essay on Alexander Pope, and the sensitive disquisition *On the Knocking at the Gate in Macbeth* (*London Magazine*, October 1823). His *Reminiscences of the English Lake Poets* are a source of gossipy as well as more deeply reflective information on Wordsworth, Coleridge and Southey. It is intriguing to hear how Wordsworth took down De Quincey's copy of *Burke's Works* (the cacophonous title offended De Quincey) and, by no means unaware, applied to its uncut leaves a knife from the breakfast table that was plastered with butter. We can understand the observation of Southey, the bibliophile: 'To introduce Wordsworth into one's library, is like letting a bear into a tulip garden.'

'Mr Landor ... is a man of genius, and, as such, he *ought*

to interest the public', De Quincey wrote, and the irony still touches us, for Walter Savage Landor (1775–1864) seems today to have been pushed firmly back within the border surrounding those who are read exclusively by students of literature. 'His first work was a poem, viz. *Gebir*,' De Quincey adds, 'and it had the sublime distinction for some time of having enjoyed only two readers; which two were Southey and myself.[10] *Gebir*, an epic in blank verse, published in 1798, was followed by a trilogy of plays (*Andrea of Hungary*, *Giovanna of Naples* and *Fra Rupert*) based on a marriage connection between the Hungarian and Neopolitan royal houses in the fourteenth century. But where Landor is known today it is chiefly for his *Imaginary Conversations*, published in the 1820s and presenting dialogues, diverse in tone and character, and sometimes idiosyncratic in viewpoint, between such congruous and incongruous pairs as *Dante and Beatrice* and *Fra Filippo Lippi and Pope Eugenius IV*. In his poetry his high literary ideals, his craftsmanship and his cultivated sense of style are evident, but the content suffers from what today might be called 'remoteness', if not 'irrelevance' – except, ironically enough, in such ironical little squibs as *Ireland never was contented* ('Say you so? You are demented') and in those lyrics where personal love, nostalgia or melancholy break through, such as the elegiac verses, *Rose Aylmer*, *Twenty Years Hence* and *Late Leaves* ('The leaves are falling; so am I'). Landor welcomed the vigorous new voice of Browning in a sonnet ('There is delight in singing') in the *Morning Chronicle* in 1845. Shelley, Wordsworth and Lamb, as well as Shakespeare and Milton, were among those to whom he paid poetic tribute. He spoke his own epitaph with simple dignity:

> I strove with none, for none was worth my strife.
> Nature I loved, and next to Nature, Art:
> I warm'd both hands before the fire of life;
> It sinks and I am ready to depart.

[10] *De Quincey's Literary Criticism.*

There is perhaps even less in currently remembered literature to recall the immense contemporary significance of Leigh Hunt (1784–1859), the journalist, essayist and poet, who at different stages of his life edited the *Reflector*, the *Examiner*, *The Liberal* (in collaboration with Byron, who contributed *The Vision of Judgment* to the first issue), the *Indicator* and *Leigh Hunt's London Journal*. His championship of Keats and Shelley was discerning and influential, though in Keats's case it provoked the politically motivated critical backlash from the Tory *Quarterly Review* that was so hurtful to the poet. His poems, *The Story of Rimini* (1816, derived from the Paolo and Francesca episode in Dante), *Hero and Leander* (1819) and the anti-war *Captain Sword and Captain Pen* (1835) are little read, but until recently every schoolchild used to recite *Abou ben Adhem* ('May his tribe increase!') and 'Jenny kissed me when we met'. Hunt was still turning out books in the 1850s (there was an *Autobiography* in 1850).

We have looked in turn at major poets, minor poets and men of letters. A writer who resists any classification is James Hogg (1770–1835), 'The Ettrick Shepherd', who touched greatness at two extreme points in contrasting studies of evil and of goodness, in prose and verse respectively. The *Private Memoirs and Confessions of a Justified Sinner* (1824) is the prose work. The 'justified sinner' is the product of antinomianism, the doctrine that perverts Pauline teaching into the belief that grace frees the Christian from obligation to the moral law. 'I wept for joy to be thus assured of my freedom from all sin, and of the impossibility of my ever falling away from my new state', Robert says in the autobiographical second half of the book. His jealousy of his own brother and greed for his money are exploited by the Devil, who induces him to murder him for his supposed worldliness, overcoming qualms by 'religious' persuasion: 'Whether are the bonds of carnal nature or the bonds and vows of the Lord strongest?' Gruesome irony is achieved by Hogg's design of putting a third-person account of events alongside the sinner's blinkered autobiographical record of his career ('My sorrows have all been for a slighted gospel, and my vengeance has been wreaked on its adversaries'). Since Hogg first came to notice through the assistance he gave to Scott in gathering material for his *Minstrelsy of the Scottish Border*, it is interesting that Scott has a less sombre and eerie exposé of antinomian thinking in the 'Familist', Tomkins, in *Woodstock*.

Hogg's ballads (*The Mountain Bard*, 1807) first established his name: *Familiar Anecdotes of Sir Walter Scott* (1834) was his last original work. *The Queen's Wake* (1813) presents a song contest at the court of Mary Queen of Scots. Among the varied narrative poems sung by competing minstrels is the justly famous *Kilmeny*. It tells how the bonnie girl ('For Kilmeny was pure as pure could be') goes up the glen, fails to return, and is presumed dead. Eventually she comes back with a lovely grace and still mystery about her, for she has been in a sinless land of love and light. It is her spotless purity that has earned her a welcome in the glory and radiance of 'the land of thought'. There she has a vision of the poisoning of the world by war and evil, then the passing of man's sorrows into love and harmony. She is allowed to return home:

> To tell of the place where she had been,
> And the glories that lay in the land unseen.

But her return is short-lived. She soon goes back to the 'land of thought'.

When Hogg died, Wordsworth paid tribute in the *Extempore Effusion upon the Death of James Hogg* (1835), noting that within a few years there had died also Scott ('the Border-minstrel'), Coleridge ('The rapt one of the godlike forehead'), Lamb ('the frolic and the gentle'), Crabbe and Felicia Hemans ('a holy Spirit / Sweet as the spring, as ocean deep'). Wordsworth's regard for Mrs Hemans (1793–1835) draws attention to a now unread poet. *Casabianca*, a poem about the French admiral whose son stuck to him when their flagship caught fire and went down at the Battle of the Nile, is still quoted ('The boy stood on the burning deck'). Otherwise her immense output is largely unremembered. 'She is a clever person, and has been pretty,' Scott wrote in his *Journal* for 17 July 1829, 'I had a long walk with her *tête-a-tête*. She told me of the peculiar melancholy attached to the words *no more*.' What follows in the *Journal* is hilarious. Scott replied with a masculine anecdote of a drunk wife who fell off the pillion on the seashore while she and her drunk husband were riding home from a party. The husband did not miss her for some time. A search party discovered her later, with the incoming tide washing over her. She was still mentally at the party and waved away her rescuers, assuming that they were coming to fill up her cup, with the allegedly melancholy words, 'No more'.

William Lisle Bowles (1762–1850), parish priest and later canon of Salisbury, made a mark with his first work, *Sonnets* (1789), which had sufficient technical merit to stimulate a new interest in the form in Wordsworth, Coleridge, Southey and many other contemporaries. They are mellifluous, gentle and highly sentimental. Tuneful bells bid him 'many a tender thought recall'. The cliffs of Dover remind him of the lonely wanderer who parts from 'friends he lov'd most dear'. As for time, he rests his only hope on time, trusting to 'meet life's peaceful evening with a smile'. 'Harmonious Bowles', Byron called him in *English Bards and Scotch Reviewers*, 'great oracle of tender souls' and 'maudlin prince of mournful sonneteers'.

Highly productive among the now Great Unread was Joanna Baillie (1762–1851) whose *Plays on the Passions* are a series 'in which it is attempted to delineate the stronger passions of the mind; each passion being the subject of a tragedy and a comedy'.[11] The stilted blank verse (some, however, are in prose) is a ready-to-wear poetic garb derived

[11] Joanna Baillie, *The Dramatic and Poetical Works* (London, 1851), Introductory Discourse.

from Elizabethan declamation and eighteenth-century bombast:

> These nightly watchings much retard your cure ...
> How goes the hour? is it the second watch? ...
> And does the fearful night still lie before me
> In all its hideous length?
>
> (*Ethwald*, a tragedy, Act V scene v)

Joanna Baillie's poems have adventitious interest in some instances. In the 'Miscellaneous Poetry' added to the *Fugitive Verses* (first published 1790), there are *Lines on the Death of Sir Walter Scott* ('pleasant noble Bard, of fame far spread') and *Recollections of a Dear and Steady Friend*, none other than Lady Byron:

> I see her mated with a moody lord ...
> I see her next in agony of soul ...
> I see her from the world retired caressing
> Her infant daughter, her assured blessing.

We have already seen the child from another's angle:

> Is thy face like thy mother's, my fair child!
> ADA! sole daughter of my house and heart?
>
> (Byron: *Childe Harold's Pilgrimage*, Canto III)

17
Scott and contemporary novelists

In the general preface to the collected Waverley Novels Scott mentions Maria Edgeworth's Irish novels as one of the influences that caused him to take up the neglected manuscript of *Waverley* and turn novelist. Maria Edgeworth (1767–1849) was the daughter of Richard Edgeworth, the educationist, and collaborated with him in his *Practical Education* (1798). The educator's urge to use fiction for the moral improvement of mankind is evident in Maria Edgeworth's *Moral Tales* (1801) and *Popular Tales* (1804), but they are not therefore uninteresting, and she writes with wider social motives too. *Castle Rackrent* (1800) pictures the fortunes of an Irish estate through several generations of extravagant and dissipated landlords. The story is told in the form of reminiscences by an old retainer, Thady Quirk. His viewpoint gives a sharp bite to the satire, for everything is seen from the angle of 'the family', its dignity and prosperity; while the sufferings of the tenants and the oppressive mismanagement by the landlords are implicit. Satire is more widely directed in *Belinda* (1801). The young heroine, sent up to town for the first time, is too wise to slip into its frivolous dissipations. She falls in love with Clarence Hervey, a high-souled young man who is bringing up his female ward, Virginia St Pierre, on the educational theory of Rousseau. He at first intends her for his wife and is determined that she shall be uncontaminated by the vices and vanities of society. The mystery surrounding this project provides suspense and delay in Belinda's progress towards marriage. Through Vincent, Belinda's unsuccessful suitor, generous and warm-hearted, frank and handsome but perilously devoid of principle, we are taught that the Man of Feeling is unreliable: 'So fallacious is moral instinct unenlightened or uncontrolled by reason and religion.' The other moral is that fashionable society, being dissipated, is unhappy. Virtue brings happiness: 'How wisely has Providence made the benevolent and generous passions the most pleasureable.' In Harriott Freke there is a satirical study of early nineteenth-century feminism: she is dreadfully devoted to frolic and self-advertisement. Other social heterodoxies are discredited too: Lady Delacour is recalled from a delirious orgy of Methodism to 'the consolations of mild and rational piety'.

Yet Maria Edgeworth keeps returning to social problems that we can get more excited about. *The Absentee* (1812) traces Lord Colambre's struggle between his love for Grace Nugent and a supposed impediment to marriage. The impediment is her assumed illegitimacy, and a *deus ex machina* proves that it was all a mistake. The most shocking incident in the book is when Lady Oranmore discovers that she has suffered the humiliation of entertaining to dinner a gentleman and his mistress, whom she had assumed to be his wife. But the serious social purpose of the novel is faithfully served – to represent the plight of the Irish tenantry at the mercy of unscrupulous absentee landlords and their oppressive deputies, and to urge the happiness of a landlord's life in conscientious superintendence of his estate and its tenants, in contrast with the rottenness of the social rat-race in London. In *Harrington* (1817) the young hero faces parental opposition to his matrimonial plans, and one of the obstacles is the assumption that Berenice, the heroine, is a Jewess. As in *The Absentee*, the hero's dilemma is washed away, for Berenice turns out to be a Christian after all. Nevertheless there is a serious plea for toleration towards the Jews, and old Mr Harrington's obtuse and muddle-headed anti-Semitism is shown up as stupid. The account of the accidental emotional antipathy towards Jews bred in young Harrington during childhood is interesting. From his mother Harrington inherits excessive sensibility; childhood loneliness fosters it; stories told by a foolish servant direct his fears into a phobia about Jews.

Maria Edgeworth is at her best in *Ormond* (1817), a riotously packed novel brimming over with interesting people. King Corny, the warm-hearted, eccentric king of the Black Islands, who revels in the squandering of misdirected talent, is a delight. The variety of scene and of *dramatis personae* is remarkable. We are introduced to decadent Paris society, to the backwaters of diehard feudalism in eighteenth-century Ireland, to Catholic-Protestant dissension in country drawing rooms and village schools, to wreckers on the Irish coast, and to struggling Irish aristocrats sustained by opportunist political jobbery. Ormond himself is the impetuous, frank, rebellious hero. He reads *Tom Jones* and immediately desires the life of the popular, good-hearted rake. A perilous liaison with a village girl ensues. But Richardson soon rectifies the damage done by Fielding. By reading *Sir Charles Grandison* Ormond is inspired with the new ideal of the useful gentleman loved by women – by the best of women – for his goodness. A pure-hearted idealization of Dora, the heroine, is the clean outcome.

History, politics, social problems and religious problems pack Maria Edgeworth's books. Neither subtle psychology nor righteous reforming indignation is lacking. That material is insufficiently integrated in a total pattern is her main artistic deficiency.

Sir Walter Scott (1771–1832) solved the problem of integration in the Waverley Novels. Scott came at the right time to capitalize on the various individual contributions that had enriched the novel form between Fielding and Edgeworth. He read his predecessors and used them intelligently. In several books he adopted the principle of organizing his material around two sides locked in conflict. His method was to position the hero in detachment from the 'excesses' of either of the antagonistic parties and then to get him involved with one side or the other through special personal or convictional pressure. Scott did this in such a way as to represent the tug-of-war, emotional and intellectual, endured by every man in all ages while his contemporaries are at each other's throats. The duality tones in with the traditional, Western, Christian account of the human situation, where choosing man is torn between opposing forces: it gives a philosophic depth, a moral thrust and an artistic coherence to Scott's best work.

The conflict varies from novel to novel in range and intensity, and also in the strength of its ideological content. In *Wavereley* (1814), which centres on the Jacobite rising of 1745, the victory of Prince Charles Edward at Prestonpans and the subsequent collapse, the mighty opposites are the Jacobites and the Loyalists. Romantic idealism surrounds the former: reason and good sense favour the latter. The hero, Edward Waverley, has been brought up alternately by a Jacobite uncle and a Whig father, and there is an elaborate psychological explanation of how he gets onto the 'wrong' side, succumbing to the romantic appeal of High-

land adventure and the lure of Flora MacIvor. A deeper
level of conflict is plumbed in *Old Mortality* (1816), which
centres on the rising of Scottish Covenanters in 1679. Their
zeal comprehends, at the one extreme, a genuine need for
religious liberty, and at the other extreme, a readiness to
assassinate archbishops. By diversifying the characters on
either side, Scott is able to present the conflict between
government and Covenanter, monarchy and republicanism,
episcopacy and Presbyterianism, as rooted in antitheses
between justice and freedom, between oppression and
anarchy. Reason is arrayed against intuition, order against
individualism, culture and ceremony against piety and
asceticism. Each side has its humane moderates as well as
its fanatics, and when William III comes to the throne,
bringing a reign of tolerance, there is an appropriate re-
grouping.

Royalist and republican clash again when Montrose's
rebellion of 1644 on behalf of Charles I is pictured in *A
Legend of Montrose* (1819). The romantic duke, a man of
iron constitution, graceful and athletic, overflowing with
'the energy and fire of genius', is up against the republican
Duke of Argyle, a morose, ambitious and mean man of
politics rather than of battle. The Catholic-Protestant conflict dominates *The Abbot* (1820) in the contrasting persons
of Mary Queen of Scots and Murray, while Roland Graeme,
the everyman hero, is torn between the two opposing ways
of thought. Scott reverts to the same pattern in *Woodstock*
(1826) for his picture of the English Civil War and Charles
II's adventures after the Battle of Worcester. Sir Henry Lee
is the perfect symbol of Stuart loyalty, while the study of
Cromwell gives expression to an inextricable blend of piety
and cant, religious feeling and personal ambition, crispness
and coarseness.

Scott sometimes plays down the public in favour of the
private conflict: what is ideological fades into the background and what is personal comes to the fore. The world
of business is in opposition to the world of romance in *Rob*

Roy (1817), city commerce in opposition to Highland free-booting. The house of Osbaldistone is the stronghold of one set of values and the clan MacGregor the fortress of another. Francis's adventures between the two extend and deepen the conflict in terms of private and moral obligation, and not in terms of political or religious controversy. Bailie Jarvie is a humane and steady-minded representative of the business world ('I maun hear naething about honour – we ken naething here but about credit'), but for all his prudence, his heart is touched by Rob Roy, the romantic king of blackmail with his law of the dirk and his grand adventurous forays ('... I think the Hieland blude o' me warms at these daft tales'). For Rob has declared honourable vengeance on the world of legalized greed that he despises. Die Vernon, the object of Francis's romantic passion, is a vital study in candid womanhood. Indeed a cluster of powerfully projected characters gives the book personal intensity.

One might label as *personal* (as opposed to *public*) the novels in which Scott repeats this emphasis. It would be just as meaningful an artistic distinction as that between the Scottish and non-Scottish novels. In *The Bride of Lammermoor* (1819) the conflict between Tories and Whigs, Ravenswood and Ashton, once more opposes the heart to the head, romance to careerism; but the study of Ravenswood outreaches any ideological schematization. His sullen gloom and decayed fortunes are matched by the gaunt tower of Wolf's Crag, an ancient stronghold built on a rock but lashed by wind and wave. The personal conflict runs deep, for family honour demands vengeance on the house of Ashton, while Lucy's love and beauty cry for Christian forgiveness. This is *Romeo and Juliet* with a difference. Ravenswood's fierce, aristocratic nature unfits him for the timid daughter of his rival. Kith and kin conspire against her and the burden is too much. The tragic sequence escalates remorselessly. After the wedding imposed upon her, piercing cries draw the guests to the door of her bridal chamber. They find the bridegroom on the threshold in a pool of blood, while Lucy is a gesticulating lunatic, crouched in the chimney, her eyes glazed, her nightclothes bloody and torn. The use of symbolism and supernaturalism is fine and sensitive. This is a book that could have been written only by a poet. It is our first great tragic novel. Greater still, and even less given to public dualities, is *The Heart of Midlothian* (1818). Effie Deans is imprisoned on a charge of child murder at a time when Scots law made this the appropriate charge against a girl who could not produce a child born after a concealed pregnancy. Jeanie Deans, her sister, can gain her acquittal by falsely asserting in court that her sister revealed her pregnancy. The conflict in Jeanie between expedience supported by the strongest motives of affection, and the duty of honesty, backed up by religious conviction, is powerfully and subtly handled. She cannot bring herself to lie, but she saves her sister by a heroic journey to London to seek a royal pardon.

Among the other Scottish novels highly prized for their sharp characterization is *Guy Mannering* (1815), in which we have a usurpation story followed seventeen years later by the emergence of the lost heir. The villainies of lawyer Glossin and smuggler Dirk Hatteraick are ultimately defeated by the mysterious prophetic gipsy, Meg Merrilies. Her saving role is matched in *The Antiquary* (1816) by Edie Ochiltree, a wandering devotee of the simple life. The 'antiquary' himself is the learned laird of Monkbarns, Jonathan Oldbuck, a garrulous fellow reputed to be something of a self-portrait by Scott. And there is a fine array of varied character studies in *Redgauntlet*, a story of the 1760s involving the aprocryphal return to Scotland of Prince Charles Edward to try his fortunes again.

Scott forsakes Scotland for England in *Ivanhoe* (1819). It is based on a plan to contrast the spirit of Saxon and Norman, to pit the 'plain, homely, blunt manners, and the free spirit' against the code of the 'Flower of Chivalry'.[1] The con-

[1] Introduction to *Ivanhoe*, Collected Edition of Waverley Novels.

flict between honest, independent simplicity and a new, more sophisticated civilization, is rather a conflict of manners than of ideals, a duality of externals rather than of moral or philosophical stances. Scott is too much outside the struggle, and so is the reader. The embarrassing 'ye olde' English dialogue is hard to judge fairly. It was a considerable invention at the time, but now that it has been done to death by over a century of imitation in weekend comics and the like, it is bound to look threadbare. Yet when Scott leaves Scotland for the France of Louis XI in *Quentin Durward* (1823) he produces a magnificent gallery of living portraits assembled for the working out of conflict between the fifteenth-century heirs of the old spirit of chivalry (like Charles, Duke of Burgundy) and the new diplomatic exponents of machiavellian opportunism, like King Louis. Again, on a personal as well as a public level, *Kenilworth* (1821) recreates the England of Elizabeth I all the more powerfully because Scott turns the story of Amy Robsart's murder into something like an Elizabethan tragedy. Leicester's struggle between love and ambition has a Shakespearian flavour, and Varney is a villain after the model of Iago. Similarly the celebrated study of James I is only one among the portraits in *The Fortunes of Nigel* (1822) that give a picture of the age notably enriched by Scott's reading in Jacobean drama.

It might be argued that Scott is at his best when basic human interests are fused with, and not submerged under, the reconstruction of history. In *Peveril of the Peak* (1823) history gets out of hand and Scott gives a detailed picture of the Restoration court, the Titus Oates trial and eccentrics like Geoffrey Hudson, at the expense of a well-knit story. In *The Fair Maid of Perth* (1828), *Anne of Geierstein* (1829) and *Count Robert of Paris* (1831) the historical material gradually assumes the kind of interest which leaves one conscious of the 'plot' as something separable – a technical necessity rather than an integrated essential. *The Fair Maid of Perth* is set in the reign of Robert III at the end of the fourteenth century and includes the murder of the king's son, the Duke of Rothsay, at the instigation of his uncle, the Duke of Albany. *Anne of Geierstein* is set in the late fifteenth century, the period of *Quentin Durward*, and indeed the Duke of Burgundy appears again, to be defeated by the Swiss at the battles of Granson and Marat. For feudal chivalry is up against something different this time – not the machiavellian intrigue of King Louis, but the new spirit of independence and tolerance of the Swiss. The central plot all but disappears behind elaborate pictures of personages like Queen Margaret of Anjou, extravagances like King René's Court of the Troubadours, and horrors like the sinister Vehmegerichte. The lesser known Waverley Novels are full of riches.

We have scarcely touched, in this brief survey, on Scott's gifts for handling dialogue and manipulating narrative technique, for ranging convincingly over vast panoramic backgrounds peopled with an immense variety of vitally active human beings, and for threading through his work poetic correspondences and symbolic configurations that conduce to orderliness of vision and force of impact. It must be accepted, of course, that Scott often wrote well below his best. Nevertheless his imaginative world is one of the richest and the fullest we have to deal with in this book.

The Life of Sir Walter Scott by Scott's son-in-law, John Gibson Lockhart, is one of our greatest biographies. One needs it in order to understand the remarkable events resulting from the anonymous publication of *Waverley* and its successors. Scott actually reviewed his own *Old Mortality* in the *Quarterly Review* for January 1817, and the mystery of the long-concealed authorship provoked a fascinating book by John Adolphus (*Letters to Richard Heber, Esq*, 1821), attempting by internal evidence to prove the Waverley novels 'to have been written by the author of *Marmion*'. Scott refers to the book in his Introduction to *The Fortunes of Nigel*. He entertained Adolphus at Abbotsford but gave nothing away. Lockhart's biography is movingly detailed too on the financial crash of Constable and Ballantyne that all but ruined Scott in 1826, when he had built up his grand house and estate at Abbotsford. The disaster provoked a heroic determination to write unceasingly to pay off the creditors. Much of the debt was cleared by the time he died, and the subsequent settlement of copyrights paid off the remaining liabilities.

On 14 March 1826, soon after the financial crash, we find Scott recording in his *Journal* that he has just read *Pride and Prejudice* 'and for the third time at least', finding Miss Austen's talent 'most wonderful'. 'The Big Bow-wow strain I can do myself like any now going', he says, but not 'the exquisite touch' that transforms the commonplace. Jane Austen (1775–1817) was the daughter of a country rector and she spent her life largely between Hampshire villages and Bath, having access to the social exchanges of the lesser landed gentry and professional classes, and these became her main material as a writer. She worked and reworked her early manuscripts, so that order of publication does not parallel order of composition. *Sense and Sensibility* came out in 1811. One of its themes is the contrasting responses of two sisters, Elinor and Marianne Dashwood, to disappointment in love. Marianne, the creature of sensibility, cannot keep her sufferings to herself as Elinor manages to do by virtue of her good 'sense'. But the novel is far more than an exercise on this moral contrast; and it includes comically satirical studies of selfish and brash personalities deftly presented in dialogue. *Pride and Prejudice* (1813) of course perfects the technique of satirical portraiture. Piquancy is added by the cunning management of a dislikeable young man, Darcy, who is rude and offensive to Elizabeth Bennet at a ball and strengthens against himself the girl's prejudice – a prejudice which, like his own pride, will have to be corrected before the author can bring them to an engagement. The family life of the Bennets is an adroitly manipulated counterpoint on the themes of generation gap and generation bond. There are five daughters. Mr Bennet takes refuge in his library from the silliness of his wife. It is the easy way out and leaves his giddy young daughters, Kitty and Lydia, unchecked in their empty-headed flirtatiousness. Jane, the eldest daughter, is an earnest, modest, unselfish girl, who suffers uncomplainingly from the family's private and public foolishness. Elizabeth has a strong sense of humour and a sharp awareness of the ridiculous: she is a spirited, witty, resourceful young lady, acutely embarrassed by the behaviour of her relations, by no means infallible in her judgement, but genuine and winning, surely one of the half dozen most captivating heroines of English fiction. Her father's dry sarcasms, half-disguised as innocuous civilities, salt many a page with humour. There is a delightful undercurrent of understanding between father and favourite daughter (Elizabeth) and Mr Bennet quietly relishes the absurdities he illuminates for her and for the reader. His shafts are not always wise or kind. Catherine and Lydia ought not to be just laughed at by their father. But he is a man in a woman's world and has to endure a sequence of surprises as his daughters Lydia, Jane and Elizabeth in turn find remarkable husbands. His equanimity is equal to the strain: 'If any young men come for Mary or Kitty, send them in, for I am quite at leisure.' We are given an unforgettable study in self-satisfied pomposity in the person of the Reverend William Collins, who is grotesquely obsequious to his ecclesiastical patroness, Lady Catherine de Bourgh. He is male heir by entail to the Bennets' property, and as a complacently condescending suitor to Jane (and, failing Jane, Elizabeth) he is hilariously inappropriate.

Mansfield Park (1814) is an exploration of character and relationships in a situation where a poor girl (Fanny Price) from a crowded home has been adopted by a well-to-do family (the Bertrams). The overall design treats with some subtlety the havoc that can be wrought by the introduction of a wholly unselfish and honest girl into a human circle rhat is not outstandingly virtuous. Lady Bertram's sister, Mrs Norris, is as malicious and hard a woman as one can find in Jane Austen. There is underlying gravity in the working out of the contrast between the worldly and the unworldly. Edmund Bertram (the young clergyman) and Fanny are united only after Edmund has been compulsively involved with the shallow Mary Crawford and Fanny sought by her unscrupulous brother. Mellower and more relaxed judgements on humanity are implicit in what many regard as Jane Austen's finest work, *Emma* (1816). Emma Woodhouse is infuriating and loveable. She has got her own (single) future firmly and happily worked out, and now the dutiful and unselfish thing to do is to work out everybody else's future equally happily and even more firmly. And so she makes a start by preparing an appropriate match for Harriet Smith. A lot has to happen before she learns how foolish her interference has been. Jane Austen achieves to perfection the ironist's feat of containing her heroine within a double vision of judgement and affection, that sees her laughably silly yet none the less dear. Surrounding portraits constitute a wide range of shrewdly observed personalities, none more fascinating than Emma's father, Mr Woodhouse, a valetudinarian of mediocre understanding and self-indulgent amiability. He is nervously unequal to such immense strains as a change in the weather or in an acquaintance's marital status:

> His own stomach could bear nothing rich, and he could never believe other people to be different from himself ... and he had therefore earnestly tried to dissuade them from having any wedding-cake at all, and when that proved vain, as earnestly tried to prevent anyone's eating it.

A literary motive was the starting point of *Northanger Abbey* (1818, but written as early as 1798–1803), whose heroine Catherine is invited to the Tilneys' medieval home, Northanger Abbey, and, her head being stuffed full with expectations aroused by reading gothick novels like *The Mysteries of Udolpho*, persuades herself that just such horrors and mysteries surround her as befell Emily de St Aubert. The literary satire is eventually submerged under the healthily unarchaic progress towards marriage. By contrast Jane Austen's last novel, *Persuasion* (1818), operates at a deeper psychological level than any of its predecessors. The much retarded love story of Anne Elliott is handled with an earnestness and compassion that inevitably tone down the shafts of the comic spirit and have raised speculation about the kind of writer Jane Austen might have become had she lived longer. There is a rare artistic wholeness about her novels. The marriage plot, which largely restricts action to the advances and retardations, the hesitations, doubts and intrigues involved in love affairs, imposes its own order. Armies clash and governments totter in Scott. In Jane Austen the crises are of the drawing room, and the agonies are smothered away behind the brave daily performance of domestic duties. The drama resides in an unanswered letter, an unspoken word, a silent doorknocker or an averted face.

The year of the publication of *Persuasion* also saw the publication of Peacock's *Nightmare Abbey*. Thomas Love Peacock (1785–1866), after living on his own means until 1819, then entered the service of the East India Company and became thereafter another amateur of literature. He links two ages of writers. His close friendship with Shelley dated from 1812 and took him into the poet's innermost councils at the time of the crisis over the marriage with Harriet. Yet his elder daughter, Mary Ellen, became the first wife of George Meredith in a disastrous marriage that culminated in her elopement with an artist and provoked the moving series of sonnets, *Modern Love*. Something of the cheerfully combative strain of anti-romanticism in Peacock can be seen in the book that provoked Shelley's *Defence of Poetry*, namely *The Four Ages of Poetry* (1820), for it trounces contemporaries: 'A poet in our times is a semi-barbarian in a civilised community', for the 'highest inspirations of poetry are resolvable into three ingredients:

the rant of unregulated passion, the whining of exaggerated feeling, and the cant of factitious sentiment'.

Peacock had tried his hand at poetry himself, but his importance lies in his short novels, if that is the right name for books in which the narrative interest is submerged beneath conversation, and the text often takes the form of dramatic dialogue. *Headlong Hall* (1816) sets the pattern with a gathering of mixed and highly idiosyncratic personalities, each ready to expound eccentric views. There is a grotesque farcicality in action and discussion that often has its point in terms both of literary burlesque and of satirical topicality. Peacock's target is pretentious humbug in cranks who want to set the world to rights, in crotchety theorists and in sentimental dreamers. *Melincourt, or Sir Oran Haut-ton* (1817) figures Sir Oran Haut-ton (Orang-utan) a primitive who can play the flute, live the fashionable life, acquire a baronetcy and a seat in Parliament, but has not yet advanced so far as to be able to speak. Southey and Wordsworth are pilloried as Mr Feathernest and Mr Paperstamp, while Coleridge is Mr Mystic. At the house party in *Nightmare Abbey* (1818) we meet some of these again under different names. Coleridge is Mr Flosky and Byron is Mr Cypress, who announces:

> Sir, I have quarrelled with my wife; and a man who has quarrelled with his wife is absolved from all duty to his country. I have written an ode to tell the people as much, and they may take it as they list.

The fullest such portrait is that of Scythrop Glowry, namely Shelley, who develops a passion for Marionetta Celestina O'Carroll.

> But when Marionetta hinted that she was to leave the Abbey immediately, Scythrop snatched from its repository his ancestor's skull, filled it with Madeira, and presenting himself before Mr Glowry, threatened to drink off the contents, if Mr Glowry did not immediately promise that Marionetta should not be taken from

the Abbey without her own consent. Mr Glowry, who took the Madeira to be some deadly beverage, gave the required promise in dismal panic. Scythrop returned to Marionetta with a cheerful heart, and drank the Madeira by the way.

Shelley took it all in good part and praised Peacock in his verse *Letter to Maria Gisborne*: 'his fine wit / Makes such a wound, the knife is lost in it.' *Crotchet Castle* (1831) is another exercise in the same vein, though this time the party takes a trip to Wales, and Scott is under fire from Dr Folliott for producing a 'literature of pantomime' told 'in the worst dialects of the English language'.

While new ground was being broken by writers we have named, the output of sentimental and horror novels continued. Charles Robert Maturin (1782–1824) kept alive the tradition of 'Monk' Lewis. His *Melmoth the Wanderer* (1820) is his most horrific work, dealing with Melmoth's sale of his soul to the Devil in exchange for continuing life. The compact is such that Melmoth shall be able to transfer the bargain to another, if anyone can be found who is willing. We meet a series of characters in dire distress to whom the offer is made and by whom it is rejected. More subtly gruesome perhaps is the novel that Mary Shelley (1797–1851) wrote when the Shelleys and Byron agreed to while away some wet weather by writing terror stories. In *Frankenstein, or the Modern Prometheus* (1818) a student, Frankenstein, discovers how to create life, collects the bones of corpses, assembles them and gives vitality to a gross and loathsome fabrication that eventually murders Frankenstein's brother and friend, and then the creator himself.

William Godwin records Mary Shelley's birth and her mother's subsequent death in *Memoirs of Mary Wollstonecraft*. This moving tribute to the author of *The Rights of Woman* tells how Godwin and she did not at first marry because they thought it improper to mark the climax of what is 'most sacredly private' with ceremony and noise.

This scorn of marriage as an institution became the target of an interesting propaganda novel by Amelia Opie (1769–1853), who published her *Adeline Mowbray* in 1804. It is a critical condemnation of Godwinism but written with sympathy and understanding. Adeline is the child of a woman whose feministic and progressive educational ideas occupy her so earnestly that she neglects to instruct her daughter. Adeline grows up with her mother's ideas, then horrifies everyone by putting them into practice, embarking on free cohabitation with the very philosopher whose thinking her mother imbibed – Glenmurray. Glenmurray and Adeline are unselfish, pure-souled idealists in a world whose hostility is sordid and slanderous. Nevertheless their individualism produces unnecessary secret agonies for both. Through poverty and hostility they are in turn hounded out of life. (The sequence seems to foreshadow Hardy's *Jude the Obscure*.) Their own suffering and remorse speak the moral. Adeline's conclusion is that 'if the ties of marriage were dissolved or it were no longer to be judged infamous to act in contempt of them, unbridled licentiousness would soon be in general practice ...' The message is hammered home, but Mrs. Opie has psychological insight, a command of humorous irony, and a breadth of human sympathy.

18
Victorian poetry

On Wordsworth's death in 1850 Alfred Tennyson (1809–92) was made Poet Laureate. We are apt to think of the award as officializing his identification with the spirit of the age and to consider him the literary representative of Victorianism: but his brilliance as a poetic craftsman and the readiness with which, in his finest work, he voiced perturbations and aspirations of the mind and spirit that come to men in all ages, make the 'Victorian' tag ultimately dispensable.

The son of a Lincolnshire rector, Tennyson was educated at Cambridge and there became a member of a group of idealists who called themselves 'Apostles', having embraced a self-chosen prophetic mission to crusade for culture. A leading light in the group was Arthur Hallam who became Tennyson's friend and his sister's fiancé. Hallam's sudden death in Vienna in 1833 at the age of twenty-two profoundly shocked Tennyson and exercised a lasting influence on his poetic career. The *Poems* which came out in 1833 already included work of staggering technical virtuosity, like *The Lady of Shalott, Oenone* and *The Lotos-Eaters*. In *The Lady of Shalott* it is as though Keats's sensuous richness and acute verbal sensitivity have coalesced with the haunting, incantatory magic of Coleridge; and the symbolic overtones add a mysterious dimension with a deeply felt personal implication. For the Lady, weaving her magic web and seeing only 'shadows of the world' outside passing by in her mirror, brings the curse of destruction upon herself (and her mirror) by leaving her loom and looking down on the real world. We recognize the underlying dilemma of the poet before the competing claims of art and the living world. And we are aware of a comparable dichotomy, and a comparable technical mastery, when we see how the languid atmosphere in the imagery and music of *The Lotos-Eaters*:

> Music that gentlier on the spirit lies
> Than tir'd eyelids upon tir'd eyes –

can be shattered in a flash at a momentary glimpse of the turbulent world that drugged contentment has escaped from:

> Blight and famine, plague and earthquake, roaring
> deeps and fiery sands,
> Clanging fights, and flaming towns, and sinking ships,
> and praying hands.

After the death of Hallam this virtuosity meets with the discipline of a personal purpose so deeply felt that it must eschew exhibitionism and flamboyance, for Tennyson grapples with the problem of coming to terms with bereavement and death. His elegiac tribute, *In Memoriam* (1850), was begun in 1833. The sections were written at different times and in different places. The chaste metrical form adopted (four-foot iambic quatrians, rhyming *abba*) had been used by Lord Herbert of Cherbury, but Tennyson was unaware that it was not his own invention. Tennyson deftly exploited its metrical possibilities and, as he gave periodic vent to his private grief, brooded on its larger significance, and explored the answering consolations of Christian faith, the stanzas accumulated and the poet decided to arrange them in a meaningful sequence so that the whole should show the gradual conquest of suffering and doubt. It was to be at once an autobiographical record, the 'Way of the Soul', and, as Tennyson himself said, 'a kind of *Divina Commedia*, ending with happiness.'[1] Thus the scattered laments, probing reflections and fitful reckonings of grief's continuance culminate in a marriage song that celebrates the wedding of his sister. The hope is expressed that an offspring of the union will be born to be a 'closer link' between men of the present and those of the future for whom nature will be 'an open book'. For Hallam has finally become, in the eyes of the poet, a 'noble type' treading this planet prematurely and providing a foretaste of the future humanity that will shake off its animal affiliations.

Those who follow the poet's spiritual pilgrimage sympathetically will perhaps find the wayward development of mood and response throughout the body of the poem more genuinely in accord with man's inner dignities than this closing attempt to overlay it with a forward-looking philosophy. But the poem's greatness lies in the way the poet re-creates such scenes as the calm of a soundless morning with only 'the chestnut pattering to the ground' and the mood of calm despair that accompanies it. The concentrated character of grief, often sharply particularized, has rarely been so finely defined:

> Be near me when my light is low,
>   When the blood creeps, and the nerves prick
>   And tingle; and the heart is sick,
> And all the wheels of Being slow.

[1] Tennyson, *In Memoriam, Annotated by the Author* (1905).

The reasoning which wrestles with this grief convinces because it is everyman's reasoning, not because it is watertight. Piece by piece, there is much writing that is authentic and irresistible. Moreover here, as elsewhere, Tennyson is aware of current scientific thinking and the need to accommodate it. For all the flaws that arise from Tennyson's philosophic over-simplifications, *In Memoriam* surely stands after *The Prelude* and alongside *The Ring and the Book* among the big poems of the century.

Tennyson called *Maud* (1855) a 'monodrama'. It is a collection of diverse lyrics, many of them intensely passionate in rhythm and expression, which recount a tragic story of frustrated love. The violence and turbulence of tone match the state of mind of the narrator. His father and family were ruined by the lord of the Hall, whose daughter Maud he has now fallen in love with. Her brother is contemptuous of him and though he gains Maud's love, the brother's insults provoke a confrontation in which the brother is killed, and the narrator is compelled to flee. Through the impassioned rhythm and high register of the outcry an archetypal force is given to the experience of deep devotion countered by worldly arrogance that is inimical to genuineness and purity when they are devoid of rank and wealth. Yet it is also evident that a personal and particular awareness of rejection underlies the agitation. Agony and rapture alike are voiced with superb vigour.

Tennyson's most ambitious work was *The Idylls of the King*. It came out piece by piece between 1859 and 1885. The long-pondered scheme to present the story of Arthur and the Knights of the Round Table in poetry squares with the kind of ambition that possessed Milton and Wordsworth to fashion a work of epic proportions and significance. Tennyson delivered himself of his *magnum opus* tale by tale, and not in the order which was eventually theirs. Between *The Coming of Arthur* and *The Passing of Arthur* are sandwiched the ten tales, beginning with the cheerful story of *Gareth and Lynette*, working through the saddening rhythm of demoralization and collapsing hopes to the events of *The Last Tournament* and *Guinevere*. The blank verse is finely and melodiously handled, but it has an archaic stateliness that helps to distance the adventures and their participants. There is richness of colour and detail, but it is a tapestried richness, far from the monochromatic, but somehow bi-dimensional. This does not mean that the tales do not touch the emotions: they do, and with something more than sentiment, for even forsaken Elaine's over-sweet song to sweet love and sweet death tears at the heart:

> High with the last line scaled her voice, and this,
> All in a fiery dawning wild with wind
> That shook her tower, the brothers heard.

The high peak of the work is *The Passing of Arthur* where, against an uncannily sensitized natural background, masterly cadences measure out the grievous approach of the king's end – his burden of lost hopes and broken loyalties, his haunting reminiscences, his last exhortation, and his committal to the queens, the barge and the lake.

Much has been said of the Victorianization of Malory's values and the expurgation of his substance. Tennyson's determination to turn Arthur into an almost quasi-divine incarnation of 'Ideal manhood' involved sanctification of the king in accordance with current mores. When Arthur stands with sinful Guinevere at his feet:

> I did not come to curse thee, Guinevere,
> I, whose vast pity almost makes me die
> To see thee, laying there thy golden head ...

the husband is momentarily lost in the embodied moral and religious authority:

> Lo! I forgive thee, as Eternal God
> Forgives.

And as the penitent queen grovels at his feet, she perceives in the darkness the waving of his hands in blessing: the husbandly parting is merged in sacerdotal benediction. To imagine that Tennyson wanted Victorian cuckolds to address their faithless wives in these lofty terms is surely to miss the point.

Anyone who has studied the metrical force and versatility of *The Charge of the Light Brigade, Locksley Hall* and the *Tribute to Virgil*, and anyone who has savoured the imagery of 'Now sleeps the crimson petal, now the white' or the music of 'The splendour falls on castle walls' knows that their impact is one of unique technical accomplishment covering every variety of orchestration from the majestic and the urgent to the delicate and the ethereal. Yet this is only one aspect of Tennyson's versatility. In *Enoch Arden* (1864) the story of the long-lost, shipwrecked wanderer's return, to find wife and children in the keeping of his boyhood friend and rival, is handled with frank simplicity, if not with Wordsworthian force, and the blank verse keeps an unobtrusive grip on feeling and dialogue. Dialect poems like *Northern Farmer* (*Old Style* and *New Style*) are vigorous and entertaining. Lastly, the magnificent monologue *Ulysses*, in which the old hero determines in age on one more venture before life is done, indicates Tennyson's capacity, within a very small compass, to extend the import of an individual's impulse transcendentally by investing it with potently mythic images:

> The long day wanes: the slow moon climbs: the deep
> Moans round with many voices. Come, my friends,
> 'Tis not too late to seek a newer world.

Tennyson did not lack a sense of humour. When Browning published his *Sordello* in 1840 – over 5,000 lines of the most difficult poetry in the English language – Tennyson quoted the first line and the last:

> Who will, may hear Sordello's story told. . . .
> Who would, has heard Sordello's story told.

They were the only two lines in the poem that he under-

stood, Tennyson said, and they were both lies. Robert
Browning (1812–89) was difficult partly because he was
learned in out-of-the-way branches of study like the thirteenth-century struggle between the Guelphs and the Ghi-
bellines that provides the background to the story of Sordello
– of 'the development of a soul', as Browning called it. He
was difficult too because of his eccentricities of style. He
relied on oblique implications and innuendoes for conveying
impressions and information, especially in the form that was
his speciality – the dramatic monologue, in which a character reveals himself and his past, sometimes, like the Duke of
My Last Duchess, without any intention of doing so. The
last (and least creditable) aspect of Browning's difficulty was
his penchant towards sheer display of expertise in the forcing of excruciating rhyme ('fabric' with 'dab brick', 'Italy'
with 'fit ally') and in other parodic or semi-parodic caricatures of his own verbal dexterity. When the tongue is
fully in the cheek, one can have a good laugh at this kind of
thing; but the jokes seem to be little different from the
apparently serious gymnastics that occur in earnest poems
like *Rabbi ben Ezra*:

> Irks care the crop-full bird? Frets doubt the maw-
> crammed beast?

Browning had begun his poetic career with the anonymous
publication of *Pauline* in 1833. It is a sickly and confused
outburst of pseudo-Shelleyan sentiment unanchored to
reality and punctuated largely by dashes. Browning's aunt
financed its publication, but no one bought it. *Paracelsus*
followed, a blank-verse drama dealing with a sixteenth-
century magician-cum-scientist, a serious chemist who was
denounced as a quack. His fervent pursuit of the secret of
things, which puts him at loggerheads with his unadven-
turous fellows, is Browning's theme. After Browning's next
venture, the blank-verse tragedy *Strafford,* failed, the poet
worked on *Sordello*; but his potential only began to be
realized in the pamphlets issued between 1841 and 1846,

called *Bells and Pomegranates*, and beginning with *Pippa Passes*. Pippa's song ('The year's at the spring. ... God's in his heaven, All's right with the world') is the delighted cry of a girl from the silk mills of Asolo on her annual day off. As she goes singing through the town, her cheerful voice is overheard by four parties whom she is envying for their happiness, each of whom at the time is ironically involved in tragedy or near-tragedy, and each of whom is moved by her voice to appropriate remorse, forgiveness, action or compassion. Other numbers of the series contained *Dramatic Lyrics* (1842) and *Dramatic Romances* (1845). These, together with *Men and Women* (1855) and *Dramatis Personae* (1864), contain most of Browning's best poetry, apart from *The Ring and the Book*.

Browning's imaginative skill with dramatic monologue is notably evident in *Fra Lippo Lippi* and *Andrea del Sarto* (*Men and Women*), companion studies of Florentine painters: Filippo Lippi was a fifteenth-century Carmelite monk who abducted a nun and whose frescoes are remarkable for the colourful detail and composition, and Andrea del Sarto, a generation younger, was known for his faultless technique ('Andrea senza errore'). Browning brings these two to life in portrayals which at once match the character of their work and incidentally serve to press home Browning's preference for the restless aspiration of an effervescent if wayward enthusiast like Lippi over the perfection achieved by one too ready to take the easy way. Brother Lippi is caught by the watch, sneaking home to Cosimo de Medici's after a night of frolic, and tells his own story, as one who cannot accept inhibitions on his zest for living or on his artistic vocation to show spiritual beauty through physical beauty. The poem ends with daybreak; but the background of *Andrea del Sarto* is evening twilight, and the painter muses regretfully yet resignedly on the weaknesses which offset his technical achievement. His 'low-pulsed forthright craftsman's hand' shuts him off from the heaven that more inspired artists reach. A less obvious contrast on comparable lines might be detected between the self-revelation of the Renaissance bishop looking back on his self-indulgent life in *The Bishop Orders His Tomb At Saint Praxed's Church*, where the worldly old reprobate and aesthetic connoisseur is surrounded by his sons ('nephews') and is still brooding, at the hour of death, on his jealousies, animosities and petty vanities; and *A Grammarian's Funeral*, which reproduces the funeral procession of a sixteenth-century German scholar. The mourners march to the heights to bury on a mountain top a man who has spent all his life studying, careless of earthly success. Aspiration, even in failure, has a transcendental value for Browning, never more buoyantly reflected than in *The Last Ride Together*. The rejected lover begs one last ride with his mistress; then, as they ride together, favourably compares his brief, immediate achievement-in-failure with the supposed achievements-in-success of great statesmen, soldiers, poets, artists and musicians, and finally senses the present happiness as a foretaste of Heaven:

> What if we still ride on, we two,
> With life for ever old yet new,
> Changed not in kind but in degree,
> The instant made eternity ...

Like the lover's, the musician's experience can be, in Browning's eyes, a sacramental entry to the eternal vision. In *Abt Vogler* the organist extemporizes and the human touches the infinite at the moment of musical climax ('For earth had attained to heaven, there was no more near nor far').

In *Saul* Browning achieves argumentative clarity and emotional power attractively blended in David's dramatically recalled account of how he brought back Saul from the depths of despair by singing to him. David sings in praise of life and Saul stirs; gradually the trance is broken, but the gloom remains. How shall David further restore him? The agony of loving him and wanting to do all for him at any cost itself provides the answer, and he sings it rapturously. For if God surpasses man immeasurably in all other respects he must also surpass him in the single respect of wanting (like David now) to sacrifice himself for man's restoration. With this prevision of the necessity for God's incarnation in the saving Christ, the work is done:

> 'O Saul, it shall be
> 'A Face like my face that receives thee, a Man like to
> me.'

Overwhelmed with the glory of his vision, David returns home, and one of Browning's most moving climactic paeans settles down to peace and calm.

Browning's vigorous lyricism is vibrant in *The Lost Leader* ('Just for a handful of silver he left us') and *How they brought the good news from Ghent to Aix*. There are gems of a gentler kind among the love lyrics – perhaps nothing more concisely managed than the capsulated drama of *Meeting at Night* and *Parting at Morning*. At the other extreme the *magnum opus*, *The Ring and the Book* (1868-9) has forbidding dimensions and has been unduly neglected. Browning picked up the 'book' from a stall in Florence. A goldsmith mixes alloy with gold to make a 'ring', and Browning fashions his work by adding to the basic story of the book – a seventeenth-century murder case. Guido Franceschini, an impoverished count, marries Pompilia Comparini, only to discover that the bride's wealth is not what he thought – nor indeed her parentage. He persecutes her cruelly, accusing her of unfaithfulness with the priest, Caponsacchi, who takes her away. Then she faces a charge of adultery, but protests her innocence. Caponsacchi, however, is banished and Pompilia is placed in a convent. Later, back at her old home, she is murdered along with her 'parents' (they adopted her). Guido is executed. Browning presents the story in a series of monologues. 'Half-Rome' represents the case from Guido's side and 'The Other Half-Rome' represents Pompilia's side. After 'Tertium Quid' has voiced a further point of view, Guido makes his public case as the wronged husband, then Caponsacchi his, and Pompilia's own dying confession follows: it is made with touching faith:

> Marrriage on earth seems such a counterfeit,
> Mere imitation of the inimitable:
> In heaven we have the real and true and sure.

Rival advocates sum up – at great length (the vein is lighter here); and then, in Book X, the Pope considers the case and delivers judgement. Guido is to be beheaded next morning, the Pope nourishing the faint hope that the blow of death may flash out the truth

> 'And Guido see, one instant, and be saved.'

Thereupon Guido is given a second monologue – this time a private attempt at self-justification. At the end of it he hears the messengers of execution on the prison stairs and, just as the Pope had hoped, the imminence of death wrings from him in his very last line a cry that reveals the truth by its implicit claim for Pompilia's goodness:

> 'Pompilia, will you let them murder me?'

Browning was completely unknown when he found himself named favourably alongside Wordsworth and Tennyson in Elizabeth Barrett's *Lady Geraldine's Courtship* (*Poems*, 1844):

> Or from Browning some 'Pomegranate' which, if cut
>   deep down the middle,
> Shows a heart within blood-tinctured, of a veined
>   humanity.

Browning wrote to Elizabeth Barrett, whose fame was already established, and there followed the famous courtship that whisked the poetess from sofa and sickroom and imprisonment under a gaoler-father to years of married happiness and health in Italy. Elizabeth Barrett Browning (1806–

61) is a poet whose reputation has slumped inordinately. One can understand why: her defects are a strain on the patience; her poems often seem too long; for all their accomplishment, one puts them aside unfinished. Good passages, culled and gathered, look impressive: they mark a poet of learning and dexterous verbal sensitivity. But they leave behind much unevenness and much diffuseness. In some of the *Sonnets from the Portuguese* – so called to veil the fact that they were a private record of Elizabeth's love for Browning – the sonnet form disciplines the thinking and the expression admirably, as in 'If thou must love' (XIV) with its neatly perceptive psychological conceits:

> Neither love me for
> Thine own dear Pity's wiping my cheeks dry,
> Since one might well forget to weep who bore
> Thy comfort long, and lose thy love thereby.

And there is firmness and directness, along with subtlety enough, in some of the urgent declarations of love, like 'How do I love thee? Let me count the ways' (XLII); but others are weakly and redundantly rhetorical and verbally self-indulgent.

Oddly perhaps, in view of her prolixity elsewhere, Mrs Browning's longest poem is readily readable. *Aurora Leigh* (1856) is a narrative poem with some 10,000 lines of blank verse, spirited in idiom and vigorous in rhythm. In its dedication the poet describes it as 'the most mature of my works, and the one into which my highest convictions upon Life and Art have entered'. Aurora is a poet, and her cousin Romney Leigh an ardent social reformer whose proposal of marriage she refuses, being hurt by his proud demand for a 'helpmate' rather than a 'mistress'. Romney sets up a socialistic community on his estate, rescues a tramp's daughter, Marian Erle, plans to marry her, but loses her when she is tricked and taken to a brothel. His community breaks up, his hall is burnt, and he loses his eyesight. The final recon-

ciliation between Romney and Aurora (one is inevitably reminded of *Jane Eyre*) represents a mellowing and blending
of conflicting approaches, social and public, individual and
personal, to the cause of humanity :

> Beloved, let us love so well,
> Our work will still be better for our love,
> And still our love be sweeter for our work.

If Tennyson and Browning strove to voice the victory of
faith over doubt in the Victorian Age, Matthew Arnold
(1822–88) may be said to have voiced the victory of doubt
over faith. A dour melancholy broods over his work as a poet.
The son of a forceful and famous headmaster of Rugby, he
laments the loss of his father in *Rugby Chapel*, stressing his
cheerfulness and zealous strength. By contrast we on earth
'strain on' with 'frowning foreheads' and lips 'sternly compress'd'. Father kills son in *Sohrab and Rustum*, a sombre
and stately 'epic' fragment. The disaster is a grievous instance of accident and misunderstanding prior to the revelation of identities, pitiable rather than tragic. There is a
pervasive sorrowful dignity, but the dispirited fatalism deprives the conflict and catastrophe of emotional spine. The
deficiency is perhaps a correlative of that tormenting doubt
by which Arnold's imagination seems sometimes to be de-
energized. There is comparable enervation in *Balder Dead*.
This Norse myth of the god of light, whose release from
the abode of the shades is conceded provided that all things
on earth weep for him, involves a preoccupation with universal lamentation symptomatic of Arnold's spirit. The
lachrymose tone recurs in *The Scholar Gipsy*. Here Arnold
resurrects a seventeenth-century legend of a student drop-out
who joined the gipsies and still haunts the Oxford countryside. Arnold's aim is to pin-point the 'strange disease of
modern life, / With its sick hurry, its divided aims' and to
versify envy of the unspoilt singleness of purpose that keeps
the young scholar away from the 'sick fatigue, the languid
doubt', the disintegration and hopelessness of the nine-

teenth-century urban mind and spirit. And *Empedocles on Etna* presents dramatically the last reflections of the disillusioned Sicilian philosopher before suicide in the volcano. Empedocles's great lyrical outburst in Act I scene ii warns men against fabricating gods to be blamed for human suffering or to provide imaginary satisfactions, and gives the lie to Browning's consolatory way of reading even failure and dissatisfaction as corroborative of faith:

> Fools! that in man's brief term
> He cannot all things view,
> Affords no ground to affirm
> That there are gods who do ...

Man must face life's harshness honestly, look inwards, and discipline his will to reality.

Arnold's prose works represent an extended crusade against the materialism and philistinism of the Victorian Age. In works like *Culture and Anarchy* (1869) and *Essays In Criticism* (1865 and 1888) he strove to exercise a prophetic influence by bringing a surgically critical judgement to bear on society and literature. Culture is the only brake on current worship of wealth. English Protestantism has emphasized the moral at the expense of the cultural. We have relied on faulty religious organizations with inadequate ideas of perfection. 'The pursuit of perfection is the pursuit of sweetness and light.' The whole of society must be 'permeated by thought, sensible to beauty, intelligent and alive'. Arnold's idealism would do away with classes and 'make the best that has been thought and known in the world current everywhere' (*Culture and Anarchy*).

In such poems as *Thyrsis* a fine apparatus of authentic poetic ceremonial is brought into play, but it serves chiefly to probe the nerve of disquietude and stir the pool of uncertainty, and one is left in a mood of pensive nostalgia and poignant regret. Yet Arthur Hugh Clough (1819–61), whom *Thyrsis* commemorates, was himself a man of some toughness, as his much-quoted verses, 'Say not the struggle naught availeth' indicate. He resigned his Oxford fellowship in rejection of required Anglican orthodoxy: he wrote in hexameters a bright and lively long-vacation pastoral called *The Bothie of Tober-na-Vuolich* (1848) in which Oxford students visit Scotland in a party with a tutor and one of them falls in love with a Highland lassie, Elspeth Mackaye. Clough's vigour contrasts with Arnold's calculated deflation:

> Philip returned to his books, but returned to his Highlands after;
> Got a first, 'tis said; a winsome bride, 'tis certain.
> There while courtship was ending, nor yet the wedding appointed,
> Under the father he studied the handling of hoe and of hatchet.

Hexameters are employed again in the *Amours de Voyage* (1858), the product of a summer in Italy. The teasing contemporaneousness and the evasion of commitment have been seen as anticipatory of twentieth-century trends:

> But for the funeral train which the bridegroom sees in the distance,
> Would he so joyfully, think you, fall in with the marriage-procession?
> But for the final discharge, would he dare enlist in that service?

It is a far cry from the academic and literary world of Clough and Arnold to the Northamptonshire village in which John Clare (1793–1864) was brought up in poverty, the son of a labourer. He published *Poems Descriptive of Rural Life and Scenery* in 1820 with considerable success, and followed it with three other volumes, the last of them being *The Rural Muse* (1835). But by this time he was struggling to look after a wife and seven children. His mind gave way, and he spent the last twenty-three years of his life in Northampton lunatic asylum. Clare's power and precision as a descriptive poet are striking; and his observant exactitude is animated by an imaginative transference of human attitudes into creatures of earth and sky:

> And note on hedgerow baulks, in moisture sprent,
> The jetty snail creep from the mossy thorn,
> With earnest heed, and tremulous intent,
> Frail brother of the morn.
>
> (*Summer Images*)

His knowledge and love of the country are a part of him, essential to the play of his senses and his mind. By comparison Mathew Arnold's responsiveness to the country must be labelled 'literary'. In Clare's *February* the response of natural life to the first peep of February sunshine and the first hint of spring is detailed in image after image of expertly etched clarity – the misty smoke reeking from behind the running sheep and the new coyness of the no longer hungry robin. In his more subjective poems, like *A Vision* and *The Peasant Poet*, Clare grasps at mythic symbols that give an impression of visionary depth ('I snatch'd the sun's eternal ray / And wrote till earth was but a name'), and the moving verses *Written in Northampton County Asylum* ('I am! yet what I am who cares, or knows?') give voice to agony and need:

> I long for scenes where man has never trod –
> For scenes where woman never smiled or wept –
> There to abide with my Creator, God,
> And sleep as I in childhood sweetly slept.

A poet whose work is no less vividly rooted in the life of the country was William Barnes (1801–86):

> While snowy night winds, blowing bleak
> Up hill, made rock-borne fir-trees creak,
> And drove the snow-flakes, feather-light,
> O'er icy streams in playsome flight ...
>
> (*Burncombe Hollow*)

Barnes's is a warmly peopled environment: unforced gaiety

is captured or recaptured in present scenes or nostalgic memories. In *Shellbrook* the remembered glee of the merry young in white Maytime is counterbalanced by the frozen churchyard all white now with 'young offsunder'd from the young in sleep'. Such familiar moods, in poems of love, description and personal musing, are framed in unwasteful verses that point modestly forward to the work of poets like Thomas Hardy and R. S. Thomas. Barnes's regional affiliation naturally links him with Hardy. His poems in the Dorset dialect impose the usual obstacles to the sympathy of outsiders, but of course they plant the poet four-square in the country he is depicting and give a particularized pathos to human studies like that of the widower in *The Wife a-lost* ('Since I noo mwore do zee your feace').

Emily Brontë (1818–48), though she might be called a 'regional novelist', was not a 'regional poet'. She left behind a handful of poems of astonishing quality, charged with power, and sometimes opening up mystical dimensions:

> Then dawns the Invisible; the Unseen its truth reveals;
> My outward sense is gone, my inward essence feels.
>> (*The Prisoner*)

Her entry into the Unseen is a flight 'home' to a freedom and peace from which the return is a dreadful check, an intense agony, as senses, pulse and brain begin to work once more. In Emily's poems there is delight in nature in all moods and seasons; there is suffering tersely compressed into a handful of burning words ('If grief for grief can touch thee'); and there is one of the loveliest outcries from the heart of bereavement in our literature:

> Cold in the earth – and the deep snow piled above thee,
>> Far, far removed, cold in the dreary grave!
> Have I forgot, my only Love, to love thee,
>> Sever'd at last by Time's all-severing wave?
>>> (*Remembrance*)

Before we turn to the Pre-Raphaelites, it is fitting to mention Thomas Babington Macaulay (1800–59), the historian. His *History of England from the Accession of James II* is one of the great prose achievements of the age. As a literary critic Macaulay has been accused of wrong-headedness and insensitivity. Certainly his *Essay on Milton* contains silly as well as discerning judgements. The *Lays of Ancient Rome* (1842) display a mastery of bold rhetoric and rhythmic swing. The sledge-hammer style of *Horatius* is saved from vulgarity by a degree of metrical variety, by quick flashes of sharply delineated personal and scenic detail, and of course by the stately stanzaic procession of named warriors and dignitaries strenuously living up to the unforgettable occasion (of keeping the bridge) in deed and word.

The original Pre-Raphaelite Brotherhood was formed by a group of young artists, including Rossetti, Millais and Holman Hunt. Its aim was to combat the 'Raphaelism' of the artistic 'establishment' by drawing on the detailed naturalism of medieval frescoes. In the short-lived periodical, *The Germ*, started in 1850, the movement was extended to literature, and it was in this journal that Rossetti's *The Blessed Damozel* was first published. Dante Gabriel Rossetti (1828–82), as painter and poet, was the man through whose work the phrase 'Pre-Raphaelite Movement' came to have a bigger, vaguer, but nevertheless more useful connotation in relation to aesthetic ideals prominent in the second half of the nineteenth century.

The Blessed Damozel is a rich pictorial tapestry of literary medievalism in which the transfigured beloved leans out from 'the gold bar of Heaven', wishing for her earthly lover left behind. If the three lilies in her hand and the seven stars in her hair catch a note of idealized Dantesque symbolism, the sensuousness of other images brings us back to the colour and warmth of the real earth. A more complex essay in romantic medievalism is *The Bride's Prelude*, an unfinished narrative in which Rossetti arranges his composition with a flamboyant ease and grace:

> Against the haloed lattice-panes
>   The bridesmaid sunned her breast;
> Then to the glass turned tall and free,
> And braced and shifted daintily
> Her loin-belt through her cote-hardie.

The bride tells her story compulsively to her sister – the story of her secret passion and the suffering it has brought her as a mother bereft of her baby. The quiet tension is oppressive, eerie and vibrant with suspense. The personalities are felt as immediate presences, the sister all the more for her reticence, the bride for the hint of possession that hangs about her. And a touch of the Coleridgean magic pervades the strange haunting archaisms of ballads like *Troy Town* and *Sister Helen* with their insistent awesome refrains. By contrast *Jenny*, a poem in lively octosyllabics, is a monologue by the poet. He sits with a prostitute's hand on his knee in her room, and wonders why he is where he is. Jenny falls asleep. Touchingly, whimsically, he muses on her, doing full justice to both her wantonness and her charm, till the cold light of dawn breaks, and he steals off silently without disturbing her, laying among her golden hair the golden coins she has not earned.

Interest will always focus on Rossetti's sonnet sequence, *The House of Life*. Some of the poems record his love for Elizabeth Siddal whom he married, after intolerable delay and some faithless distraction, in 1860, and who died from an overdose of laudanum two years later. Rossetti's grief and remorse were such that he buried the manuscript of his current poems in her coffin. The lost poems were exhumed with his permission nine years later, and published in 1870; but the complete sequence, *The House of Life*, did not appear until 1881 in *Ballads and Sonnets*, and by this time Rossetti's addiction to chloral had sadly disordered him. Jane Morris (William Morris's wife) was another source of inspiration in a collection notable for emotional openness and for that blend of perceptive realism and romantic idealism that so distinguishes Rossetti:

> What of her glass without her? The blank grey
> There where the pool is blind of the moon's face.
> Her dress without her? The tossed empty space
> Of cloud-rack whence the moon has passed away.
>
> (*Without Her*)

The 101 sonnets are by no means all love poems. They include packed descriptive studies like *Ardour and Memory* (LXIV) and dramatizations of subjective psychological probing like *Lost Days* (LXXXVI), where the poet pictures himself re-meeting after death his murdered selves – representative of the lost days of his life. Perhaps the most searching and disquieting of all are those in which symbolism and passion meet to register the dreams and wastages of love frustrated – in the 'fathom-depth of soul-struck widowhood' (*Willowood*, XLIX, L, LI and LII), or the agitations and reflections of love known (*Body's Beauty*, LXXVIII and *Lovesight*, IV).

Rossetti's sister, Christina Georgina Rossetti (1830–94), differs from her brother in her poetry as in her personality. She was a devout Anglo-Catholic who refused to marry, and the chastity of her life and her poetry seems to counterbalance her brother's excesses with compensatory spiritual and artistic discipline. She is known to the young for her delightful verse fairy tale, *Goblin Market*, in which two sisters, Laura and Lizzy, are tempted by the rich fruits the goblins sell. Laura succumbs, yearns for more, and becomes gravely ill when the goblins refuse her. Lizzy saves her sister redemptively by resisting the goblins' allurements. The allegorical meaning is oddly consonant with the contrast between Christina and her brother. Some of Christina's finest poems are exquisitely wrought miniatures, giving graceful stanzaic form to descriptive scenes or reflective moods (see *Twilight Calm* or *A Birthday* – 'My heart is like a singing bird'). There is nothing in them to match her

brother's decorative lavishness, yet the comparative freedom from ornament does not produce in the best ones any
weakness in the fabric or thinness of effect. Rather simplicity and directness give translucency to the texture. The
lucidity makes for a searching poignancy in those poems
where personal relationships are at issue, regretfully or nos-
talgically ('When I am dead, my dearest / Sing no sad songs
for me' and the sonnet, 'Remember me when I am gone
away'). Many of the poems that reflect personal renunciation, or give expression to religious dedication and need,
touch the heart deeply. *Monna Innominata*, a sonnet
sequence, is her fervent record of love denied:

> Many in aftertimes will say of you
> 'He loved her' – while of me what will they say? ...
> I charge you at the Judgment make it plain
> My love of you was life and not a breath.

It was Rossetti's influence that first involved William
Morris (1834–96) in the Pre-Raphaelite Movement, and indeed Rossetti's love for Morris's wife became a sorrow and
a burden to the husband. Another crucial influence on
Morris was that of John Ruskin (1819–1900) whose three-
volume treatise, *The Stones of Venice*, exalts Gothic art and
discredits Renaissance art. Ruskin's wide-ranging en-
thusiasms committed him to richly written polemics against
contemporary philistinism and on behalf of social reform.
Of his many works he valued especially *Sesame and Lilies*
(1865) and *Unto this Last* (1862).

Morris was an artist-poet. His products extended from
furniture and wallpaper to book-production. He founded the
Kelmscott Press for issuing his own works and for reprint-
ing classics, like Chaucer, in 1890. His devotion to fine craftsmanship and his concern for aesthetic values were closely
bound up with his rejection of capitalistic industrialism and
his zealous work for the cause of socialism. The range of his
interests and achievements is formidable, the expression of
a rare and rich personality. His historical knowledge of the

Middle Ages would not allow him to be satisfied with vaguely idealized Pre-Raphaelite medievalism. Guenevere is at once lovingly and spiritedly projected in *The Defence of Guenevere*. The dramatic energy locked in *terza rima* brings the tone closer to Browning than to Arthurian Tennyson. This poem, like *The Haystack in the Floods* from the same volume (*The Defence of Guenevere and Other Poems*, 1858), has emotional tension and imaginative concentration. It may be argued that the smoother decorativeness of some of Morris's subsequent work involved a loss of intensity. The poetry becomes an intentional means of escape from contemporary ugliness.

> Forget six counties overhung with smoke,
> Forget the snorting steam and piston stroke ...

So begins the *Prologue* to *The Earthly Paradise* (1868). It tells how Norsemen, fleeing the Black Death, set sail in search of the earthly Paradise and eventually reach an unknown Western land where they settle, and exchange stories with their hosts, month by month. Thus the twenty-four tales that follow derive from alternate classical and Northern sources. They show an easy mastery and fluency in varied verse forms, including rhyme royal, octosyllabics and pentametrical couplets. Morris's sustained readability is achieved without lapses into vulgarity, though the texture of his verse is inevitably often insipid and its embellishments thinly spread. *Atalanta's Race* is probably now the best known of the tales, but *The Lovers of Gudrun* is an impressive achievement. It is a version of the Norse saga, the Laxdaela, and tells of Gudrun, daughter of the Icelandic lord, Oswif, who is loved by dear friends, Kiartan and Bodli. The rivalry brings tragic death to both.

Morris had achieved his first success with *The Life and Death of Jason* (1867), telling the story of the Argonauts, Medea and the winning of the Golden Fleece. The poem had outgrown its intended place in *The Earthly Paradise*. Its seventeen books of uncomplicated couplets are all alive with pictorial delights. It may be claimed, however, that the distanced charm of Morris's archaic settings and archaic poetic stance has a devitalizing effect on the inner spirit of his work. One senses a pervasive, languid sadness.

> Dreamer of dreams, born out of due time,
> Why should I strive to set the crooked straight?

he asked in verses prefaced to *The Earthly Paradise*, frankly adding that what he was about was the attempt to 'build a shadowy isle of bliss'. However that may be, his later epic, *Sigurd the Volsung* (1876), bred of his enthusiasm for Icelandic literature, has a more sinewy, though sombre, spirit, and the rolling, rhyming seven-footers give it external vigour that sweeps the reader along. There is energy and freshness too in the long work, *Pilgrims of Hope* (1886), at once a poem of love and of socialism. Immediate in relation to Morris's deep personal concerns, private and public, it deals with a husband-wife-lover triangle and takes us to the Paris Commune. Among Morris's numerous prose works are *A Dream of John Ball* (the poet's dream about John Ball, not John Ball's dream) and *News from Nowhere* (1890), a vision of a post-revolutionary utopian English future.

The aesthetic movement, which was orientated towards social reform in the work of writers like Ruskin and Morris, took a quite different direction in the work of the critic Walter Pater (1839–94). Pater formulated a philosophy of receptivity to works of art as a means of enriching human experience through the intensest responses of the sensibilities. The doctrine presupposes the supreme significance of art: it also isolates the individual with his 'own dream of a world'. The core of Pater's thinking can be found in the famous 'Conclusion' to his *Studies in the History of the Renaissance* (1873). His book, *Marius the Epicurean* (1885), portrays the quest for truth of a young Roman in the second century. Marius moves through various phases before finding what he seeks in an early Christian community. The force of the work lies in the important correspondence between Antonine Rome and Victorian England, and between Marius's pilgrimage and Pater's. In Pater the 'movement' drifted towards hedonistic aestheticism. He should not be credited with consciously fathering Wilde's attitudes, but he probably influenced them, and Swinburne's too.

Algernon Charles Swinburne (1837–1909) was the friend of Morris and Rossetti from his Oxford days. He was with Rossetti on the very evening of Mrs Rossetti's tragic death and indeed spoke for him at the inquest, on the love between husband and wife. But Swinburne's interests soon took him away from Pre-Raphaelite medievalism. He published *Atalanta in Calydon*, a drama on the classical Greek model, in 1865 ('It is a long day since I have read anything so fine', Tennyson said),[2] but it was the first of the three series of *Poems and Ballads* (1866, 1878 and 1889) that laid bare his poetic character and provoked the *Saturday Review* to call him 'the libidinous laureate of a pack of satyrs' with 'a mind all aflame with the feverish carnality of a schoolboy over the dirtiest passages in Lemprière'. No doubt Swinburne asked for what he got. He assumed the posture of a perverted prophet preaching pagan sensuality in negation of the religion of the 'pale Galilean'. In *Dolores* he hymned the actress Adah Isaacs Menken, known as the 'naked lady', with an abandoned sexual acclamation that parodies a litany to the Virgin:

> Could you hurt me, sweet lips, though I hurt you?
>   Men touch them, and change in a trice
> The lilies and languors of virtue
>   For the raptures and roses of vice.

Swinburne's sensual extravagances, which often amount to hints of biting and bleeding, of bruised flesh and foaming lips, of the white and the red of nudity, sweep over the reader in a swirl of sound whose basis is rhythmic and assonantal. There is an infectious, self-proliferating musicality:

[2] Edmund Gosse, *The Life of Algernon Charles Swinburne* (Macmillan & Co., London, 1917), p. 139.

phrase grows from phrase, line from line, stanza from stanza, in an intoxicating accumulation, wave after wave of cloying melody. Anapestic metres and feminine rhymes heighten the hypnotic effect. The native gift which gave Swinburne this virtuosity of unfailing aggregative versification, compelling in its vigour and unfaltering in its thrust, is one that any poet might envy. When the versification is informed with vision and directive thought, the product is good. But the process goes on of its own accord when little or nothing is being said. The poetry seems to write itself.

Swinburne turned course in *Songs before Sunrise* (1871). The *Prelude* has a new confession of purpose – to use life's opportunities for service to humanity. The poems that follow were inspired by the struggle for independence in Italy. Bitter anti-clericalism is now at the service of social revolution rather than of sexual emancipation. In *Before a Crucifix* Christ is told how our souls 'sicken' to see against his side the foul and 'leprous likeness of a bride'. The volume also contains the nearest thing in Swinburne to a basic philosophical statement – *Hertha*. The goddess of earth speaks, as animating all nature and all living things. She is the only ultimate reality. Man is urged to free himself from supernatural faiths: they are delusive superstitions that parasitically corrupt the tree of life. Swinburne's dissipation was rapidly killing him when his friend, Theodore Watts Dunton, took him over in 1879 and looked after him at The Pines, Putney, for the nearly thirty years of life left to him. The poet settled down to a steady routine of walking and eating, writing and reading, like a wild thing domesticated.

One of the poems in the first *Poems and Ballads*, *Laus Veneris*, a frankly sensual rendering of the Tannhäuser story, was directly inspired by Swinburne's introduction (at the hand of Rossetti) to Fitzgerald's *Rubáiyát of Omar Khayyam*. Its quatrains fired him with admiration. Edward Fitzgerald (1809–93) published the famous verses ('Rubáiyát' means 'quatrains') in 1859. The Persian poet and astronomer was born in the eleventh century, and Fitzgerald arranged Omar's verses in a connected sequence, translating and freely adapting the original material. The poet muses pessimistically on the passing of time and the vanity of the world's glories, and calls his beloved to fill the cup and make merry while they can. The oriental flavour disinfects the message even for rigoristic readers.

A writer who threw in his lot with the Pre-Raphaelites for a time was George Meredith (1828–1909). It is to his credit as a critic that he had reservations about Swinburne's poetry ('I don't see any internal centre from which springs anything that he does');[3] and it is to Swinburne's credit that he rose to the defence of Meredith's *Modern Love* when it was savaged by the *Spectator* on publication. *Modern Love* is a series of fifty sixteen-lined 'sonnets' recounting growing uneasiness between husband and wife, and recording the total disintegration of their relationship. In the first sonnet one is taken straight inside the bedroom where the wife is sobbing in the night at her husband's side. The immediacy of contact is sustained in scene after scene in which psychological analysis lays bare the nerves of pretence, suspicion and jealousy. It is all done with a wiry economy of expression and intermittent aphoristic force. The outer gambits of the marriage game are underscored with irony, as emotional permutations deployed under the shadow of infidelity are recorded with devastating accuracy. Finally, on the edge of a possible clarification, the wife takes poison. No doubt writing this personal record eased the tension and grief consequent upon Meredith's loss of his first wife. *Modern Love* apart, Meredith the poet is remembered chiefly for one or two items from *Poems and Lyrics of the Joy of Earth* (1883), notably *Phoebus with Admetus*, *The Woods of Westermain* and above all *Love in the Valley*, a pulsing song that gushes up like a fountain in the first stanza and goes flowing, flooding away in an innocent rapture of young love.

[3] Edmund Gosse, *The Life of Algernon Charles Swinburne*, p. 93.

> Under yonder beech-tree single on the green-sward,
>   Couched with her arms behind her golden head,
> Knees and tresses folded to slip and ripple idly,
>   Lies my young love sleeping in the shade.

Another poet with Pre-Raphaelite connections at an early stage in his career was Coventry Patmore (1823–96). His own connections were helpful to the young Brethren. During his early married life (with his first wife, Emily) his 'drawing-room became the meeting-place of such different personalities as Tennyson, Ruskin, and Browning'.[4] He was asked to contribute to the first number of *The Germ* and sent his poem *The Seasons*. Rossetti was delighted. The cultivated simplicity of the Pre-Raphaelites is evident in Patmore's *The Angel in the House*, but he has none of their taste for archaism. This substantial work came out in four parts between 1854 and 1862. It is basically a homely story of wooing and marrying Honoria, the daughter of a dean. But in tracing the growth and maturing of love, the poet adds to his homespun verses hints of the mystical significance of the sexual and marital bonds:

> This little germ of nuptial love,
>   Which springs so simply from the sod,
> The root is, as my song shall prove,
>   Of all our love to man and God.

Patmore lost his first wife, and his second marriage took him from the Church of England to the Church of Rome. His later poetry substituted for the earlier plainness of style a loose free verse that allowed greater flexibility and sometimes degenerated into diffuseness. The 'other poems' of *The Unknown Eros and Other Poems* (1877) include personal records like that of his bereavement, *Departure* ('It was not like your great and gracious ways') and *Tired Memory*. The odes *To the Unknown Eros* explore the mystical dimension of romantic love in marriage. Though there is sometimes an

[4] Derek Patmore, *Portrait of my Family* (Cassell, London, 1935).

embarrassing preciousness of concept ('Little, sequester'd pleasure-house / For God and for His Spouse', he calls the body in *To the Body*), the best passages have imaginative power. *Eros and Psyche* is ostensibly a dialogue between the two mythical figures. But it is also a dialogue between God and the human soul, illuminating the relationship of the soul to God by illuminating the sexual relationship between woman and man. The mystery of divine condescension in seeking man's love, and the pride involved in reluctant response to what is proffered, are matters finely explicated within sexual equivalents.

Two younger fellow Catholic poets closely associated with Patmore were Alice Meynell (1847–1922) and Francis Thompson (1859–1907). Patmore's admiration for Alice Meynell produced an emotional crisis for both of them. Her famous sonnet, *Renouncement* ('I must not think of thee; and tired yet strong / I shun the love that lurks in all delight'), is what she is now best remembered for. It was Alice Meynell and her husband Wilfred who rescued Francis Thompson when opium had reduced him to selling matches in the street. The subsequent friendship between Thompson and Patmore was one of intimate mutual understanding and admiration. In Thompson's verses, 'O world invisible we view thee', occurs the memorable image in which he sees 'the traffic of Jacob's ladder / Pitched betwixt Heaven and Charing Cross'. There is sometimes a vein of simplicity in Thompson:

> The faintest things have fleetest end;
>   Their scent survives their close,
> But the rose's scent is bitterness
>   To him that loved the rose.

> (*Daisy*)

But the purple prose of his *Essay on Shelley* is characteristically lavish, and his most celebrated poem, *The Hound of Heaven*, is an exercise in verbal richness in places reminiscent of Crashaw:

> I was heavy with the even,
> When she lit her glimmering tapers
> Round the day's dead sanctities.

It is a record of conversion. The hound of Heaven is the love of God pursuing the poet's soul till he surrenders to it. As he tries to evade the challenge, seeking consolation in human loves and earthly delights, the pressure of the divine demand gathers urgency in the image of following feet that pound behind him till he is beaten to his knees by the inadequacy of alternative satisfactions. The pursuit is halted when the poet realizes that the darkness of deprivation which all along he feared was really but the shadow of the divine hand stretched over him in love. He has been resisting the offer of protection and peace.

An even more fascinating literary friendship was that between Patmore and Gerard Manley Hopkins (1844–89), a friendship that was represented by few personal contacts but by a voluminous exchange of letters. Hopkins had become a Roman Catholic in 1866 and soon after joined the Jesuit Order. His self-dedication meant a total commitment of all his faculties and restricted the exercise of his poetic talent within the limits allowed by his rigorous conscience and his superiors. It may be doubted whether these restraints damaged him as a poet, for when he did write, it was poetry that measured out in concentrated form the backlog of intensely pressurized experience. For Hopkins's account of the world is indwelt not only by the sensed objective harmony of its multifariousness as it utters God's glory, but also by the subjective need to be involved in that utterance. The exciting thing about Hopkins's technique is that poetry itself has to be disciplined – subjected to open co-operation with the essential character of what it portrays. Words, syntax, rhythm, all the constituents of poetry must move in obedience to that which they are grappling to realize in all its distinctiveness and uniqueness. The image of the farrier in *Felix Randal* is a case in point. In the same way, in

Inversnaid, the burn is realized by a process which makes you feel that words have been gathered, scoured and wedged in place by a mind fiercely determined that they shall do his will in reconstituting an unrepeatable experience:

> This darksome burn, horseback brown,
> His rollrock highroad roaring down,
> In coop and in comb the fleece of his foam
> Flutes and low to the lake falls home.

Hopkins's concern with the attempt to bring to view the inner reality of the living world led to his use of the word 'inscape', which seems to connote not only the essential pattern at the heart of objects and experience but also the individual distinctiveness and uniqueness of a thing – its selfhood. Hopkins released new currents of verbal power by arranging words in a pulsing, jostling counterpoint of rhythm and image that would be right for one experience alone, but dead right for it and inseparable from it. The metrical principle which enabled Hopkins to free his stanzas from subjection to traditional patterns, and to bind rhythm and word, sound and image, together in recapturing the flow of a burn (*Inversnaid*) or the flight of a bird (*The Windhover*), he called 'sprung rhythm'. Though his most substantial work was *The Wreck of the Deutschland*, written 'to the happy memory of five Franciscan Nuns, exiles by the Falk Laws, drowned between midnight and morning of December 7th 1875', his most deeply moving poems are the last 'terrible sonnets'. They record the testing of faith by moods of desolation, and it is done with such distinction as to revivify the sonnet form:

> I cast for comfort I can no more get
> By groping round my comfortless, than blind
> Eyes in their dark can day or thirst can find
> Thirst's all-in-all in all a world of wet.

Thomas Hardy (1840–1928) is chronologically in place here by virtue of his birth date, but his poetry, though he wrote it all through his writing career, was actually published in the latter part of his long life – most of it in the twentieth century (*Poems of the Past and Present*, 1902, *Time's Laughingstocks*, 1909, and *Satires of Circumstance*, 1914). Hardy likes to versify incidents of country life, imposing on its greyer ironies and coincidences the pessimistic outlook expressed in the novels. There are powerful poems of personal observation, like *The Darkling Thrush*, characteristic in the sharp concreteness of the descriptive touches –

> The tangled bine-stems scored the sky
>> Like strings of broken lyres –

and characteristic too in that the sudden burst of joyful song which lights up the winter greyness seems so little justified by what is evident on the terrestrial scene that the poet must assume the bird to have some reason of hope not disclosed to him. It is in reflective observations of this kind, often melancholy and nostalgic, that Hardy excels. The simplicity of his style sometimes seems like a hard-won simplicity; but the sense of strain, which makes for awkwardness at times, also makes for an awareness of thoughts and words grappled with and thoroughly brought to book – as in *On The Departure Platform*:

> We kissed at the barrier; and passing through
> She left me, and moment by moment got
> Smaller and smaller, until to my view
>> She was but a spot.

In spirit, perhaps, Hardy is a twentieth-century poet. In the effects he seeks and the style he cultivates he has little in common with the Pre-Raphaelites and those close to them. His readiness, in the pursuit of directness and authenticity, to run the risk of seeming prosaic or unpolished, separates him from the Victorians.

The death of his first wife, Emma, in 1912, put an end to a relationship whose early happiness had long given way to division and even bitterness. The shock of bereavement was deepened by perusal of autobiographical papers Emma left behind, and Hardy's tangled feelings became vocal in some of his finest poems. Many of them combine a devastating honesty towards himself with poignant recollections of Emma's latest or her earliest days (like *The Going* and *Your Last Drive* or *Beeny Cliff*). They give the reader an acute and intimate encounter with his sorrow and voice an astonishing resurgence of love:

> Woman much missed, how you call to me, call to me,
> Saying that now you are not as you were
> When you had changed from the one who was all to me,
> But as at first, when our day was fair.

> (*The Voice*)

Hardy's last great work, *The Dynasts*, is largely in verse and is dramatic in form. It was published in three parts in 1904, 1906 and 1908, and makes a panoramic survey of events from Napoleon's threat to invade Britain in 1805 to the Battle of Waterloo in 1815. Scenes which depict great political and military events, like Napoleon's coronation or the ball at Brussels before Waterloo, are balanced by scenes showing the day-today reactions of ordinary countrymen and soldiers. And superimposed on the progress of human history is a commentary by supernatural beings – the Spirit of the Years, in Spirit of the Pities, the Spirits Sinister and Ironic, and accompanying Choruses. Thus something like the form of Shakespearian historical drama is fitted with over-world dimensions like those of Goethe's *Faust* and Shelley's *Prometheus Unbound*. In the background is the Immanent Will, the 'Great Foresightless' which a Semichorus of Pities hopes will one day mend its ways:

> Nay; – shall not Its blindness break?
> Yea, must not Its heart awake,
>   Promptly tending
>   To Its mending

> In a genial germing purpose, and for loving-kindness'
> sake?

A poem of even blacker gloom than this is *The City of Dreadful Night* by James Thomson (1834–82). Thomson was an atheistic free-thinker and, though there is a more cheerful vein in lesser-known poems, *The City of Dreadful Night* is charged with utter pessimism and despair. Thomson's introductory verses declare that he writes in 'cold rage' with the delusive hopes and dreams of men and because it gives him 'some sense of power and passion' to try 'in helpless impotence' to catch human woe in words. There follows the nightmare account of the city of darkness and horror. The cumulative exploration of misery is unrelieved in its bitterness by the humour and compassion that accompany Hardy's pessimism. The poetic quality of the work is uneven: there is metrical and verbal clumsiness; and one feels that literature is being ransacked to garner the vocabulary and imagery of maximum calamity.

In Oscar Wilde (1854–1900) the Pre-Raphaelite revaluation of art became caricatured in an aestheticism with a self-parodic centre. Outside the drama, Wilde's reputation depends chiefly on works of sheer charm, like *The Happy Prince and Other Tales* (1888), and works which reflect the aesthetic issue directly, like *The Picture of Dorian Grey* (1891). In the latter the dichotomy between real world and art world is clearly present: for Dorian Grey pays a terrible price for having prayed that his 'portrait should bear the burden of his days, and he keep the unsullied splendour of eternal youth'. Wilde's early poetry (he published *Poems* in 1881) is competently derivative from the Romantics and Pre-Raphaelites. In *The Garden of Eros* he pays explicit tribute to Keats and Shelley, Swinburne ('morning star / Of re-arisen England' who sang 'the Galilean's requiem') and Morris ('sweet and simple Chaucer's child'). The flashy poeticisms are abandoned in *The Ballad of Reading Gaol* (1898). Wilde's passion for Lord Alfred Douglas provoked

Douglas's father, the Marquess of Queensberry, to accuse him of perversion, and Wilde foolishly brought an unsuccessful libel suit which recoiled in a successful homosexual charge and a sentence of two years' hard labour. During imprisonment Wilde wrote the prose apologia later published as *De Profundis,* and it shows us the epigrammatist's art baptized by suffering ('... Out of sorrow have the worlds been built, and at the birth of a child or a star there is pain'). He also wrote the fine ballad marking the execution of a fellow prisoner for murder:

> I never saw a man who looked
> With such a wistful eye
> Upon that little tent of blue
> Which prisoners call the sky
> And every wandering cloud that traced
> Its ravelled fleeces by.

The compelling incantatory power sustains a portrayal of life inside at its point of maximum intensity when the death penalty is to be carried out. The poem carries an indictment burdensome to the social conscience, for which the simple ballad structure is an apt vehicle.

Among minor poets in the last decades of the nineteenth century Austin Dobson (1840–1921) deserves mention for the good-humoured verve of his light verses familiar to many a schoolchild in *A Ballad of Queen Elizabeth* on the Spanish Armada. The more earnest and ambitious poetry of John Addington Symonds (1840–93), the art historian, has perhaps worn less well. Ernest Dowson (1867–1900) had technical expertise and vitality in exploring the cross currents of wayward passion, as evidenced in the popular verses, *Non sum qualis eram* ('Surely the kisses of her bought red mouth were sweet'). Dowson was among those who contributed to the quarterly *Yellow Book* (1894–7) of which Aubrey Beardsley was the first art editor. Lionel Johnson (1867–1902), the poet of *By the Statue of King Charles at Charing Cross*, also contributed; and so did Max Beerbohm (1872–1956), caricaturist and satirist of social and literary fashion, and author of *Zuleika Dobson* (1911), whose pose provoked Oscar Wilde's claim that the gods had granted him the gift of eternal old age. Another contributor was Frederick Rolfe (1860–1913), who claimed the title of 'Baron Corvo'. His further day dreams were given fulfilment in *Hadrian the Seventh* (1905), a novel of self-revelation (not to mention revenge) in which a rejected priest is elected to the papacy.

A. E. Housman (1859–1936), classical scholar and poet, belongs to the same generation, though it was many years before his volume *A Shropshire Lad* (1896) was succeeded by the second volume, *Last Poems* (1922). In his Shropshire countryside he gave his readers an up-to-date version of pastoral. His simply structured but finely fashioned verses have appealed to musicians looking for songs to set. The much-sung *Bredon Hill* ('In summertime on Bredon') neatly miniatures the joy and sorrow of love and loss. The gale in 'On Wenlock Edge the wood's in trouble' blows us feelingly back through history from today's disquiet to 'the Roman and his trouble'. Housman's carefully moulded simplicities of form contain a contrived countryside contemplated with melancholy reflections on the sadness of things. 'Heartless, witless Nature' cares nothing for us whose lot is to 'endure an hour and see injustice done'. In a world where beauty and joy are quickly past, where soldiers' breasts find bullets, and where even the weather is against us, we have at least the certainty of knowing that we are not the first generation to have cursed 'Whatever brute and blackguard made the world'.

Robert Bridges (1844–1930) is a poet whose Victorian output made his name, though he was to become a twentieth-century Poet Laureate in 1913. His three series of *Poems* (1873, 1879 and 1880) and his *Shorter Poems* (1890) have fed the anthologies with felicitous if mannered verses like 'I will not let thee go' and *A Passer-By* ('Whither, O splendid ship, thy white sails crowding'). There is perceptive and observant descriptive work in such poems as *London Snow* and *November*. These, and such favourites as 'Awake, my heart, to be loved' and 'Spring goeth all in white', are the product of a sensitive ear. There can be no question about Bridges's metrical skill and mastery of prosody. Even when one senses a straining after borrowed dignity, in such poems as 'Beautiful must be the mountains whence ye come' (*Nightingales*), one is aware of a highly skilled practitioner fastidiously probing the pen's resources. All the sadder is the fact that Bridges moved away from reality to incarnate his mature reflections in a vast verbal mausoleum, *Testament of Beauty* (1929), a pretentious fabric of craftsmanship about whose precious idiom it is difficult to speak seriously. We described Young's *Night Thoughts* as 'semi-conversation-alized philosophy in ornate garb'. One detects an interest and a talent in Bridge's most ambitious poem that claim him as Young's successor.

By contrast Rudyard Kipling (1865–1936) puts all his poetic cards on the table face upwards. He knows what he wants to say and he speaks to his audience in a tongue they can understand. The rhythms of sturdy ballads and stately hymns undergird his vigorous rhetoric, and the fluent 'catchiness' is the product of superb control. *Departmental Ditties*, *Barrack-Room Ballads* and *The Seven Seas* belong to the nineteenth century (1886, 1892, 1896), and *The Five Nations* and *The Years Between* to the twentieth (1903, 1919). At his best his poems have an ingratiating comeliness evident in the gently archaized minstrelsy that is practised between the chapters of *Puck of Pook's Hill* and *Rewards and Fairies*. Kipling addresses himself to a mass public in racy ballads and in more cultivated if scarcely less hearty experiments in rhythmic facility like *The Flowers*. This poem might stand as a sample of Kipling's flair for rolling out the right words and leaving his artefact shipshape. The repeated chorus, 'Buy my English posies! / Kent and Surrey May', knits together an imperial nosegay; for the refrains interlock with quatrains of stirring seven-footers, devoted in turn to Canada, South Africa, Australia and New Zealand, and concluding:

> Far and far our homes are set round the Seven Seas;
> Woe for us if we forget, we that hold by these!
> Unto each his mother-beach, bloom and bird and land –
> Masters of the Seven seas, O, love and understand.

With Kipling we take dignified leave of Victorian poetry. He is a fit man to ring down a curtain. At the individual or public level, hand on shoulder as in *If*, or head bowed as in *Recessional* ('God of our fathers ... Lest we forget, lest we forget!'), Kipling makes the most of standard moral and emotional postures, and is wise enough not to outreach himself.

19
The Victorian novel

Charles Dickens (1812–70) is as central to the Victorian novel as Tennyson is to Victorian poetry. Dickens's struggling, unhappy childhood, as the son of a poor, debt-ridden dock clerk, brought him into contact with debtors' prisons and forced him into work in a blacking factory at the age of twelve. By perseverance he became office boy, journalist, and finally original contributor to periodicals. His satirical *Sketches by Boz* (in the *Old Monthly Magazine*) proved popular, and the *Pickwick Papers*, following hard after, made his name. What began as an illustrated series of episodes in the lives of the Pickwick Club evolved into a loosely knit picaresque novel.

The experience of rising from poverty to affluence put feeling into Dickens's indignant attack on the cruel exploitation of the poor, children especially, as is evident in *Oliver Twist* (1837–8) and *Nicholas Nickleby* (1838–9). In the former the savage Poor Law and the workhouse are under judgement: in the latter it is the brutal maltreatment of his charges by Wackford Squeers, schoolmaster of Dotheboys Hall. Such social passion is a continuing factor in Dickens's work and encourages reformers and revolutionaries to claim him for their own. A second strength is his keen eye for character and for the idiosyncrasies of habit (involving temperament, speech, physical peculiarities, dress and possessions) by which personality comes to life. The extent to which the wide gallery of Dickensian types, subtle or caricatured, is also the product of reading is not clear; but the influence of Smollett cannot be ignored. A third strength is the strange emotional power which makes Dickens's revelation of suffering compelling if sometimes melodramatic (a good instance is the death of young Paul Dombey in *Dombey and Son*, 1846–7), and which makes his treatment of love, generosity and unselfishness something that grabs at the heart (one might instance the final sacrifice of Sidney Carton in *A Tale of Two Cities*, 1859, Dickens's highly coloured novel of the French Revolution). It must be admitted that there is an element of artistic unreliability in Dickens's human studies. Sentimentality and moralism sometimes flatten characters out of their authenticity: emotion and rhetoric may be tastelessly over-amplified. The death of Little Nell in *The Old Curiosity Shop* (1840–1) is often cited as a case of cloying excess, though its pathos had the nation in tears. The effect of Dickens's personal life on the emotional aspect of his work is difficult to gauge. The critical habit of writing off Dickens's marriage (which produced ten children) as a 'failure' is not without foundation. Dickens's devotion to his sister-in-law, Mary Hogarth, who died at the age of seventeen, was deep and disturbing: the later liaison with the young actress, Ellen Ternan, who became his mistress after he was separated from his wife, must have been a disquieting matter for a writer who had become firmly associated with household virtues. But there can be no doubt about Dickens's profound involvement with his own created characters. 'Paul is dead,' he wrote, after working on the chapter 'What the waves were always saying' in *Dombey and Son*, 'He died on Friday night about 10 o'clock, and as I had no hope of getting to sleep afterwards, I went out, and walked about Paris until breakfast-time next morning.'[1]

Social conscience, deft characterization, emotional power – to these three strengths we must add two more; humour and poetry. The humour is universally recognized. Its force depends often on the ability to mingle pathos with comedy, tears with laughter; to undercut pomposity and pretentiousness with irony; to cartoonify oddity. It is often closely related to Dickens's mastery of the grotesque. The poetry is a more complex matter. Dickens is a poet in that his descriptive writing has an imaginative range that extends, say, the account of a London fog (*Bleak House*, chapter 1) into a rhapsody on fogginess. He is the master of atmosphere who can inject into the marshland background at the beginning of *Great Expectations* or the waterside scenes of *Our Mutual Friend* an air of sinister desolation or eerie gloom. Dickens is a poet too in that the imagery which in his early works animates scenes and human portraits becomes in his later works a unifying principle whereby characters, events and background are symbolically related. In earlier novels characters are sometimes detachable from their context: one may forget which book a memorable character belongs to. But there is a development from the inspired extemporization of *Pickwick*, through the various attempts to organize material around the skeleton of a conventional plot, to the full maturity, from *Dombey and Son* onwards, when a dominant motive, social and moral, is increasingly evident in thematic strands and correspondences that give unity to

[1] K. J. Fielding, *Charles Dickens, A Critical Introduction* (Longmans, Harlow, 2nd edition, 1965).

the work. In the last great works, *Little Dorrit* (1857-8), *Great Expectations* (1860-1) and *Our Mutual Friend* (1864-5) characters belong together by their relatedness in Dickens's poetic exploration of the human situation, an exploration overshadowed at the material level by the fortuitous distribution of wealth, at the spiritual level by the need for love and the presence of evil.

Not that the novels of the 1840s are any less rich in essential Dickensian qualities. The attempt to turn historical novelist and picture the Gordon Riots in *Barnaby Rudge* (1841) resulted in an uncomfortably manufactured product, but there are some of Dickens's most memorable character portraits in *Martin Chuzzlewit* (1843-4) and *David Copperfield* (1849-50). Mrs Pecksniff and Mrs Gamp belong to the former; Mr Micawber, Traddles, Mr Peggotty and Mrs Gummidge to the latter. *David Copperfield* begins with one of the finest recapturings of the child's view of life that we have. No doubt the considerable autobiographical element in the book accounts for Dickens's own professed fondness for it. But just as the material of *Dombey and Son* was carefully structured around the central idea of Mr Dombey's obsessive ambition for his firm and son, that overrides the claims of family love and personal need, so too in *David Copperfield*, for all its multifariousness, the imaginative fluency is matched with unity of theme. The moral heart of the design is to recommend fortitude and, in John Forster's words, 'to strengthen our generous emotions and to guard the purities of the home'.[2] At the last, in *Edwin Drood* (1870), which Dickens was working on at the time of his death, he turned to the kind of mystery at which his friend Wilkie Collins excelled. The unfinished story is all the more teasing now for the subtle suggestiveness of its atmosphere.

However, Dickens's greatness consists, not in the production of one or two masterpieces, but in the creation of an imaginative world, packed with vividly realized men, women and children, and overlapping the dividing lines between

[2] K. J. Fielding, *Charles Dickens, A Critical Introduction*.

novel and novel. His suspicion of institutions, his hatred of harsh and mean vices, and his high valuation of the gentler virtues, give him a strong appeal today. We know what decent people are up against in the Dickensian world, though it wears different masks in different novels. The powers-that-be who are represented by workhouses, debtors' prisons, courts of Chancery, brutal schools, fraudulent commercial enterprises and the like are fit objects of our hatred. So are the hypocrites, swindlers, bullies, blackmailers, humbugs, seducers, snobs and exploiters who flourish within the corrupt social machinery. And eminently lovable are, not only the gentle, tender, innocent victims of evil men, but also the warm-hearted scapegraces, fumblers, bumblers and wastrels who in various degrees manage to get by. Perhaps one secret of Dickens's success is that he gives readers a kind of moral holiday in a world where approval and disapproval, love and hate, can be congenially distributed without complexity or confusion of mind or conscience. One should add, finally, that the prodigality of Dickens's world is matched by the prodigality of his style. The ease with which Dickens changes voice and idiom, so as to chime in with every variety of human character and characteristic, strikes one as a kind of verbal wizardry. He exploits the resources of language with a whole-heartedness that spares little in the way of histrionics, but the aptness of tone and expression is Shakespearian in its range.

Dickens founded the weekly, *Household Words,* in 1849, and ten years later, *All the Year Round.* It was in *Household Words* that Wilkie Collins's novel, *The Woman in White* appeared in serial form in 1860. Dickens helped Collins and collaborated with him in stories for the journal. Collins (1824–89), who proclaimed Scott 'the God Almighty of novelists', has himself been called the 'father of the detective novel'. *The Woman in White* is an intricate tale of villainous scheming for money by Sir Percival Glyde, whose speciality is to get those women he wants out of the way locked up in lunatic asylums. The ingenuity with which the story is pre-

Conclusion

sented by various participants successively makes it a masterpiece of plotting. An even more cunning *tour de force* in
the same form is *The Moonstone* (1868). It has the additional
spice of the enormous diamond whose possession seems to
carry mysterious peril. Collins's mastery of suspense is such
that it compels eager reading. A bachelor himself, Collins
managed to surround his own private life with mystery too,
keeping two successive mistresses, but so discreetly as to tax
prying historians. And, a sufferer from gout, he gradually
became dependent on a daily glass of laudanum. His relationship with Dickens was close enough for him to be
among the first to question the reliability of the standard
Life of Charles Dickens (1872–4) by Dickens's friend, John
Forster (1812–76). The issue takes us into the heart of the
controversy about Dickens's private life, which is still disputed territory among the experts.

A year older than Dickens, William Makepeace Thackeray
(1811–63) made the same progress through journalism to
the serialized production of novels. But his upbringing and
social background gave him an obverse outlook on the
civilization of his day. Thackeray's father had money and
position in India with the East India Company. His father
died when Thackeray was four, but he soon acquired a stepfather, and the beginning of literary success conveniently
coincided with the depletion of private means left by his
father. The sureness of the position from which Thackeray
the writer surveys the world is symptomatic of his social
experience. But there were crucial personal experiences of
another kind feeding their fruits into his work. His marriage
to Isabella Shawe in 1836 was at first a happy one, but the
second of his three daughters died in infancy, and Isabella
became insane. The shadows on Thackeray's private life
threw him into society life for consolation and into assiduous
writing for preoccupation. He became a compulsive writer.
He started with *The Yellowplush Correspondence*, assuming the character of a footman for indirect satire on the
social scene (in *Fraser's Magazine*), then invented Major

Goliah O'Grady Gahagan for the purpose of recounting grossly exaggerated military adventures (in the *New Monthly Magazine*, 1838–9). The satirical vein acquires an eighteenth-century flavour in *The Book of Snobs* (*By one of themselves*) (1848), which had been issued as separate papers in *Punch* during 1846 and 1847. 'The necessity of a work on Snobs, demonstrated from History, and proved by felicitous illustrations. . . . Snobs are to be studied like other objects of Natural Science, and are a part of the Beautiful (with a large B) . . .' Thackeray's prefatory remarks remind us that he is very much Fielding's successor. Indeed the Fielding of *Jonathan Wild*, the Fielding of *Tom Jones* and the Fielding of *Amelia* are revivified as Thackeray assumes the mantle of satirist, omniscient author, and chronicler of private emotion and public destruction in his masterpiece, *Vanity Fair* (1847–8).

The story is symmetrically built on two careers, that of Becky Sharp, a gifted, calculating minx whose wit and sexuality are her means of getting a rich husband and entry into society, dissipation and vice; and that of Amelia Sedley, a gentle, earnest, loving girl who wastes her affection on George Osborne. Osborne deviates into an affair with Becky and is killed at Waterloo. There is a devoted, unselfish, would-be husband for Amelia in the wings throughout, secretly helping her; but it is ten years before Becky disenchants Amelia about her lost husband and the faithful Dobbin comes into his own. The panoramic vastness and complexity of the total picture, the superb control and the unflagging blend of satire with compassion make this one of the greatest books of the age. That Thackeray chooses to ridicule society through Becky Sharp's exploitation of its hollowness and corruption, and at the same time to hold Becky's course under severe judgement, is a subtle exercise in two-pronged moral censure.

Thackeray did not write again with such irresistible inspirational power, but he accomplished something at least as remarkable in its own kind in *The History of Henry*

Esmond (1852), a historical novel of the reign of Queen Anne, in which literary figures like Addison, Steele and Swift, as well as political figures like Marlborough and the Pretender, are convincingly pictured. The central story movingly recounts the career of a young man, Esmond, whose life is shadowed by his supposed illegitimacy, and by the altruistic scruples which prevent him, when he learns the truth, from revealing that he is in fact legitimate and an heir. The sustaining of an eighteenth-century style throughout is a considerable feat. *The Virginians* (1857–9) is a sequel. We follow the fortunes of Esmond's descendants in the New World. If one is seeking clear insight into the layers of feeling and motivation, pretence and counter-pretence, that complicate the texture of human character and human society, Thackeray has a lot to offer.

Thackeray received a disturbing compliment in 1847 when the second edition of *Jane Eyre* was dedicated to him by the unknown Currer Bell. Charlotte Brontë (1816–55) knew nothing of Thackeray's private distress – his wife's insanity – when she dedicated to him a novel whose hero is burdened with a lunatic wife. Thackeray's mind fascinated Charlotte Brontë; yet her comments show that she detected his weaknesses too. For she was no untutored genius. *Jane Eyre*, for all the use made in it of childhood memories and other personal experience, is a well-structured work, balancing two contrasting love relationships against each other; the one, with Rochester, a relationship which is deeply passionate but morally wrong until bereavement transforms the situation; the other, with St John Rivers, a relationship which is deeply justifiable on all moral and religious grounds, but devoid of passion. The tension endured by the heroine in countering these two 'temptations' (for neither can provide the basis for a true union) is finely examined and movingly conveyed. Jane, of course, is the plain heroine endowed with searing passion, steely self-control and a gift for self-irony and self-mockery that brings her very close to the reader. Charlotte Brontë's humour is important. She

sometimes caricatures fine style by comic, ironic exaggeration of it in description and dialogue.

With hindsight it is possible to pronounce *Jane Eyre* built
to a recipe whose ingredients must guarantee success.
Granted Charlotte Brontë's unerring power to lay bare the
heart of her heroine in the presence of a dominating
master, given the hyper-masculinity of the master as the
Byronic hero domesticated and baptized, and given the
torturing suspense in which the heroine's self-martyrdom to
'duty' seems all too probable, the final resolution cannot fail:
even the humbling of Rochester into physical dependence
upon Jane, artistically necessary, also helps to keep the
persons real.

The defects of *Shirley* (1849) are obvious. A duplicate hero
(there are two heroines) and a lost mother are too readily
brought out of the authorial bag. Nevertheless the book is
sprawlingly full of interest, much of it due to the background
of the Luddite riots, organized machine-breaking, and the
impact of new technology on moorland industry. Charlotte
tried to represent some of her sister Emily's traits in Shirley
Keeldar. The famous incident in which Emily, having been
bitten by a mad dog, went home and immediately cauterized
the wound herself with a red-hot iron is transferred to
Shirley. If the 'masculinity' of Shirley is not realized with
conviction, the attempt sheds interesting light on how
Emily's character struck others. The strong autobiographical
vein that Charlotte tapped in her first novel, *The Professor*,
which she failed to place with a publisher, is tapped again
in *Villette* (1853). Lucy Snowe, another plain heroine,
rigorous in control of her own feelings, comes, as a teacher
in Brussels, under the spell of a tyrannical but good-hearted
professor, M. Paul Emmanuel, and thus Charlotte works
out in her imaginative world the frustrated passion she
suffered for M. Héger.

The three Brontë sisters, Charlotte, Emily and Anne, and
their brother Branwell, brought up in the bleak parsonage
at Haworth on the Yorkshire moors, built for themselves in

childhood well-peopled imaginative worlds whose chronicles are recorded in a remarkable collection of minutely penned tales. This practice, together with their precocious habit of reading adult literature, was their way of enjoying themselves in the long winter evenings in a wild part of the north country. There were stimuli to authorship of a graver kind too. Their mother died in their infancy. Two elder sisters, Maria and Elizabeth, succumbed to tuberculosis. The three remaining sisters had to watch their brother Branwell decline into dissipation, taking drink and drugs, and dying miserably. Their story is told with compassion and clarity in one of the finest biographies in our literature, *The Life of Charlotte Brontë* (1857), by Mrs Gaskell. Mrs Gaskell had become Charlotte's trusted friend after she achieved success as a writer. The biography came too soon to tell the story of Charlotte's love for M. Paul Héger.

Charlotte's fictional material is derived from various sources, whereas Emily's seems to spring right out of the immediate moorland background. *Wuthering Heights* (1847) is a chronicle of two generations of Earnshaws and Lintons in their moorland homes. The intrusive bringer of doom is Heathcliff, a waif picked off the Liverpool streets and brought home by Mr Earnshaw senior. The strange elemental passion that binds Heathcliff and young Catherine Earnshaw is offset by brother Hindley's resentment against the intruder, a resentment that is given full play after Mr Earnshaw's death. Heathcliff's temporary disappearance and Catherine's marriage to Edgar Linton provide the basis for a careering retributive sequence when Heathcliff returns for vengeance and sets about ruining the two families. His aim is to secure the transmission of both estates to himself. His compelling obsession is the inescapable link with Catherine, who dies: 'the entire world is a dreadful collection of memoranda that she did exist, and that I have lost her.' Edgar Linton is a gentle, cultivated person whose home, Thrushcross Grange, is as refined and peaceable as Wuthering Heights is wild and unruly. Emily Brontë binds together ferocities of personality, domestic life and elemental nature, and paints counterbalancing gentlenesses of character, home and natural background. Wuthering Heights and Thrushcross Grange are the opposite poles. The book is shot through with a vein of mystic exaltation in response to moor and sky, and in analysis of compulsive love: Emily creates a symbolic pattern that reaches out to the supernatural and merges the dead with the living. The perspective of presentation is a subtle compound of the distanced and the immediate, achieved through the use of involved storytellers.

Anne Brontë (1820–49), the youngest of the three sisters, was the least gifted. Her *Agnes Grey* (1847) makes use of her experience as a governess. Her more ambitious novel, *The Tenant of Wildfell Hall* (1848), objectively considered, is a work cluttered with stilted language and clogged with moralizing. But no one familiar with the Brontë story can read it without emotion. It traces the deterioration and ruin of a man by intemperance, faithfully making use of what the girls had been through in watching and handling Branwell. And it was not the desire to capitalize on the sensational element that drove Anne to the task. 'She hated her work on it',[3] Charlotte said. But she was sensitive, pious and sincerely resolved to carry through the burdensome duty of bringing before others the lesson which had cast a shadow over her melancholy temperament.

It is characteristic of Elizabeth Gaskell (1810–65) that her biography of Charlotte Brontë should have got her into hot water for its frankness. Mrs Gaskell, the wife of a Manchester Unitarian minister, mother of four daughters (a fifth and a son died), was a warm-hearted, unassuming, homely Victorian housewife whose literary career still looks improbable. That she should have provoked the respectable by her novels was astonishing to the authoress herself. Nevertheless her novel *Mary Barton* (1848) was criticized for the harsh picture it gave of employers in a story of

[3] Mrs Gaskell, *Life of Charlotte Brontë*.

murder committed by a Manchester trade unionist and provoked by industrial distress. Mrs Gaskell returned to the theme of labour relations in *North and South*, enriching the human fabric of the tale by the intrusion of a country-bred southerner into the heart of a conflict in the industrial north. But Mrs Gaskell's most celebrated book is *Cranford* (1851–3), a study of quiet rural life in a Cheshire village modelled on Knutsford, where Elizabeth had been brought up by her aunt. The picture is an idealized one, charmingly drawn with a blend of compassion and humour. The flutterings caused in the hearts of spinster sisters, Miss Deborah and Miss Matty Jenkins, by parlour-shaking events like engagements or visits of the aristocracy, are conveyed with a faint sense of absurdity washed clean of acidity. ('Two people we know going to be married,' Miss Matty exclaims, 'It's coming very near!') There is a fairytale innocence about the portrayal of gentility zealously preserved by decorous economies, and contentment perilously sustained by rolling a ball under the bed at night – just to make sure without actually looking that no intruder lurks there. Like *North and South*, *Cranford* was published serially in *Household Words* at Dickens's request, so impressed had he been by *Mary Barton*.

The book nearest in tone and quality to *Cranford* is *Wives and Daughters* which Mrs Gaskell was still working on at the time of her death. Molly Gibson is devotedly close to her father, Dr Gibson, and his remarriage to a shallow, self-centred widow (with an attractive, impetuous daughter of her own) produces emotional cross-currents that are feelingly probed. The vain stepmother is at once deliciously and wickedly portrayed; and indeed the quiet irony and humour of chapters picturing daily provincial life have the magnetism of *Cranford*. In *Cousin Phillis* (1864) railway construction impinges on the life and ethos of a farming community and, in the person of a young engineer, on the heart of a country minister's daughter. *Ruth* (1853) is a story of an unmarried mother told with feeling and with moral emphasis on repentance, and in *Sylvia's Lovers* (1863), a historical novel centred on a Yorkshire coastal town in the days of the pressgang, Sylvia has to struggle between duty to her unloved Quaker husband, Philip, and her lost lover returned, Charley Kinraid, by Sylvia supposed dead – but Philip has known better all along.

The discomfort over social conditions manifested in *Mary Barton* was evident in two novels by Benjamin Disraeli (1804–81) published in the same decade, *Coningsby: or The New Generation* (1844) and *Sybil: or The Two Nations* (1845). The former traces the career of a young aristocratic heir whose disillusionment with the political establishment leads to his being disinherited. In *Sybil* the social concern is deeper: the two nations, rich and poor, are sharply differentiated, and the miseries of the exploited, ill-housed workers plainly depicted. The same decade saw the publication of *Yeast* (1848) and *Alton Locke* (1850) by Charles Kingsley (1819–75), country rector and scholar who was involved in the Christian movement for social reform initiated by F. D. Maurice (Tennyson's friend, and the clergyman praised by Charlotte Brontë when she spoke of memorable experiences outstanding from a few weeks spent in town – Thackeray's lectures, Rachel's acting, Maurice's preaching and the Crystal Palace). Contemporary religious controversy as well as bad social conditions impinge on *Yeast*: and similarly in *Alton Locke* Christian faith outdoes Chartist rioting as a recipe for social and spiritual betterment. Kingsley appealed to the young in retelling the stories of Perseus, Jason and Theseus in *The Heroes* (1856) and in his imaginative tale of a boy chimney sweeper's adventures under water in *The Water Babies* (1863), but perhaps he is at his best in the tale of Elizabethan adventure, *Westward Ho!* (1855) in which the Devonshire hero, Amyas Leigh, is up against the Spaniards and their Armada.

The 1840s and 1850s were a period of extraordinary productivity. Another major new name emerged in 1858 when *Scenes of Clerical Life* was published. Provincial life, as

portrayed by George Eliot in the three tales in this volume,
throws up instances of suffering and brutality and, in *Janet's
Repentance*, the third one, of a wife driven to alcohol by her
alcoholic husband's cruelty. George Eliot (pen-name of
Mary Ann Evans, 1819–80) was the daughter of a Midland
farmer who had become agent for a Warwickshire estate. As
youngest child (of a second marriage) Mary seems to have
experienced the sometimes painful devotion to an elder
brother that is so powerfully reproduced in Maggie Tulli-
ver's love for Tom in *The Mill on the Floss* (1860). The book
is heavily autobiographical both in portrayal of external
background and in exploration of the young girl's inner life.
After a devout burst of evangelical fervour under the influence of a schoolmistress, Miss Lewis, George Eliot came
later into contact with sceptical thought and abandoned
her beliefs. She stood by her father till his death in 1849,
before going to London as assistant editor of the *Westminster Review*. When she did find the person to give her
the love she seems to have hungered for, he proved to be a
married man, George Henry Lewes (1817–78), journalist,
writer and philosopher, who was separated from his wife.
George Eliot threw in her lot with him and the happy, stable
relationship lasted until his death.

Adam Bede (1859) contrasts Hetty Sorel, a pretty, foolish,
flirtatious girl, with Dinah Moris, an earnest and devout
evangelical preacher. Hetty, loved by the honest carpenter,
Adam, is seduced by the easygoing young squire, Arthur
Donnithorne. Adam is still prepared to marry her, but she
is pregnant and, after a desperate search for her seducer, she
murders her baby at birth. At the centre of the book's
appeal is the farmer's wife, Mrs Poyser, an entertainingly
humorous study of a shrewd, no-nonsense countrywoman
whose vividly fluent conversation is alive with rich imaginative exaggeration and down-to-earth wisdom. In this book,
and in *Silas Marner* (1861) – a little masterpiece in the blending of psychological and emotional analysis with a plot of
highly contrived disasters and discoveries – we see the weak-

willed young man laden with the guilt of bringing enormous suffering upon others, a moral emphasis characteristic of George Eliot. (She has no shiftless wastrel turned hero, like Sidney Carton in *A Tale of Two Cities*, no loyal good-hearted rake like Nanty Ewart in *Redgauntlet* or Roger Wildrake in *Woodstock*.) When George Eliot leaves her home area and her own period for fifteenth-century Florence in *Romola* (1863), she achieves an impressive work of historical reconstruction (involving a full-length study of Savonarola) but it is laboriously put together. It is as though the conscious pursuit of accuracy has fettered her imagination. In *Felix Holt the Radical* (1866) George Eliot returns to familiar ground with a study of a reforming idealist who purposely chooses to be a manual worker and live among the people he wants to help. Esther Lyon, much as she enjoys the good things of life, chooses poverty at his side. It will be evident that George Eliot is much concerned with people who have serious views of life, social and religious, and are determined to apply them.

Middlemarch (1871–2) represents George Eliot's powers at their maturest. These powers, when fully mustered, are formidable indeed. George Eliot is a thinker who brings reflectiveness and moral judgement to bear on the lives of those she portrays. She has an insight into the workings of the human heart and mind that shows itself in some of the most penetrating analyses of human idealism and human pettiness in our literature. The unravelling of the skein of self-deception is her forte. Yet these qualities exist alongside a sympathetic engagement with her characters. Our acquaintance with those characters is intimate, and our entry into their company made authentic by her closely observed reproduction of their environment, their habits and their manner of speech. *Middlemarch* tackles, among other issues, the problem of the gifted, idealistic nineteenth-century woman who wants to *do* something. Dorothea Brooke's enthusiasm for devoted service is misdirected into marriage with an aged, pedantic clergyman, Casaubon.

Casaubon is a sham and the marriage a failure. In symmetrical balance, Lydgate, a young doctor full of ambitious zeal for medical reform, comes to Middlemarch and marries a worthless, calculating girl, Rosamund Vincy, who runs him heavily into debt. The two stories derived from plans for two separate novels, but fusion is effected by the common theme of frustrated aspiration. Two other subordinate stories are combined with them; the one of Bulstrode, a religious hypocrite whose banking frauds catch up on him, and the other of Mary Garth, member of a delightful and contented family, whose love wins Fred Vincy from his foolishness. There has been critical disagreement about the effectiveness of the study of William Ladislaw, the artist who becomes the widowed heroine's second husband. A skeleton of the central action of *Middlemarch* could give no impression of the immense human tapestry woven of many themes and personalities whose common basis is the life of the provincial town.

By the time *Middlemarch* was published Dickens and Thackeray, as well as Mrs Gaskell and the Brontë sisters, were already dead, and George Eliot's status was supreme. But she was not to write much more. Her next novel, *Daniel Deronda* (1876), the study of another high-minded idealist, this time a Zionist, was her last. Lewes died in 1878, and she was devastated. In May 1880 she married John Cross, twenty years her junior and an old friend, but she died before the end of the year.

'One of the heartiest, most genuine, and moral men we know'[4] so George Eliot described Anthony Trollope (1815–82), a writer of very different stamp from herself. He took up his pen designedly to make money, for his mother, Frances, had kept the family by writing, after the financial failure of her husband. (Trollope also had a career in the Post Office and invented the English pillar box.) There is a

---

[4] Leslie Stephen, *George Eliot* (English Men of Letters, Macmillan, London, 1902).

carefully posed self-portrait in Trollope's *Autobiography*, and he is not reticent about his work, its aims, or indeed its rewards. The latter, he tells us, totalled £68,939 7s. 5d. His vast output included nearly fifty novels, besides biography, travel books, essays and sketches. The discipline of his regular routine of writing is reflected in a temperate uniformity of style that is not demanding but has its subtleties in the way of gentle ironic humour. He was forty when he published the successful novel, *The Warden* (1855), and it was followed by the group of related works called the 'Barsetshire Novels', *Barchester Towers* (1857), *Dr Thorne* (1858), *Framley Parsonage* (1861), *The Small House at Allington* (1864) and *The Last Chronicle of Barset* (1867).

Plot is not important in these books. Trollope himself admitted that he would start a story without the least idea whither it would lead. He was a man who dreamed up personalities and lived with them mentally, eschewing extraordinary incident, but involving them in the issues which produce life's crises in a propertied, hierarchical society, interknit with subtle etiquettes and obligations, that is ruffled by competitive personal desires – especially those of love and ambition. In *The Warden* the Reverend Septimus Harding, precentor of the cathedral and warden of Hiram's Hospital, an earnest, gentle and unassuming fellow, eventually resigns his office after a young local reformer, John Bold, has made a national issue out of the question whether the terms of the original charitable foundation are being honestly observed in the provision of what amounts to a comfortable sinecure for the warden. Bold's love for Harding's daughter, Eleanor, provides an effective cross-current. The fact that the twelve old almsmen on whose behalf the agitation was supposedly undertaken are the chief sufferers – in that they lose their kind overseer, and the hospital is neglected – indicates the balance of human sympathies that Trollope preserves and his refusal to become a satirical social critic. Archdeacon Grantly, married to Harding's elder daughter and son of the old bishop, a masterful and not unambitious dignitary, is a key figure in the tale and in its sequel, *Barchester Towers*. The archdeacon is disappointed in his ambition to succeed his father on his death, and the new bishop, Dr Proudie, is very much under the thumb of his formidable wife. These things take their toll. Appointment to the wardenship is still at issue and Mrs Proudie's candidate, Mr Quiverful, father of fourteen children, gets the job. Mr Slope, arch-manipulator, fails in his designs on power behind the episcopal throne, on preferment and on the hand of the now widowed Eleanor Bold. The Proudies and the Grantlys turn up again in *Framley Parsonage*. The series is completed by *The Last Chronicle of Barset* and Mrs Proudie's domineering personality is stilled in death. The author overheard two fellow clubmen criticizing the persistent use of the same characters in one novel after another, and Mrs Proudie was cited. Trollope intervened. 'I will go home and kill her before the week is over', he said. And he did.

Another group of related novels is the so-called 'political' series, *Can You Forgive Her?* (1864), *Phineas Finn* (1869), *The Eustace Diamonds* (1837), *Phineas Redux* (1874), *The Prime Minister* (1876) and *The Duke's Children* (1880). Trollope was particularly proud of the portrayal of Plantagenet Palliser, nephew of the Duke of Omnium, and his wife Lady Glencora. Their personal and public life is the main interest of *The Prime Minister* and *The Duke's Children*. Like his study of ecclesiastics, Trollope's study of political and society figures is penetratingly aware of the pragmatic considerations and personal interests that bear down heavily on spheres of public action or inaction. Trollope has no bitterness and no axe to grind; but life is humanely held in view in his work by a large-minded, shrewd and good-humoured observer.

Among the lesser writers in the middle years of the century Frederick Marryat (1792–1848), with *Peter Simple* (1834), *Mr Midshipman Easy* (1836) and *Masterman Ready* (1841), produced lively yarns, nautically knowledgeable. Edward

Bulwer Lytton (1803–73) touched a variety of literary categories, but his historical novels like *The Last Days of Pompeii* (1834), *Rienzi* (1835) and *The Last of the Barons* (1843) have survived best. They deal respectively with events in the ancient world, in medieval Rome and in fifteenth-century England and are the product of sound scholarship. A quarter of a century later Charles Reade (1814–84), after several years of successful writing, published one novel which has certainly lived, *The Cloister and the Hearth* (1861), a sweeping, romantic tale also set in the fifteenth century. *Lorna Doone* (1869), the highly popular story of an Exmoor yeoman, John Ridd, by Richard Doddridge Blackmore (1825–1900), has a lightly sketched historical canvas as the background to Ridd's feud with the robber clan, the Doones, and his love for Lorna. Charlotte M. Yonge (1823–1901), a devout and proselytizing Anglo-Catholic disciple of John Keble (1792–1866, himself the author of a vastly popular book of sacred verse, *The Christian Year*), wrote over 150 books, one of which, *The Heir of Redclyffe* (1853), is still read. The self-sacrificial young heir allows himself to be disgraced as a gambler rather than compromise the unworthy recipient of his bounty. A tragic pattern is rigorously worked out. The heir forgives his enemy, and nurses him back from sickness to health before dying through infection. George Borrow's (1803–81) famous accounts of life with gipsies and other inhabitants of the rural underworld, *Lavengro* (1851) and *The Romany Rye* (1857), are rather romantic autobiography than novels, but the re-creation of the wandering life in zestful pursuit of the open road is imaginatively alive. A travel book very different in character is *Eothen* (1844) by William Alexander Kinglake (1809–91). It is a record of travels in the Near East by an inquiring and genuinely interested visitor.

A gap separates George Meredith (1828–1909) from his great contemporaries, George Eliot and Trollope. They made money: he did not. Writing in a letter of 1862 about the forthcoming publication of *Romola* in the *Cornhill Maga-*

zine, Meredith exclaims, 'I understand they have given her an enormous sum – £8,000 or more! she retaining copyright – Bon Dieu! will aught like this ever happen to me?'[5] He might well ask. *The Ordeal of Richard Feverel* (1859) was one of the most inspired novels of the century, yet twenty years passed between its first edition and its second. Meredith was fiercely determined to resist the pressures of commercialization and to reject any compromise of his literary ideals in pursuit of popularity; but it must be conceded that those ideals involved the cultivation of a style so packed with virtuosities as to make the maximum demand on even the most intelligent reader. He does not spare classical allusions, learned references, witty epigrams, philosophical generalizations, convoluted syntax and rapid transitions of thought through a kind of metaphorical shorthand. His books contain characters who are distinguished for their witty conversation or their private anthologies of profundities. Diana Warwick (*Diana of the Crossways*) instances the former, Sir Austen Feverel, with his much-quoted compilation, 'The Pilgrim's Scrip', instances the latter. These indirect vehicles for adding to the direct authorial aphorisms, which themselves are by no means scarce, weight the books heavily with intellectual glitter, hard if brilliant.

But Meredith was a poet; and if the powerful brain explodes in showers of verbal fireworks, the imagination floods some pages with rapturous lyrical prose that soars like music. It is at once sensuous and yet almost mystical in exaltation. 'Golden lie the meadows; golden run the streams: red gold is on the pine-stems. The Sun is coming down to Earth and walks the fields and waters.' So the idyll between Richard Feverel and Lucy is preluded. Sir Austen Feverel brings up his son on a system that fails when Richard falls in love with Lucy Desborough, niece of a local Roman Catholic farmer. The attempt to force parental policy through is productive

[5] Letter to Frederick Maxse, quoted in M. S. Gretton, *The Writings and Life of George Meredith* (OUP, London, 1926).

ultimately of tragedy – searing tragedy, for Lucy's death ironically postdates the reconciliation that ought to have forestalled it. Meredith's fascination with the father-son relationship is exercised in very different guise in *The Adventures of Harry Richmond* (1871). Harry's father, illegitimately descended from royalty, wildly seeks status for himself and his son. He is an engaging charlatan who has good-humouredly wrought havoc in Squire Beltham's family by marrying his daughter and driving her to her grave with his antics and his thriftlessness. The struggle for Harry's soul between the honest, bluff squire, and the roving, unscrupulous but mesmerizing adventurer, his father, is the central theme, worked out with profundity and complexity. There had been a lighter touch about the struggle for the soul of the hero in the earlier book, *Evan Harrington* (1861). The daughters of Melchizedek Harrington, the flamboyant tailor, are desperate to shake off their affiliations with trade and to marry brother Evan into high life. Louisa has become the Countess de Saldar de Sancorvo, and she is one of the most captivating creations of that comic spirit which Meredith defined and analysed so brilliantly in his essay, *On the Idea of Comedy and the Uses of the Comic Spirit*. The deceased 'Great Mel' pervasively haunts this playful novel, of particular interest in that Meredith's grandfather, a naval outfitter at Portsmouth, provided the model for Mel.

Meredith's most penetrating novel is *The Egoist* (1879). In Sir Willoughby Patterne we have a consummate study of vanity and self-centredness, firmly masked as altruism and generosity. The cracking of the shell is the work of Clara Middleton, who has been selected for the high honour of becoming Sir Willoughby's bride – and cunningly bound to the fatal privilege by a network of formal and informal obligations. She is assisted by Laetitia Dale, Sir Willoughby's oldest and most loyal standby, now overlooked, downtrodden and graciously treated like a piece of furniture, but intelligent enough to see through the fraud. Meredith represented his father-in-law, Thomas Love Peacock, in the character of Clara's father, Dr Middleton, a pedantic, good-hearted old scholar too easily swayed by the charms of vintage port. *Diana of the Crossways* (1885) takes up one of Meredith's key themes: it celebrates the courage and independence of Diana Warwick in breaking away from a husband who is commonplace in taste and mediocre in intelligence. Her own brilliance makes the union totally incongruous, though Meredith is careful to render her entry on it fully understandable. An old statesman (representing Lord Melbourne) is cited in an unsuccessful divorce case against her. Intertwined with the championing of woman's rights is a counterbalancing theme of woman's unwisdom in communicating a crucial political secret to the press for personal reasons. Thus Percy Dacier, a young statesman on the brink of his career, who is urgently pressing his love upon her, has his confidence betrayed. This, and the death of Diana's husband, opens the way for a worthy man, with shares in railways, who has been at hand in the wings throughout.

Meredith first met Thomas Hardy (1840–1928) when a manuscript Hardy had offered to Chapman and Hall came into his hands as publisher's reader. They became firm friends and by the end of the century were together recognized as the two greatest novelists of the age. They complement each other remarkably. Meredith is cosmopolitan, Hardy local; Meredith is the flamboyant stylist, Hardy a penman who sometimes knocks sentences roughly together like a man building a dry stone wall; Meredith has a superbly gay and mercurial intellect, Hardy a mind that soberly and patiently dredges out wisdom from the deeps of aberrant human destiny; Meredith can portray aristocrats, intellectuals and social stars with devastating brilliance, controlling their talk as a conductor directs an orchestra; Hardy knows his Wessex countrymen like the back of his hand but has little skill with characters of the more sophisticated classes.

Hardy had to pay to get his novel *Desperate Remedies*

(1871) into print: it made a loss but met with some approval. *Under the Greenwood Tree* (1872) followed. It is a delightful pastoral comedy, though not without its graver moments. The doings of the Mellstock musicians, whose rightful place in the church gallery is threatened by a new-fangled harmonium, provide a homely background to the love of Fancy Day and Dick Dewy – also under threat from the vicar for a time. The light cheerfulness of the book is rarely recaptured in later novels, though there is an undercurrent of rustic humour threading its way through *Far from the Madding Crowd* and *The Mayor of Casterbridge. The Trumpet Major* (1880) has some exhilaration as well as pathos. Sailor Bob, brother-rival with trumpeter John for the love of Anne Garland, carries the freshness of the seven seas about him, and the showing up of the arrogant boor, Festus, is comedy stuff.

After *A Pair of Blue Eyes* (1873) the pattern of the great Wessex novels is laid down in *Far from the Madding Crowd* (1874). The contrast established between earnest, patient, unselfish Gabriel Oak, the shepherd, and his rival for the love of Bathsheba Everdene, Sergeant Troy, the flashy, unreliable girl-charmer, forms a dichotomy used by Hardy time after time for either sex interchangeably: and all too often the wooed or the wooer falls at least temporarily for the wrong partner. So Bathsheba marries Troy, Farfrae marries Lucetta (*The Mayor of Casterbridge*) and indeed Anne Garland marries Bob instead of John (*The Trumpet Major*). Such entanglements have their roots in basic drives of human character persuasively analysed by Hardy. Men and women of passion and impulse are projected with a temperamental intensity which gives his novels a pulsing emotional force, distinctive and inescapable. Yet this is only half the story. For the perverseness which overtakes human beings in their pairing arrangements is an instance of the crossgrained resistance of circumstance to the human desire for happiness. Michael Henchard, in *The Mayor of Casterbridge* (1886), has been a reformed man for eighteen years, and has risen from hay-trusser to corn-factor and mayor, when the wife he 'sold' to a sailor in a fit of drunkenness returns with a daughter. A man of engrained stubbornness, he loses his business, his partner, his supposed daughter and his reputation. But the wilfulness and wrong-headedness of the man are a sure recipe for disaster only when aided and abetted by accumulating circumstantial coincidences. The constant rigging of eventualities in the interests of human misery (not to mention divine shamefacedness) is a pity because Hardy's central figures are realized with a rare concentration on what is essentially human. The backgrounds are convincingly realized too, whether sombre and elemental (like Egdon Heath in *The Return of the Native*) or urban and peopled (like Casterbridge). Hardy's clarity of visual description and his taste for concrete imagery serve him well in relating character to event, emotional situation to locale. He likes the symbolic act whereby, for instance, rival suitors for Lucetta (*The Mayor of Casterbridge*) pick up the same slice of bread and butter at her tea table and, neither letting it go, cause it to break. This kind of correspondence, in miniature here, as vastly elsewhere, enriches the poetic quality of his work.

Hardy's tragic power is perhaps at its most intense in *Tess of the D'Urbervilles*. Alec D'Urberville seduces Tess: a baby is born and dies. Starting a new life away from home, Tess is wooed by Angel Clare and loves him; but the burden of her past weighs upon her. He presses for marriage, and circumstances prevent a clarification of the past until the wedding night, when Tess tells all. Clare (though he himself has a confession to make) is stunned and leaves her. Tess is faithful, and when Alec appears again to pester her, she is resistant. But accumulating difficulties finally drive her to accept his support. This is the signal for a repentant Clare to return, seeking only to make Tess happy. Driven to despair by the bitterness and irony of her lot, Tess murders Alec, the cause of all her miseries. There is a brief period in hiding with Clare before she is arrested and executed. Responsibility for the tragic persecution of the girl is laid firmly at God's door at the end when the black flag rises over Wintoncester (Winchester) gaol. The 'President of the Immortals ... had ended his sport with Tess'.

The horrors let loose on suffering humanity in *Jude the Obscure* (1896) surpass the sufferings of Tess, and it may be argued that they surpass Hardy's control of his medium. Jude Fawley, apprentice to a Wessex stonecutter, has intellectual power and is anxious to study and take orders. His heart is set on the University of Christminster (Oxford). He is trapped into marriage with a sensual woman, Arabella; then falls deeply in love with Sue Bridehead, a young and neurotic teacher with intellectual interests. Discovering Jude's marriage, she marries an older man, Phillotson, on the rebound. Jude and Sue both get divorces and come together, poor, despised, increasingly burdened in the struggle to look after their three children. The climax of their sufferings is when the eldest boy, aware of his parents' difficulties, helps them out by hanging his younger sister and brother on two hooks at the back of a closet door and himself on a nail nearby. A pencilled message reads, 'Done because we are too menny'. Sue's remorse awakens religious scruples and drives her back to Phillotson, while Jude's weakness allows him to be reclaimed by the bottle and by Arabella. The justifiable aim of displaying the enormous odds ranged against the aspiring young villager by nineteenth-century institutions, social structures, moral codes and modes of thought is put at risk by overloading the mechanisms of disaster.

Coincidences do happen in real life. The writer, George Gissing (1857–1903), was present at a meeting where Hardy described his first interview with Meredith, and Gissing added that he himself had also had such an interview with Meredith while not knowing who he was. Hardy was impressed by Gissing's study of society's failures in the novel, *The Unclassed* (1884). It was followed by a series of novels dealing realistically with the sufferings and frustrations caused by poverty. The indignities which slum conditions inflict on the human spirit and their deleterious effect on character and morale are represented without varnish. In *New Grub Street* (1891) aspiring young writers are hamstrung by lack of means while the cheap reviewer who comes to terms with commercialization prospers. *The Private Papers of Henry Ryecroft* (1903), a fictional journal, owes much to Gissing's own autobiographical recollection and reflections. His experience of privation and frustration had been acute. His attempts to identify himself with the working class included two unhappy marriages, the first with Marianne Harrison, a prostitute. Gissing had his own test for a good writer. When a new name came before him, he first asked, 'Has he starved?'[6] Gissing never achieved a wide public (except for his critical book, *Charles Dickens*, 1898), but his work has a small band of steady admirers.

Like Gissing, George Moore (1852–1933), the Irish writer, gave a faithful account of life, but while Gissing had his personal grievances and rebelliousness to work off, Moore was a careful recorder. There is flatness and insipidity as well as cold detachment about his early work, though the direct, matter-of-fact account of a scullery maid's career in *Esther Waters* (1894), written when Moore was striving to emulate the realism of French writers like Zola, makes an impact by the freshness of its reportage. The girl takes service in a household dominated by racing stables and gambling, is seduced, loses her post, and goes through the unmarried mother's hardships. There are mitigations of her lot: the child's father eventually marries her; but he dies and she is left in want again. The drab tale carries its own brand of implicit sympathy. Moore's frankness in *Confessions of a Young Man* (1888) and in novels prior to *Esther Waters* kept him off respectable library shelves. There is candid autobiographical self-revelation again in the trilogy, *Hail and Farewell* (*Ave, Salve, Vale,* 1911–14), a mine of gossipy chatter about writers of the Irish movement, such as Yeats, Lady

---

[6] Frank Swinnerton, *The Georgian Literary Scene* (Dent, Everyman's Library, London, 1938).

Gregory and Synge. Moore's later historical novels, *The Brook Kerith* (1916), a reconstruction of the life of Jesus, and *Heloise and Abelard* (1921), are exercises in a totally different genre from his nineteenth-century works. The plainness has gone. Based on careful research and devised with consistent artistry, they are rich in detail and colour, and insinuatingly polished in style.

Robert Louis Stevenson (1850–94) was one of Meredith's friends and correspondents and considered the climactic meeting between Richard and Lucy towards the end of *Richard Feverel* as the strongest written thing since Shakespeare. One wonders how many books are more widely and clearly stamped on the memories of English readers than Stevenson's *Treasure Island* (1883). The achievement of rock-bottom memorability for the detail of a tale, its personages, its tang and its thematic phrases is granted to few writers. A storyteller with a vigorous narrative style, a command of bold characterization, and the capacity to envelop adventurous exploits or personal tensions in an atmosphere of moral earnestness, Stevenson is of course one of Scott's successors (and it was his pride to be such). The lung weakness from which he suffered drove him from his native Scotland to warmer climes several times and eventually permanently to Samoa, where he settled, to become a loved and revered figure among the natives. The two historical novels, *Kidnapped* (1886) and *Catriona* (1893), are concerned with events following the Jacobite rising of 1745. The substance of *Kidnapped* is summed up on the title page:

> Memoirs of the Adventures of David Balfour in the Year 1745: How he was kidnapped and cast away; his sufferings in a desert isle; his journey in the West Highlands; his acquaintance with Alan Breck Stewart and other notorious Highland Jacobites; with all that he suffered at the hands of his uncle, Ebenezer Balfour of Shaws, falsely so-called; written by himself, and now set forth by Robert Louis Stevenson.

The book that made Stevenson's worldwide reputation was *The Strange Case of Dr Jekyll and Mr Hyde* (1886). The strangeness is Dr Jekyll's discovery of a drug by which he can isolate the evil in himself in a distinct personality: hence Mr Hyde, a person of unalloyed evil. Dr Jekyll becomes Mr Hyde several times, but as the evil personality gains in power, it gets more difficult for the doctor to reassume his original identity. Hyde commits murder and ultimately suicide. Once more we have a book unforgettable in its impact and one which has bequeathed an indispensable phrase to our conversation. It is interesting that the duality here explored should recur, this time embodied in two brothers, in the powerful novel, *The Master of Ballantrae* (1889). We are back in eighteenth-century Scotland to witness a long struggle between personalities doomed by nature to collide – an impetuous and unscrupulous rogue and an honest, pacific individual. The rogue, James, is the elder brother. He was assumed dead at Culloden and his younger brother Henry has entered upon his estate and married the woman intended for him. James returns to pursue a course of extended persecution and blackmail. The harassment gradually brings about the disintegration of Henry's own character, and the final tragedy involves the death of both.

Stevenson was also successful as travel writer and essayist, notably in *Travels with a Donkey in the Cévennes* (1879), a record of an expedition made in 1878, and in *Virginibus Puerisque* (1881). The studied directness of his style – which was the product of sensitive self-discipline – enabled him to produce neat poems for children in *A Child's Garden of Verses* (1885). Stevenson was engaged upon a book whose imaginative strength and maturity promised even greater achievements (*Weir of Hermiston*) when he died from a sudden cerebral haemorrhage in 1894.

The famous literary friendship between Stevenson and Henry James (1843–1916) might seem at first sight incongruous, but both were conscious stylists and neither of them thought much of Hardy's *Tess*. 'But oh yes, dear Louis, she is vile!' James wrote in a letter, contrasting the 'abomination of the language' with Hardy's 'reputation for style'.[7] James came of a wealthy American family, but settled in England in 1875. Previous visits to Europe had stimulated his life-long interest in European culture. One of his persistent themes is the contrast between the richness of European culture and the crudity of America; but this is counterpoised by awareness of an underlying European decadence and of American innocence and enthusiasm.

Critics divide James's output into three periods, facetiously differentiated as James I, James II and the Old Pretender. *Roderick Hudson* (1876) and *Daisy Miller* (1879) belong to the first period, which culminated in *Portrait of a Lady* (1881). Roderick Hudson is a promising young sculptor brought from Massachusetts to Rome to nurture his talents, who does not justify the opportunity and comes to a tragic end. Daisy Miller is a guileless American girl whose ingenuousness and eagerness make her the victim of European misunderstanding and censure. But the most fascinating of the innocents abroad is Isabel Archer (*Portrait of a Lady*), said to be based on James's much-loved cousin, Minny Temple, who died of tuberculosis. Isabel's genuine attractiveness is counterbalanced by the uncompromising forcefulness of Henrietta Stackpole, the hearty American journalist. Isabel rejects marriage proposals from worthy men she has captivated, only to become the prey in Italy of a sinister American, Madame Merle, and the unscrupulous showman, Gilbert Osmond. Osmond marries her for money, bringing her a 'stepdaughter' who turns out to be the child of Osmond and Madame Merle.

James attained subtle mastery in the art of registering failures of human adjustment at the social and cultural level and at the level of personal relationships, where clarification and mutual understanding can so easily be impeded by inadequate awareness. This inadequacy, over that area of ambiguity where codes and values are undefined, and where

Edmund Blunden, *Thomas Hardy* (Macmillan, London, 1941).

tacit assumptions can easily collide, is registered by James in hints and implications conveyed through the subtlety of his presentation. The ultrasensitive style suits the analysis of hypersophisticated personalities, and James's balanced accumulation of tentative inferences often enables him to present those psychological moments whose complexity defies resolution into understanding, let alone judgement. Such moments are the stuff of mental life, it might be argued, and to try to recapture their evanescent flavour in exquisitely fastidious phrasing is an essential business of art. There is enough truth in this view to have made James a powerful influence on later writers.

James's middle period is concerned with decisively English themes. To this phase belong *The Tragic Muse* (1890) and *The Awkward Age* (1899). But in the last period, by many considered his greatest, the old American/European dichotomy returns in works of distinct poetic power – *The Wings of the Dove* (1902), *The Ambassadors* (1903) and *The Golden Bowl* (1904). Granted James's gifts, the idea on which *The Ambassadors* is based is a brilliantly apt one. Mrs Newsome, a wealthy and respectable American lady, despatches her somewhat ingenuous ambassador and future husband, Strether, to recall her son Chad, reputed to be involved in Paris with an undesirable woman. The family business needs him at home in Woollett, Massachusetts. The delicacy of the mission and of the ambassador makes it possible for Strether to have the wool pulled over his eyes, and anyway the 'beautiful' character of the relationship between Chad and the gracious Countess de Vionnet shakes him free of the values that belong to Woollett. Sarah Pocock, Mrs Newsome's daughter and spy number two, is an ambassador of a different breed, for whom Strether is now a lost man. There is humour underlying many of the civilized fragilities among which the probing and the probed Americans pick their way. A graver and more passionate intensity marks James's last work, *The Golden Bowl*. An Italian prince, Amerigo, marries an American girl, Maggie Verver. Her father is wealthy and the prince needs financial security. But Amerigo has previously had an affair with Maggie's friend, Charlotte Stant, an affair terminated by lack of means on either side. Charlotte eventually marries Maggie's widowed father. The subsequent psychological and emotional intricacies which entangle the quartet are registered with teasing finesse and a wary manipulative sensitivity.

If one were looking for a writer with affinities to Stevenson one might more readily have lighted on Rudyard Kipling (1865–1936) than on Henry James. Certainly Kipling has Stevenson's skill in the narrative of adventure; but his forte is the short story, though he also wrote the novels, *The Light that Failed* (1891), *Captains Courageous* (1897) and *Kim* (1901). The light that fails is the eyesight of an artist who wants to complete a great work while there is yet time. Kim is an Irish orphan in Lahore who goes travelling with a Tibetan lama, runs into the English and gets involved with the secret service. Kipling wrote very successfully for the young. His two *Jungle Books* (1894 and 1895) introduce us to Mowgli, a boy brought up by a mother wolf through being lost in a forest in infancy. The wolf pack and other animals eventually accept him, and through contact with highly personalized (and named) creatures – bears, tigers, elephants and monkeys – he acquires the lore of animal kind and learns that justice of the jungle which puts human justice to shame. *Just So Stories* (1902) is a collection of animal tales directed at younger children, whereas *Puck of Pook's Hill* (1906) and its sequel, *Rewards and Fairies* (1910), use the device of a meeting with Puck so that children can be told tales of past ages in England, going back as far as British/Roman days. Kipling's stories for adults are diverse; but the themes in which men are put to the test are favourites, and emphasis on action is strong. The sheer inventiveness and the capacity to 'plant' a tale within a context that adds to its significance do not fail him. There is of course much to justify his image as an imperialist, but his emphasis on the price, in terms of personal discipline and morale, that ruling the lesser breeds extorts is a rigorous one. One notes a considerable development from the early collections of stories, like *Life's Handicap* (1891), to the later ones, like *Debits and Credits* (1926) and *Thy Servant a Dog* (1930), in which the old directness is gone and interpretation is no longer always obvious.

The growing market for children's books brought an additional literary category into being at this time. Among the pioneers was Lewis Carroll (the pseudonym of Charles Dodgson, 1832–98), mathematics don at Christ Church, Oxford. He published *Alice's Adventures in Wonderland* in 1865. This tale of the little girl who chases a White Rabbit down a rabbit hole into a wonderful adventure land answers children's taste for talking animals in a vastly different world from Kipling's, a world where you can take a drink to make you grow enormous and another to make you shrink diminutively. There is a jumble of fantastic characters – animals like the March Hare and the Cheshire Cat; 'human' oddities like the Mad Hatter; and animated playing cards like the King and Queen of Hearts. The sequel, *Through the Looking-Glass* (1872), brings pieces from a chess set to life along with Humpty Dumpty and Tweedledum and Tweedledee. Carroll's adult appeal relies partly on the clever wordplay, the mock-logic and the pseudo-solemnities that dignify the interviews, trials and the like which constitute the action. Carroll's taste for verbal gymnastics that break through the tedious inhibitions imposed by the dictionary makes him an accomplished writer of nonsense verse (*The Hunting of the Snark*, 1876).

Among the children who were privileged to hear all about Alice before Carroll's manuscript was published were those of his friend George MacDonald (1824–1905), a writer who has himself lived chiefly through his children's stories, *At The Back of the North Wind* (1871), *The Princess and the Goblin* (1872) and *The Princess and Curdie* (1883). MacDonald's use of symbolism in these works is at once derivative from a long poetic tradition and yet freshly adjusted to the child mind. Though his underlying purpose is didactic and Christian, this is not intrusively registered. The same impulse inspires his novels for adults, some of which reproduce the homely life of rural Scotland, and his better-known allegorical romance, *Phantastes* (1858). A fellow Scot, Andrew Lang (1844–1912), had a scholarly interest in folklore which produced not only learned work in the anthropological field but also a series of collections of fairy stories. The series began in 1889 when he published the *Blue Fairy Book*, and he continued to issue these simply told stories, volume by volume, rapidly exhausting the primary colours and ending with the *Olive Fairy Book* in 1907. Lang also published poetry and novels, and he collaborated with Rider Haggard (1856–1925) in *The World's Desire* (1890). Haggard, of course, specialized in 'thrilling' romances. *King Solomon's Mines* (1885), *She* (1887) and *Allan Quatermain* (1887) were immensely popular as fast-moving, far-ranging stories for a not too discriminating readership.

A literary appetite of a distinct kind was served by the detective stories of Sir Arthur Conan Doyle (1859–1930), who capitalized on the taste for mystery and problem-solving in the sphere of criminal investigation. Wilkie Collins and Stevenson had spiced their most popular books with mystery and criminality. Conan Doyle's achievement was to hit upon a formula that allowed him to exercise the intellect without too much strain, to locate the deductive procedures in the mind of a fascinating personality, and then to reproduce the atmosphere of a Victorian environment that is somehow more nineteenth-century than the nineteenth century could possibly have been. Sherlock Holmes has a nice blend of acuteness over what matters with donnish withdrawal from what does not, a super-professionalism that denotes the super-amateur, an awesome reticence and an unerring capacity to sort the world out after the fashion of our own dreams; and we are just sufficiently distanced by reverence to feel privileged when, in company with Dr Watson, we are admitted into the great man's confidence. It is, after all, a dream world in which all the resources of metropolis and provinces – railways, post office, cabs and the specialized knowhow of every department of officialdom – are at our immediate disposal for getting on with the job. This sort of thing answers a lot of frustrations. Holmes's career began with *A Study in Scarlet* (1887) and from 1891 he made regular appearances in the *Strand Magazine*. Collected stories were published as *The Adventures of Sherlock Holmes* (1892), *Memoirs of Sherlock Holmes* (1894) and *The Return of Sherlock Holmes* (1905). In the meantime the full-length detective novel, *The Hound of the Baskervilles*, had been serialized. Doyle's historical novels include *Micah Clarke* (1889), which covers the Monmouth Rebellion and the Bloody Assize, as well as *The White Company* (1891) and its sequel, *Sir Nigel* (1906).

Rather than take leave of this disturbing century on so complacent a note, it would be appropriate to indicate the disquiets it left behind by pointing to Samuel Butler (1835–1902), whose rejection of his religious upbringing and the career in the Church he was destined for by his father was a textbook instance of filial rebellion. Butler's satirical novel, *Erewhon* (1872) – the word is an anagram of 'nowhere' – introduces us to a society where illness is criminal and criminality a disease to be cured. Churches are represented as musical banks. The book points forward to an important twentieth-century fictional genre, the utopias (or 'anti-utopias') like *Brave New World* and *1984*. Similarly *The Way of All Flesh* (1903), published after Butler's death, points forward to the twentieth-century novels of growing up, like *Jacob's Room* (Woolf), *Sons and Lovers* and *A Portrait of the Artist as a Young Man*. The sombre, ironic account of the Pontifex family shows the catastrophic effects of hypocritical parental bullying. The work has had its influence. Symbolically it satisfies that yearning to gaze at the Victorian Age we have happily escaped from, as opposed to Doyle's Victorian Age that we have sadly lost. Whether the one is more real than the other is a moot point.

20
Twentieth-century drama

The late ninetenth century witnessed a revolution in the European theatre. The Norwegian dramatist, Henrik Ibsen (1828–1906), broke through the slick conventionalities of the theatrical norm – ingenious plots, easy dialogue well tuned to the contemporary ear, and themes undemandingly congenial to the theatregoing public. His plays analysed the social and moral prejudices of small-town life and the frustrations they imposed on men and women of spirit and integrity. His attack was widened into a judgement on the social and political fabric of ninetenth-century society, with its pseudo-respectabilities, its corrupt go-getters and its denial of love.

The theatrical revolution was reflected in England in the change from the theatre of the early Pinero to that of Shaw. Sir Arthur Wing Pinero (1855–1934) was a master of dramatic construction with a fine theatrical sense. His early plays were highly successful farces and comedies. Later, in *The Second Mrs Tanqueray* (1893) for instance, he showed some susceptibility to the new interest in themes involving social comment, but he remains best known for his more sentimental *Trelawny of the Wells* (1898), whose story harks back evocatively to the theatrical life of the 1860s. Another dramatist who gently probed the social consciousness was Henry Arthur Jones (1851–1929). In *Michael and his Lost Angel* (1896) the wealthy and forceful Mrs Lesdon seduces the young priest, Michael Faversham, with inner consequences that even a public confession cannot resolve.

The most celebrated dramatist of the 1890s was Oscar Wilde, whose comedies abound in polished wit and epigram that compel the reader to make direct comparison with the work of Sheridan 100 years earlier. *Lady Windermere's Fan* (1892) trembles on the edge of serious social criticism; for Mrs Erlynne, the woman who is 'absolutely inadmissible into society', self-sacrificingly pretends to have brought Lady Windermere's fan by mistake when its discovery at Lord Darlington's incriminates the woman who dropped it there; and in *A Woman of No Importance* (1893) Lord Illingworth's questionably motivated attempt to make reparation by marriage, after twenty years, to the unimportant woman who bore his son meets with a dignified and moving rebuff. But Wilde, unlike Sheridan, does not satirize hypocrisy and selfishness, foible and eccentricity, against a background of implicit respect for moral values and social proprieties. His wit and irony are exercised at the expense of worthless and worthy postures alike: the clever mind scintillates where scintillation is an end in itself. 'You should study the Peerage, Gerald,' Lord Illingworth advises his son. 'It is the one book a young man about town should know thoroughly, and it is the best thing in fiction the English have ever done.'

Thus Wilde's masterpiece, *The Importance of Being Earnest* (1895), is the product of sheer virtuosity in the exploitation of farcical situations and of vivid characters whose entertaining vagaries make no concessions to psychological subtlety or seriousness. But the glittering wit, with its characteristic exploration of amoral paradox, keeps the play alive from beginning to end.

George Bernard Shaw (1856–1950) was born in Dublin but came to London at the age of twenty. He embraced the cause of socialism and joined the Fabians. As a music critic he advertised Wagner (*The Perfect Wagnerite*, 1898) and as a dramatic critic he advertised Ibsen (*The Quintessence of Ibsenism*, 1891). From the start his plays tackled social problems – slum-landlordism in *Widower's Houses* (1892), the false glamorization of war in *Arms and the Man* (1894), and living indirectly on the profits of prostitution in *Mrs Warren's Profession* (production delayed by the censor until 1902). Ibsen's influence is evident in Shaw's study of Candida Morell (*Candida*), the wife of a muscular socialist clergyman, genial and popular, who is doing good work among the London poor but is heavily dependent on his wife. The young poet, Marchbanks, loves Candida and rebukes Morell for taking her for granted. At the crisis Morell's assurance is shaken and when Candida is bidden to choose between the two men, she sticks to her husband on the grounds that he is the weaker of the two and needs her more. Of course the dice are heavily loaded against expected conventionalities, so that the investigation of contrived relationships is less effective than the entertainment, but the rival spokesmen are lively specimens from the Shavian casebook and the spokeswoman is made in her maker's image. In *You Never Can Tell* well-worn comic situations are reinvigorated by the intrusion of the theme of how to educate children and uphold women's rights. Mrs Clandon has brought up her children away from the infection of an old-fashioned, dictatorial husband; but her daughter Gloria, supposedly insulated by her upbringing as the New Woman, proves an easy victim of an impecunious dentist. The comedy runs riot, swamping the message, and one feels that it is all to the good.

Polished as the Shavian comic apparatus may be, one must not forget that Shaw's drama of ideas compelled his audiences to think. There is fusion of social and economic theory with human interest in *Major Barbara* (1907). Barbara Undershaft is the daughter of a wealthy armament manufacturer and she holds office in the Salvation Army. She resigns over the discovery that tainted money made from munitions and whisky is sustaining Army social work. The central theme is that poverty, not sin, is the cause of evil. Medical men are entertainingly baited in *The Doctor's Dilemma* (1906), where Sir Colenso Ridgeon has to choose between saving a poor GP with his new cure for tuberculosis or saving Dubedat, a talented, amoral artist. Shaw achieved a brilliant and still reverberating success by working on a story from Smollet's *Peregrine Pickle* in *Pygmalion* (1913). Higgins, a professor of phonetics, accepts a challenge to turn Eliza Doolittle, a cockney flower girl, into a lady indistinguishable from a duchess within six months. The interference with a living girl's personality on the basis of phonetic experimentation produces an emotional backlash, and Shaw once more displays the supposedly dominant male in some bewilderment before the roused powers of womanhood. The turning of the tables is comedy's most basic device, and Shaw exploits it in novel ways, often in struggles between the sexes, but also in displaying unselfishness and heroism in the supposedly wicked (Dick Dudgeon in *The Devil's Disciple*) and weakness in the supposedly strong (Morell in *Candida*).

Shakespeare's mature queen of Egypt becomes a kittenish young girl in Shaw's *Caesar and Cleopatra*, while his unimpressive Julius Caesar becomes a superman strong in his own natural virtue; but a meatier and more shapely exercise in the historical chronicle is *St Joan* (1923). The saint is transmuted into a premature Protestant challenging the Church's authority where it conflicts with the guidance of her conscience, and paying the price of the progressive thinker who threatens established institutions with peril. It is good polemics and good theatre, but it does not plumb tragic depths or move wholeheartedly into the religious dimension. Indeed, though potent in putting the brain to work, Shaw was a great humorist rather than a profound teacher. His social thinking is important because it provides such a fine basis for the interplay of human relationships, such excellent material for thoughtful and witty conversation. Human beings are more interesting when they have ideas and beliefs, programmes and platforms, as well as contacts at the level of meeting and mating, loving and hating. Men and women who read books and espouse causes are enriched human material for the writer to work on. Shaw's instinct as artist is often sounder than his polemical purpose, and his humour saner than his seriousness. That is why *Back to Methuselah* (1921), a vast panoramic forecast of evolutionary developments on the human scene, does not have the irresistible appeal of the light-hearted comedies: nor does *Man and Superman* (1905), in which woman and the Life Force catch up with the long-resistant revolutionary Jack Tanner, for all his fervent rationality. It might be argued that Shaw's serious judgement on his age is at once most powerful and most palatable in dramatic terms when it is allegorized behind the witty comedy of wayward love relationships in *Heartbreak House* (1913–16); for the household of heartbreak portrays the national drift towards the abyss of war. However that may be, Shaw certainly gave the English theatre a much-needed shot in the arm from the needle of his intellect. An important name in the story of his success was that of the actor, Harley Granville-Barker (1877–1946), who played many Shavian characters on the stage and who himself wrote *The Voysey Inheritance* (1905) and *Waste* (1907), the latter a tragedy of a politician's suicide after a death from abortion.

John Galsworthy (1867–1933) also put immediate social problems before his audience and compelled them to feel as well as to think about them. *Strife* (1909) gives a disturbing picture of the bitterness engendered by a strike at a Welsh tin plate works. Galsworthy registers the moods and attitudes of employers and workers alike with a scrupulous impartiality, laying stress on the stubbornness of the two protagonists, each in his way a man of principle and fortitude. That suffering weighs more heavily on the starving men and their families is forcefully brought home; yet the emphasis on those aspects of underlying humanity and vulnerability common to opponents across the barriers of social class is strong here, as it is in *The Skin Game* (1920), where the struggle is between Hillcrist, the aristocrat, and his neighbour, the newly rich manufacturer, Hornblower, a crude, uncultivated fellow who threatens to ruin the locality with a factory. Unease with class conflicts and divisions is tellingly probed in *The Eldest Son* (1912). Sir William Cheshire orders his under-keeper to marry a pregnant village girl or get out. But Sir William's own son Bill has made the lady's maid pregnant and proposes to marry her. 'I utterly forbid this piece of nonsense', Sir William says and, when the obvious parallel is drawn, adds, 'I don't see the connection.' Galsworthy uncovers disquiets deeper still in *Justice* (1910) where the machinery of justice ruins a clerk who is trying to rehabilitate himself after a prison sentence. And in *The Silver Box* (1906) a drunken young gentleman and an unemployed labourer are both involved in what are technically 'thefts' but only the latter carries the can. Galsworthy's compassion, his sensitivity to suffering, his sympathy for the underdog, and his alert awareness of the precarious equilibrium of the social fabric make his message a compelling one, and his insight is matched by a telling economy of expression and a deft management of substantial casts through tidily engineered situations. If Shaw put problems on the stage, Galsworthy put people there.

A vein of social satire is discernible in some of the work of J. M. Barrie (1860–1937). *The Admirable Crichton* (1902) shows Lord Loam's party shipwrecked on a desert island, and it is the butler, Crichton, who has the resourcefulness and authority to take charge of the situation, while the peer turns handyman. Rescue, of course, restores the *status quo* – with a difference. Barrie's reputation has been entangled in reaction against his taste for fantasy and whimsy. In *Dear Brutus* (1917) a number of people are magically granted the opportunity to live their lives over again: but they do not thereby answer their dissatisfactions ('The fault, dear Brutus, is not in our stars but in ourselves'). *Mary Rose* (1920) takes us to a magic island and *Peter Pan* (1904) is a riot of escapism from the threat of adulthood to a Never-Never Land, whither the elfin boy who never grows up and Tinker Bell the fairy waft the children of the Darling family.

Meantime there had been a vastly different break with naturalism on the other side of the Irish Sea. William Butler Yeats (1865–1939) turned to the heroic cycle of Cuchulain and Conchubar in *On Baile's Strand* (1904) for a tragic instance of a challenge reluctantly taken up that leads to Cuchulain's slaughter of his son (and we are reminded of *Sohrab and Rustum*). Gaelic legend was again tapped in *Deirdre* (1907). King Conchubar lures back Deirdre and her husband Naoise with a promise of forgiveness for the marriage that deprived him of his young bride-to-be. Naoise is treacherously murdered, but Deirdre defeats Conchubar by suicide. Before these verse plays (though the former contains some prose), Yeats had already written the forceful nationalistic one-acter, *Cathleen ni Houlihan* (1902) largely in prose. Cathleen, a poor and mysterious old woman, symbolizes Ireland. She promises glory to those who can assist in recovering her land from strangers, and lures young men to forsake home and sweetheart in her cause. Many years later Yeats asked the moving question:

> Did that play of mine send out
> Certain men the English shot?

Prose was used again in *The Words Upon The Window-Pane* (1934), in which a Dublin spiritualist seance brings the conversation of Swift, Vanessa and Stella to us through the voice of the medium.

Yeats worked in a crusading spirit. In collaboration with Lady Gregory and others he founded the Irish National Theatre Company, and the group established itself at the Abbey Theatre in Dublin in 1904. Lady Gregory was herself a writer and Yeats admitted that she supplied much of the dialogue of *Cathleen ni Houlihan*. Her competence in presenting emotional situations formed in the backwash of momentous events is evident in her *Devorgilla* and *The White Cockade*, the one revealing the remorseful queen of Breffny at Mellifont forty years after her infidelity, and now an octogenarian near to death, and the other picturing James II escaping ignominiously after the Battle of the Boyne. Lady Gregory's comic playlets are neat and lively. The backchat of the two old men in their beds in *The Workhouse Ward*, with its repetitious circularities, reminds us that Beckett is her compatriot. John Millington Synge (1871–1909) was the most gifted dramatist of the Irish movement. He immersed himself in the peasant life of the Aran Islands and emerged with stories, characters, and a vital oral idiom at his fingertips. His famous one-act tragedy, *Riders to the Sea* (1904), is a deeply moving study of an old woman, Maurya, who has lost her husband at sea and now loses her two sons in turn. Synge's most popular play is the comedy, *The Playboy of the Western World* (1907). Christie Mahon arrives at a village inn in County Mayo. He is on the run, having, as he thinks, fatally struck his father. The villagers are fascinated by the privilege of harbouring a real live 'murderer', he is lionized by the girls, and it is the making of him. 'In a good play every speech should be as fully flavoured as a nut or an apple', Synge wrote in his preface, and the vitality and poetic richness of the dialogue are as irresistible as the theme; but the play provoked riots at the Abbey Theatre, so offensive did it seem to the good name of Irish women. (The trouble seems to have lain partly in the assumption that Irish girls like parricides and partly in the public utterance of the five-letter word 'shift'.) Synge's last play was left completed but unpolished when he died, and it was one more recasting of the Deirdre story, *Deirdre of the Sorrows*. Another collaborator in the Irish movement had also taken up the story. A. E. (George William Russell, 1867–1935) had written his *Deirdre* (1902) for the group from which the National Theatre was formed.

The next milestone in the literary history of the Abbey Theatre was the work of Sean O'Casey (1880–1964) which followed after the war. *Juno and the Paycock* was put on in 1924. The action takes place in a Dublin tenement against the background of the civil war between Free Staters and republicans in 1922. Juno Boyle's practicality and fortitude in hardship is set against her husband's showy thriftlessness and drunkenness (he is the 'Paycock'). Apprised of a surprise bequest, lazy 'Captain' Boyle spends freely and piles up debts. When the will in question is discovered to be worthless, bailiffs cart the furniture away. By this time daughter Mary is pregnant and her schoolmaster lover has left her. Finally son John, one-armed and neurotic after action with the republicans, is shot by his own comrades for informing. The play is a rich tapestry of action and emotion, for the sharp constrasts between human worth and worthlessness in confronting disaster comprehend both the humorous and the tragic. O'Casey was brought up in the Dublin slums and the dialogue has vitality and pathos. If 'Captain' Boyle, with his crony, Joxer, becomes an almost pantomimic symbol of empty show and self-deception, wasting all he lays hands on, Juno is the archetype of suffering Irish womanhood, remembering at the end that a casualty is not 'a Diehard or a Stater, but only a poor dead son', and praying, 'Sacred heart o' Jesus, take away our hearts o' stone, and give us hearts o' flesh! Take away this murdherin' hate, an' give us Thine own eternal love.'

The Plough and the Stars (1926) shows even more explicitly the cost of fanatical nationalism in the violence it engenders. The background is the 1916 rising. We see men moved to bloodshed by patriotic rhetoric which appeals more to vanity than to good sense, and the consequent suffering, endured by the women especially, is agonizing. Since O'Casey made verbatim use of the oratory of Pearse with ironic purpose (intensifying its extravagance), it is not surprising that there was a disturbance at the first performance and civic guards had to be called in to carry protesting women off the stage. O'Casey's relationship with the Abbey Theatre came to an unhappy end in 1928 when Yeats turned down his more expressionist play, *The Silver Tassie*, a harrowing exposure of the damage trench warfare in France did to men's hope and happiness. The play experiments with non-naturalistic dialogue and presentation. After this disappointment O'Casey became an exile in England. Later plays tended to be overlaid with symbolism for propaganda purposes (often Marxist – but a Marxism increasingly brought into relationship with Christianity), but he returned to a more authentic personal subject in *Red Roses for Me* (1943), where the setting is once more Dublin. Autobiographical memories are exploited and the hero seems to be a self-portrait. Of the six books of autobiography with which O'Casey occupied his later years it is generally agreed that the fourth, *Inishfallen, Fare Thee Well* (1949), covering the years 1917 to 1926, is the most interesting, though its predecessor, *Drums under the Windows* (1945), deals with the crucial period from 1906 to 1916 – and the chapter 'Song of a Shift' makes great sport of the fuss over Synge's *Playboy*.

O'Casey, like Shaw, was a dramatist first and foremost; but many of the playwrights of the inter-war period were either primarily novelists or primarily poets and, to a certain extent, the struggle between naturalistic drama and more stylized drama represents the interplay of novelist-dramatist with poet-dramatist. Not that poets always write their plays in verse. John Drinkwater (1882–1937) used prose for his chronicle play *Abraham Lincoln* (1918) and for *Oliver Cromwell* (1921), though the action of the former is periodically

interrupted by two Chroniclers who philosophize in sometimes turgid verse. There is a milk-and-water quality about
these plays both in substance and in style. John Masefield
(1878–1967) also used prose for his historical play, *The
Tragedy of Pompey the Great* (1910), but the dialogue,
intended no doubt to be taut, vigorous and sinewy, in
fact jerks and spurts abruptly and unrhythmically.
Masefield used verse for *Good Friday* (1916) and *The Trial
of Jesus* (1925), but it does not achieve sustained dramatic
vitality.

More accomplished theatrically are the more naturalistic
comedies of Somerset Maugham (1874–1965), which recapture something of the flavour of Oscar Wilde's. In *Our
Betters* (1917) the target is American women who buy their
way into European aristocracy by marriage, and the husbands who allow themselves to be purchased. In this, and in
The Circle (1921), a drawing-room comedy of middle-class
relationships, there is the psychological sharpness one ex-
pects from so observant a novelist. In Maugham's plays
generally the wit and verve are spiced with a controlled
cynicism, and one feels that he keeps his eye on the box
office. Maugham the dramatist has been called the link
between Wilde and Noël Coward (1899–1973), whose talent
for keeping the pot of verbal flippancy at simmering point
can be entertaining in short doses. His work raises the question whether flippancy can be labelled 'satire' in the absence
of a morally anchored viewpoint. Another novelist who
turned playwright was J. B. Priestley (1894–   ). He proved
his skill in light domestic comedy (*When We Are Married*,
1938) and experimented with more thoughtful themes in
Johnson over Jordan (1939), in which a man is followed into
his experience after death, and in the 'Time' plays. In
Dangerous Corner (1932) the opening of the first act is repeated in summary at the end of Act III, but the dangerous
corner (a remark which led to devastating revelations) is
this time smoothly negotiated. In *Time and the Conways*
(1937) the lives of the Conways leap forward twenty years

in Act II, to return in Act III to the 'present' of 1919. *I have been here before* is the third of the 'Time' plays. Priestley is not a profound thinker, but his directness of idiom and his steady competence as a craftsman have ensured his appeal to the middlebrow public.

James Bridie (the name is a pseudonym for O. H. Mavor, 1888–1951), the Glasgow writer, achieved a remarkable feat in his biblical plays, *Tobias and the Angel* (1930) and (to a lesser extent) *Jonah and the Whale* (1932), for he managed to attain modernity, vigour and naturalness without sacrifice of dignity and without whittling away the supernatural element or the religious thrust. But a large part of Bridie's output consisted of 'plays of ideas', like *Mr Bolfry* (1943) in which the Devil puts in an appearance at a Scottish manse where the minister's visitors are disputing their host's theology. Another Scot who went in for pseudonyms, Elizabeth Mackintosh (1897–1952), had a brilliant London success when she wrote *Richard of Bordeaux* (1933) under the name 'Gordon Daviot'. (She was also known in the field of detective fiction as Josephine Tey). This rewriting of the story of Richard II has a certain freshness (people like to hear Shakespeare's most poetically eloquent monarch saying 'Cheer up' and 'Pull yourself together'), and the sure-fire simplicities of inter-war psychological currency were not yet recognized as clichés except by the perceptive. Middlebrow historical chronicle, which dresses up fashionable psychological formulas in period costume, recurs on the boards from time to time, and *Richard of Bordeaux* has easily assimilable post-war successors in Osborne's *Luther* and Bolt's *A Man for All Seasons*. A contemporary success very different in motive and content was the 1934 dramatic version of *Love on the Dole*, the novel by Walter Greenwood (1903–) who brought the realities of unemployment in the industrial north before the public in this and other books, like *His Worship the Mayor* (1934). The impact of Greenwood's unsparing gloom and satirical bluntness was uncomfortable. Greenwood's imaginative range was limited, but his Lancashire upbringing gave him first-hand knowledge of the conditions he represented.

When *Murder in the Cathedral* was commissioned for the Canterbury Festival in 1935, T. S. Eliot (1888–1965) initiated a resurgence of poetic drama. His study of the martyrdom of St Thomas à Becket at the instigation of Henry II is more than a 'historical' play in that Thomas's temptation and sacrifice are made symptomatic of every man's vocation to surrender to the divine will. The struggle between Church and state reflects the conflict between the spiritual and the temporal that threads its way through all human experience. The pattern of movement through trial and suffering to sanctity is paralleled with the pattern of Christ's atonement and resurrection, with the seasonal pattern of movement through the death of winter to the birth of spring, and even with the sexual pattern of human creativity whereby woman 'dies' in love to man in order to give birth. This is but to touch the fringe of the poetic substance of a profound play. In terms of theatrical history, one notes the influence of Greek tragedy, of *Samson Agonistes*, and of the medieval morality. Moreover the liturgical element in text and staging powerfully authenticates the religious content.

Whether Eliot's later plays fulfil the promise of this masterpiece is arguable. More concessions are made to current theatrical modes in *The Family Reunion* (1939). The members of the Monchensey family have psychological histories; but the curse (recurrently characterized in a vision of the Eumenides) resting on Harry, Lord Monchensey, seems to break out of the framework of pathological cause and effect devised to contain it. The burden of inherited guilt carries its religious implications, and indeed the more one examines the text of this play at the points where it plainly echoes Eliot's other poetry, the more cross-reference suggests allegorical readings of themes and situations. The same must be said of Eliot's later plays, *The Cocktail Party* (1949), *The Confidential Clerk* (1953) and *The Elder States-*

man. The verse moves acceleratingly towards the undoctored rhythms of conversation: surface obviousness of substance is ever more suspiciously 'obvious'; religious implications are conveyed in light overtones and half-pressed ambiguities (the significance of the 'Family' in *The Family Reunion* or of the 'Party' in *The Cocktail Party*), and underscored by acts of spiritual commitment (like Celia's martyrdom in *The Cocktail Party*). The threatening estrangement between Edward and his wife, Lavinia, in *The Cocktail Party* is averted by the guidance and wisdom of the unidentified stranger (Sir Henry Harcourt-Reilly): just so there are disjointed human relationships that divine assistance can put right at a price. *The Confidential Clerk* eschews even this degree of explicable symbolism. It is at first sight a farce of labyrinthinally complex mysteries and counter-mysteries over the identities of illegitimate offspring and over the obligations of parents whose interchangeability of parenthood explores an entertaining sequence of permutations. But the histories of parents and offspring alike, together with their changing uncertainties as the action develops, present a parable on the themes of human vocation, the need for self-knowledge, for openness of understanding, and for commitment of the will: these themes have their force at the level of natural human relationships and of the so-called search for identity; but they carry too their implications for the spiritual life.

A good deal of poetic drama followed in the wake of *Murder in the Cathedral*. Among the better religious plays of the forties was *The Old Man of the Mountains* (1946) by Norman Nicholson. It plants the story of Elijah firmly in the Cumberland area. The dialogue (verse and prose) is wiry and disciplined, the blending of Cumbrian and Old Testament interests fruity and alive. Dorothy Sayers (1893–1957) played her part in the movement with *The Zeal of thy House* (1937) (also written for Canterbury), a play dealing with events at the time of the cathedral's construction and managing to move with some dramatic power while yet exploring the theme of divine and human creativity. Miss Sayers's work for radio, *The Man Born to be King* (1941), is a prose play cycle on the life of Christ, a sequence of twelve episodes covering events from the Nativity to the Resurrection in a presentation that is at once direct, in period, yet attuned to the modern mind. There is more literary than theatrical artistry in the verse plays of Charles Williams (1886–1945). The poetry often lacks the quality of lending itself naturally to the speaking tongue and the listening ear. There are passages in the historical play, *Cranmer*, that are at once metaphysically fascinating and theatrically unspeakable (verse given to the Skeleton, for instance). Ronald Duncan experimented interestingly with masque and antimasque in *This Way to the Tomb* (1946), the masque presenting a fourteenth-century martyrdom, the antimasque revisiting the scene with television crew alert for the saint's anniversary revisitation. The Nativity play by Anne Ridler, *The Shadow Factory* (1946), made a distinctly contemporary impact with its setting in 'a factory, a year or two after the last war'.

After Eliot, Christopher Fry (1907–) has given the biggest stimulus to poetic drama. His pre-war play, *The Boy with a Cart* (1939), chronicles the life of a Cornish saint who has lost his father and who pushes his mother about in a cart until he finds a place to fulfil his aim and build a church. The poetry extends the implications of persistent faith and church-building. *A Phoenix Too Frequent* (1946) retells Petronius's story of a young widow who is religiously resolute on starving herself in the tomb of her husband till a young soldier reasserts for her the power of light and life. The contrast between life and love on the one hand, and sophisticated disillusionment on the other, is the theme of *The Lady's not for Burning* (1949), the play which established Fry with the theatrical public. The setting is medieval. Thomas Mendip is determined to be hanged for murder – though there has been no crime. What restores his resolve to live and his sense of purpose is the encounter with a young woman who has been seized on a charge of witchcraft and is to be burnt.

The springlike mood of *The Lady's not for Burning* is in contrast with the autumnal mood of *Venus Observed* (1950), a second 'comedy of seasons'. The Duke of Altair is a middle-aged widower determined to put an end to a lifetime's philandering by marrying one of his many past sweethearts. The aid of his son Edgar is invited for the selection of his new 'mother'. Three contestants are due, the Venus, Juno and Minerva of the competition. The surprise arrival of one, Perpetua, focuses the Duke's attention elsewhere and for the first time puts son in active rivalry with father. There is more individuality in the psychological studies in this play than in its predecessors. The poetry too, sometimes excessively fluent at the cost of dramatic thrust in the earlier plays, is generally more disciplined, and its metaphorical overtones contribute to the fashioning of a coherent symbolic fabric. If the Duke is seeking a point of repose and stability for desires and dreams endlessly teased but unsatisfied by the teeming world of beautiful women, so all men are in search of that eternal rootedness that Perpetua offers. The symbolic searching of the heavens, through a 'phallic' telescope, is delicately linked with the Duke's probings of other would-be 'heavens'. His observatory is equipped with a bed and serves a double purpose. All in all the detailed symbolic pattern, at which we have hinted, is a rich and relevant one. Though *The Firstborn* (1946) is a sombre study of Moses and his vocation at the time of the Egyptian plagues, and *A Sleep of Prisoners* (1951), an anti-war play, is tragic in tone, Fry must be accounted a spokesman for wonder, buoyancy and gaiety, for acceptance and delight, at a time when more fashionable attitudes pointed in the opposite direction.

The work of Samuel Beckett might be cited in contrast. Beckett (1906–) has confessed his special concern with human impotence. His early discipleship of Joyce left him, artistically, with a vast overshadowing literary achievement against which he must assert himself. He had to break away from the Joycean abundance and the Joycean omniscience, and he sought out the extreme limits of economy, ignorance and inhibition. From the packed world of *Ulysses* he turned to create the bare world of *Waiting for Godot* (1954). Beckett takes away man's property, family, place in society, function in society, and then begins to strip him of the normal human equipment (legs and mobility, for instance). At the same time his characters go through the motions of reasoning and planning and use the vocabulary of experiencing the emotions of failure and success. It is not just that Estragon and Vladimir, the two tramps in *Waiting for Godot*, have no home and no locale; but they seem unaware that they have no home and locale. They do not expect the normally expectable. Just as their continuing bewilderment and uncertainty is punctuated by moments of comic confidence, so, in the case of Pozzo, the pantomimic representative of power and possessions, continuing confidence and assurance are punctuated by moments in which the sense of precariousness intrudes. The servitude of his roped, human beast of burden, Lucky, is grotesquely unreal and idiotic, yet the idiocy is the basis of Pozzo's 'security'. Moreover Pozzo's assurance is related to a vocabulary that presupposes a civilization and a placing in it: such a vocabulary is irrelevant in the 'world' which the idiom of the tramps has established and into which Pozzo intrudes.

Man's identity, his limitations and his place in the universe are at issue in Beckett's plays. In *Happy Days* (1961) we find a woman, Winnie, buried waist-deep in sand against a background that suggests the aftermath of an atomic holocaust. Her companion, Willie, is barely visible behind the mound. The conversation of the two (it is mostly monologue by Winnie) is outrageously out of keeping with their situation. Our familiar postures and verbal habits, the standard poses of human wisdom and consolation, are subjected to a ruthless scrutiny in being adopted by the half-buried woman. The counters of contemporary discourse – pretentious and unpretentious – are employed in a situation of impotence and near total negation in which they bear the weight of sheer tragedy and comedy at the same time. *Krapp's Last Tape* (1958) and *Endgame* (1958) continue the same preoccupations, the latter with Nagg and Nell in dustbins and their blind son chairbound. Against paralysis and powerlessness of this kind Beckett brilliantly deploys a dialogue that is at once tragically and farcically at loggerheads with the immediate. It moves to tears and to laughter, yet compassion persists through nightmares of negation and absurdity.

A Dubliner of the next generation, Brendan Behan (1923–64) gives an inside picture of prison life in *The Quare Fellow,* a play rich and fresh in dialogue and laced with grim Irish humour. *The Hostage* (1959) has great sport over the predicament of an English soldier held captive in a Dublin brothel by the IRA. The action is punctuated by songs, dances and fights. Belly-laughs at the verbal exchanges compensate for the lack of finesse in structure and characterization, and, against the reality of bloodshed, make their point. The fifties were also represented by the projection of the 'angry young man' in John Osborne's (1929–) *Look Back in Anger* (1956), in which rebelliousness and disillusionment shout themselves hoarse for no reason at all in the person of Jimmy Porter. A more sensitive voice was heard in the plays of Harold Pinter (1930–). *The Birthday Party* (1958), *The Caretaker* (1959) and one-act plays like *The Dumb Waiter* have established him as master of a new conversational tonality in which the phrases and rhythms of day-to-day talk are reproduced with uncanny fidelity; yet so planted that their very ordinariness, their reiteration and their illogicality carry overtones of menace mingled with humour. The label 'comedy of menace' has been used to categorize his work. It does justice to the suggestively oppressive uncertainties that overhang his sojourners in tenements and basements. In *The Birthday Party*, when two hearty guests descend upon the seaside boarding house to victimize poor

Stanley, the audience is not sure how deep in criminality, brutality or insanity various characters may be, what sinister recoil from the past or what threat from the future it is that shadows the acridly comic celebrations and cross-examinations. The basis of menace and humour alike is the inadequacy of communication, captured in many a deft inconsequentiality:

MEG: That boy should be up. He's late for his breakfast.
PETEY: There isn't any breakfast.
MEG: Yes, but he doesn't know that.

It is too soon to sum up current dramatists, but where John Arden (1930–) appealed to devotees of post Brechtian theatrical experimentalism in *Serjeant Musgrave's Dance* (1959) and Arnold Wesker (1932–), author of *Chicken Soup with Barley* (1958) and *Roots* (1959), has given himself to the crusade for working-class culture, Pinter seems to have steadily consolidated a reputation on more demonstrably literary grounds.

21
Twentieth-century poetry

Yeats and Eliot, Irish and American, are the greatest English poets of our age. William Butler Yeats (1865–1939) came of a Sligo Protestant family. In London he associated with Dowson and Lionel Johnson in the Rhymers' Club. Back in Ireland, he became a leader of the Celtic Revival. He was in love with Maud Gonne, the nationalist, and remained deeply attached to her in spite of her refusal of him. The practical passions of his life were poetry, Irish culture and occult literature. What he drew from Irish folk lore and myth, and from interest in theosophy, hermetic studies, magic and cyclic theories of history, has made some of his poetry fully comprehensible only with the aid of annotations, but his central human concerns, the vigour of his imagery, and the personality stamped on his style carry the reader unresisting through formidable substance.

The young Yeats, represented in earlier anthologies by 'I will arise and go now, and go to Innisfree' and by 'When you are old and grey and full of sleep', was a master of rhythmic patterns and colourful, suggestive imagery:

> I would that we were, my beloved, white birds on the
>   foam of the sea!
> We tire of the flame of the meteor, before it can fade
>   and flee;
> And the flame of the blue star of twilight, hung low on
>   the rim of the sky,
> Has awaked in our hearts, my beloved, a sadness that
>   may not die.
>
> (The White Birds, 1893)

The three poems cited above indulge moods of nostalgia, sadness and dreamy escapism that suggest inability to cope. The indulgence of such moods, the use of Irish legend, and the entanglement of the immediately personal in the mythical by a rather staged self-projection mark Yeats's poetry with a rich and mysterious suggestiveness. But the early reliance on appeals to vague yearnings and unease gives little indication of the immense poetic stature Yeats was to achieve as he developed. The maturing was both a personal and a technical matter. The frustrated love for Maud Gonne played its part, and no doubt the sacrifice of life in the 1916 rising transformed Yeats's personal involvement with his fellow countrymen, as the lines in Easter 1916 indicate:

> All changed, changed utterly:
> A terrible beauty is born.

But the development was essentially that of a rigorous and ambitious craftsman who worked and reworked the drafts of his poems with persistent thoroughness.

The upshot was that Yeats made poetry his servant: it

became a vessel that could hold whatever he wanted to put into it, instead of a garment which he donned to address the world. There was eventually no limit on the moods and topics, no restriction to specific poses, to particular vocabulary or idiom. Yeats strenuously added to the interests and accents that poetry could cope with till the whole man seemed to have all modes of utterance on the tip of his tongue. The passive melancholy and swooning music to be found among the exquisitely phrased lyrics of *The Wind Among the Reeds* (1899) were purged from his mature work. A sinewy strength is evident in *Responsibilities* (1914) and in *The Wild Swans at Coole* (1919) (Coole Park was Lady Gregory's home). Thereafter Yeats is a poet of sharp-edged complexity with a ruthless honesty and a reverberating striking-power:

> What shall I do with this absurdity –
> O heart, O troubled heart – this caricature,
> Decrepit age that has been tied to me
> As to a dog's tail?
>
> > (*The Tower*, from *The Tower*, 1928)

His Platonic reverence for works of art as 'monuments of unageing intellect' inspires in him the cry to be gathered through his work 'into the artifice of eternity' in *Sailing to Byzantium* (*The Tower*).

The use of astonishingly varied rhythmic and verbal patterns that are daily to hand in living conversation is now achieved without any sense of strain and sustained without any flagging of vitality. In the work of no other modern poet do we get the same sense of a master moving with consummate ease through all conceivable varieties of expression:

> Now his wars on God begin;
> At stroke of midnight God shall win.
>
> > (*The Four Ages of Man* from
> > *A Full Moon in March*, 1935)

> Yesterday he threatened my life.
> I told him that nightly from six to seven I sat at this
>   table,
> The blinds drawn up.

(*Beautiful Lofty Things*, from
Last Poems, 1936-9)

The crisp and the casual, the formal and the informal, are equally his natural utterance. It is the versatility of form that compels wonder at one moment; at the next it is the fervour and frankness of reflection. Poems like *A Prayer for my Daughter* (*Michael Robartes and the Dancer*, 1921), *A Dialogue of Self and Soul* (*The Winding Stair and Other Poems*, 1933) and *The Circus Animals' Desertion* (*Last Poems*, 1936-9) are as busy and alert as the best Metaphysical poetry. The last named looks back on the 'masterful images' of his early poetry (the circus animals he put on show) from his now enforced reliance on 'the foul rag-and-bone shop of the heart'. In such work heart and brain move dynamically from line to line, and the reader is swept along by the current. With Yeats you are always in the company of an interesting and interested man.

A near contemporary whose fame has scarcely stood the test of time was Sir Henry Newbolt (1862-1938). His rollicking nautical verses, *Drake's Drum* ('Drake he's in his hammock an' a thousand miles away' – one of the *Songs of the Fleet* aptly set to music by Sir Charles Stanford) and his melodramatic ballad, *He Fell Among Thieves*, out-kipling Kipling. (The murderous thieves condemn him to die at dawn in north-west India, but he pictures the 'gray little church' and 'the School Close' and faces it bravely.) *Vitai Lampada* ('There's a breathless hush in the Close tonight') has become a national joke about the public schools ('Play up! Play up! and play the game!')

John Masefield (1878-1967), Bridges's successor as Laureate, was a true master of nautical bluster, as is evident from *The Tarry Buccaneer* and *A Ballad of John Silver*:

> We were schooner-rigged and rakish, with a long and
>   lissome hull,
> And we flew the pretty colours of the cross-bones and
>   the skull.

Both poems are from *Salt-Water Ballads* (1902). *Sea-Fever*
('I must go down to the seas again') has the emotional spine
that Yeats's *Innisfree* lacks, while *Cargoes* has the imaginative clarity that Bridges's *A Passer-By* lacks. Masefield's
easy fluency led him to narrative poetry. His *Dauber* (1913)
is the story of an artist who goes to sea so that he can paint
nautical scenes with inside understanding. The more vibrant tale, *The Everlasting Mercy* (1911), presents in the first
person the evangelical conversion of Saul Kane from prize-
fighting, drink and debauchery. Racy idiom and octosyllabics blend exhilaratingly:

> From '61 to '67
> I lived in disbelief of heaven;
> I drunk, I fought, I poached, I whored,
> I did despite unto the Lord.

First to be recognized among the war poets of 1914 to
1918 was Rupert Brooke (1887–1915), though in fact he died
so early in the struggle that little of his work was concerned
with the war. Nevertheless his handsomeness of body and
character, and his untimely death at Scyros, after leaving
behind him at home the prophetic sonnet, *The Soldier* ('If I
should die, think only this of me'), made him a symbol of
youth and promise heroically sacrificed at the call of country.
The idolization of Brooke was justified by outbursts like
that of the sonnet, *Peace* ('Now, God be thanked who has
matched us with this hour'). But he was the poet of delicately mannered nostalgia for idealized Englishness (un-
official roses and honey for tea) in *Grantchester,* and the
eulogist of the simplest sensuous delights (white plates
ringed with blue lines and the rough male kiss of blankets)

in *The Great Lover*. The whimsical tendency is contained, the technical promise considerable.

Another young soldier who became a legend at his death was Julian Grenfell (1888–1915). His poem, *Into Battle* ('The naked earth is warm with spring'), was published in *The Times* when he fell. It speaks nobly of the fighting man's calling, his zest and his readiness in the face of destiny. This, and Brooke's sonnet, and Laurence Binyon's (1869–1943) *For the Fallen* ('They shall grow not old, as we that are left grow old') represent the traditional rhetoric of tribute to heroism. But a different note was sounded as early as 1915 by Charles Hamilton Sorley who had once acclaimed young life as delightedly as Brooke in *The Song of the Ungirt Runners*, but who now wrote of the 'millions of mouthless dead', adding, 'Say not soft things as other men have said.' This was to be a more characteristic comment of English poetry on the slaughter of the trenches.

Siegfried Sassoon (1886–1967) saw to that. Sassoon's prose works, *Memoirs of a Fox-Hunting Man* (1928) and *Memoirs of an Infantry Officer* (1930) reveal the well-to-do background of culture and sportsmanship from which Sassoon was pitchforked into the trenches. His reaction was to pitchfork the true vocabulary, implements and events of trench war into poetry. Sandbags and sludge, mud and blood, trench-boards, sodden buttocks and mats of hair, clotted head and plastering slime – in *Counter Attack* (1918) the reality of war was put in such terms on the printed page. We hear a hearty general's morning greeting as men go up the line:

> 'He's a cheery old card,' grunted Harry to Jack
> As they slogged up to Arras with rifle and pack. ...
> But he did for them both with his plan of attack.

The soldier in the middle of it all has intonations both harsh and comic. The intolerable is made more tolerable by a grim humour that distances interminable discomfort ironically. Hear a soldier greeting the dawn after a night on guard duty in the rain (*Stand To: Good Friday Morning*):

> O Jesus, send me a wound today
> And I'll believe in Your bread and wine,
> And get my bloody old sins washed white.

There is comparable frankness in the scenes from the front painted by Isaac Rosenberg (1890–1918); wheels lurching over sprawled dead and crunching their bones (*Dead Man's Dump*), dark air spurting with fire, a man's brains splattered on a stretcher-bearer's face. And, by contrast, there is a sudden incongruous moment of joy when the song of a lark drops from the sky instead of bombs (*Returning we hear the larks*).

In 1917 Sassoon was wounded and sent home. (His attempt to get himself court-martialled as a pacifist unwilling to fight on was unsuccessful.) Another wounded poet, Wilfred Owen (1893–1918), was a patient in the same hospital and he sought Sassoon's company and advice. Both were to return to the front, Sassoon to survive, Owen to be killed a week before the Armistice. His *Dulce et decorum est* directly attacks the 'lie' that it is fine to die for one's country, by picturing the death of a soldier when a gas attack overtakes men struggling back from the front line – 'bent double, like old beggars under sacks', some with boots lost limping bloodshed. One man fails to get his gas mask on in time. We see him 'guttering, choking', then flung in a wagon, white eyes writhing, blood gurgling up from 'froth-corrupted lungs' at every jolt. 'I am not concerned with poetry,' Owen wrote, 'My subject is War, and the pity of War. The Poetry is in the pity.' But his poetic gifts were distinctive. The contrast presented in *Greater Love* between sexual love and the soldier's sacrifice is sharp and profound. The red lips of the beloved are not as red as the 'stained stones kissed by the English dead'.

> Your slender attitude
> Trembles not exquisite like limbs knife-skewed.

Full warm-heartedness is seen in the hot, large 'hearts made great with shot'. This imaginative penetration in sustaining correspondences is evident time and time again in his work. In *Strange Meeting* the poet has a visionary encounter with an enemy he has killed and who shares his sense of waste. The use of consonance and half-rhyme is impressive:

> Courage was mine, and I had mystery,
> Wisdom was mine, and I had mastery.

Before the war began, in 1912, an anthology of contemporary verse called *Georgian Poetry* was published and sold well. Four further volumes were published during the next ten years, and the term 'Georgian poets' has been applied to contributors, though sometimes there has been a tendency to use the term pejoratively of the residue that remains when the poets of distinction have been creamed off. One naturally associated with the war poets is Edmund Blunden (1896–1974), whose reminiscences of service, *Undertones of War*, included some poems. His affinities are plainly with those who have observantly and lovingly done justice in verse to the detailed beauty of the country and its life. Delicately he describes a barn with its rain-sunken roof and its smell of apples stored in hay, or a pike in a pool quiveringly poised for slaughter (*The Barn* and *The Pike*). These, and such gently etched exercises in fastidious pastoralism as *Forefathers* and *Almswomen*, as well as poems that reflectively take stock of life or literature, betray a consistent refinement of sensibility and technique.

Blunden's delicacy is the delicacy of a strong mind at work with a disciplined pen. This distinguishes his poetry from that of contemporaries like John Drinkwater (1882–1937) whose lack of imaginative sturdiness and verbal concentration produces that smooth, diluted and undemanding versification that has coloured overmuch our concept of the 'Georgian'. There is more economy and dexterity in the best poems of Lascelles Abercrombie (1881–1938), and he brought considerable familiarity with the English poetic tradition to bear upon his work. And there is more indi-

viduality in the verse of Wilfrid Wilson Gibson (1878–1962):
his transparency and directness allow a decisive impact to be
made when he records the momentous in controlled verses
in *Lament* (on the war dead). In *Breakfast* soldiers are eating supine because shells are bursting over them:

> I bet a rasher to a loaf of bread
> That Hull United would beat Halifax. ...
>   Ginger raised his head
> And cursed, and took the bet, and dropped back dead.

Gibson's control of words was often slacker and his ideas
less exciting than this; nevertheless there is a deep appeal in
some of his longer narrative work, in *Money* for instance. It
tells how £4 7s. 6d. is found tied round the neck of a poor
woman who has died from starvation. The mystery of the
incongruity is uncovered. A miner, killed in a pit disaster,
was found with that sum on his corpse. It was destined for
his girl to spend on furniture for their future home, and
she duly took it. But she has preferred to die rather than to
keep herself alive by spending it.

W. H. Davies (1871–1940) has transparency too. An air
of spontaneity surrounds his unpretentious praise of the
simple life and country delights. An engaging freshness
makes for memorability in *Leisure*:

> What is this life if, full of care,
> We have no time to stand and stare,

and in *Truly Great*, where Davies lists the modest needs for
happiness (garden without, books within, a convenient legacy
and a gentle wife). Davies lived as a tramp and lost a leg
while jumping a freight train in America. His *Autobiography of a Super-Tramp* (1907) gained the attention
merited by a hobo-turned-poet who had smoked his pipe
while his leg was amputated without the use of anaesthetic.
As a personality Ralph Hodgson (1871–1962) was less forthcoming than Davies, though he too was a lover of nature and
he took the cause of animals to heart. *The Bells of Heaven*

neatly voices indignation against cruelty to circus animals, pit ponies and hunted hares, and *The Bull* surveys in compassionate retrospect the past days of youth and leadership now departed from a deposed and dying bull.

Edward Thomas (1878–1917) – another writer who fell in the war – came to poetry from years of work on books about the English countryside, English literature and highly congenial writers like Richard Jefferies and George Borrow. He fell under the personal and poetic influence of Robert Frost, but his poetry belongs only to the last five years of his life. Much of it is nature poetry, though there are also poems that recapture a complex emotional mood with a disarming personal frankness and directness, like *The Owl* and *No One Such As You*. In either vein Thomas's work is so sensitive and unforced that it conveys the impression of a writer who became a mature poet overnight. He is the kind of poet who lays himself open, then seems to withdraw unobtrusively. He imposes nothing on the reader in the way of conviction or passion.

More consonant with what the term 'Georgian' has come to imply is the work of James Elroy Flecker (1884–1915) who had posts in the foreign service in Constantinople and Beirut and who died early of consumption. He is remembered chiefly for some well-tuned lyrics of nostalgia for England and of patriotic sentiment which, if they are not imaginatively exciting, are not slack or self-indulgent; also for *The Golden Journey to Samarkand* (1913) and the verse play, *Hassan* (1922). His pulsing, seductive rhythms effectively evoke an atmosphere of oriental mystery and strangeness.

A master among twentieth-century poets in the art of creating atmosphere is Walter De la Mare (1873–1956). For over fifty years he poured out poetry and stories that won him the respect of fellow writers for the finish and precision of his artistry and the steady consistency of his imaginative power. De la Mare can readily conjure up an atmosphere of uncanny mystery. He can make eeriness palpable through images of spellbinding suggestiveness. In *The Listeners* a

Traveller knocks on a moonlit door and calls, 'Is anyone there?', to receive no reply, and to shout, 'Tell them I came ... That I kept my word', before riding away into the silence. That is all. But a tremulous awareness is evoked of meaning undisclosed and momentous, of strange happenings and stranger beings. The technique depends on negatives as well as positives, on what is not said and on what is not denied. No one comes down to the Traveller. No one leans out. No one stirs. It depends too on the clarity of the images – a bird flying up out of a turret, the horse champing in the quiet, its hoofs finally plunging into silence. The technique is effective over a wide area of experience involving magic and mystery, and it makes De la Mare an interesting writer for children. His poetry is poetry of events and experiences uninterpreted. He is much concerned with what is not understandable, not known:

> Oh, no man knows
> Through what wild centuries
> Roves back the rose.

> > (All that's Past)

He is concerned with what is not cleared up, not finished ('He said no more that sailor man ...' The Englishman). His 'meaning' is not separable from its utterance. His mode of expression functions like the character of Martha who used to 'tell us her stories / In the hazel glen':

> Her voice and her narrow chin,
> Her grave small lovely head,
> Seemed half the meaning
> Of the words she said.

> > (Martha)

D. H. Lawrence (1885–1930) is a poet of a different breed. There is no lack of opinionated assertion in poems that begin 'There is no point in work / unless it absorbs you' (Work) or 'How beastly the bourgeois is ...' The much-valued immediacy of impact, whether it be a proposition or an experience of the natural world that is laid before you, precludes all holding back. Lawrence strives for the fullest disclosure. In doing so he moves from stanzaic verse to free verse, and he seems to bind all rules, forms and modes of expression to his service in recapturing the full sensuous and emotional flavour of an encounter with a snake, a humming-bird or a mountain lion (*Snake, Humming-Bird, Mountain Lion*), in reproducing what is stirred in thought and mood by the sight of gentians in a house or by the bite of a mosquito (*Bavarian Gentians* and *The Mosquito*).

There were other poets born in the eighties and nineties who are too diverse in gifts to be grouped and generalized about. Edith Sitwell (1887–1964) – whose brothers, Osbert and Sacheverell, also distinguished themselves as writers – was a poet of cultivated technical sensitivity who indulged in the delighted display of metrical and musical virtuosity in *Façade* (1922), moved through romantic reminiscence of childhood in *The Sleeping Beauty* (1924), to become concerned in her later work with the pain and misery in the world about her (*Gold Coast Customs*, 1929). The imaginative and rhythmic intensity of this work gives it a macabre and harrowing power as a picture 'of a world where all the natural rhythms of the spirit, of the soil, of the seasons, have broken down', to quote the poet's essay prefaced to her *Selected Poems* of 1936. Miss Sitwell's last volumes of poetry owe much to the awareness of wartime suffering and to the strength of her Christian faith. Her study of Alexander Pope is one fervent technician's tribute to another. Robert Graves (1895–) made himself known to a huge reading public by his fictional reconstructions of first-century Roman history, *I Claudius* and *Claudius the God*. Graves's poetry is carefully structured rumination anchored in sharply realized response to experience. It is ruthlessly unpretentious: it is rarely joyful even though it is quite often funny. The wit of 'metaphysical' word-play (*Lost Acres*), of jocular ambiguity (*Down, Wanton, Down!*), and of post-Freudian irreverence (*Ulysses*) are all at his disposal. There is no sense of a cultural past (as in Eliot) or of mysteries half glimpsed (as in De la Mare). Indeed there seems to be a conscious depreciation of anything that might add significance to the locked-in events of the individual's temporal experience ('To evoke posterity / Is to weep on your own grave'), but these events are analysed acutely and accepted by a dynamic poetic intelligence. The poetic voice of Edwin Muir (1887–1959) is more restrained than Graves's. Muir, an Orkneyan who knew poverty in his youth, was sadly alert to the civilizational condition of his time, as the long allegorical poem, *The Labyrinth* (1949), indicates. Hugh MacDiarmid (properly C. R. Grieve) (1892–   ) is a more volcanic spirit than either. A Scot who hates England and much of what passes for 'Scotland' in the minds of readers and tourists, MacDiarmid has embraced orthodox Communism and Scottish Nationalism, and looks for a Celtic revolution against English economic and cultural tyranny. MacDiarmid's use of Scottish vernacular, crucially different from Burns's in Scottish eyes, but less obviously so to the Sassenach, makes it difficult for English readers to get the natural feel of what is no doubt some of his best work. But MacDiarmid has used standard English too. In his later work he is explosively discursive, especially when he lets fly at what he hates. The lash of his tongue is scathing and wholesale.

If Thomas Stearns Eliot (1888–1965) is the greatest English poet of his age it is not just because he fashioned a distinctive and individual utterance to be at his service for the most diverse needs (Yeats too did that), but because he employed it to produce masterpieces. Eliot, like Beckett, is post-Joycean. The enrichment of meaning by amplification, overtone and frequent cross-reference is pushed to an extreme stage in Joyce's *Ulysses*. We have spoken of Beckett's reaction against the Joycean abundance. Eliot's reaction was not to strip down the imagery of life to bare equations ('Let immersion in a sand-dune equal human impotence'), but to preserve amplification alongside economy by condensing the verbal machinery of amplification. Joyce gradually builds up a series of correspondences to establish parallels between Stephen Dedalus and Hamlet (*Ulysses*). Eliot makes use of key phrases ('Those are pearls that were his eyes', and 'The chair she sat in, like a burnished throne ...', *The Waste Land*, 'And faded on the blowing of the horn', *Little Gidding*) to echo unforgettable moments crucial to the dramatic patterns of *The Tempest, Antony and Cleopatra* and *Hamlet* respectively. Such a practice of allusiveness enables a hundred lines to carry the weight of meaning most poets would convey in five or ten times that number. And of course the allusiveness is exploited much more briefly and intensively than in the above quotations. Moreover double allusiveness can complicate the practice, adding multiple dimensions to connotation.

Eliot's multidimensionalism is based partly on internal, partly on external cross-reference. Internally the poet uses, say, the word 'rock' repeatedly to carry the religious connotation of Christ or the Church (*The Rock*). Then usages of the word elsewhere, ostensibly in natural description or arid incantation (*The Dry Salvages* or *The Waste Land* V), can sound overtones from outside the particular context to add connotative enrichment.

Multidimensionalism based on external cross-reference is perhaps a more difficult matter to pin down. We may cite a single instance of the difficulty. In *The Fire Sermon* (*The Waste Land*), the fire we pray to be plucked from is the fire of lust and greed, the fire of Hell. There is a cold blast at our backs in Hell. In it we hear the 'rattle of the bones' which is at once macabre and skeletonic and also hints at dancing with bones, as the following image of the grinning face indicates ('The rattle of the bones, and chuckle spread from ear to ear'). 'Chuckle' is the giveaway word. One does not *see* a chuckle; one hears it. What spreads from ear to ear (cf. *'year to year'*, nine lines later), as everyone who has sung hymns or psalms knows, is the wind through the cornfield at harvesting (the harvesting of souls that brings them into Heaven) – the wind that 'Crosses the brown land, unheard' ('unheard' rings a loud connotative bell in *Ash Wednesday* and *Four Quartets*) but can set the valleys laughing and singing and turn a cornfield into a golden grin. Eliot has strengthened his picture of Hell (cosy as well as hot) by the paradox of the cold wind that also carries faint echoes of heavenly music and the garnering of saved souls.

Eliot's work is consummated in a *Paradiso* that gathers the scattered leaves of experience and literary memory into a patterned fabric, an epic in miniature (*Four Quartets*). The work is preceded by a *Purgatorio* (*Ash Wednesday*) closely related to it in texture and thought. And *Ash Wednesday* is preceded by early work that has qualities of an *Inferno* (*The Waste Land*), to which it may well be that the rest of the early poems act as a commentary or an integrated accompaniment. Eliot's epigraph to *The Waste Land* suggests that he was as much interested in the image of the scattered leaves of the Sibyl's prophecy as he was in the gathered and folded leaves of rose and book and beatific vision at the end of *Little Gidding*. The torn and scattered leaves are as appropriate to the representation of a dismembered civilization and a dismembered humanity as the flower and the musically patterned poem are to the representation of order recovered and restored. To sort and arrange the torn and scattered fragments is the reader's task – parallel to his real life duty to recover and restore our fragmented culture and humanity.

Eliot has earned respect as one of the greatest of our literary critics. The precision and authority of his judgements, not only on literature but on wider questions of culture, commands attention; and of course his critical *dicta* help to illuminate his poetry. (See *The Use of Poetry and the Use of Criticism*, 1933, and *Notes towards the Definition of Culture*, 1948.)

The American poet, Ezra Pound (1885–1972), chief exponent of the 'imagist' movement that reacted against the sentimental rhetoric and metaphorical imprecision of late

Victorian and Georgian verse, was closely involved with Eliot in the poetic revolution he effected. Pound's major work, also of epic proportions, *Cantos* (1925 and following), along with his earlier poetry, is that of a volcanic temperament allied to massive erudition and sharply responsive to the evils of twentieth-century commercialism, injustice and philistinism. Eliot dedicated *The Waste Land* to Pound as *il miglior fabbro* (the better craftsman). The phrase is used by Dante of Arnaut Daniel, a twelfth-century poet. It not only pays tribute to Pound but, intentionally or otherwise, it parallels Eliot with Dante.

Another contemporary whom Eliot praised is David Jones (1895–   ). In his introduction to Jones's *In Parenthesis* (1937; but the introduction came later) Eliot speaks of Jones's 'affinity' with Joyce, Pound and himself. Though prose in form, *In Parenthesis* is poetic in quality. It is an epic of the 1914–18 war, whose literary and historic overtones extend its significance, bringing events into relation with those of Arthurian legend and Roman Britain in which Jones is especially interested. Here again, as Eliot observes, is work whose full dimensions of meaning are yet to be explored. Even more so is this the case with the more taxing work, *The Anathemata* (1952). Here the use of Welsh and Latin terms and motifs thickens the texture, and the influence of *Finnegans Wake* is evident in oral rhythm and verbal configuration.

We take leave of poets born in the nineteenth century and turn to the 'poets of the thirties'. Some of them remained just that: but one of them has become a poet of the century, Wystan Hugh Auden (1907–73). Eliot, born in St Louis, Missouri, settled in England and took British nationality. Auden, born in York, bred in the Midlands, settled in New York and took United States citizenship. Auden's early work seemed to put him close to the Marxist camp. He was the poet of unidealized contemporary urbanism, of starving cities, rolling prams, moaning saxophones and talkie-houses, of

The judge enforcing the obsolete law,
The banker making the loan for the war.

This world, and the complex 'metaphysical distress' it engendered in his generation, are realized in *Look, Stranger* (1936) with striking boldness of rhythm and angularity of idiom. But, like Eliot, Auden became a Christian, and the conversion determined the character of his later work. His technical versatility and virtuosity are immense: moreover he is irresistibly readable. An engaging fluency takes possession of the reader: it is one half the secret of Auden's compulsion. The other half is uncanny memorability, a gift of epigrammatic conversationalism that blends the casual and the contrived, the vulgar and the literary, in juxtapositions that prove inevitable against all laws of predictability. The composite style perhaps reflects the Christian paradoxes of sin and salvation, nature and grace, worldly ephemerality and sacramental significance, in which theology has immersed Auden's thought and experience moulded his sensitivities. The deep currents of his thought and experience flow under cover; while the speaking voice is given to emotional and spiritual understatement. Auden's output was vast and various, from *Look, Stranger* and *The Ascent of F6* (a drama written in collaboration with Christopher Isherwood), through *New Year Letter* (1941), *For The Time Being, A Christmas Oratorio* (1945) and *The Age of Anxiety, A Baroque Eclogue* (1948), to later volumes like *The Shield of Achilles* (1955) and *About the House* (1966). It also included prose works, notably *The Dyer's Hand and Other Essays* (1963), that are invaluable for the study of his poetry.

In poems of direct approach Auden makes you feel that you are in his presence, but not that you know him well. He is not remarkable for self-revelation, or for transference onto paper of what is sharply felt in human relationships: but his voice is always a poet's voice, in love with words. A verbal plutocrat, he has turns of expression within his reach in such multitude that the reader tends to feel swamped. Like Eliot, Auden grapples with a great range of thought and experience, and grapples in parallel with the resources of utterance. One is conscious of the grappling. But Auden rejects the prophet's stance: he does not instruct; and he does not buttonhole the reader. The take-it-or-leave-it air does not betoken a lack of concern but a healthy sense of proportion. The reader often finds himself eavesdropping as a modest practitioner thinks aloud:

> ... After all, it's rather a privilege
> amid the affluent traffic
> to serve this unpopular art which cannot be turned into
> background noise for study
> or hung as a status trophy by rising executives ...
> *(The Cave of Making: About the House)*

So Auden writes in the memorial verses to Louis MacNeice (1907–63), one of the poets loosely grouped with him as spokesmen for the young in the uneasy thirties. MacNeice's conversational style is looser and easier than Auden's, the texture more fluid, the tone more lyrical. His facility is winningly easy on the eye and the ear: if it lapses sometimes into versified reportage, it does not try to disguise its banality:

> Frivolous, always in a hurry, forgetting the address,
> Frowning too often, taking enormous notice
> Of hats and back-chat – how could I assess
> The thing that makes you different?

This is *Autumn Journal* (1939) and one can defend a journal for being journalistic. The evocative, nostalgic appeal of its account of the autumn of 1938 for those who lived through it is undeniable. MacNeice has no political axe to grind: he is not at loggerheads with the world he reports on. He observes and ruminates like a verse-essayist. There is something of the scholar in his detachment, much of the Irishman in his melancholy and in his comic irony:

> Mrs Carmichael had her fifth, looked at the job with
>   repulsion,
> Said to the midwife, 'Take it away; I'm through with
>   over-production'.
>
> (Bagpipe Music)

MacNeice came from Belfast, and Cecil Day Lewis (1904–72) came from Ballintogher (his mother could trace a family connection with Goldsmith). Lewis shared the social disenchantment of Auden and Spender, but his gifts as a lyric poet made the personal love sequence, *From Feathers to Iron* (1931), particularly memorable. In 'Do not expect again a phoenix hour', celebrating conception, and 'Come out into the sun, for a man is born today', a cry of delight at birth ('Take a whole holiday in honour of this!'), Lewis's lucidity and imaginative inventiveness are charmingly blended. And though his metaphysical bent sometimes leads elsewhere to a thickening of texture that makes for stumbling reading, the same powers are applied to a wide range of personal and public topics in *Overtures to Death* (1938). The slick stanzas of capsulated wit was one of his media from the earliest days:

> With me my lover makes
>   The clock assert its chime:
> But when she goes, she takes
>   The mainspring out of time.
>
> (Transitional Poems, 1929)

Day Lewis divides the critics. His early work has been criticized for its immaturity, his later work for its lack of intensity. The translation of Virgil is often laboriously and infelicitously fabricated. There seems to be a ceiling to his verbal awareness, and it is below the level at which precise connotative illumination can astonish and excite.

A useful impression of the poetic situation in the thirties can be gained from *World within World* (1951) by Stephen Spender (1909–   ). Spender, who more than any of the group has been a life-long propagandist for progressive social causes, nevertheless emerges in his poetry as a reflective lyrist, musing and brooding on the human victims of civilization and on the problem of being (see *The Edge of Being*, 1949). Two South-African-born poets of the same generation, Roy Campbell (1901–57) from Natal and William Plomer (1903–73) from Northern Transvaal, have been anthologized side by side with the 'Auden group'. Campbell's politics, however, were of the Right (he fought for Franco in Spain). He is a poet with a vigorous voice, prodigal of word and image, sometimes to a fault, a South African Hemingway in some of his postures, and given to satire. In this last respect he matches Plomer, but Plomer's satire is comic and explores the absurdity of the human scene, not ignoring the tragic but undercutting it with a blade of irony (and even with a jocular 'hey nonny nonny'). Meet the heroine of *Mews Flat Mona, A Memory of the Twenties*. On a sofa upholstered in human skin Mona did researches in original sin, and so on. Finally, hooked on the hard stuff, she stepped from the top of an Oxford Street store, falling like a bomb on an elderly curate:

> When they came with a shovel to shift her remains
> They found a big heart but no vestige of brains.

Other poets of the same age group are William Empson (1906–   ), who has perhaps pursued his ideal of maximum verbal concentration beyond the point of maximum demand upon the reader, James Reeves (1909–   ), who has distinguished himself as a writer of verse and prose for children, and John Betjeman (1906–   ), whose limpid directness and swinging rhythms have given him a deserved popularity. More than any other contemporary's poetry, Betjeman's speaks for itself at first encounter with lambent clarity. It ranges over a wide variety of likes and dislikes proper to a sensitive personality in love with Victorianism, fascinated by people and keenly nostalgic for the private and public past.

Among the poets born in the second decade of the century there are three for whom the Christian basis of their life has been crucial to their literary output: Norman Nicholson, R. S. Thomas and David Gascoyne. Let us put at their side a poet born as far back as 1885 who has made himself known more recently than his own contemporaries, Andrew Young. Canon Young was a naturalist as well as a priest; and he is a poet who can compress acutely observed impressions of the natural world into concise and thoughtful lines, often strong in sustained metaphorical ramification, as is the picture of the crab (*The Dead Crab*) with its 'well-knit cote-armure', and legs with 'plated joints' ending in 'stiletto points':

> I cannot think this creature died
> By storm or fish or sea-fowl harmed
> Walking the sea so heavily armed;
> Or does it make for death to be
> Oneself a living armoury?

This imaginative grasp of the real world is blended with spiritual vision in *Out of the World and Back* (1958), which pursues the soul's pilgrimage after death.

Young had botanical interests, Norman Nicholson has geological ones. His sense of the interrelationship between the writer's vision of life and his religious position is evident in the critical work, *Man and Literature*. As a poet he is a Cumbrian of Wordsworthian breed, rooted in his home area, sensitive alike to its rural and urban aspects, writing of *Cleator Moor* and *Ravenglass Railway Station* with an unsparing accuracy, descriptive and emotional. The collection, *The Pot Geranium*, was published in 1954.

R. S. Thomas (1913–   ), Welsh poet and parish priest, is a writer of sparser output, whose unromantic studies of unromanticized rural life are the work of a man deeply concerned with the physical and spiritual needs of the people he writes about. Studies of men like Iago Prytherch (*A Peasant*) make no concessions to sentimentality. Thomas accepts the 'frightening vacancy of his mind' yet recognizes him as prototype of human endurance. Thomas's concern with the dual power of nature to brutalize and to heal is rooted in his awareness of the openness of man's nature to the bestial and the spiritual. If the men of the moors have not yet 'shaken the moss' from their savage skulls or 'prayed the peat from their eyes' (*A Priest to His People*), nevertheless men of the farm survey the girl evacuee with 'earth's charity, patient and strong' (*The Evacuee*). A religious awareness of the cost of healing and creativity, natural and spiritual, in the life of earth and the life of man, asserts a powerful consistency. There is deep faith behind the confrontation – in evident tension of heart and mind – with the repellent harshness of the countryman and his lot.

David Gascoyne (1916–) has shown a remarkable development in his work. The surrealistic imagery of some of the earlier poems has an almost garish extravagance. But, from the time of the moving poem on the suicide of a friend in 1941 (*An Elegy*), Gascoyne has been represented by work in which his lavish gifts have been disciplined. The religious concern is potently aware and contemporary. His Christ in *Ecce Homo* is one who weeps over Jerusalem and over the bombed cities of Europe. Gascoyne brings wit, irony and penetration to the diagnosis of our ills and his religious cry is never evasive of the true human situation:

> Not from a monstrance silver-wrought
> But from the tree of human pain
> Redeem our sterile misery,
> Christ of Revolution and Poetry ...

One of Gascoyne's anthologized poems is *The Sacred Hearth*, addressed to a fellow poet George Barker (1913–). Barker's poetry has always aroused controversy. It is a torrent of words in which every trick of the verbal conjuror is skilfully played. There is an indiscriminate extravagance in the use of technical and metaphorical devices and in the juxtaposition of incongruous tones of voice. For all that, the impact is undeniable: there is plenty of fine writing, and the welter, notably perhaps in *Eros in Dogma*, (1944), and *The True Confessions of George Barker* (1950), can be irresistible.

While poets like Nicholson and R. S. Thomas, Gascoyne and Barker, were steadily developing their gifts, Dylan Thomas (1914–53) rose rapidly to fame, his genius blazed, and he died at thirty-nine. The flamboyant character of his gifts and his personality, the ostensibly fatalistic addiction to alcohol, and the resultant untimely death, left behind a legend of artistic self-immolation. Thomas's *Portrait of the Artist as a Young Dog* (1940) has lively autobiographical information about a poet whose childhood and youth in South Wales left him with an intensely aware zest for its life and its scenery. His first volume of poems, *Eighteen Poems,* came out in 1934. His reputation was widely established by the time *Deaths and Entrances* was published in 1946. The radio play, *Under Milk Wood,* got into print in 1954. Thomas's tumultuous verse is rich in rhetorical imagery of great suggestive force, and voices a visionary sense of the wonderful as he pounds away at the basic experiences of life and death. Syntax and logic are displaced by interwoven music and metaphor, and the complex verbal patterns, with their extraordinary rhythmic force and resounding Celtic superabundance, inevitably recall both Hopkins and Joyce. Whether Thomas's intellectual core justifies the former affinity or his inner artistic discipline justifies the latter is a question which evokes controversy, for Thomas's work inaugurated a neo-romantic phase that later fashion repudiated. But Thomas's poetic persona has stamped itself indelibly on the cultural consciousness of our age with lines and verses that compulsively convey the urgency of man's need and of his faith amid the elemental confrontations of life in time. One might cite *A Refusal to Mourn the Death, by Fire, of a Child in London, And death shall have no dominion* or *Do not go gentle into that good night.*

The reaction against neo-romanticism took visible shape

in 1956 with the publication of *New Lines*, edited by Robert Conquest. The label, 'The New Movement', gained currency, but it would be unjust to blur the individualities of the poets involved by subsuming their efforts under a common banner. The anti-romantic movement eschewed rhetorical extravagances, prophetic postures and claims to insight. But the ascetic spirit and the cynical spirit are both anti-romantic: the poets of the fifties and sixties are a mixed bag.

Philip Larkin (1922–) has been the most respected of the group since *The Less Deceived* was published in 1955. He writes little, and tends to shun publicity. He has been compared with Hardy. His words catch the commonplace experience, deftly in respect of its impact on the senses, disquietingly in its half-realized implications for men and women unsure of their significance. The feeling recurs that man has lost his footing amid natural and civilizational instabilities. The 'positive' corollary is not propositional support for faith or unfaith, but an implicit hint at fellow feeling among fellow victims. See how, in *Ambulances,* children in the road and women coming from shops suddenly catch sight of

> A wild white face that overtops
> Red stretcher-blankets momently

and sense the 'solving emptiness / That lies just under all we do'. Larkin's *Church Going*, in which the unbeliever enters an empty church in curiosity, and lingers in worried bewilderment, teased by his own attitude, has become his best-known poem.

The cultivation of a casual tone that seems to say 'I'm not a poet' was tried by several poets. Those who have done it best, like Kingsley Amis (1922–) in *A Bookshop Idyll*,

> Man's love is of man's life a thing apart;
>   Girls aren't like that,

have used the tone sparingly against more sophisticated utterance. D. J. Enright (1920–) has adopted the offhand stance and the low-key idiom to catch the modish air of 'sincerity' in *Bread Rather Than Blossoms* (1956). Poets with a sense of humour, such as he has, can do so to good effect. The directness of John Wain (1925–) in *A Word Carved on a Sill* (1956) is a highly cultivated directness. Wain has been criticized for over-cleverness, but it is not the cleverness of ostentation. He uses words like a wit, well educated in English poetry, and able to give bite and vitality to the most obvious stanzaic forms.

None of the *New Lines* poets has used simple diction and stanza forms with a finer touch than Elizabeth Jennings (1926–). Her limpid clarity has rare charm, and the naturalness she achieves within conventional metrical design is the result of consummate artistry. The stanza always seems to flow in unobtrusive obedience, yet its contrapuntal interplay with her beautifully shaped sentences (in *The Old Woman*, for instance) gives a rich spice to the verse. One savours the stanzas lingeringly on the tongue like a vintage wine. But one must not hint at anything precious or contrived. Miss Jennings sincerity (it has been aptly called 'chastity') of speech is as authentic as the daylight. This is a statement about what she says as well as how she says it. The engagingly open self-analysis in *To a Friend with a Religious Vocation* or *At a Mass* is testimony to this and to the fineness of her poetic sensitivity.

A totally different talent emerges in the work of James Kirkup (1923–). He moves with accomplishment among the technical terminology in his memorable poem, *A Correct Compassion*, a careful first-hand description of a heart operation ('Mitral Stenosis Valvulotomy') observed in the General Infirmary at Leeds. The inclusion of the surgeon's explanatory commentary for the benefit of medical students, and other dramatic interventions, give the poem the air of a documentary; but the poet's own observations frame the experience within a reflective consideration of the character of compassion.

When we turn to poets born in the 1930s we come to

writers who are still comparatively young and whose work must yet have great potentiality for development. That Ted Hughes (1930–) and Thom Gunn (1929–), who were paired in a Faber paperback in 1962, are poets of distinction and power is evident from Hughes's reflection on the six war dead (of the First World War) preserved in celluloid (*Six Young Men*) and Gunn's *The Unsettled Motorcyclist's Vision of his Death*. But it would be unjust to try to 'place' poets whose work is far from finished. And it would be invidious and misleading lightly to select for reference a sample of the numerous poets now at work. That the task would be so formidable is something to be thankful about.

22
The twentieth-century novel

Of the writers who launched themselves about the turn of
the century none is more remarkable than Joseph Conrad
(1857–1924). A Polish orphan, he conceived a passion for the
sea, was twenty years a seafarer, and became a British subject and a master-mariner. He settled down on land in 1894
and his first two novels, *Almayer's Folly* (1895) and *An Out-
cast of the Islands* (1896) have a common Malayan background. But it is in *The Nigger of the 'Narcissus'* (1897) and
more especially in *Lord Jim* (1900) that Conrad's quality
first shows up. He is now master of his adopted language and
is able to add to his control of atmosphere and his rather
melancholy concern with broken men (such is Almayer) a

new depth of psychological insight. 'Lord' Jim instinctively leaps to join other officers who take to a boat when their ship, laden with pilgrims, appears to be sinking. In fact it is saved and towed to harbour. Jim is a romantic and an idealist: the jump is his 'fall'; and his incapacity at the crisis is one version of that impulsive departure from habitual standards which fascinates Conrad. The burden of the almost involuntary cowardice stays with Lord Jim until his life ends in a final expiatory act of redemption.

Though Conrad's experience as a seaman provides the stuff of his novels, and the sea itself – its changefulness, enmity in storm and reposefulness in calm – had moulded his spirit, his overriding interest is in human beings, and sea life provides a background and a symbolism for exploring their behaviour and their worth. The 'worth' is tested in situations of stress such as life at sea or on the edge of the jungle or among violent men readily provokes. Faithfulness, whether in sudden peril or before an exacting demand or under the corrosive strain of long isolation in remote parts of the world, is what proves men. So Captain MacWhirr (in *Typhoon*, 1903) rides the storm in the *Nan-Shan* and deals courageously with 200 fighting Chinese coolies and the danger of mutiny: and so Tom Lingard (in *The Rescue*, 1920) saves the upper-class people perilously stranded in their yacht; while Mr Kurtz (in *Heart of Darkness*, 1902), an ivory-trader in the Congo, succumbs to the strange evils of the jungle and proves a hollow man. *Heart of Darkness*, like *Lord Jim*, is one of the stories told by Marlow. Conrad's ironic power is strengthened by his use of a narrator whose comments distance events and supply an additional point of judgement. The oblique method is needed to contain the intricacies of the psychological and moral investigations Conrad undertakes.

Nostromo (1904), often regarded as Conrad's most masterly work, is a vast study of a South American country, 'Costaguana'; and in it Conrad works out a complex pattern of conflicts and mysteries on a philosophical basis whose central symbol is the 'Gould Concession', a silver mine. Charles Gould's wealth and power have enabled him to prop up a shaky capitalist government, but revolution breaks out. Nostromo, a trusted foreman, conveys silver away under instructions, hides it, and then pretends the vessel carrying it has sunk. Silver is the demonic influence, political and personal, rotting the governing system, the domestic virtues of Gould and the integrity of Nostromo: and of course many others are touched by it in life and personality too. Conrad's created world is immense – the republic of Costaguana with its politics, its trade and its teeming personalities. The intricacy of the imaginative presentation is such that every sensitivity of the reader's poetic and psychological understanding is appealed to. Man clashes with nature, value with value, man with man; and all public enterprise and private virtue are at war with the corrosive dominion of time. Among novels in which the sea plays no part is *Under Western Eyes* (1911) with its setting in Tsarist Russia. Razumov runs into difficulties when trying to aid a fugitive fellow student who has thrown a bomb and killed a minister in St Petersburg, and he betrays the revolutionary to the police. As so often, Conrad's central concern is the testing of a man's soul in crisis, the laying bare of his ultimate resources in lonely confrontation with a perilous question mark.

Two of Conrad's earlier works (*The Inheritors*, 1901, and *Romance*, 1903) were written in collaboration with Ford Madox Ford (1873–1939), a writer whose work is now being increasingly appreciated. A friend of Pound and a champion of Joyce, Ford was anxious to free the novel from narrative techniques that do violence to the mind's encounter with life's disordered impressions, and also to exploit further the technique of oblique reportage, so that reading can never lead to single-track interpretation that falsifies the character of experience. Thus Dowell, the narrator of *The Good Soldier* (1915), is himself a protagonist. He is heavily involved in all he speaks of, and his own oddities of act and response tease our curiosity; but there is no guidance from an omniscient author to help us to a decisive judgement on the reliability of his record or the accuracy of his self-revelation. The book is something of a *tour de force*: it was a fit precursor to the tetralogy of novels, together called *Parade's End*, which were published between 1924 and 1928 and which investigate the effect of the First World War on English society by tracing the career of one of the gentry (Christopher Tietjens) damaged by it.

A very different literary career started almost simultaneously with Conrad's when H. G. Wells (1866–1946) published *The Time Machine* in 1895, thus beginning a series of prophetic books in what we now call science fiction. The time machine carries its inventor forward to a horrific future of evolutionary regress. In addition to Wellsian fantasies (*The Shape of Things to Come*, 1933, was a later one), Wells wrote social novels with a message. In *Kipps* (1905) a young man who works at a draper's suddenly acquires great wealth, and a good deal of fun (not to mention propaganda) accompanies his entry into a different social class. Humour and human interest remain predominant, as they are in *Tono-Bungay* (1909) and *The History of Mr Polly* (1910), two books which contain autobiographical material. 'Tono-Bungay' is the name of a patent medicine, 'slightly injurious rubbish at one and three halfpence a bottle', that makes a fortune by effective sales promotion. Mr Polly is a bankrupt shopkeeper who fails to commit suicide, takes to the road, and settles down with the landlady of a country pub. There are later novels, like *The World of William Clissold* (1926), in which fiction is a vehicle for argument. Since Wells was the apostle of scientific progress, socialism and emancipation from monogamy, his polemics brought him into conflict with his contemporaries.

Among them was G. K. Chesterton (1874–1936), whose good-humouredly aggressive Christianity (Roman Catholicism eventually) made him the lively foe of scientism, humanism and rationalism. His imaginative work is impregnated with his beliefs. Love of paradox and fertility in aphorism mark his inimitable style. The detective stories featuring the shrewd priest, Father Brown (eventually collected in *The Father Brown Stories*, 1929), were immensely popular for their unpredictability, and, like all else Chesterton wrote, they are judiciously laden with wisdom. *The Man Who Was Thursday* (1908) is his best novel. A tale of anarchists and secret agents that unexpectedly makes a serious point at the end, it excellently exemplifies Chesterton's brilliance at leading the reader up the garden path. For the turning of tables and the rocking of glibly held assumptions is Chesterton's forte. His poetry keeps its place in the anthologies by virtue of his mastery of rousing balladry at once rhythmically sophisticated and rhetorically ablaze (*Lepanto* and *The Ballad of the White Horse* especially). As a critic GKC is zestful, brimming with ideas, an unapologetic chaser of hares and dispenser of illumination (see *Robert Browning,* 1903, *Charles Dickens,* 1906, and *Bernard Shaw,* 1909). As a biographer and thinker Chesterton is the kind of popularizer who does not cheapen what he touches, as his *St Thomas Aquinas* (1933) and his *Orthodoxy* (1908) will show.

Chesterton's friend and fellow Catholic, Hilaire Belloc (1870–1953), completes the quadrumvirate (Shaw, Wells, Chesterton, Belloc) who challenged settled assumptions, social and economic, though from vastly different angles. The Chesterbelloc (Shaw's term) also challenged the established reading of history in respect of the value of the Reformation and the presupposed continuity of progress. Belloc's output of satire, travel books, history and polemics was prolific: but the topicality of much of it has dated it, and he is now read chiefly for his light verse. A famous couplet now reads ironically:

> When I am dead, I hope it may be said:
> 'His sins were scarlet, but his books were read.'

On Conrad's last voyage as captain of the *Torrens* in 1893, one of his passengers was the young John Galsworthy (1867–

1933). Galsworthy has described how the 'great teller of tales' and he spent evening watches together and how Conrad asked him to his cabin on the last evening. They were to become friends as writers later. Galsworthy's field of documentation was that of the upper class to which he himself belonged. In creating the Forsyte family he found a medium for expressing his disturbed awareness of the limitations that the values of the propertied classes impose on their lives, particularly on their finer sensitivities in human relationships. Soames Forsyte's arid incompatibility with his wife Irene, who rejects her status as a piece of property, represents the failure of beauty to impinge on the world of the possessive. Galworthy's thinking is clear and unpretentious, his fictional world honestly and compassionately constructed. The three volumes of *The Forsyte Saga* (*The Man of Property*, 1906, *In Chancery*, 1920, and *To Let*, 1921) were succeeded by two further trilogies, *A Modern Comedy* (1929), and *The End of the Chapter* (1935).

What Galsworthy did for the upper classes Arnold Bennett (1867–1931) did for a shopkeeper's family in the Potteries in *The Old Wives' Tale* (1908), a long chronicle of the lives of two sisters, Constance and Sophia Baines. They are the children of a draper in Bursley, one of the Five Towns. Bennett's sense of reality and his understanding of women's minds gives the reader a close familiarity with his people and their world. Of his other novels, *Anna of the Five Towns* (1902) and *Clayhanger* (1910), also Potteries novels, have a comparable authenticity. (The latter, the first of a trilogy, is set in the 1870s and 1880s and takes in the Jubilee of Queen Victoria in 1887.) The influence of French realism (Balzac and Flaubert) lies behind the careful recording of Midlands life. Another highly successful novelist, Somerset Maugham (1874–1965), qualified as a doctor before turning to writing. There is a clinical detachment in his study of human character and a surgical precision in ironic judgement. His narrative is not always disinfected of authorial involvement and commitment. *Of Human Bondage* (1915) contains autobiographical material. Philip Carey, an orphan with a club foot, tries vainly to become an artist. And artistic vocation is the theme too in *The Moon and Sixpence* (1919) in which Charles Strickland, a stockbroker, forsakes his wife because of an urge to paint. Eventually he goes to Tahiti where he lives with a native woman (the book is based on the life of Gauguin).

A writer of totally different temperament and outlook was John Buchan (1875–1940) who had experience as a war correspondent and an intelligence officer in the First World War and eventually became Governor-General of Canada as Lord Tweedsmuir. His adventure stories are sturdy yarns. *Prester John* (1910) has its setting in South Africa, *Huntingtower* (1922) and *John Macnab* (1925) have theirs in Buchan's native Scotland. Perhaps his most distinctive books are the stories of espionage featuring Richard Hannay. In *The Thirty-Nine Steps* (1915) Hannay is made aware of a German plot and becomes the quarry of plotters and (by error) of police alike: the appears again in *Greenmantle* (1916) and *Mr Standfast* (1919). It is fair to compare Buchan with Stevenson for the liveliness and directness of his narrative technique, and he is a master of suspense. His verve in fiction makes him a readable historical biographer too, as his studies *Marquis of Montrose* (1913) and *Augustus* (1937) show.

Two writers who began to make themselves known before the First World War and attained immense popularity later were Hugh Walpole (1884–1941) and Compton Mackenzie (1883–1972). Both were encouraged by Henry James. *Mr Perrin and Mr Traill* (1911), a study of hatred between two schoolmasters, drew attention to Walpole's talent, and *Sinister Street* (1913), a thoughtful study of a middle-class boy's adolescence and development, drew attention to Mackenzie's. If Mackenzie's facility, the readiness of his humour, and his narrative inventiveness guaranteed continuing success as an entertainer, Walpole's earnest ambition stirred him to more challenging enterprises. *The Cathedral* (1922) gave him success with a wide public and invited comparison with Trollope, centring as it does on the public and private downfall of the Archdeacon of Polchester. The book has an attractive fluency but events and characters are too contrived: one is conscious of authorial effort operating towards a predetermined end. Walpole eventually gave himself to the ambitious task of writing a monumental family saga chronicling the history of a family, the Herries, over 100 years. *Rogue Herries* (1930) was the first volume of *The Herries Chronicle*. The region is that around the Solway Firth. The saga has always had its devotees.

Mackenzie might claim that the desire to entertain and the facility to do so in a lifetime's productivity need not cheapen a writer's gifts. P. G. Wodehouse (1881–   ) might be cited to prove the point. His humorous novels exploit farcical situations involving a group of characters as well known as any in English literature – the Hon. Bertie Wooster and his butler Jeeves, Psmith and Aunt Agatha, and lots of idle gentry and their satellites. The style brilliantly caricatures gentlemanly finesse and aristocratic dignity, with earthier tones appropriate to the lower orders. The *dramatis personae* are put through their paces in situations of adroitly contrived absurdity, yet naturalness of sequence and dialogue is unbroken for the reader who enters Wodehouse's world on its own irresistible terms. *Leave it to Psmith* (1923), *The Inimitable Jeeves* (1924) and *Carry on, Jeeves* (1925) show the author at full tide.

Before we turn to E. M. Forster and the 'giants' we might well look briefly at a current of fiction that has flowed richly this century – that of children's fiction. The wider diffusion of culture has made the child-readership an important one; and it may well be that imaginative writers of quality will turn increasingly to this public if adult fiction turns irrecoverably sour. Of course some writers for children are not people, one feels, who *might* have written for a different age group. Beatrix Potter (1866–1943) is a case in point. *The Tale of Peter Rabbit* (1902) was the first of a series of animal stories, finely illustrated in water-colour, which blended a knowledge of real animals and what one can only call a reverence for their animal individualness with the gift for dressing them up and making them talk. As there is no condescension to rabbits, ducks, hedgehogs and cats (to Benjamin Bunny, Jemima Puddleduck, Mrs Tiggy-Winkle or even naughty Tom Kitten), so there is no condescension to children. When the meaning of 'credit' is explained in *The Tale of Ginger and Pickles* (a cat and a terrier who keep a shop), the explanation, you feel, leaves the children understanding the system a good deal more profoundly than those adults who practise it. Beatrix Potter's style is inimitably businesslike and to the point. The narrative line is richly filled out by the illustrations, notable for scenes of the Lake District, where Beatrix Potter lived for much of her life.

The Lake District also provided the setting for some of Arthur Ransome's adventure stories for children of a higher age group. Ransome (1884-1967) had an interest in outdoor activities like camping and sailing boats and this, together with his knowledge of nature and topography, gave body to his adventure stories like *Swallows and Amazons* (1931). The children use the vocabulary of adult enterprise and seem conversant with the technical terminology of fairly advanced seamanship, but their explorations are realistic holiday activities and there are reliable, kissable parents in the background.

A. A. Milne (1882-1956) had worked as journalist and dramatist before his children's books took the country's middle-class families by storm in the 1920s. It was the birth of Milne's son, Christopher Robin, and the parental need to turn bedtime entertainer that initiated the uncovering of Milne's immense talent for vivifying toy animals. Appropriate human characteristics – lovable slow-wittedness (Pooh Bear), plaintive self-pity (Eeyore), pathetic ineffectiveness (tiny Piglet) and diminutive 'cheekiness' (Roo, pocket edition of Kanga) – are read into the toy animals according to their appearance. Stuffed limbs, suitably bedraggled, and stitched eyes were vividly realized by E. H. Shepard's illustrations.

The two prose volumes, *Winnie-the-Pooh* (1926) and *The House at Pooh Corner* (1928), built upon the reputation already firmly established by Milne's charmingly versatile verses for children in *When We Were Very Young* (1924), to which *Now We Are Six* was added in 1927.

The reputation of E. M. Forster (1879–1970) is founded on four novels published in his first thirty-one years and a fifth published when he was forty-five. He is a writer with a keen eye for idiosyncrasies of temperament and for the capacity of people to deceive themselves. Like Hardy, he is fond of turns of events which make the most of the misunderstandings that readily arise between people of contrasting upbringing, social and cultural, but whereas in Hardy such moments are given full dramatic force, in Forster they are given what has been called the 'tea-table' treatment. Forster organizes his material in a dualistic pattern whereby opposed attitudes to life collide and their respective representatives in various degrees fail, with the best will in the world, to bridge the gap between them. This pattern is strengthened by correspondences between people, background and events that have symbolic consistency. It is interesting, in view of Forster's professed dislike of Scott, that the dualistic patterning and the symbolic enrichment are fundamental to many of the Waverley Novels. But whereas Scott's use of the framework is designed to bring readily recognized ideologies into conflict, Forster's aim is to uncover conflicts of attitude which have never been explicated, or even fully recognized, but which have damaged human life and interfered with honest relationships. In this sense Forster must be regarded as a novelist with a message.

In *Where Angels Fear to Tread* (1905) the conflict is between English middle-class respectability (Forster's favourite target) which, under a hypocritical exterior, is narrow-minded, provincial and crudely insensitive, and Italian frankness and impetuosity. The English family, the Herritons, is itself a little miniature of the England Forster dislikes – dominating mother, frustrated children, daughter self-righteous, son sentimental, and all out of touch with life. The widowed daughter-in-law marries Gino, an uninhibited Italian, then dies in childbirth. The life of the baby – symbol of the linking of incompatibles – is ultimately sacrificed to the competition for possession launched by the Herritons. Fools rush in where angels fear to tread. In *Howards End* (1910) the collision is between the Wilcox family (Howards End is their family home and, as such, stands like Shaw's Heartbreak House for England) who are solidly efficient but narrow in their sensitivities, and the half-German Schlegel sisters who are deeply interested in culture and sensitive to human needs. The Wilcoxes' world is that of commerce, imperialism and philistinism, while the Schlegels are socialists and go to symphony concerts. Forster's motto is 'Only connect', and the need for cross-fertilization is made plain. The pattern of connections that cross the frontiers of class and culture is complicated by the representative of the aspiring underprivileged, Leonard Bast, whom Helen Schlegel befriends. The book's design is a subtle fabric of event and symbol, giving expression to the price paid when the well-meaning impulses of blinkered personalities go awry. Its more extravagant turns (such as Helen's affair with Bast and her pregnancy) have been criticized as too improbable, but Forster's narrative power goes far towards making improbabilities acceptable.

Forster's very various characters are vibrant individuals who catch the reader's sympathies (or antipathies) as knowable people in their own right. The plane on which suffering or failure is enacted is one on which the larger human predicament is at issue as well as the more easily definable queries about whether English middle-class culture, public school education, and immersion in conventionalities unfit one for the finer commerce of human contact. *A Passage to India* (1924) explores the difficulty of reaching understanding and full communication between the English and the natives in British India. Cyril Fielding, a college principal, and Dr Aziz are friends whose relationship is shaken when Adela Quested concludes that Aziz has assaulted her in the Marabar Caves – a charge which she later retracts. The repercussions in public feeling and in personal dilemmas are articulated with fidelity and insight. At the end Fielding and Aziz remain divided by racial and historical facts which their mutual affection cannot obliterate. Forster's message throughout his work is based on respect for 'passion and truth', for 'personal relations', for 'integrity', as opposed to conventionalism and rule by accepted 'catchwords'. Of course the dichotomies he relies upon are open to question, and indeed they have now become the clichés of a new 'liberal' conventionalism perhaps due in its turn for demolition.

Forster was associated with the 'Bloomsbury Group', a coterie of writers and intellectuals with a common interest in love, art and truth, and a common revulsion against the cramping inhibitions of the middle-class Victorian mind. A key figure in the group was the biographer, Lytton Strachey (1880–1932), who gained a reputation for debunking by frankly deflating the 'heroes' of recent history in his spicy studies of Florence Nightingale, Cardinal Manning and Thomas Arnold in *Eminent Victorians* (1918). He applied the same ironic technique, in some respects less devastatingly and more sentimentally, to the queen, Prince Albert and others in *Queen Victoria* (1921). A writer at the centre of the group was Virginia Woolf (1882–1941), wife of the political thinker, Leonard Woolf. She was a woman of great sensitivity, subject to mental depression, and she took her own life at the height of the air war in England.

Virginia Woolf felt that standard fictional techniques of narrational plotting and character projection constituted an artistic servitude to the crude external sequence of events. To this extent she has affinities with Proust and Joyce. She replaced the standard techniques of presentation – description, narrative and dialogue, arranged in sequential chunks – with a 'stream of consciousness' which could represent the fluidity of the inner life and the sharp richness of the little experiences and sensations that stimulate it. Virginia Woolf thus evolved a technique in which characters are not 'presented' to the reader: rather the content of their inner lives impinges on the reader. In *Mrs Dalloway* (1925) events take place on a single summer day in the life of Clarissa Dalloway, but the substance of the book is contained in mental reflections and flashbacks that reconstruct Mrs Dalloway's past. *To the Lighthouse* (1927) extends the technique, handling a group of people centred on the Ramsay family in their seaside home. The party plan to visit the lighthouse in Part One of the book but do not go. Only after the passage of ten eventful years is the trip made; and by now the lighthouse has become a powerful symbol of the shifting light and darkness in human life. *Orlando* (1928) is technically a *tour de force*, for Orlando's lifetime extends over four centuries. Orlando, at first an Elizabethan nobleman, is a projection of the human spirit and as such changes sex *en route* through history. Brilliant sketches of succeeding ages help to make this an illuminating and vital book. In *The Waves* (1931) the externals of action and dialogue are totally submerged, and the reader is taken into the minds of a group of growing characters who know one another when young, but whose ways diverge for many years. The personality of each is reflected in the minds of the others so that a kaleidoscopic pattern emerges, corresponding in its glittering fluidity to the movement of the sea.

Virginia Woolf distrusted the masculine world of practical action and the commercialized fiction that flattered its superficialities. With something of the passion of the mystic she valued rather the 'reality' of the perceptive moment and of inner wonder. Her novels juxtapose mighty opposites – isolation and relatedness, rejection and acceptance, randomness and pattern – and reconcile them in an aesthetic harmony which at least suggests that meaning underlies appearance.

A vastly different innovator was D. H. Lawrence (1885–1930). His working-class background, his obsession with sexual passion, his open determination to preach, and his casual attitude to the novel as an art form are four characteristics that distinguish him from E. M. Forster and Virginia Woolf. His father was a Nottinghamshire miner, barely literate, and his mother an ex-schoolteacher increasingly dissatisfied with her husband's cultural level and desperately anxious for 'Bertie' (David Herbert), her favourite, to rise above his origins. Mrs Lawrence's possessive devotion to her son and the tension of the family situation are represented autobiographically in the novel, *Sons and Lovers* (1913). In a finely realized account of mining life in the Midlands, the situation of the Morel family parallels that of the Lawrences. Mrs Morel's background was middle-class and the passion that caused her to marry her miner husband has died, to leave her love wholly directed at her sons, especially at Paul. Paul's psychological development is traced with subtlety, especially the growth of his interest in books and painting and the course of his early love affairs with Miriam and Clara. The boy cannot escape the overpowering emotional bond imposed by his mother's love and he fails to achieve a fulfilling relationship with either girl. The personality of Miriam ('nearly sixteen, very beautiful, with her warm colouring, her gravity, her eyes dilating suddenly like an ecstasy'), pitted against the competitive emotional demand of Paul's mother (who dies of cancer), is movingly alive; and Jessie Webster, whom Miriam represents, has written her own reminiscences of Lawrence since his death. (See *D.H. Lawrence, A Personal Record*, by E. T., 1935.)

After teacher training at University College, Nottingham, and subsequent teaching at Croydon, Lawrence turned to full-time writing, publishing *The White Peacock* in 1911 and *The Trespasser* in 1912. In the meantime his mother had died and in 1912 Lawrence fell in love with Frieda Weekley. He took her away from her husband (a professor at Nottingham) and her three children to the Continent. Sexual passion thus had a practical primacy for him over other obligations, and it was again his preoccupation in *The Rainbow* (1915) and in *Women in Love* (1920). The former covers the lives of three generations of a Nottinghamshire family, the Brangwens, but is especially concerned with the emotional career of Ursula Brangwen, a sensitive woman who rejects the deadening mechanization of spirit and environment by the mining industry. The theme ramifies in the sequel, *Women in Love*. Here Gudrun and her sister, Ursula, are paired with Gerald Crich, son of a mine-owner, and Rupert Birkin, a school inspector. Gerald is representative of the industrial ethic and Birkin spokesman for the passionate self that must assert its integrity against the cramping pressures of mechanized industrialism and the domination of intellect. Lawrence was now using the novel form to hammer out a view of life and to exercise a radical effect on his readers' thinking. Sex-based anti-intellectualist theories are extravagantly developed in the non-fiction work, *Fantasia of the Unconscious*. But one must remember that Lawrence was not a static thinker. He does not hesitate to pit idea against idea: even theories that he likes may be propounded by one character and taken to pieces by another. He lives his own problems on paper. The marital difficulties of Richard Lovat Somers and his wife in *Kangaroo* (1923) are projected from Lawrence's own experience with Frieda. The book gives a rich portrayal of Australian life and scenery. Cooley, the underground fascist leader, is a Nietzschean devotee of 'blood-consciousness', but Somers in the end rejects his leadership. *The Plumed Serpent* (1926), set in Mexico, develops the Nietzschean theme and gives it a religious dimension. Set against the alien Catholic culture is an Aztec cult that is rooted in sex and blood-consciousness and exalts the dominant male over the passive female. One is aware of an almost demonic urge driving Lawrence towards the assertion of unexplored naturalistic allegiances to replace the civilizational values he hated and had rejected. The frank sexuality of *Lady Chatterley's Lover* (1928) made it his most notorious book. It takes us back to Nottinghamshire.

Sir Clifford Chatterley has returned from the war paralysed below the waist. His impotence is made symbolic of the sterile upper-class establishment. Mellors, the gamekeeper, representative of lower-class virility, provides the sexual satisfaction Chatterley's wife, Connie, desperately needs. In attempting to intensify the collision between what is vital and what is moribund, Lawrence made free use of 'four-letter' words in the love relationship. The urge to rescue such words from the slough of comic obscenity was vain.

In 1914 Ezra Pound was already describing Lawrence and Joyce as 'the two strongest prose writers among *les jeunes*'.[1] James Joyce (1882–1941) was born and educated in Dublin. His incorrigibly thriftless father and struggling mother brought up their children (ten of them) ever nearer the edge of poverty, but Joyce was thoroughly educated at Catholic schools and at University College, Dublin. Then, after a year in Paris, and a return to Dublin on his mother's death, he went abroad with Nora Barnacle in 1904 and kept himself by teaching until he was able (with the help of patronage) to be a full-time writer.

It was not until 1914 that Joyce managed to get his book of short stories, *Dubliners*, published. The stories are written with deceptive simplicity and deal successively with events of childhood, youth and adulthood. Some show the nullifying effect of the Dublin social and mental environment on characters whose dreams, hopes and ambitions are pathetically or tragically unfulfilled. The rhythm of aspiration and disappointment or resignation recurs at various levels of sophistication; and the element of stylization in the patterning of the material, together with the evident recourse to symbolism, foreshadows Joyce's later work.

A Portrait of the Artist as a Young Man had been long a-writing when it came out in 1916. It reworked much material in *Stephen Hero*, a manuscript that has been post-

[1] Quoted in Stuart Gilbert (ed.): *Letters of James Joyce* (Faber and Faber, London, 1957).

humously published (1944). It is as much rooted in autobiographical experience as Lawrence's *Sons and Lovers*, yet
the artistic technique is so different that it can easily be mis-
read. Joyce at once hugs his hero close in sympathy and
distances him in irony: the resultant blend of pathos and
humour is piquant. Of course Stephen's recollections of
home, school, first love, and awakening cultural interests
have an unmistakably authentic core; but the final artistic
self-dedication is to 'silence, exile, and cunning', and silence
and cunning imply abandonment of direct openness. The
adoption of literary subterfuges – symbolism, labyrinthinism,
and formality hidden inside naturalism – are as important in
the total artistic vocation as the need by exile to escape Irish
politics, religion and sentimentality. Joyce's presentation
of Stephen's experience from within Stephen's own mind
involves use of styles in tune with infant thought, childhood
thought, adolescent thought and student thought successively. Sensitive adjustment of idiom to the thinker's moods
and understanding, whether they are healthy or not, involves walking on a stylistic tightrope stretched precariously
between involvement and detachment. The thematic use
of images establishes continuing symbolic connections.
Stephen Dedalus's own name brings together that of the first
Christian martyr and that of the arch artificer of classical
legend.

With *Ulysses* (1922) we reach a masterpiece of epic proportions. The framework is linked to the *Odyssey*. Odysseus's
years of wandering, his son Telemachus's search for him, and
the return to Penelope, are echoed in the story of Leopold
Bloom, Dublin advertisement canvasser, Stephen Dedalus
(who is in search of spiritual fatherhood), and Molly,
Bloom's much-loved but sexually neglected wife. For wanderings about the world of ancient myth we have wanderings about the city of Dublin. All is compressed within one
June day (the 16th) in 1904. The full development of the
'stream-of-consciousness' technique enables Bloom's past life
to be grasped in retrospect. The technique faithfully records

the flow of thought and feeling, doing justice to persistent emotional currents and logical randomness alike. The natural flow of mental reflection, the shifting moods and impulses that constitute the fabric of inner life, are represented with uncanny penetration. But readers who see only thus far miss much of Joyce's power. For as the outer and inner action proceeds, Joyce's 'poetry' continuously throws up metaphors, symbols, ambiguities and overtones which gradually link themselves together so as to form a network of connections and cross-connections binding the whole edifice in unity.

Leopold Bloom has been sexually separated from his wife for ten years since the birth and tragic death, eleven days later, of their longed-for son, Rudy. Leopold is a Jew. His separation from Molly is not only comparable to Odysseus's separation from Penelope, for the upgrading of Bloom to epic status is part of a wider enrichment of significance. Joyce's imagery makes Bloom the focus of universal human tensions. His hunger for Molly is an aspect of everyman's hunger for his earth goddess, for his mother, for the warmth and security and fulfilment which earth can never permanently provide. Therefore it corresponds with man's idealistic turning to Church and Madonna, mystical Bride and Divine Spouse. The imagery gives Molly a changing status: she may correspond to mother country, Mother Church, or mother of the Son of Man. Similarly her infidelity with Boylan may correspond now with Ireland's betrayal of her children, now with Eve's betrayal of Adam, and now (via a symbolic reading of *Hamlet*) with betrayal by the frail, erring human flesh of the manhood it has mothered. The system of correspondences enables Joyce to take a panoramic (even encyclopedic) view of the human situation while never for a moment relaxing his grip on the particular: for *Ulysses* is alive throughout with the savour and salt of life in Dublin in 1904. The reader is deeply immersed in the currents of its private and public life. But Joyce makes Dublin everyman's city. In its association with Molly it is a potential reflection of *Urbs Beata*, the New Jerusalem, though Bloom, materialistic twentieth-century everyman, whose eye is on the main chance, would prefer to see it turned into the New Bloomusalem, with electric dishscrubbers, bonuses for all, universal brotherhood and free love thrown in.

The eighteen episodes are divided into three books (three, twelve, three) with an implicit Dantean structure, in that the central section, Bloom's wanderings in Dublin, takes us spiralling down the circles of modern 'unreality' (in newspaper office, library and the like) to the depths of the twentieth-century Inferno in the brothels of Nighttown. The moral pattern is clear. In Molly's adultery we see the home betrayed from without and within (by Boylan's intrusion, by Bloom's fastidious neglect). Molly is Eve seduced by Satan, Ireland usurped by the British, the Church betrayed from within, the flesh of man let down by the selfish masculine intellect. Ireland is betrayed by those who rend her dedicated prophetic leaders, by those who sell her horses to the enemy for cash, by those who sell her artistic soul for cash (as establishment writers do) and by those who sell her young womanhood for cash in the Dublin brothels.

The humour of the book balances its profundity; the stylistic virtuosity matches the magnitude of the conception. Each episode displays Joyce's literary skill in a distinct style appropriate to the substance of that episode alone. Joyce spent seven years writing *Ulysses*. Its delights and its illuminations for the reader are excitingly added to with every reading, however many. At the end of several, the reader will wish to try *Finnegans Wake* (1939) where new techniques of verbal ambiguity allow for the accumulation of simultaneous meanings at a new level of complexity. Joyce had experimented in *Ulysses* with new words like 'menagerer' which derives a threefold connotation from 'manager', 'ménage' and 'menagerie'. By developing this method of compression and calling in the aid of other languages than English, he gave additional dimensions to the tale of a Dublin publican and his family, touching the cosmic and the archetypal at one extreme and the personal (autobiographical) at the other. The text is difficult. Joyce could justify his method on the grounds that the world of *Finnegans Wake* is the dream world in which we spend a good part of our lives, and where shifting identities, multiple significances and absurdly incongruous composite impressions are commonplace.

An exciting writer in close touch with Joyce, Eliot and Pound was Wyndham Lewis (1884–1957). He shared the 'anti-romantic' drive towards reinstating artistic impersonality and the values of intelligence; for he hated current indulgence of the artistic personality and sentimental denigration of intellect and objectivity. He had no sympathy with Lawrence's cultivation of the primitive and the unconscious nor with the 'stream-of-consciousness' technique because of its internality and intuitiveness. As an artist he led a movement known as 'Vorticism', yet he wrote prolifically as novelist and polemicist. *Time and Western Man* (1927) has perhaps been most celebrated among his polemical books. The summit of his work as a novelist is represented by the trilogy, *Childermass* (1928), *Monstre Gai* and *Malign Fiesta* (both 1955), a fantastic satirical epic in which we first see the mass of humanity gathered outside Heaven and facing supernatural judgement before a peculiar authority (half man, half dwarf) known as the Bailiff. Great claims are now made for Wyndham Lewis: certainly his vast achievement is yet to be generally granted the status it deserves. He has been compared to Swift for the intellectual passion of his satire, and to Blake for his lonely, prophetic mission of judgement.

Another extraordinary personality of the same generation was T. E. Lawrence (1888–1935), who led the Arab revolt against the Turks in the First World War and thereby became a legendary figure in his own lifetime. The glamour of his personality casts its aura over his personal record of the Arab revolt, *The Seven Pillars of Wisdom* (1926). T. E. Lawrence's letters were edited in 1938 by David Garnett: they do not help to sustain the legend of a discerning warrior-artist. David Garnett (1892–   ) is a novelist who first specialized in transitions from the naturalistic to the fantastic effected with total lack of fuss. In *Lady into Fox* (1922) a country gentleman keeps up appearances as best he can while his wife is gradually transformed into a fox. In *A Man in the Zoo* (1924) a man manages to get himself included among the creatures on display as a specimen of his kind. The Lawrence myth came under fire from Richard Aldington (1892–1962) in *Lawrence of Arabia* (1955). Aldington wrote on D. H. Lawrence too (*Portrait of a Genius, But . . .*, 1950). His service in the army in the First World War gave him a very different picture of warfare from T. E. Lawrence's and indelibly marked his subsequent novels, especially *Death of a Hero* (1929), which draws a bitter contrast between civilian life at home and the harrowing experience of the front-line soldier that cuts him off from meaningful communication with those left behind.

Aldous Huxley (1894–1963) edited D. H. Lawrence's letters in 1932. The grandson of T. H. Huxley, the scientist, and connected through his mother with Matthew Arnold, he came of a good family and was essentially a man of intellect and culture. His early novels were witty satirical studies of the fashionable cultural circles of the 1920s. Huxley's casual display of erudition and his capacity to give highbrow status to cleverness about current cleverness (and wickedness) gave him a cult appeal to the student as a kind of educated Noël Coward. The technique at first owes something to Thomas Love Peacock in its emphasis on the conversation of eccentrics (*Crome Yellow*, 1921), though *Antic Hay* (1923) offsets the cynical representation of highbrow chatter with the activities of Theodore Gumbril who markets Gumbril's Patent Small-Clothes – with built-in pneumatic seats. Gumbril senior's pride is his model of London as it would have been had Wren's plan for rebuilding it after the Fire been carried out. ('My men, like satyrs grazing on the lawns, / Shall with their goat-feet dance the antic hay', says Gaveston, the king's favourite in Marlowe's *Edward II*.) *Point Counter Point* (1928) represents the early vein at its richest.

It experiments with the interplay of themes (chiefly disturbed marriages and liaisons) on a musical pattern, and the writer Philip Quarles is working on a novel counterpointing what is happening. Huxley draws on Lawrence and Frieda for Mark Rampion and his wife, on John Middleton Murry (Lawrence's biographer in *Son of Woman*) for Burlap, and on Sir Oswald Mosley for Everard Webley.

Brave New World (1932) is a fantasy of the future. The year is 632 AF (After Ford). Totalitarian scientific control governs everything from the incubation of babies in bottles to the assignment of each (preconditioned) being to his appropriate (predetermined) function in society. Culture is suppressed. Standardized pleasures are laid on through the contentment media. Hygiene is the supreme moral value ('Mother' is a dirty word). The accuracy of the forecasting is still worrying. Huxley's later work is strongly influenced by successive concern with non-violence and the philosophy of non-attachment (*Ends and Means*, 1937), with mysticism (*The Perennial Philosophy*, 1946) and with the occult. Practical interest in mysticism sidetracked him into experimentation with drug-induced hallucination.

Huxley's struggle between scientific and religious leanings, between physiological obsessions and cultured idealism, is not so much resolved as conducted full-circle. There is comparable tension between the satirical and the religious impulse in the work of T. F. Powys (1875–1953), brother of John Cowper Powys (1872–1963), himself a novelist with imaginative energy and wide-ranging percipience, and of Llewelyn Powys (1884–1939), a writer of fiction and miscellaneous prose. T. F. Powys lived quietly in a village in Dorset and the novels that emerged from his seclusion indicate the complexity of his response to life. There is harsh irony, ruthless exposure of the realities of village life (sex life notably), and a macabre sense of humour in *Mr Tasker's Gods* (1925) for instance: but there is a seductive vein of symbolism in *Mr Weston's Good Wine* (1927) where God figures as a travelling vintner.

We find a lively scorn of foolery and knavery in the work of Rose Macaulay (1881–1958). *Potterism* (1920) brought her to notice for its withering ridicule of current go-getting philistinism. *Told by an Idiot* (1923) is a three-generation family study in similar vein. Aubrey Garden's six children, named acording to his enthusiasm of the hour in pursuit of religious truth, are permanent living witnesses to his giddy career ('Rome' and 'Una' – for Unitarianism – are but two of them). Rose Macaulay's deeper personal concerns push their way to the surface in later books, notably in *The Towers of Trebizond* (1956) where her own emotional crisis in worried love for a married man is known to be reflected. (The dilemma of conscience is movingly recorded in *Letters to a Friend*.) No soul-searing tensions visit the world of J. B. Priestley (1894–   ) in *The Good Companions* (1929), a frank attempt to resurrect the zestful bounce and comic gusto of the three-decker picaresque novel. It oozes with aggressive Yorkshire warm-heartedness, and Jess Oakroyd of Bruddersford is a substantial human study. Later novels have sustained the tale of success it initiated. Priestley is also a critic with books on Meredith and Peacock to his credit, as well as the more comprehensive study, *Literature and Western Man* (1960). And he is an agreeable essayist (*Delight*, 1949).

If Priestley's literary lineage harks back to the eighteenth century, that of Elizabeth Bowen (1899–1973) derives more immediately from the Bloomsbury Group. Her detailed exploration of the inner emotional life and her interest in tangled relationships reflected through the minds of children, as well as her conscious artistry, inevitably remind one of Virginia Woolf. She is acute in rendering the maturing emotional experience of sensitive women and the transmutation of innocence and idealism into wounded understanding (as in *The Hotel*, 1927, and *The Death of the Heart*, 1938). Rosamond Lehmann (1903–   ) is often linked with Elizabeth Bowen, for she shared her indebtedness to Virginia Woolf and her first novel, *Dusty*

Answer (1927) traces the development of a sensitive girl – a theme she has continued to probe (see *The Echoing Grove*, 1953).

Among other successful and accomplished novelists of the same generation, who exerted no exacting demand on the reader's understanding or sensibilities, one should mention Eric Linklater (1899–   ), a Scotsman whose gift is for light-hearted wit and satire (like *Juan in America*, 1931, and its successors), Naomi Mitchison (1897–1964), who combined genuine historical authenticity with updated raciness of conversational idiom in stories of Greece and Rome (like *The Conquered*, 1923), and Margaret Kennedy (1896–1967) whose immensely successful novel, *The Constant Nymph* (1924), shows spiritedness and love in (ultimately tragic) conflict with conventionalized society. Storm Jameson (1897–   ) helped to feed the appetite for family chronicles with her trilogy on a Yorkshire shipbuilding family, *The Triumph of Time* (1932). Charles Morgan (1894–1958) directed cultivated penmanship at an audience with intellectual pretensions. The ostentatiously literary tone and the affected concern with supposed moral and philosophical dimensions, in novels like *The Fountain* (1932) and *Sparkenbroke* (1936), imposed on some readers the notion of rare profundity and artistry.

A writer who had no need to strive after profundity was Helen Waddell (1889–1965), a medieval scholar who wrote a study of medieval Latin poets (*The Wandering Scholars*, 1927) and returned to the twelfth century to reproduce the story of Abelard and Heloise in the novel, *Peter Abelard* (1933). Because of her scholarship Helen Waddell was able to handle the emotional story lyrically without cheapening it. She faithfully reproduces the intellectual climate of the age, doing justice to the philosophical and theological controversies Abelard was involved in and binding them so closely with his personal dilemma that the whole acquires the status of an archetypal study in Christian self-surrender such as Eliot made in *Murder in the Cathedral*.

Theology gives depth of a different kind to the novels of Charles Williams (1886–1945). Williams presented the human being as supernaturally involved in a cosmic conflict between the powers of light and of darkness. He was penetratingly subtle in detecting the ease with which the misorientated ego can become virtually possessed by potencies demonically motivated. His novels open up the daily twentieth-century lives of his characters to the full range of spiritual influences from without – whether divine or diabolical in origin. His supernatural mythology is not just fictional machinery but credible Christian symbolism. The later novels like *Descent into Hell* (1937) and *All Hallows' Eve* (1945) are the best. Williams's work in the field where theology and literary criticism meet (*The Figure of Beatrice, A Study in Dante*, 1943) is stimulating. Williams had interesting literary connections, being both a friend of T. S. Eliot and a member of the Oxford circle associated with C. S. Lewis (1898–1963). It was Lewis who, in *Arthurian Torso* (1948), recommended and elucidated Williams's sequences of Arthurian poems, *Taliessin Through Logres* (1938) and *The Region of the Summer Stars* (1944).

Lewis's own work as a literary critic and Christian apologist (especially the famous correspondence between devils, *The Screwtape Letters*, 1942) has been enormously influential. His novels give the weight of moral and religious significance to tales of interplanetary travel and biological experimentation such as are now generally called science fiction (*Out of the Silent Planet*, 1938, *Perelandra*, 1943, *That Hideous Strength*, 1945). Lewis's frank use of allegory in *The Pilgrim's Regress* ('An Allegorical Apology for Christianity, Reason, and Romanticism', 1933) deserves more attention than it has had, but perhaps his finest work as an imaginative writer is in the chronicles of Narnia, seven stories for children, of which the first, *The Lion, The Witch, and The Wardrobe*, represents the divine power of redeeming love in the person of the awesome lion, Aslan. In these stories the finely articulated symbolism shadows aspects of the Christian faith and, in *The Silver Chair* for example, brings a shrewd prophetic wisdom to bear on contemporary civilization.

Dorothy Sayers's work as dramatist, apologist and translator of Dante brought her within Lewis's circle. Her reputation as detective novelist predates the connection. In this field she added to the necessary expertise in criminal investigation a power to give vitality to men and women of taste and culture who have plenty to talk about in addition to corpses and clues. The spice her wit and sophistication provided for the educated reader relied a good deal on the character of her amateur sleuth, Lord Peter Wimsey, an urbane, donnish aristocrat: but she also laid on meatily digestible backgrounds such as the advertising agency in *Murder Must Advertise* (1933). It is of course a woman who has become one of the most popular and prolific of all English detective novelists, Agatha Christie (1891–   ), largely, it would seem, by virtue of the skilfully engineered complexity of her plots.

Of all that emerged from Lewis's circle the most astonishing success has attended the work of J. R. R. Tolkien (1892–1973). His fairy story, *The Hobbit* (1937) proved to be forerunner of a massive mythical epic in three parts, *The Lord of the Rings* (1954–5). The hobbit is a little, two-legged being, whose encounter with dwarfs takes him from his cosy home to dangerous adventuring in forests and mountains and a perilous introduction to the dragon, Smaug. This adventure is enriched by hints of a mighty 'history' in the background, but scarcely prepares us for the colossal expansion of the fantasy world that follows in the trilogy. The vast work takes us into a world strangely alive with unspoken meanings and unseen presences. The magic ring is the token of corruption, for its possession means power. It has been captured from Sauron, Dark Lord of the evil and desolate land of Mordor, who would recover it and enslave all living beings. A key foe is Aragorn, heir to the rival kingdom of Gondor. Among the inhabitants of the Middle-

Earth in the Great Year of its Third Age, whose history Tolkien is chronicling, we meet dwarfs, elves, wizards, and unfamiliar species like the Orcs and the Ents, as well as the hobbits. Tolkien has not of course elucidated the meaning of the underlying symbolism. That the modern world of technology and mechanization seems to be under judgement is evident, and the awareness of good and evil in conflict is palpable throughout. Tolkien's imaginative inventiveness is extraordinary, and his flair for name-making a great bonus of adornment. His epic is the product of a rich fusion between scholarship in older languages and in mythology, and a Christianly orientated imagination (he was a Roman Catholic).

Another trilogy of epic quality is that by Mervyn Peake (1911–68) – *Titus Groan* (1946), *Gormenghast* (1950) and *Titus Alone* (1959). Peake too creates a fantasy world, but its inhabitants are, at least in shape, human beings however grotesque. Moreover it has no flavour of the primitive. Its horrors belong to a post-civilizational mythology. Life in Gormenghast (Titus's home) proceeds according to a complex ritual anciently established and now fully understood only by Sourdust who has devoted a lifetime to mastering it. Lord Sepulchrave (Lord Groan) gazes at the world 'through a haze of melancholia'. The Countess lives amid a swarm of cats and birds. The curator, Rottcodd, presides over the Hall of Bright Carvings. But a young radical emerges to question, murder and destroy – one Steerpike. Mervyn Peake was an artist and the pictorial power of his work is stirringly eerie and sinister. There is a cartoonery of gravity and momentousness as well as of the ridiculous, and Peake's characters loom larger than life. In the last volume, when Titus escapes from Gormenghast, we find a more savage brand of satire depicting a nightmare world uncomfortably like our own.

As Peake's stylistic virtuosity bears the marks of the artist, so too does the work of Joyce Cary (1888–1957). Here is one more writer of whom it is sometimes said that his verve and vitality put his novels outside the main stream of twentieth-century fiction: but it is possible to misidentify the 'main stream'. Some of his work harks back to the packed, rollicking world of Smollet or Dickens. Cary was born in Londonderry and the gift of colourful Irish fluency is plainly his. He has the capacity to assume a style as an actor puts on a costume. It is not only a manner of speech that he adopts: he enters into the mind and heart of characters so that they emerge obtrusively alive and subject to criticism, yet inwardly felt and sympathized with. This is the recipe for a collision between the comic and the pathetic, between the hilarious and the tragic, that makes his books awesomely perceptive yet often riotously funny. In *Mister Johnson* (1939) the Nigerian clerk, a mission-school product, aspires to the white man's ways with a naïvety and roguery that are irresistibly touching and vibrant. He deceives himself with his own grandiose pretensions ('a poet who creates for himself a glorious destiny', Cary said of him). In the trilogy, *Herself Surprised* (1941), *To Be a Pilgrim* (1942) and *The Horse's Mouth* (1944), it is first the earthy, warm-hearted cook-housekeeper, Sara Monday, whose experience is explored. She has gone into domestic service and married into the family, but after her huband's death she becomes the mistress, successively, of Gulley Jimson, a compelling but unprincipled artist, and of Thomas Loftus Wilcher, an aged solicitor. Wilcher's family history is explored in the second novel, and in the third Gulley Jimson's career is before us. Rascally, scurrilous, irrepressible as ever (after a term in gaol), he battens on Sara touchingly, on 'patrons' consciencelessly. The high farce at the end is unforgettable. A later trilogy handles a very different triangle. Nina Nimmo tells the story of her husband, Chester Nimmo, in *Prisoner of Grace* (1952). Nimmo is a dedicated and self-mesmerizing radical politician, dominant by that thrust of self-confidence that makes Mister Johnson and Gulley Jimson what they are. In *Except the Lord* (1953) Nimmo tells his own story at the end of his life (he rose to be a cabinet minister). Jim Latter, Nina's lover, a soldier of the old school, writes *Not Honour More* (1955) in the death cell for the shooting of Nimmo. One senses an archetypal rendering of the history of twentieth-century political England patterned movingly at the personal level. Nimmo's idealism is not unrelated to the flamboyant self-deception of Mister Johnson and Gulley Jimson. The last two at least, it may be argued, are Irishmen in disguise.

There are two more novelists who were born before the turn of the century, and both are writers whose artistry operates within a narrow range. One of these is L. P. Hartley (1895–1972). His trilogy about Eustace and Hilda does not have the limitless splendours of Cary's abundance, but it is a sensitively controlled study of a brother-sister relationship (*The Shrimp and the Anemone*, 1944, *The Sixth Heaven*, 1946, and *Eustace and Hilda*, 1947). The overpowering emotional link with his sister is something Eustace, the younger, cannot snap: the attempt brings tragedy. The range of Ivy Compton-Burnett (1892–1969) can be precisely defined. Her characters are members of upper-class families who speak a stereotyped 'Victorianese' that smacks of drawing rooms where good manners prevail. The tone of the mannered sentences is in ironic contrast to what they gradually reveal – tales of bitter internecine conflict between kindred, or between masters and servants. There is tyranny and murder, malice and blackmail, cruelty and hypocrisy in what emerges from under the verbally unruffled surface. No horror is spared. A devastatingly vitriolic view of family groupings is conveyed with witty graciousness of utterance. *Brothers and Sisters* (1929), *Elders and Betters* (1944) and *Mother and Son* (1955) are of this genre.

Of the English novelists born since 1900 perhaps Graham Greene (1904–) is the most considerable. His conversion to Roman Catholicism in 1927 has determined the character of his best work. In *Brighton Rock* (1938) he makes a study of a teenage delinquent who runs a gang and commits murder, but Pinkie has been brought up as a Catholic and is aware of sin. Greene is especially powerful in distinguishing between the Catholic ethic, which is rooted in the idea of grace and of dependence on the sacraments, and humanistic notions of virtue which lack spiritual dimension and supernatural orientation. When ill-handled, this distinction leads to the dangerous trick of surrounding wicked Catholics with an aura of superiority to good, unselfish unbelievers – a superiority that seems to have been purchased on the cheap in the religious market. But the clear identification of salvation as open to the sinful man who clings to his faith and at least tries to repent leads to fine and moving pictures like that of the 'whisky priest' persecuted in Mexico in *The Power and the Glory* (1940). Perhaps Greene's fullest sketch of a Catholic sinner whose sin is so tied up with humility, penitence and self-sacrifice that it begins to smack of godliness is that of Scobie in *The Heart of the Matter* (1948). He is a District Commissioner of Police in West Africa, desperate over non-promotion. His compassion and sensitivity lead him to adultery: his desire not to injure his mistress or his wife lead him knowingly to take communion unabsolved: then he kills himself. The implication is that he is more virtuous than the virtuous, and holier than the holy: and it is well done. Yet Greene leaves one sometimes feeling sorry for the people in his books who manage, not without cost, to be more conventionally decent and get no authorial thanks for it. Greene's style does not draw attention to itself: there is no waste of words. He lays bare the anguish and weakness of human beings on the edge of despair; but he restores to human experience the status of the contingent. The heart breaks under the eye of God, and it is not just happiness, but salvation, that is at issue.

Evelyn Waugh (1903–66), like Greene, was a Roman Catholic convert. He made his name as a satirical novelist, scathing in his representation of upper-class types, but spicing the mixture with cartoonery and farce. The picture of life in a bad private school in *Decline and Fall* (1928) is riotously funny; though ironies are cheerfully pushed beyond the bounds of plausibility. Waugh's later work is more serious. The distrust of modern values grows, and it is not unmixed with contempt. The Catholic leaning is linked with nostalgia for aristocratic culture in *Brideshead Revisited* (1945). An upper-class Catholic family chronicle is unfolded retrospectively when Captain Ryder is posted on wartime duty to the former family home of his friends, the Marchmains. The sense of institutional Catholicism is strong in Waugh, and a code of updated militaristic chivalry is aired sometimes at the expense of the benighted products of modern egalitarianism. Waugh's service in the army in the Second World War was the basis of his war trilogy, *Men at Arms* (1952), *Officers and Gentlemen* (1955) and *Unconditional Surrender* (1961).

The social system is under judgement from a very different angle in the work of George Orwell (pseudonym of Eric Blair, 1903–50). A scholarship boy at Eton, Orwell became excessively conscious of his disadvantages, physical and financial. Police experience in Burma added to his class sensitivity, and the backlash took him into voluntary participation in poverty at and below the working-class level. From such self-immersion among the social dregs emerged books like *Down and Out in Paris and London* (1933) and *The Road to Wigan Pier* (1937). Orwell's most important books came late in his short life. Disillusioned with Communism (after fighting in Spain), he wrote *Animal Farm* (1945), a satirical fable on revolution that has turned totalitarian. The animals oust tyrant Jones and take over the farm themselves, but the pigs get on top, convinced of their own superiority. It is for the good of the community as a whole that, being the brains of the state, they should be well served by the others. The revolutionary slogan, 'All Animals are Equal', is amended to suit the new situation: 'But Some Animals are More Equal than Others'. *1984* (1949) looks prophetically into the future and foresees the triumph of totalitarianism so complete that individual thought is eradicated. A Ministry of Truth feeds the nation with lies and propaganda in the name of education, culture and news. A Ministry of Love operates the insidious Thought Police, while the Ministry of Plenty cuts the rations down and the Ministry of Peace runs the permanent war. An instrument of repression is 'New-speak', the approved language from which concepts dangerous to the prevailing non-thought are eliminated. The reader follows gloomily the crushing of a rebel, Winston Smith, who deviates into the pursuit of privacy and love. Monochrome relentlessness gives the book a certain sourness.

Among other writers born into the first decade of the century T. H. White (1906–64) gave a rendering of the Arthurian cycle in the tetralogy, *The Once and Future King* (1958). The version is at once in key with Arthurian mores and updated in psychological treatment. It began in 1938 with *The Sword in the Stone*, dealing with Arthur's boyhood and the entry on his calling. The third book in the series, *The Ill-Made Knight* (1941), is a convincing and moving reconstruction of the Lancelot and Guinevere story. White's *The Goshawk* (1951) describes how he tried to train a hawk according to the ancient practice of falconry. Henry Green (pseudonym of Henry Vincent Yorke, 1905–73) has established a reputation as a conscious stylist, sensitive in recording the minutiae of experience, aware of the comic, and versatile in experiment. *Blindness* (1926) is written from the point of view of John Hayes, blinded as a boy by a stone thrown through a railway carriage window. In *Party Going* (1939) a group of people are fog-bound at a railway station, and their frustrations mirror the larger human predicament. We are immersed in class conflict at a factory in *Living* (1929): we are at an Irish castle in wartime in *Loving* (1945), and much preoccupied with the world of Raunce, the self-important butler. Green manages to be objective in the representation of such unattractive characters and yet to keep them very real. Stella Gibbons (1902–) scored a popular success in 1932 with *Cold Comfort Farm*, a hilarious skit on the over-solemn treatment of rural life in fiction. Nancy Mitford (1904–73) made her name with *The Pursuit of Love* (1945) and *Love in a Cold Climate* (1949). Upper-class personalities converse freely on her lively pages: she has a sharp ear and a keen wit. It was a volume of essays of which Miss Mitford was joint editor (*Noblesse Oblige: An Enquiry into the Identifiable Characteristics of the English Aristocracy*, 1956) that launched the terms 'U' (Upper class) and 'Non U' on their career. As labels for distinguishing (not too seriously) smart from vulgar ways of speaking and behaving, they have been a source of entertainment since. Miss Mitford's excursions into historical biography (*Madame de Pompadour*, 1954, and *The Sun King*, 1966) give intimate pictures of life at the courts of Louis XIV and Louis XV.

Anthony Powell (1905–), a low-key recorder of our decaying twentieth-century civilization, has undertaken a complex connected series called *The Music of Time*. It began with *A Question of Upbringing* (1951) and includes *The Acceptance World* (1955) and *Casanova's Chinese Restaurant* (1960). There is much futility, much drinking, much marrying, remarrying and not marrying in this vast symphonically structured panorama of middle-class existence in a world lurching vainly on. The extended scope of the work, the patterning of the characters' entries and exits, and the overall melancholy at the flight of time have together invited comparison with Proust. The work is matched, at least in magnitude, by Snow's necropolitan annals of the grey men of power, *Strangers and Brothers*. C. P. Snow (1905–) has been varsity scientist and civil servant and knows all about what goes on behind Cambridge senior common room doors and within Whitehall corridors. His revelations may not stir the appetite for either academic or administrative status, but it is a privilege to have a knowledgeable, firsthand account of life away at the top. The chronicle (the title of the first book is *Strangers and Brothers*, 1940) centres on the life of Lewis Eliot; a lawyer. Ethical questions are portentously at issue as hands reach out to grab at office or at the levers of power.

Perhaps the most accomplished recent achievement in the way of grouped novels is *The Alexandria Quartet* by Lawrence Durrell (1912–). Durrell is a poet and the luxuriance of his prose style is well suited to the task of immersing the reader in the soporific atmosphere of the Near East. Landscapes tend to be overwritten, but the sensuous verbal denseness does justice to the physical feel of the Alexandrian world as well as to the pervasive air of the mysterious and the sinister. The tetralogy is not a chronological sequence, but explores the interplay of relationships between the main characters from different viewpoints in turn. We see the strangely compelling Justine through the infatuated eyes of Darley (a writer) in *Justine* (1957), but her character and behaviour emerge in a totally different light in *Balthazar* (1958). *Mountolive* (1958) and *Clea* (1960) complete the work. The theme of political espionage and gunrunning is entangled with that of rivalries and duplicities in love. Inevitably again comparisons have been made with Proust; but, though the *Quartet* is a highly accomplished work, reflection does not run deep. The tetralogy effects no profound awakening or transformation of response to life.

Oddly enough a novelist definitely, if negatively, influenced by Proust is Samuel Beckett, whose critical study, *Proust* (1931), provides insight into his own convictions as a writer and indicates his literary affiliations. Beckett seems to have realized that what Proust and Joyce had done was not imitable but must be a stimulus to the exploration of new ground. *Murphy* (1938) is at once a burlesque on an exhausted fictional technique and an attempt to revivify the novel from 'non-literary' verbal sources. The description of Celia by catalogue makes a mockery of millions of stereotyped introductory descriptions of heroines: the detailed measurements are like a dressmaker's notes. Miss Counihan is parodically presented:

> Standing in profile against the blazing corridor, with
> her high buttocks and her low breasts, she looked not
> merely queenly, but on for anything.

The plot is a send-up of the Hardyesque pattern of crossed
amorous relationships. Neary loves Miss Dwyer, who loves
Elliman, who loves Miss Farren, who loves Father Fitt, who
loves Mrs West, who loves Neary, and so on. There is Irish
fun at the expense of everything in sight or in print. Yet the
loosening of Murphy's tenuous hold on sanity and life is
movingly registered, and the prostitute, Celia, preserves a
touching dignity in her love and in her bereavement. On
the basis of burlesque and of an all-inclusive range of verbal
manipulation (technical, poetic, conversational, philosophical, idiotic, obsessional, inarticulate, etc.) Beckett later explores the minds and feelings of characters in states of impotence, frustration and imbecility so gross that their emergence as full-length, inwardly sensed personalities in fiction is
disturbing. Such characters are not figures on the objective
periphery but central to the action – or inaction. (See *Malone
Dies*, 1956, *Molloy* and *The Unnameable*, 1958.) Increasingly
Beckett makes use of serial irony. In *Watt* ironical postures
or devices are used tellingly, then ironically overstretched
so that irony is undercut by a new layer of irony, and there
is no resting place for conviction or steady response. But
the humour is irresistible. What arises, with devastating im-
becile logic, out of the need to feed Mr Knott and regularly
get rid of the remains in his bowl, is one of the funniest
things in our literature.

As Beckett has written on Proust, so Angus Wilson
(1913–) has written on Zola (*Emile Zola: An Introductory
Study*, 1952), a master of naturalistic documentation and
close psychological analysis. Wilson has the gift for minute
investigation of inner questioning and unrest on the part
of men and women at grips with personal inadequacies and
broken hopes, with confused relationships and with such
problems as homosexuality (a successful novelist, Bernard

Sands in *Hemlock and After*, 1952, and an aged historian, Gerald Middleton, in *Anglo-Saxon Attitudes*, 1956). The *Old Men at the Zoo* (1961) is something of a satirical fable, the issue being the care of the animals at the London Zoo in an atomic war.

William Golding (1911–) established his individual genre in *Lord of the Flies* (1954), in which a group of boys, stranded on a desert island after an air crash, regress to savagery. In reversing the pattern of children's adventure stories and locating evil in the boys themselves, Golding re-energized the notion of original sin. Facile fashionable doctrines of progress and evolution are up-ended in *The Inheritors* (1955) where we see a crucial stage in the rise of our species through the eyes of Neanderthal man (and hear a good deal of his primitive utterance too). Golding makes no concessions to the novelist's natural desire to work to a promising brief. In *Pincher Martin* (1956) a shipwrecked sailor imagines that he is clinging to a bare rock desperate to survive. His past is recalled; but at the end we learn that he died in the wreck and that the whole recollection has taken place at the point of drowning. *Free Fall* (1959) is the study of Sammy Mountjoy, a successful artist, how he loses his soul and is brought up against the consequences when the girl he has seduced goes insane. Golding's later use of symbolism (that of the cathedral spire in *The Spire*, 1964) is not unlike Iris Murdoch's in *The Bell* (1958). If Golding's spire gives expression to the dean's labours, Miss Murdoch's bell expresses the ideals of the new lay community at a convent, which is the object of the author's interest. But the comparison stops there. Golding is an experimenting artist at grips with obdurate material; Iris Murdoch (1919–), for all her versatility elsewhere, is here uneasily half-funny about other people's seriousness. An air of faint contrivance lingers alike about her symbolism, her assemblages of freaks, perverts, sexualists and deluded idealists, and about her knowing psychological categorizations.

The symbolic vein in Muriel Spark (1918-) is subtler

and her implicit sense of the human situation more earnest. Dimensions of awareness are lightly opened up in her books through evanescent glimpses of a beyond. Each novel satisfying makes its point. *Memento Mori* (1959) explores the reactions of the elderly to mysterious telephone calls reminding of death. The Devil turns up at a London factory in the shape of a lively Scotsman in *The Ballad of Peckham Rye* (1960), and the consequences give ample scope for Miss Spark's vibrant inventiveness. *The Bachelors* (1960) is a quieter study of what the title suggests: the intrusion of the unknown Other is in this case represented by spiritualism.

One perhaps ought not to leave the twentieth-century novel without referring to the literary phenomenon which journalists conceptualized for a mass public with the phrase 'Angry Young Men'. That post-war socialism gave university education to young men from the working classes and then left them cut off from élitist circles, social and cultural, no doubt helps to explain the rise of the anti-hero, venomously, comically or patronizingly dismissive of establishment mores and inhibitions. William Cooper (1910–) has been credited with ushering in the anti-hero of the fifties with Joe Lunn in *Scenes from Provincial Life* (1950), but it was *Lucky Jim* (1954) by Kingsley Amis (1922–) that provided the journalists with a protest hero to partner Osborne's Jimmy Porter. In fact, of course, Amis is essentially a comic writer and Jim Dixon, the young university lecturer, is up against a target as much represented by pretentiousness and phoney dilettantism as by anything likely to get under the skin of an ardent social egalitarian. Amis, developing his comic talent in later novels, has taken up the handy sex recipes. Science fiction, another of his interests, is surveyed in *New Maps of Hell* (1960). A more standard specimen of *iuvenis iratus* is Joe Lampton, a West Riding hero with his eyes on the money, in *Room at the Top* (1957) by John Braine (1922–). Arthur Seaton, in *Saturday Night and Sunday Morning* (1958) by Alan Sillitoe (1928–), is a Midlands factory hand who lacks a meaningful place in society and whose physically dirty working hours are balanced by morally seedy weekends. But a more thought-out study in the search for social adjustment is provided by John Wain (1925–) in *Hurry on Down* (1953). Charles Lumley, a young university graduate, faces difficulties supposedly due to the fact that (in Wain's words) 'there is an unhealed split between the educational system and the assumptions that actually underlie life'. The fifties and their foibles, however, have now receded, and one may question whether the fashionable trends of that decade ought to carry much weight in a summary covering a field as wide as that of English literature from Chaucer's day to our own.

Chronological table of writers (by date of birth)

born		died	born		died
1295	Richard Rolle	1349	1488	Miles Coverdale	1568
?1316	John Barbour	1395	1489	Thomas Cranmer	1556
c.1330	John Gower	1408	c.1490	Sir Thomas Elyot	1546
c.1332	William Langland	c.1400	?1494	William Tyndale	1536
c.1340	Geoffrey Chaucer	1400	?1497	John Heywood	?1580
1342	Julian of Norwich	1416	1503	Sir Thomas Wyatt	1542
?1370	John Hoccleve	?1450	1505	Nicholas Udall	1556
	John Lydgate	1452	1515	Roger Ascham	?1568
1394	King James I	1437	1517	Henry Howard, Earl of Surrey	1547
c.1408	Sir Thomas Malory	1471			
c.1430	Robert Henryson	1506	c.1520	Raphael Holinshed	c.1580
c.1460	John Skelton	1529	?1525	John Stow	1605
	William Dunbar	c.1530	c.1530	George Gascoigne	1577
1475	Gavin Douglas	1522	1532	Thomas Norton	1584
1478	Sir Thomas More	1535	1534	William Harrison	1593

born	died	born	died
?1535	Thomas North ?1601	1592	Francis Quarles 1644
1536	Thomas Sackville 1608	1593	George Herbert 1633
1537	Thomas Preston 1598		Izaak Walton 1683
c.1543	Thomas Deloney 1600	?1594	Thomas Carew 1640
?1552	Edmund Spenser 1599	1596	James Shirley 1666
c.1552	Sir Walter Ralegh 1618	c.1600	John Earle 1665
1553	Richard Hakluyt 1616	1605	Sir Thomas Browne 1682
c.1554	Richard Hooker 1600	1606	Sir William D'Avenant 1668
	John Lyly 1606		Edmund Waller 1687
1554	Sir Philip Sidney 1586	1608	Thomas Fuller 1661
1555	Lancelot Andrewes 1626		John Milton 1674
1556	George Peele ?1597	1609	Edward Hyde, Earl of Clarendon 1674
1558	Thomas Kyd 1594		Sir John Suckling 1642
	Thomas Lodge 1625	1612	Samuel Butler 1680
c.1560	George Chapman ?1634		Richard Crashaw 1649
	Robert Greene 1592	1613	John Cleveland 1658
1561	Francis Bacon 1626		Jeremy Taylor 1667
	Robert Southwell 1595	1615	Sir John Denham 1669
1562	Samuel Daniel 1619	1618	Abraham Cowley 1667
1563	Michael Drayton 1631		Richard Lovelace c.1657
1564	Christopher Marlowe 1593	1620	John Evelyn 1706
	William Shakespeare 1616	1621	Andrew Marvell 1678
1567	Thomas Nashe 1601	?1622	Henry Vaughan 1695
c.1569	Barnabe Barnes 1609	1626	John Aubrey 1697
1569	Sir John Davies 1626	1628	George Villiers, Duke of Buckingham 1687
?1570	Thomas Dekker 1632		John Bunyan 1688
1572	John Donne 1631	1631	John Dryden 1700
	Ben Jonson 1637	1632	John Locke 1704
1574	Joseph Hall 1656	1633	Samuel Pepys 1703
c.1574	Thomas Heywood 1641	?1635	Sir George Etherege 1691
c.1575	Cyril Tourneur 1626	1637	Thomas Traherne 1674
1576	John Marston 1634	1638	Charles Sackville, Earl of Dorset 1706
1579	John Fletcher 1625	?1639	Sir Charles Sedley 1701
1580	Thomas Middleton 1627	1640	Aphra Behn 1689
c.1580	John Webster ?1625		William Wycherley 1716
1581	Sir Thomas Overbury 1613	1643	Gilbert Burnet 1715
1582	Phineas Fletcher 1650	1647	John Wilmot, Earl of Rochester 1680
1583	Philip Massinger 1640	c.1649	Nathaniel Lee 1692
	Lord Herbert of Cherbury 1648	1650	Jeremy Collier 1726
1584	Francis Beaumont 1616	1652	Thomas Otway 1685
1585	William Drummond 1649	1660	Daniel Defoe 1731
	Giles Fletcher 1623		Thomas Southerne 1746
c.1586	John Ford 1640	1661	Anne Countess of Winchilsea 1720
1588	Thomas Hobbes 1679	1664	Matthew Prior 1721
	George Wither 1667		Sir John Vanbrugh 1726
1591	Robert Herrick 1674		
	William Browne 1643		

born	died	born	died
1667	Susannah Centlivre 1723	1729	Edmund Burke 1797
	Jonathan Swift 1745		Bishop Thomas Percy 1811
1670	William Congreve 1729		
1671	Colley Cibber 1757		Clara Reeve 1807
1672	Joseph Addison 1719	1730	Oliver Goldsmith 1774
	Sir Richard Steele 1729	1731	Charles Churchill 1764
1674	Nicholas Rowe 1718		William Cowper 1800
?1675	Ambrose Philips 1749	1732	Richard Cumberland 1811
1676	John Philips 1709		
1678	George Farquhar 1707		William Falconer 1769
1679	Thomas Parnell 1718	1736	James Macpherson 1796
1683	Edward Young 1765	1737	Edward Gibbon 1794
1685	George Berkeley 1753	1739	Hugh Kelly 1777
	John Gay 1732	1740	James Boswell 1795
1686	Allan Ramsay 1758	1745	Thomas Holcroft 1809
	William Law 1761		Henry Mackenzie 1831
?1687	Henry Carey 1743	1750	Robert Fergusson 1774
1688	Alexander Pope 1744	1751	Richard Brinsley Sheridan 1816
1689	Samuel Richardson 1761		
	Lady Mary Wortley Montagu 1762	1752	Frances Burney 1840
			Thomas Chatterton 1770
1692	Joseph Butler 1752	1754	George Crabbe 1832
1693	George Lillo 1739	1756	William Godwin 1836
1694	Lord Chesterfield 1773	1757	William Blake 1827
c.1696	Richard Savage 1743	1759	William Beckford 1844
1697	Robert Paltock 1767		Robert Burns 1796
1700	John Dyer 1758		Mary Wollstonecraft 1797
	James Thomson 1748	1762	Joanna Baillie 1851
1705	David Mallet 1765		William Lisle Bowles 1850
1707	Henry Fielding 1754		
1709	John Armstrong 1779	1763	Samuel Rogers 1855
	Samuel Johnson 1784	1764	Ann Radcliffe 1823
1711	David Hume 1776	1767	Maria Edgeworth 1849
1712	Edward Moore 1757	1769	Amelia Opie 1853
1713	Laurence Sterne 1768	1770	James Hogg 1835
1714	Lord Monboddo 1799		William Wordsworth 1850
	William Shenstone 1763		
1716	Thomas Gray 1771	1771	Sir Walter Scott 1832
1717	David Garrick 1779		Dorothy Wordsworth 1855
	Horace Walpole 1797		
?1719	Charles Johnstone ?1800	1772	Samuel Taylor Coleridge 1834
1720	Gilbert White 1793		
1721	Mark Akenside 1770	1774	Robert Southey 1843
	William Collins 1759	1775	Jane Austen 1817
	James Grainger 1766		Charles Lamb 1834
	Tobias Smollett 1771		Walter Savage Landor 1864
1722	John Home 1808		
	Christopher Smart 1771		Matthew Gregory Lewis 1818
	Joseph Warton 1800		
1728	Robert Bage 1801	1777	Thomas Campbell 1844
	Thomas Warton 1790	1778	William Hazlitt 1830

born	died	born	died
1779	Thomas Moore 1852	1819	John Ruskin 1900
1782	Charles Maturin 1824	1820	Anne Brontë 1849
1784	Leigh Hunt 1859	1822	Matthew Arnold 1888
1785	Thomas De Quincey 1859	1823	Coventry Patmore 1896
	Thomas Love Peacock 1866		Charlotte M. Yonge 1901
1788	George Gordon, Lord Byron 1824	1824	Wilkie Collins 1889
			George MacDonald 1905
1792	Thomas Jefferson Hogg 1862	1825	R. D. Blackmore 1900
	John Keble 1866	1828	George Meredith 1909
	Frederick Marryat 1848		Dante Gabriel Rossetti 1882
	Percy Bysshe Shelley 1822	1830	Christina Rossetti 1894
	Edward John Trelawny 1881	1832	Lewis Carroll 1898
1793	John Clare 1864	1834	William Morris 1896
	Felicia Hemans 1835		James Thomson 1882
1794	John Gibson Lockhart 1854	1835	Samuel Butler 1902
1795	John Keats 1821	1837	Algernon Charles Swinburne 1909
1797	Mary Shelley 1851	1839	Walter Pater 1894
1799	Thomas Hood 1845	1840	Austin Dobson 1921
1800	Thomas Babington Macaulay 1859		Thomas Hardy 1928
1801	William Barnes 1886		John Addington Symonds 1893
1803	George Borrow 1881	1843	Henry James 1916
	Bulwer Lytton 1873	1844	Robert Bridges 1930
1804	Benjamin Disraeli 1881		Gerard Manley Hopkins 1889
1806	Elizabeth Barrett Browning 1861		Andrew Lang 1912
1809	Edward Fitzgerald 1883	1847	Alice Meynell 1922
	Alexander William Kinglake 1891	1850	Robert Louis Stevenson 1894
	Alfred Lord Tennyson 1892	1851	Henry Arthur Jones 1929
1810	Elizabeth Gaskell 1865	1852	Lady Gregory 1932
1811	William Makepeace Thackeray 1863		George Moore 1933
1812	Robert Browning 1889	1854	Oscar Wilde 1900
	Charles Dickens 1870	1855	Sir Arthur Wing Pinero 1934
	John Forster 1876	1856	Rider Haggard 1925
1814	Charles Reade 1884		George Bernard Shaw 1950
1815	Anthony Trollope 1882	1857	Joseph Conrad 1924
1816	Charlotte Brontë 1855		George Gissing 1903
1818	Emily Brontë 1848	1859	Sir Arthur Conan Doyle 1930
1819	Arthur Hugh Clough 1861		A. E. Housman 1936
	George Eliot 1880		Francis Thompson 1907
	Charles Kingsley 1875	1860	J. M. Barrie 1937
			Frederick Rolfe 1913
		1862	Sir Henry Newbolt 1938
		1865	Rudyard Kipling 1936
			W. B. Yeats 1939

born	died
1866	Beatrix Potter 1943
	H. G. Wells 1946
1867	Arnold Bennett 1931
	Ernest Dowson 1900
	John Galsworthy 1933
	Lionel Johnson 1902
	A. E. (George Russell) 1935
1869	Laurence Binyon 1943
1870	Hilaire Belloc 1953
1871	W. H. Davies 1940
	Ralph Hodgson 1962
	J. M. Synge 1909
1872	Max Beerbohm 1956
	John Cowper Powys 1963
1873	Walter De la Mare 1956
	Ford Madox Ford 1939
1874	G. K. Chesterton 1936
	Somerset Maugham 1965
1875	John Buchan 1940
	T. F. Powys 1953
1877	Harley Granville Barker 1946
1878	Wilfred Gibson 1962
	John Masefield 1967
	Edward Thomas 1917
1879	E. M. Forster 1970
1880	Sean O'Casey 1964
	Lytton Strachey 1932
1881	Lascelles Abercrombie 1938
	Rose Macaulay 1958
	P. G. Wodehouse
1882	John Drinkwater 1937
	James Joyce 1941
	A. A. Milne 1956
	Virginia Woolf 1941
1883	Compton Mackenzie 1972
1884	James Elroy Flecker 1915
	Wyndham Lewis 1957
	Llewelyn Powys 1939
	Arthur Ransome 1967
	Hugh Walpole 1941
1885	D. H. Lawrence 1930
	Ezra Pound 1972
	Andrew Young 1973
1886	Siegfried Sassoon 1967

born	died
1886	Charles Williams 1945
1887	Rupert Brooke 1915
	Edwin Muir 1959
	Edith Sitwell 1964
1888	James Bridie 1951
	Joyce Cary 1957
	T. S. Eliot 1965
	Julian Grenfell 1915
	T. E. Lawrence 1935
1889	Helen Waddell 1965
1890	Isaac Rosenberg 1918
1891	Agatha Christie
1892	Richard Aldington 1962
	Ivy Compton-Burnett 1969
	David Garnett
	Hugh MacDiarmid
	J. R. R. Tolkien 1973
1893	Wilfred Owen 1918
	Dorothy Sayers 1957
1894	Aldous Huxley 1963
	Charles Morgan 1958
	J. B. Priestley
1895	Robert Graves
	L. P. Hartley 1972
	David Jones
1896	Edmund Blunden 1974
	Margaret Kennedy 1967
1897	'Gordon Daviot' 1952
	Storm Jameson
	Naomi Mitchison 1974
1898	C. S. Lewis 1963
1899	Elizabeth Bowen 1973
	Noël Coward 1973
	Eric Linklater
1901	Roy Campbell 1957
1902	Stella Gibbons
1903	Walter Greenwood
	Rosamond Lehmann
	George Orwell 1950
	William Plomer 1973
	Evelyn Waugh 1966
1904	Graham Greene
	Nancy Mitford 1973
	C. Day Lewis 1972
1905	Henry Green 1973
	Anthony Powell
	C. P. Snow
1906	Samuel Beckett
	John Betjeman

born		died	born		died
1906	William Empson		1916	David Gascoyne	
	T. H. White	1964	1918	Muriel Spark	
1907	W. H. Auden	1973	1919	Iris Murdoch	
	Christopher Fry		1920	D. J. Enright	
	Louis MacNeice	1963	1922	Kingsley Amis	
1909	James Reeves			John Braine	
	Stephen Spender			Philip Larkin	
1910	William Cooper		1923	Brendan Behan	1964
1911	William Golding			James Kirkup	
	Mervyn Peake	1968	1925	John Wain	
1912	Lawrence Durrell		1926	Elizabeth Jennings	
	Anne Ridler		1928	Alan Sillitoe	
1913	George Barker		1929	Thom Gunn	
	R. S. Thomas			John Osborne	
	Angus Wilson		1930	Ted Hughes	
1914	Norman Nicholson			Harold Pinter	
	Dylan Thomas	1953		John Arden	
			1932	Arnold Wesker	

Bibliography

The book-lists below should be used in conjunction with the index for, where important works are known to be currently available in standard popular editions, they will not necessarily appear in the bibliography, but an appropriate symbol, directing the reader to one such edition, will be found against the titles of these books in the index. This applies especially to many of the plays referred to in chapters 4, 5, 10 and 20, and to many of the novels and prose works referred to in chapters 8, 11, 14, 17, 19 and 22. Readers should therefore consult the index, where the following abbreviations are used against appropriate titles:

Ar   The Arden Shakespeare, Methuen
CC   Collins Classics

EL	Everyman's Library, Dent
ELP	Everyman's Library Paperback, Dent
FP	Faber Paperback
Hd	Hodder
MMP	Methuen's Modern Plays
NM	The New Mermaids, Ernest Benn
OP	Oxford Paperbacks, OUP
Pg	Penguin Paperback
Pm	Papermac Series, Macmillan
Rg	Regents Renaissance Drama Series & Regents Restoration Drama Series, Edward Arnold
Rv	The Revels Plays, Methuen
WC	The World's Classics, OUP

Throughout the bibliography itself the symbol 'Pb' indicates 'Paperback'.

CHAPTER I   THE FOURTEENTH CENTURY

GEOFFREY CHAUCER, *Complete Works*, ed. W. W. Skeat (with glossarial indexes), Oxford Standard Authors, OUP

GEOFFREY CHAUCER, *The Canterbury Tales* (with a glossary), The World's Classics, OUP

JOHN GOWER, *Selections*, ed. J. A. W. Bennet, Clarendon Medieval and Tudor Series, OUP (Pb)

WILLIAM LANGLAND, *Piers Plowman*, The Prologue and Passus I–VII, ed. J. A. W. Bennett, OUP (Pb)

Pearl and *Sir Gawain and the Green Knight*, ed. A. C. Cawley, Everyman's Library, Dent

Revelations of Divine Love (Julian of Norwich), *The Fire of Love* (Richard Rolle), *The Cloud of Unknowing*, each translated by C. Walters, Penguin

Everyman and Medieval Miracle Plays, ed. A. C. Cawley, Everyman's Library, Dent

G. G. COULTON, *Chaucer and His England*, University Paperbacks, Methuen

S. S. HUSSEY, *Chaucer: An Introduction*, University Paperbacks, Methuen

W. P. KER, *Medieval English Literature*, Oxford Paperbacks University Series, OUP

c. s. lewis, *The Allegory of Love*, Galaxy Books (OUP New York) (Pb)

CHAPTER 2 FIFTEENTH-CENTURY POETRY AND PROSE

The Middle Scots Poets, ed. A. M. Kinghorn, York Medieval Texts, Edward Arnold (Pb)

The Poems of William Dunbar, ed. W. M. Mackenzie, Faber (Pb)

john skelton, *Poems*, ed. R. Kinsman, Clarendon Medieval and Tudor Series, OUP (Pb)

English and Scottish Ballads, ed. Robert Graves, The Poetry Bookshelf, Heinemann (Pb)

Medieval English Lyrics, ed. R. T. Davies, Faber (Pb)

sir thomas malory, *Le Morte d'Arthur*, Everyman's Library, 2 vols, Dent

geoffrey of monmouth, *Histories of the Kings of Britain*, trans. S. Evans, Everyman's Library, Dent

e. k. chambers, *English Literature at the Close of the Middle Ages* (Oxford History of English Literature), OUP

CHAPTER 3 THE EARLEY SIXTEENTH CENTURY

sir thomas more, *Utopia* and *Dialogue of Comfort Against Tribulation*, Everyman's Library, Dent

r. w. chambers, *Thomas More*, Penguin

sir thomas elyot, *The Governor*, Everyman's Library, Dent

Silver Poets of the Sixteenth Century, ed. G. Bullett, Everyman's Library, Dent (includes Wyatt, Surrey, Ralegh, Sir John Davies) (Pb)

sir thomas wyatt, *The Collected Poems*, ed. K. Muir, Muses' Library, Routledge and Kegan Paul (Pb)

Gorboduc and *Ralph Roister Doister* are included in *Minor Elizabethan Drama*, see page 483

c. s. lewis, *English Literature in the Sixteenth Century*, Oxford Paperbacks, OUP

maurice evans, *English Poetry in the Sixteenth Century*, University Library, Hutchinson (Pb)

CHAPTER 4 ELIZABETHAN DRAMA

WILLIAM SHAKESPEARE, *Complete Works* (with a glossary), ed. W. J. Craig, Oxford Standard Authors, OUP

CHRISTOPHER MARLOWE, *Plays*, ed. R. Gill, Oxford Paperbacks, OUP

Minor Elizabethan Drama, 2 vols, Everyman's Library, Dent (includes *Gorboduc, Ralph Roister Doister, Arden of Feversham*, and plays by Kyd, Lyly, Peele and Greene)

Holinshed's Chronicle as used in Shakespeare's Plays, ed. A. and J. Nicoll, Everyman's Library, Dent

Shakespeare's Plutarch, ed. T. J. B. Spencer, Penguin

E. M. W. TILLYARD, *The Elizabethan World Picture*, Pelican

IRVING RIBNER, *Patterns in Shakespearean Tragedy*, University Paperbacks, Methuen

CAROLINE SPURGEON, *Shakespeare's Imagery and what it tells us*, Cambridge University Press (Pb)

SIR EDMUND CHAMBERS, *A Short Life of Shakespeare* (abridged by Charles Williams), OUP

Dr Johnson on Shakespeare, ed. W. K. Wimsatt, Penguin

WILLIAM HAZLITT, *Characters of Shakespeare's Plays*, The World's Classics, OUP

For editions of individual plays see titles in the index.

CHAPTER 5 JACOBEAN DRAMA

Jacobean Tragedies, ed. A. H. Gomme (Marston, Tourneur and Middleton are represented), Oxford Paperbacks, OUP

Five Stuart Tragedies, ed. A. K. McIlwraith (Chapman, Beaumont and Fletcher, Webster and Ford are represented), Oxford Paperbacks, OUP

BEN JONSON, *Five Plays*, The World's Classics, OUP

FRANCIS BEAUMONT and JOHN FLETCHER, *Select Plays*, ed. M. C. Bradbrook, Everyman's Library, Dent

JOHN FORD, *Five Plays*, ed. Havelock Ellis, MacGibbon and Kee (Pb)

JOHN WEBSTER, *Three Plays*, Penguin

JAMES SHIRLEY, *The lady of pleasure* 1637 (facsimile reprint), Scolar Press (Pb)

J. B. BAMBOROUGH, *Ben Jonson*, University Library, Hutchinson

UNA ELLIS-FERMOR, *The Jacobean Drama*, University Paperbacks, Methuen

T. S. ELIOT, *Elizabethan Essays*, Faber

For editions of individual plays see titles in the index.

CHAPTER 6   ELIZABETHAN POETRY

SIR PHILIP SIDNEY, *Poetry and Prose*, Signet Poetry, New English Library (Pb)

EDMUND SPENSER, *Poetical Works*, ed. J. C. Smith and E. de Selincourt, Oxford Paperbacks, OUP

EDMUND SPENSER, *The Faerie Queene: Book I* and *Book II* (separate volumes), ed. P. C. Bayley, OUP (Pb)

WILLIAM SHAKESPEARE, *The Poems*, ed. F. T. Prince, The Arden Shakespeare, Methuen (Pb)

The Penguin Book of Elizabethan Verse, ed. E. Lucie-Smith

Longer Elizabethan Poems, ed. M. Seymour Smith, The Poetry Bookshelf, Heinemann (Pb)

SAMUEL DANIEL, *Delia* 1592 (facsimile reprint), Scolar Press (Pb)

PETER BAYLEY, *Edmund Spenser, Prince of Poets*, University Library, Hutchinson (Pb)

F. INGLIS, *The Elizabethan Poets*, Literature in Perspective Series, Evans (Pb)

CHAPTER 7   METAPHYSICAL AND CAVALIER POETRY

JOHN DONNE, *Poetical Works*, ed. Sir Herbert Grierson, Oxford Paperbacks, OUP

GEORGE HERBERT, *Poems*, intro. H. Gardner, The World's Classics, OUP

Jonson and the Cavaliers, ed. M. Hussey, The Poetry Bookshelf, Heinemann (Pb)

English Poetry 1550–1660, ed. F. Inglis, University Paperbacks, Methuen

The Poems of Andrew Marvell, ed. H. Macdonald, Muses' Library, Routledge and Kegan Paul (Pb)

RICHARD CRASHAW, *Selected Works*, ed. M. Cayley, Fyfield Books, Carcanet Press (Pb)

ROBERT HERRICK, *Selected Poems*, ed. J. Hayward, Penguin

HENRY VAUGHAN, *Silex scintillans* (facsimile reprint), Scolar Press (Pb)

EDMUND WALLER, *Poems &c* 1645 (facsimile reprint), Scolar Press (Pb)

IZAAK WALTON, *Lives of Donne, Wotton, Hooker, Herbert and Sanderson*, ed. G. Saintsbury, The World's Classics, OUP

D. BUSH, *English Literature in the Early Seventeenth Century* (Oxford History of English Literature), Oxford Paperbacks, OUP

BASIL WILLEY, *The Seventeenth-Century Background*, Penguin

CHAPTER 8   ELIZABETHAN AND SEVENTEENTH-CENTURY PROSE

Green's groatsworth of witte 1592, Dekker's *The guls horne-booke* 1609 and Nashe's *Pierce Penilesse* 1592 are separately available in facsimile reprints (paperbacks) from the Scolar Press

FRANCIS BACON, *Essays*, Everyman's University Library, Dent (Pb)

JOHN DONNE, *Sermons*, selected by L. Pearsall Smith, OUP

EARL OF CLARENDON, *Selections from the History of the Rebellion* and *The Life by Himself*, ed. G. Huehns, The World's Classics, OUP

The Pelican Book of English Prose Volume 1, ed. Roger Sharrock

Aubrey's Brief Lives, ed. O. L. Dick, Penguin

JOHN EVELYN, *Diary*, ed. W. Bray, 2 vols, Everyman's Library, Dent

SAMUEL PEPYS, *Diary*, ed. J. Warrington, 3 vols, Everyman's Library, Dent (Pb)

For popular editions of individual works by Bacon, Bunyan, Browne, Stow, Hakluyt, Hobbes, Hooker and Walton, see titles in the index.

CHAPTER 9   MILTON TO DRYDEN

JOHN MILTON, *Poetical Works*, ed. D. Bush, Oxford Paperbacks, OUP

JOHN MILTON, *Prose Writings*, ed. K. M. Burton, Everyman's Library, Dent (Pb)

Poetry of the Restoration, ed. V. de Sola Pinto, The Poetry Bookshelf, Heinemann (Pb)

JOHN WILMOT, Earl of Rochester, *Poems*, ed. V. de Sola Pinto, Muses' Library, Routledge and Kegan Paul (Pb)

JOHN DRYDEN, *Poems and Fables*, ed. J. Kinsley, Oxford Paperbacks, OUP

JOHN DRYDEN, *Selected Criticism*, ed. J. Kinsley and G. A. E. Parfitt, Oxford Paperback English Texts, OUP

E. M. W. TILLYARD, *Milton*, Penguin

C. S. LEWIS, *A Preface to Paradise Lost*, Oxford Paperbacks, OUP

HARRY BLAMIRES, *Milton's Creation, A Guide through Paradise Lost*, University Paperbacks, Methuen

K. M. S. BURTON, *Restoration Literature*, University Library, Hutchinson

CHAPTER 10   RESTORATION DRAMA

Restoration Plays, intro. Edmund Gosse, Everyman's Library, Dent (Pb) (Dryden, Congreve, Wycherley, Otway, Farquhar, Vanbrugh and Etherege are represented)

For ADDISON's *Cato* and ROWE's *Jane Shore* see *Eighteenth-Century Plays*, p. 487

Congreve: Complete Plays, ed. A. C. Eswald, MacGibbon and Kee (Pb)

George Farquhar: Four Plays, ed. William Archer, MacGibbon and Kee (Pb)

GEORGE VILLIERS (Duke of Buckingham), *The Rehearsal* 1672 (facsimile reprint), Scolar Press (Pb)

COLLEY CIBBER, *Apology for His Life* (not known to be currently available in an inexpensive edition)

BONAMY DOBRÉE, *Restoration Tragedy 1660–1720*, OUP

BONAMY DOBRÉE, *Restoration Comedy 1660–1720*, OUP

For editions of individual plays by Restoration dramatists see titles in the index.

CHAPTER 11 ORIGINS OF THE NOVEL

Elizabethan Love Stories, ed. T. J. B. Spencer, Penguin

Shorter Novels: Elizabethan, intro. G. Saintsbury, Everyman's Library, Dent (Pb) (Deloney, Nashe and Greene are represented)

Shorter Novels: Seventeenth Century, ed. P. Henderson, Everyman's Library, Dent (Pb) (Forde, Behn and Congreve are represented)

THOMAS LODGE, *Rosalynde* 1592 (facsimile reprint), Scolar Press (Pb)

JOHN LYLY, *Euphues* 1578 (facsimile reprint), Scolar Press (Pb)

IAN WATT, *The Rise of the Novel*, Penguin

For popular editions of individual novels by Defoe, see titles in the index.

CHAPTER 12 THE AGE OF SWIFT AND POPE

JONATHAN SWIFT, *Gulliver's Travels and Selected Writings in Prose and Verse*, Nonesuch Library, Bodley Head

ALEXANDER POPE, *Poetical Works*, ed. H. Davis, Oxford Standard Authors, OUP

JOSEPH ADDISON and RICHARD STEELE, *Selections from the Tatler and the Spectator*, ed. R. J. Allen, Rinehart Paperback, Holt, Rinehart and Winston, New York

Eighteenth-Century Plays, ed. J. Hampden, Everyman's Library, Dent (Pb) (Addison and Rowe are represented as well as Fielding, Lillo and Cumberland)

JAMES THOMSON, *The Seasons and The Castle of Indolence*, ed. J. Sambrook, Oxford Paperback English Texts, OUP

The Early Augustans, ed. Francis Venables, The Poetry Bookshelf, Heinemann (Pb)

The Oxford Book of Eighteenth-Century Verse, ed. D. Nichol Smith, OUP

R. QUINTANA, *Swift: An Introduction*, Oxford Paperbacks, OUP

BONAMY DOBRÉE, *English Literature in the Early Eighteenth Century* (Oxford History of English Literature), OUP

For popular editions of individual prose works or plays by Swift, Steele, Cibber, Centlivre, Lillo, Law, etc. see titles in the index.

CHAPTER 13   THE AGE OF JOHNSON

DR SAMUEL JOHNSON, *Poetry and Prose*, ed. Mona Wilson, The Reynard Library, Rupert Hart-Davis (Pb)

JAMES BOSWELL, *Life of Johnson*, ed. R. W. Chapman, Oxford Paperbacks, OUP

JAMES BOSWELL, *Boswell's London Journal 1762–1763*, ed. F. A. Pottle, Penguin

Johnson's Journey to the Western Islands and Boswell's Journal of a Tour of the Hebrides, ed. R. W. Chapman, Oxford Paperbacks, OUP

OLIVER GOLDSMITH, *Poetry and Prose*, selected by Richard Garnett, The Reynard Library, Rupert Hart-Davis (Pb)

OLIVER GOLDSMITH, *Two Plays* (and also *An Essay on the Theatre*), MacGibbon and Kee (Pb)

The Late Augustans, ed. D. Davie, The Poetry Bookshelf, Heinemann (Pb)

THOMAS GRAY, *Poems: With a Selection of Letters and Essays*, ed. J. Drinkwater, Everyman's Library, Dent

Eighteenth-Century Tragedy, ed. M. R. Booth, The World's Classics, OUP (includes Johnson's *Irene*, Moore's *The Gamester* and Home's *Douglas*)

LORD CHESTERFIELD, *Letters to His Son: and Others*, Everyman's Library, Dent (Pb)

EDWARD GIBBON, *The Decline and Fall of the Roman Empire*, abridged by D. M. Low, Penguin

JOHN DYER, *Poems* 1761 (facsimile reprint), Scolar Press (Pb)

For popular editions of individual works see titles in the index.

CHAPTER 14   THE EIGHTEENTH-CENTURY NOVEL

Consult the index for popular editions of novels by the major eighteenth-century writers.

FRANCES BURNEY, *Evelina*, ed. E. A. Bloom, Oxford Paperbacks, OUP

FRANCES BURNEY, *Diary* (1842–6), selected by Lewis Gibbs, Everyman's Library, Dent

HENRY MACKENZIE, *The Man of Feeling*, ed. B. Vickers, Oxford Paperbacks, OUP

Three Gothic Novels, ed. P. Fairclough and M. Praz, Penguin (*The Castle of Otranto, Frankenstein* and *Vathek*)

ANNE RADCLIFFE, *The Mysteries of Udolpho*, Oxford Paperbacks, OUP

MATTHEW GREGORY LEWIS, *The Monk*, Oxford English Novels, OUP

HORACE WALPOLE, *Selected Letters*, ed. W. Hadley, Everyman's Library, Dent

SIR WALTER SCOTT, *Lives of the Novelists* (not known to be currently available in an inexpensive edition)

WALTER ALLEN, *The English Novel: a short critical history*, Penguin

CHAPTER 15   THE CLOSE OF THE EIGHTEENTH CENTURY

THOMAS CHATTERTON (poems), selected by G. Lindop, Fyfield Books, Carcanet Press (Pb)

RICHARD B. SHERIDAN, *Six Plays*, ed. L. Kronenberger, MacGibbon and Kee (Pb)

WILLIAM COWPER, *Poems*, ed. H. L'A Fausset, Everyman's Library, Dent

Selected Poems of Robert Burns, ed. G. S. Fraser, The Poetry Bookshelf, Heinemann (Pb)

Selected Poems of William Blake, ed. F. W. Bateson, The Poetry Bookshelf, Heinemann (Pb)

GEORGE CRABBE, *Tales, 1812 and other selected poems*, ed. H. Mills, Cambridge University Press (Pb)

The Life of George Crabbe by his Son, Barrie and Jenkins

DAVID CECIL, *The Stricken Deer* (life of Cowper), Constable

S. FOSTER DAMON, *A Blake Dictionary: The Ideas and Symbols of William Blake*, Thames and Hudson (Pb)

CHAPTER 16   WORDSWORTH AND THE ROMANTICS

WILLIAM WORDSWORTH, *Poetical Works*, ed. T. Hutchinson, Oxford Paperbacks, OUP

DOROTHY WORDSWORTH, *Journals*, ed. M. Moorman, Oxford Paperbacks, OUP

S. T. COLERIDGE, *Poetical Works*, ed. E. H. Coleridge, Oxford Paperbacks, OUP

SIR WALTER SCOTT, *Selected Poems*, ed. T. Crawford, Oxford Paperback English Texts, OUP

LORD BYRON, *Poetical Works*, ed. F. Page, Oxford Paperbacks, OUP

LORD BYRON, *Letters*, intro. A. Maurois, Everyman's Library, Dent

PERCY BYSSHE SHELLEY, *Selected Poetry*, ed. N. Rogers, Oxford Paperbacks, OUP

JOHN KEATS, *Poetical Works*, ed. H. W. Garrod, Oxford Paperbacks, OUP

LETTERS OF JOHN KEATS, ed. R. Gittings, Oxford Paperbacks, OUP

WILLIAM HAZLITT, *Selected Writings*, ed. C. Salvensen, Signet Classics (Pb)

A Choice of Southey's Verse, ed. G. Grigson, Faber (Pb)

THOMAS HOOD, *Whimsicalities and Warnings: Selected Poems*, ed. J. Ennis, Panther (Pb)

JAMES HOGG, *The Private Memoirs and Confessions of a Justified Sinner*, ed. J. Carey, Oxford Paperbacks, OUP

W. S. LANDOR, *Poems*, ed. G. Grigson, Centaur Press (Pb)

MARY MOORMAN, *William Wordsworth: A Biography*, 2 vols, Oxford Paperbacks, OUP

ANDRÉ MAUROIS, *Byron*, Bodley Head

Poets and their Critics, vol 2: From Blake to Browning, ed. H. Sykes Davies, Hutchinson

For popular editions of prose works by De Quincey, Hazlitt, Lamb, etc., see titles in the index.

CHAPTER 17   SCOTT AND CONTEMPORARY NOVELISTS

MARIA EDGEWORTH, *Castle Rackrent and The Absentee*, intro. B. Matthews, Everyman's Library, Dent

CHARLES MATURIN, *Melmoth the Wanderer*, Oxford Paperbacks, OUP

Jane Austen: Selected Letters 1796–1816, ed. R. W. Chapman, The World's Classics, OUP

M. LASCELLES, *Jane Austen and her Art*, Oxford Paperbacks, OUP

J. G. LOCKHART, *Life of Sir Walter Scott* (abridged), Everyman's Library, Dent

For popular editions of novels by Scott, Jane Austen and Peacock see titles in the index.

CHAPTER 18 VICTORIAN POETRY

ALFRED, LORD TENNYSON, *Poems and Plays*, Oxford Paperbacks, OUP

ROBERT BROWNING, *Poems*, selected by H. Milford, The World's Classics, OUP

ROBERT BROWNING, *The Ring and the Book*, Everyman's Library, Dent (Pb)

The Essential Matthew Arnold (poetry and prose), ed. L. Trilling, Chatto and Windus (Pb)

A Choice of Swinburne's Verse, ed. Robert Nye, Faber (Pb)

Victorian Poetry: Clough to Kipling, ed. A. J. Carr, Rinehart Paperbacks, Holt, Rinehart and Winston, New York (includes Clough, Meredith, the Rossettis, Morris, Patmore, etc.)

The Oxford Book of Nineteenth-Century Verse, chosen by J. Hayward, OUP

WILLIAM MORRIS, *Selected Writings*, Nonesuch Library, Bodley Head

Selected Poems of John Clare, ed. James Reeves, The Poetry Bookshelf, Heinemann (Pb)

Poems of Thomas Hardy: A Selection, ed. T. R. M. Creighton, Papermac, Macmillan

THOMAS HARDY, *The Dynasts*, intro. John Wain, Papermac, Macmillan

Selected Poems of G. M. Hopkins, ed. James Reeves, The Poetry Bookshelf, Heinemann (Pb)

A Choice of Kipling's Verse, ed. T. S. Eliot, Faber (Pb)

CHARLES TENNYSON, *Alfred Tennyson*, Papermac, Macmillan

G. K. CHESTERTON, *Robert Browning*, Papermac, Macmillan

CHAPTER 19 THE VICTORIAN NOVEL

The main novels by major Victorian writers are available in popular editions. Consult the index.

DAVID CECIL, *Early Victorian Novelists*, Constable

MICHAEL SADLEIR, *Trollope: A Commentary*, Oxford Paperbacks, OUP

JOHN LUCAS, *The Melancholy Man: A Study of Dickens's Novels*, University Paperbacks, Methuen

A Century of George Eliot Criticism, ed. G. S. Haight, University Paperbacks, Methuen

DAVID CECIL, *Hardy the Novelist*, Constable

LYTTON STRACHEY, *Queen Victoria*, Collins

CHAPTER 20   TWENTIETH-CENTURY DRAMA

OSCAR WILDE, *Plays, Prose Writings and Poems*, ed. H. Pearson, Everyman's Library, Dent (Pb)

JOHN GALSWORTHY, *Ten Famous Plays*, Duckworth

W. B. YEATS, *Selected Plays*, ed. N. Jeffares, St Martin's Library, Macmillan (Pb)

C. B. PURDOM, *A Guide to the Plays of Bernard Shaw*, University Paperbacks, Methuen

Shaw on the Theatre, ed. E. J. West (letters, speeches and articles), MacGibbon and Kee (Pb)

The Plays and Poems of J. M. Synge, ed. T. R. Henn, University Paperbacks, Methuen

SEAN O'CASEY, *Three Plays: Juno and the Paycock, The Shadow of a Gunman, The Plough and the Stars*, Papermac, Macmillan

UNA ELLIS-FERMOR, *The Irish Dramatic Movement*, University Paperbacks, Methuen

RAYMOND WILLIAMS, *Drama from Ibsen to Eliot*, Penguin

Popular editions of individual plays are available in many cases. Publishers are indicated below: Barrie: Hodder (Hd), Shaw: Penguin (Pg), Eliot and Beckett: Faber Paperbacks (FP), Fry; Oxford Paperbacks (OP), Pinter, Behan and Arden: Methuen's Modern Plays (MMP). *Consult the index.*

CHAPTER 21   TWENTIETH-CENTURY POETRY

W. B. YEATS, *Selected Poems*, ed. A. N. Jeffares, Papermac, Macmillan

A. N. JEFFARES, *W. B. Yeats: Man and Poet*, Routledge and Kegan Paul (Pb)

Georgian Poetry, ed. James Reeves, Penguin

Up the Line to Death – The War Poets: 1914–1918, ed. B. Gardner, intro. E. Blunden, Methuen

WILFRED OWEN, *Collected Poems*, ed. C. Day Lewis, Chatto and Windus (Pb)

T. S. ELIOT, *The Complete Poetry and Plays*, Faber

GROVER SMITH, *T. S. Eliot's Poetry and Plays: a study in sources and meaning*, University of Chicago Press (Pb)

HARRY BLAMIRES, *Word Unheard, A Guide through Eliot's Four Quartets*, University Paperbacks, Methuen

W. H. AUDEN, *Selected Poems*, Faber (Pb)

DYLAN THOMAS, *Collected Poems, 1934–52* and *A Portrait of the Artist as a Young Dog*, Aldine Paperbacks, Dent

The Oxford Book of Twentieth-Century Verse, chosen by P. Larkin, OUP

The Faber Book of Twentieth-Century Verse, ed. J. Heath-Stubbs and David Wright, Faber (Pb)

Modern Poets on Modern Poetry, ed. James Scully, Fontana, Collins (Pb)

The following are among the poets represented by volumes in Faber Paperbacks (general selections): Auden, Rupert Brooke, De la Mare, Eliot, MacNeice, Edwin Muir, Norman Nicholson, Sassoon and Spender. Andrew Young and R. S. Thomas are published by Rupert Hart-Davis.

CHAPTER 22 THE TWENTIETH-CENTURY NOVEL

Many twentieth-century novels referred to are available as Penguins. Consult the index.

JAMES JOYCE, *Ulysses*, Bodley Head

RICHARD ELLMAN, *James Joyce*, Oxford Paperbacks, OUP

HARRY BLAMIRES, *The Bloomsday Book, A Guide through Joyce's Ulysses*, University Paperbacks, Methuen

F. R. LEAVIS, *D. H. Lawrence Novelist*, Penguin

J. I. M. STEWART, *Eight Modern Writers* (Oxford History of English Literature), Oxford Paperbacks, OUP (Hardy, James, Shaw, Conrad, Kipling, Yeats, Joyce, Lawrence)

FREDERICK R. KARL, *A Reader's Guide to the Contemporary English Novel*, Thames and Hudson

Index

The index supplements the bibliography by indicating, after certain titles (especially of important novels and plays), that texts are available in popular editions. A key to the abbreviations used for this purpose is to be found on pp. 480–1.